READERS IN HISTORY

READERS
IN
HISTORY

Nineteenth-Century
American Literature and
the Contexts of Response

EDITED BY JAMES L. MACHOR

THE JOHNS HOPKINS UNIVERSITY PRESS   BALTIMORE AND LONDON

© 1993 The Johns Hopkins University Press
All rights reserved
Printed in the United States of America on acid-free paper

The Johns Hopkins University Press
2715 North Charles Street
Baltimore, Maryland 21218-4139
The Johns Hopkins Press Ltd., London

Library of Congress Cataloging-in-Publication Data

Readers in history : nineteenth-century American literature and the
  contexts of response / edited by James L. Machor.
        p.   cm.
    Includes bibliographical references.
    ISBN 0-8018-4436-3 (cloth : acid-free paper). — ISBN 0-8018-4437-1
(pbk. : acid-free paper)
    1. American literature—19th century—History and criticism—
Theory, etc.   2. Authors and readers—United States—History—
19th century.   3. Books and reading—United States—History—
19th century.   4. Reader-response criticism.   5. Historicism.
I. Machor, James L.
PS201.R37   1993
810.9′003—dc20   92-14471

A catalog record for this book is available from the British Library

Contents

Introduction: Readers/Texts/Contexts

JAMES L. MACHOR

Writing about the history of literary studies, Terry Eagleton in 1983 offered a characterization of the turns in that history by pointing out that if a focus on the author and the autonomous text had dominated earlier periods, "a marked shift of attention to the reader" has occurred "over recent years."[1] Though broadly drawn, such an assessment not only articulates a perception that is now widely held but also accurately reflects a major reorientation in critical theory and practice during the last twenty years. Indeed, there is no denying that the "return of the reader," as one critic has called this shift, has had a major impact on literary studies.[2] Arguing that the significance of texts consists of more than their structural and thematic patterns, reader-oriented criticism has directed attention to the interaction between textual signals and interpretive practices as the motor behind the creation of meaning and the formation of the literary canon. Yet, if literary studies have been marked by this particular revival of late, they have more recently been affected by another redivivus: what has been termed the "return to history," most noticeably in the form of the New Historicism. What is interesting, however, is the way these two "returns" have remained at a considerable distance from one another. For despite its accomplishments, reader-oriented criticism has exerted its influence at the expense of obfuscating a key question: who is the "reader" at the center of its analysis? When engaged in practical criticism, most reader-response critics have not provided analyses of the reading process and the textual construction of the audience's role as products of particular historical factors but instead have offered accounts that privilege the critics' own responses by positing themselves as the ideal readers of the text(s) in question. The problem with such strategies is not only that they have essentialized reading by framing it within an unvarying set of interpretive codes but that such practices have ignored the historically specific conditions by which reading proceeds and through which audiences are engaged.[3]

Despite this general tendency, however, the historical aporia in reader-oriented criticism has not taken the same shape, or existed in the same degree, throughout the range of methods that have come to be grouped under this critical movement, particularly when we consider its own changing history. In its 1970s version, focus on the reader paid scant attention to anything but the textual construction of audience, whether that readership was conceived as the narratee, the implied reader, the characterized reader, the model reader, the fictionalized reader, or the ideal reader. Identifying the reader as a construct within the text itself, or as a largely passive respondent to linguistic and structural signals, or as a function of literary competence synchronically defined, this form of reader-oriented criticism engaged in analysis divorced from consideration of the way interpretive, ideological, and material contexts governed the forms of reader activity in various ways for different historical audiences. Even critics such as Wolfgang Iser, who acknowledged theoretically that "the reading process . . . will vary historically from one age to another," produced accounts of response that posited the reader as a formalized function of the text itself or as a transhistorical receptor whose practices are everywhere and always the same.[4]

Partly as a result of charges against its ahistorical propensity, reader-oriented criticism began to take a "turn" toward history in the 1980s. Nor was it a surprise that such a swerve came simultaneously with the return to history in criticism at large, which stemmed from a general reaction to what was perceived as a hermetically sealed concept of discourse and textuality in post-structuralism, as well as from the growing impact of women's, ethnic, and Afro-American studies, all of which emphasized the role of specific social and material factors in shaping both literature and critical studies.[5] This shift was perhaps most prominent in the first book-length studies available in the United States of Hans Robert Jauss's theory and practice of reception aesthetics as well as in the new and growing fields of *l'histoire du livre* and, to a lesser degree, the New Historicism. But the results of these efforts often have been disappointing in terms of advancing our understanding of the dynamics of reading or the textual engagement of audience as historical phenomena. Although professing an interest in historical conditions governing response and the reader's role, the leading practitioners of reception aesthetics, particularly Jauss, have been concerned with tracing the history of theories of aesthetic response or with the changing history of the concept of the fictive—in effect a traditional history of ideas approach—or in analysis of historical representations of certain paralinguistic texts (for example, the myth of the Fall or the Platonic dialectic) in subsequent texts. Indeed, even Jauss's most important contribution—his reformulation of the hermeneutic concept of the "horizon of expectations"—has taken shape primarily through analyses of the way literary works reformulate horizons that had been created "intraliterarily" by previous aesthetic texts.[6] When Jauss has talked about the reader as a processor of texts, moreover, he has sounded very much like a version of Iser, positing a transcendent receptor whose work in no way depends on historically specific reading strategies.[7] More concerned with production than with response, *Rezeptionästhetiks*, as its name implies, has also been limited by its privileging of the aesthetic dimensions of reception, thus neglecting the manner in which ideological, political, and material factors define and structure the reader's role.

Other problems, in some cases related ones, have characterized the work in the history of the book and in the New Historicism, at those places where the latter has considered the role of the reader. Although New Historicists have been concerned primarily with vectors of power and ideological containment/subversion within texts themselves, some practitioners—in particular, Stephen Greenblatt—have sought to relate these issues to the question of audience. In doing so, however, Greenblatt simply has extracted from a text a conception of how its readers read—a traditional formalist analysis of thematized audience—or has emphasized the way "the reader is virtually created by the text he absorbs," a strategy strikingly reminiscent of earlier 1970s approaches such as Stanley Fish's affective stylistics or Iser's concept of textualized response.[8] Studies in the history of the book have presented a different kind of shortcoming in relation to the question of reading. There is no doubt that the work of Cathy Davidson, Michael Anesko, William Gilmore, Christopher Wilson, and Robert Darnton, among others, represents a significant contribution to our understanding of both reading as a sociological activity and the material conditions affecting the availability of reading material.[9] Because this field is concerned with the history of publication, print, and distribution, with authors' relations to their publishers, and/or with literacy (i.e., who read, what they read, and why they read), it discloses much about the relation between readers and books as commodities and artifacts—that is, with how readers in the past *used* reading materials. But it has been able to reveal little if anything about the process of response and the dynamics of audience engagement in earlier periods—little, in other words, about *how* people read and how texts semantically delivered themselves to historically specific audiences. These questions are precisely the ones that lie at the core of reader-response criticism.[10]

While the brief history I have just given of reader-directed criticism is accurate in a general sense, it nonetheless needs to be amended in two ways. First, it does not take into account the psychological approaches to reading by such critics as David Bleich and Norman Holland or the ethnographic method of a critic such as Janice Radway, all of whom have examined reading within specific contextual frameworks.[11] Yet even in these areas the same gap remains: that is, because of its focus on contemporary readers and reading conventions, this work likewise does not address reading within past historical contexts. Second, the neat dichotomy between the ahistorical formalism of seventies reader-oriented criticism and the limited but nonetheless clear historical gestures of the eighties versions is not as sharp as it may appear. If the 1980s witnessed many critics continuing to offer studies of response that relied on the 1970s transhistorical, textual notion of the reader,[12] several of the earlier seventies forms had made their own sorties into the historical. These took the shape of constructing broad homologies of the historical reader, which invoked audience as a collection of general ideas and conceptions drawn from traditional intellectual and cultural history. Thus we had Stanley

Fish's Protestant reader of *Paradise Lost* and Wolfgang Iser's rational, Enlightenment reader of *Tom Jones*.[13] What is striking, moreover, is that if there has been a continuity between the seventies and the eighties discussions of readers, it has been this tendency to rely on such critically constituted hypostatizations of audience when attempting to mount response within a historical frame. Hence the 1970s homologies of Iser and Fish have found their counterparts in such constructs as Michael Denning's working-class reader in nineteenth-century America, Jauss's bourgeois audience of French lyrics, and Jane Tompkins's Christian woman reader of antebellum American fiction.[14] As a result, these sorties into history remain far from two major objectives of a historicized study of response: (1) the exploration of reading as a product of the relationship among particular interpretive strategies, epistemic frames, ideological imperatives, and social orientations of readers as members of historically specific—and historiographically specified—interpretive communities; and (2) the analysis of the way literary texts construct the reader's role through strategies necessitated and even produced by particular historical conditions. The historical gap in reader-oriented criticism, in other words, largely has remained.

I do not mean to suggest, however, that previous ventures into examining the history of reading and response have been without value. On the contrary, such efforts as James Wallace's analysis of the historical conditions affecting Cooper's attempts to fashion a readership for his early novels, Nina Baym's study of the poetics of antebellum American reviewers, Steven Mailloux's work on the cultural rhetoric by which readings have been negotiated, debated, and disseminated, and Susan Harris's recent study of women's subversive reading in mid-nineteenth-century America have begun to move reader-response criticism in a direction it had been slouching toward for too long only in theory.[15] But reader-oriented criticism needs both to pursue these paths more fully and to push out in new directions by engaging in practical criticism that explores the dynamics of reading and the textual construction of audience as products of historically specific fields, where social conditions, ideologies, rhetorical practices, interpretive strategies, and cultural factors of race, class, and gender intersect. Engaging in that kind of work through a specific focus on nineteenth-century American literature and discourse is the purpose of the essays in this collection.

The American 1800s provides an especially appropriate context for such work. That century witnessed an unprecedented upsurge in reading activity owing to improvements in literacy, major advances in printing and book production, and improved methods of transportation, which facilitated the distribution and availability of printed matter. In the face of such developments and the new mass market they created—a combination that marked the advent of modern print culture—reading as a social and cognitive act took on growing significance for producers of printed material and the mass audience that began consuming it. Significant social, cultural, and material changes—including massive urbanization, industrialization, the growth of professionalism, new patterns of cultural homogenization and diversification, and changes in the social role and status of women and minorities—also had a major impact on both the formation of audiences and the way texts were read. These developments in turn affected the ways American writers engaged their audiences, forcing their discourse to take into account and address in often complex and problematic ways the interpretive practices, ideologies, and social positions of readers within this varying context. Nineteenth-century America thus offers a rich and important ground on which to explore reading as a historical act.

In addressing a range of relations between texts, authors, and readers within specific contexts of the nineteenth-century, the essays in this collection bring to bear a variety of methods—from New Historicism and feminist criticism to deconstruction and hermeneutics—in practical criticism that also confronts, either directly or implicitly, theoretical questions regarding the methodology of historicizing response. To provide a sense of the types of concerns at the center of each, the essays have been grouped into three divisions. Part One consists of works that theorize about the shape of historical approaches to response while turning theory into practice or that engage in a historical study of particular elements of nineteenth-century response through analyses that carry theoretical implications. In the second part, four essays explore the relation between the manner in which nineteenth-century texts addressed, thematized, or were received by their cultural readership and the constitutive conditions that shaped those strategies. The three essays in Part Three share a concern with the intersections of race, gender, textual production, and reader response as both subject and context for historical analysis. While these divisions are useful for indicating shared concerns among several of the contributors, they should not obscure the fact that most of the essays address issues beyond the boundaries suggested by such divisions. For example, the essays by Susan Harris and Stephen Railton, though appearing in the second and third sections, also make the relation between theory and practice an important element of their discussions. Likewise, questions of race and gender are central concerns of several essays in Parts One and Two. Taken as a whole, that is, these essays repeatedly demonstrate the multifaceted connections among theory and practice, writing and response, ideology and interpretation, historical conditions and reading activities.

These interconnections are apparent in Steven Mailloux's "Misreading as a Historical Act," which begins Part One. Pointing out the turn toward history in the reader-oriented criticism of the 1980s, Mailloux builds upon his previous work in the rhetoric of response to argue that studies of reading need to pursue more vigorously the way reading is "historically contingent, politically situated, institutionally embedded, and materially conditioned." Maintaining that such an effort should focus on the rhetorical practices through which interpretations of texts are constructed, circulated, exchanged, and debated, Mailloux pursues precisely that method in examining a particular historical act of reading: Margaret Fuller's 1845 review of Frederick Douglass's *Narrative of the Life*. Exploring the way Fuller's interpretation was historically situated in the mid-century rhetoric of "Bible politics," Mailloux shows how Fuller's response to Douglass's text was a reading of the cultural debate over Christianity and slavery even as her response to that debate constituted her reading of the *Narrative*. In the process, Mailloux develops a double-edged discussion that both reveals Fuller's response as a product of specific historical contexts and demonstrates his own theoretical project: how "rhetorical hermeneutics uses rhetoric to practice theory by doing history." Arguing that Fuller's response cannot be understood apart from a "historically specific, politically charged configuration of cultural rhetoric," this analysis of Fuller's hermeneutic act becomes for Mailloux a trope for redefining reader-response theory as a flexible praxis attuned to the cultural conditions constituting specific rhetorical histories.

John Carlos Rowe's "Swept Away: Henry James, Margaret Fuller, and 'The Last of the Valerii'" shares with Mailloux's contribution more than a concern with the relation between reading and Fuller. Like Mailloux, Rowe provides an analysis that theorizes through practice, but Rowe does so by a method of historicizing reading that, it suggests, cannot be done through other forms of reader-oriented criticism. Problematizing the distinction between production and reception, Rowe treats several of James's texts as readings or interpretations of Fuller embedded within a psychopoetics involving James's literary "fathers" and the cultural issue of the "New Woman." Unlike reception aesthetics, however, Rowe's analysis of James's responses to Fuller does not focus on aesthetic horizons but on the relationship between ideology and the poetics of gender in the late nineteenth century. For Rowe, James's writings as readings are the effect of the interpretations of Fuller by male writers generally identified within the nineteenth-century literary canon. From this perspective, James's responses can be seen as projections of both his own literary anxiety and his position within that historical hierarchy. By unpacking James's response to "Fuller" as a function of a particular historical phase in the patriarchal construction of women—a phase exemplified in James's unconscious projections of the figure of the "Margaret ghost" as a condensation of the texts of previous "fatherly" readers such as Hawthorne, Emerson, and Henry James, Sr.—Rowe deconstructs the canonical reading of the "Woman artist" in nineteenth-century America. The result is not only an anatomy of a specific dimension of James's psychological career as a cultural reader but a penetrating analysis of how a writer such as James is produced from a chain of historically specific readings with discernibly different connotations for the "woman intellectual" and the "New Woman" as cultural texts. Simultaneously, Rowe's analysis suggests that traditional approaches to reading and those that seek to historicize response through empirical investigations of reception need to be supplemented by analyses of reading "attitudes" produced by such historical linkages.

The concern with gender and its relation to both the theory and the practice of historicizing response characterizes James Machor's "Historical Hermeneutics and Antebellum Fiction: Gender, Response Theory, and Interpretive Contexts." Because feminist critics concerned with reading have tended toward the same kind of ahistorical analysis characterizing reader-response criticism as a whole, Machor maintains that we have little sense of what it meant to read as a woman in any period before our own. Arguing that an effective way to begin historicizing reading is through a study of the connection between gender and responses to fiction in antebellum America, Machor seeks to do so by defining the relation between specific interpretive codes and the ideological assumptions of an especially powerful reading community in that period: the reviewers in popular periodicals, who constituted the primary vehicle for the public dissemination and assimilation of ideas about how to read fiction in an "informed" manner. Machor shows that many of these strategies were based on gender-specific assumptions, as reviewers sought to instruct women to respond to fiction according to codes deemed appropriate to their sex. In doing so, reviewers characterized women readers in contradictory ways and promoted a strategy of response that denied women full participation in a community of (ultimately) phallocentric reading. Yet while this reduction of the female reader was confining, Machor points out how it nonetheless gave women novelists a set of assumptions they could redefine and challenge to engage their female audience. Demonstrating that turnabout by reconstructing part of an antebellum "informed" response to Susan Warner's *The Wide, Wide World*, Machor simultaneously explores the theoretical implications of such a reconstruction as a method for historicizing response.

The question of gender continues as an important element in Wai Chee Dimock's "Feminism, New Historicism, and the Reader," which concludes the opening section by addressing a concern shared by the previous essays: the interconnections between theory and practice. Arguing that the relation between feminism and the New Historicism can be productively explored through the practice of reading, Dimock approaches that relation by focusing on the role of the reader in Charlotte Perkins Gilman's "The Yellow Wallpaper" in the context of the historically specific "structures of authority" at the end of the nineteenth century. The particular reader Dimock locates as both immanent in Gilman's text and capable of making it meaningful in late Victorian America is an interpreter whose codes are grounded in the new authority of professionalism evolving in the culture. This "professional" reader, however, is no mere historical homology in Dimock's analysis, no mere hypostatization composed by the historian from general cultural practices. Rather, Dimock reveals that such a reader is a product of Gilman's own model of the female professional as a competent reader of her text—a model that is significant for its historical absence. Since the female professional constituted a role that was virtually nonexistent in late-nineteenth-century America, the historical embeddedness of Gilman's text reveals less its accommodation to this new cultural authority and more its own authority as transformative agency, shadowing forth for its Victorian female audience the "distance between what the female reader is and what she might become." Dimock, however, goes beyond this reading of reading formulated through the disjunction of feminist and New Historicist criticism by destabilizing that formulation as itself a product of a specific phase of contemporary feminist thought. Deconstructing that disjunction by problematizing the relation between history and feminist analysis, Dimock argues that a feminist reading in any form—including a reading of reading—"must be a historical reading" if it hopes to avoid reifying and essentializing gender. But if history can help feminists reconceive what engendered reading means, reading through gender, she asserts, can itself be an important strategy for redefining what it means to be historical. Through this last metacritical maneuver, Dimock's essay bears an affinity with Rowe's, since both insist that historical approaches to reading and gender need to address the diachronic process of historical continuity and change.

As the opening essay of Part Two, Robert Daly's "Cooper's Allegories of Reading and 'the Wreck of the Past'" makes the nature of change and continuity the center of a different focus. Seeking first to reconsider Cooper within the context of the renewed interest in historicism in literary studies as a whole and the more specific movement toward historical inquiry in reader-oriented criticism, Daly uses this reorientation as a basis for analyzing Cooper's novels as interpretive acts enmeshed within the cultural debates of their time. For Daly, reading historically is a recuperative act that can enable us to move past— by moving back before—the Twainian dismissal that has persisted in twentieth-century responses to Cooper's fiction. In one sense, then, Daly continues the recovery project begun by Jane Tompkins in her work on *The Last of the Mohicans*. But Daly takes this recuperative project a step further by locating in Cooper's fiction a historically generated concern with reading itself. Thematizing reading in his narratives, Cooper presented an allegory of response as a cultural dilemma, in which a hegemonic code, fashioned by Whig reformers and Jacksonian democrats, was replacing, in Cooper's view, the formerly rich multiplicity of reading codes in America. As Daly demonstrates, Cooper's fictions sought "to stage modes of reading" that would "influence the interpretive codes" his contemporary audience used to read their culture, in a manner that would "complicate and enlarge their own modes of reading." Arguing that preserving a multiplicity of reading codes was Cooper's goal for his contemporary readers, Daly reveals that to read Cooper historically requires responding to his texts as historical readings in which history itself is inextricably tied to transformations in the culture's interpretive practices.

Daly's concern with the relation between critical debate and thematized reading is shared by Stephen Railton in his essay "The Address of *The Scarlet Letter*." Arguing that reader-oriented critics need to make a strategic distinction between audience and reader if historical inquiry into reading is to proceed productively, Railton provides such a distinction to investigate the way Hawthorne's novel contains within it an audience—embodied in the Puritan community—whose responses constitute a pattern of flawed reading. Identifying that community's codes as an inverted or negative example of the kind of response Hawthorne sought for *The Scarlet Letter*, Railton locates this allegory of reading in a historically specific context: the literary conventions, self-images, and gender assumptions embedded in genteel fiction of the 1840s and 1850s and embraced by the middle-class audience that consumed those narratives. Using the horizon of expectations inferred from this audience, Hawthorne sought to move his readership to the kind of interpretive work that would reveal this community to itself, an end that ultimately accommodates—though in a flexible and disturbing way for his contemporaries— Victorian respect for its own "laws." Yet that accommodation, Railton reminds us, is an important vehicle for recognizing our own distance as readers from the admonitory relation between Hawthorne and his contemporary audience. For Railton, then, there is an ideal addressee for *The Scarlet Letter* as well as an "ideal" way to read it—one quite different from those constructed by modern readers—but not because there is a transhistorical "right" reader whose response is definitive for an "essential" *Scarlet Letter*. Rather, Railton's point is that the concept of an ideal audience can be a viable vehicle for historicizing response once we recognize that that audience, as conceived in *The Scarlet Letter*, was a function of Hawthorne's own relation to the historically constructed interpretive horizon of middle-class Victorian Americans.

Like Railton, Willis Buckingham concerns himself with a dual purpose in "Poetry Readers and Reading in the 1890s: Emily Dickinson's First Reception." As he explains, part of his concern is to "illuminate the readership to which Dickinson herself belonged" by examining reviewers' responses to her first published collection of poetry. But Buckingham is concerned with more than just exploring a phase of the history of response to a canonical author, a tactic that would be just one more version of the traditional "critical heritage" idiom. Rather, Buckingham's second and larger purpose is to investigate how an influential community of late-nineteenth-century readers "formulated norms of valuation" and defined the relation between poetry and its readers. As Buckingham points out, the most noticeable feature of nineties reading strategies was the conception of poetry as an "affect" grounded in emotional pleasure. Central to this notion was the idea of "sacred tears"—a response code linked to gender assumptions about women as readers and writers of the poetic. Although such a connection caused some reviewers to read Dickinson as a "type" of womanhood, Buckingham demonstrates that such assumptions also were accompanied by identification of her masculine power—a correlation that led some women reviewers to read her poems as a testimony against the patriarchal repression of women. While these "social constructions of femininity and masculinity" thus "worked on Dickinson's behalf" with the reviewing community of the nineties, the emphasis on pleasure also signaled an effort among reviewers to deal with larger cultural issues: the new threat of scientific rationalism and the question of poetry's role in a democratic age. Read within the context of these issues, the responses to Dickinson's *Poems* by reviewers of the 1890s disclose a rarefied conception of poetic pleasure as the sacred prerogative of an elite class of knowing respondents.

The need to reconceive the reader in the text by reconstructing that role in relation to an extratextual historical audience is the subject of Raymond Hedin's "Probable Readers, Possible Stories: The Limits of Nineteenth-Century Black Narrative," which explores the filiations between the "intratextual" audience of black narratives and the white audience to which these texts were addressed. Tracing this relationship through a series of narrative encounters, from the ventriloquist work of Thomas Gray's *Confessions of Nat Turner* (1831) to Sutton Griggs's *Imperium in Imperio* (1899), Hedin examines how black writers sought to make a genuine black voice audible to a nineteenth-century white audience through the use of a mediating white auditor that doubled as narrator. Because the black story had to "look like a white story" to be acceptable to that audience, the white narrator/observer became both a buffer for engaging that sometimes hostile and often indifferent readership and a strategy of subversion. Like the Puritan misreaders Railton locates in *The Scarlet Letter*, the white frame narrators/auditors of black narratives functioned as racial misreaders whose flawed responses performed cultural work: undermining the white audience's racist ideology. Hedin points out, however, the severe restrictions on both teller and tale that this strategy had, thereby signaling the repressive power the nineteenth-century white audience had over the thematization of reading in black narratives. In disclosing both that power and its impact, Hedin's essay demonstrates that analysis of thematized reading can be a valuable practice provided it proceeds through an examination of sociopolitical contexts—contexts which, in the case of black narratives, constituted the conditions of reception governing such thematization of racial reading throughout the nineteenth century.

Confronting the nexus of reading and race through a narrower but equally illuminating focus is the task of Marva Banks's "*Uncle Tom's Cabin* and Antebellum Black Response," the first essay of the third section. Banks points out that reader-response critics, though attending to a variety of interpretive communities, have largely ignored the black reading audience, and she identifies the reception of *Uncle Tom's Cabin* as a case in point. When Stowe's novel was first published in book form, over two hundred responses by black readers appeared in the antebellum black press, yet those responses have received little notice. Banks's goal, therefore, is to disclose the meaning of *Uncle Tom's Cabin* for its contemporary black audience by examining the way African American responses were profoundly influenced by their historical moment—particularly the racist policies in the North that culminated in the Fugitive Slave Law and the equally invidious work of the American Colonization Society. Although black readers first welcomed Stowe's novel as a powerful antislavery document, the threat of emigration posed by the racist machinations of the Colonization Society became the primary interpretive lens through which black readers reconceived *Uncle Tom's Cabin* as a propagandistic text promoting sentimental racism. Yet Banks notes that the black reaction was not monolithic; besides changing over time, it was characterized by some heated debates over the political implications of Stowe's novel and her own life. Printed responses, however, suggest that for the majority of antebellum blacks, who read the novel through and against the midcentury politics of racial oppression, *Uncle Tom's Cabin* became "a curse that encouraged continuation of the doctrine of white supremacy in America."

Moving from an examination of race and response to the connections among race, class, gender, and reading, Christina Zwarg's "Reading before Marx: Margaret Fuller and the *New-York Daily Tribune*" also signals a shift away from the politically charged reading of a popular novel to a specific politics of reading articulated in an organ of mass culture at midcentury. On one level, Zwarg's analysis of Fuller's interest in reading strategies represents the most orthodox approach among the essays in this collection, in that its focus on the history of a writer's ideas about response bears a certain resemblance to traditional reception aesthetics. But Zwarg moves beyond this narrow preoccupation of previous criticism by disclosing Fuller's interest in reading, not primarily as a form of aesthetic theorizing, but as a cultural practice inherently connected to ideology—a discursive space where, as Zwarg explains, "those who have been denied access to the dominant forms of power could reassert themselves." Fuller, moreover, saw reading as a process embedded in historical conditions and implicated in the question of history, a question which itself became for her "radically enmeshed in reading." Although revealing that Fuller's concerns with the historicity of reading antedate our own contemporary concerns with contextuality—and thereby implicitly admonish our postmodern critical hubris—Zwarg does not bend Fuller's discourse into service as a precursor to contemporary critical practice. Rather, she discloses Fuller's theory of reading, articulated and enacted in her columns of the *New-York Daily Tribune*, both as a product of the material and ideological conditions in the 1840s and as a radical political act confronting questions of race, gender, and hegemonic power.

As the final essay of Part Three, "Responding to the Text(s): Women Readers and the Quest for Higher Education" by Susan Harris serves in one sense as a coda to the entire collection by returning to a concern that figures prominently in the essays by Mailloux, Rowe, Machor, and Dimock: the inescapable linkage among theory, practice, ideology, and history for the study of reading. Expanding on her recent investigation of subversive female reading and writing in the 1860s and 1870s, Harris seeks, as one of her goals, to enlarge the methodological boundaries of reader-response criticism by using it as a passageway to a historical examination of consciousness. The particular history she explores, accordingly, is the nineteenth-century cultural debate over women's education, which elicited a range of responses in private and public discourse by women. Identifying through letters and diaries the historically specific reading "schemata" and gender experiences that served women as a framework for interpreting that debate, Harris illuminates the dynamic interplay of response and production as reciprocating components in the changing contours of the debate itself. Showing how women's novels and essays in the mid-to-late century constituted both products through which women readers engaged in the debate and interpretive acts in their own right, Harris overtly challenges the conventional distinction between production and reception by examining each as a form of the other. In the process, Harris locates in these reverberating responses a powerful and problematic interpretive tension generated by nineteenth-century definitions of gender, which these interpretive acts both accommodated and covertly questioned.

As this commentary suggests, the essays in this collection, while varying substantially in their methods and conclusions, share a conviction about the need and value of historicizing response. But it is also useful to point out what they do not do—and perhaps what they indicate about what cannot be done—in approaching reading historically. Placing reading in historical contexts can yield fruitful analyses about interpretive strategies and conceptions of reading as cultural practices in the past, but what remains elusive finally is a clear sense of what the actual reading experiences were for the numerous nineteenth-century readers whose encounters with literature took place, not in public forums, but alone in the bedrooms of middle-class homes in suburban Boston, or in barn lofts in rural Virginia, or between stolen moments of leisure at factory workbenches in Pittsburgh and Chicago. Few of the essays in this collection deal with these historical acts of reading, and even when the analyses move in this direction, they do so obliquely and speculatively. This omission in part results from the sparseness of the historical archive: these readers simply did not leave many records of their experiences, and what they did provide represents only the barest traces of the shapes those experiences took. But limited analysis of what might be called "common readers" also reflects the fact that reading in the nineteenth century already had become, in one sense, what it largely is today: an extremely private activity that can never be fully recorded in performance because such a "recording" is always selective, always a reconstruction, and hence always a reconstitution. Thus the impossibility of full and unmediated access to historical readers ineluctably limits efforts to "recapture" reading as a historical act.

Even if a full and unadulterated archive were available, however, the assumption that it would provide a more direct and accessible picture of past reading experiences is itself problematic. For the supposition that such an archive would bring us closer to history ignores the way that even the most complete historical record never discloses a pure presence but depends on our own mediating activities as interpreters and readers of the past. To speak of an omission in these essays is thus to engage in a certain amount of wishful thinking that sidesteps the larger issue intrinsic to employing history as a critical tool in our post-structuralist age: the question of the status and nature of history and historical inquiry. Because that issue bears directly on the premises behind this collection, it needs to be addressed here.

In the wake of post-structuralism, it is no longer possible to innocently invoke history as an authoritative marker that provides an unchallengeable register for critical practice. Derrida's oft-quoted assertion that there is nothing outside the text, that all is a discourse constructed and interpreted, has not only problematized the distinction between text and context by collapsing both as forms of textuality, but has led to the recognition that all textuality emanates from a particular set of interpretive, theoretical, and ideological conditions. In other words, if all history is textual, then—to use the formulation that has become the virtual byword of the New Historicism—all textuality, including that of historical practice, is historical. To do history is thus already to be implicated in a system of historically specific strategies that constitute the thing they propose to describe.

By identifying the work of the historian itself as a construct embedded within a particular historical field of discursive practices, epistemic frames, and interpretive codes, this formulation has undermined the ground on which history stands by deconstructing its claim to reveal accurately the facts and the "truth" about the past. The result has been what Dominick LaCapra, Frederic Jameson, and others have termed the current "crisis in history"—a crisis that gives pause to the assumption that a return to history can be a consolation through which we can bypass the problems of essentialism and presentism in reader-response criticism. For if deconstruction, as Jonathan Culler has maintained, "explores the problematic situation to which stories of reading have led us,"[16] it also severely undermines our attempts to lead ourselves through historical analysis out of the conundrums of that situation.

The general problem I raise here, of course, has been debated and struggled with at least since the appearance of Roland Barthes's essay "The Discourse of History" in 1967. Moreover, it is a problem with its own extensive history, a history reminding us that this crisis, far from being only contemporary, reaches back to the 1930s in the relativist arguments of Becker and Beard, which themselves had grown from the "crisis in history" that had been materializing in Europe since the late nineteenth century.[17] But that pedigree hardly alters the fact that today this crisis continues to raise crucial questions. For if history, as Derrida asserts, "is never a gesture that is neutral, innocent, transparent, disinterested," can never reveal the past but can only produce a textual mediation constituted by its own historical conditions,[18] what warrants the continuation of historical practice? What kinds of claims can history legitimately make, and what justification exists for its legitimacy? Or to put the matter another way, why bother to practice history—particularly a historical version of reader-response criticism—at all?

One answer to these questions is that despite post-structuralist theory, history continues to be produced. By this I do not mean that historians as a whole have not stopped writing but that even those who have approached the question of history through post-structuralist theory have continued to make historical claims. Hence, even as he deconstructs history, Derrida asserts that "the history of the West, is the history of . . . metaphors and metonymies"—a concept that Hayden White has made central to his post-structuralist metahistory of historical discourse.[19] Like the New Historicists, White and Derrida continue to speak of history as something which we can identify and about which we can speak because antifoundationalist theory does not eradicate the possibility of *producing* histories. As Stanley Fish has pointed out in his analysis of the New Historicism and of the warrant for historical inquiry in general (an analysis especially relevant here, given Fish's seminal contribution to reader-response criticism), the textuality of history does not preclude our ability to ask and answer the historical question, "What happened?" because the principle of the textuality of history—and the constructed status of all historical fact—

operates on a different (i.e., metacritical) level from that on which the question of historical occurrences is answered. For that reason, the metacritical principle of historical constructedness can have no *practical* consequences for historical practice.[20]

Fish's argument here, of course, is another version of the theoretical "against theory" position, but one which, in this instance, does not deny the power of theory by undermining the legitimacy of its claim to govern practice from the outside. Rather, Fish asserts, in effect, that theory is so powerful that its claims must be declared irrelevant if any truly consequential work, such as the investigation of the past, is to proceed. In characterizing Fish's analysis in this way, I do not mean to caricature it in order to dismiss it. On the contrary, his arguments are both attractive and in several ways convincing, particularly his assertion that no matter how much we may believe in the constructed nature of all discursive practices—including all histories and all historical facts—as the products of particular historical conditions, the knowledge produced by those practices remains cogent for us as long as those particular conditions are not under challenge. Moreover, even when such challenge occurs, "the result will not be an indeterminacy of fact, but a new shape of factual firmness underwritten by a newly, if temporarily, settled perspective."[21] What is less satisfying and less convincing, however, is Fish's attendant claim that the principle of the historical textuality of all discourse has no consequences for practice itself. The danger of such a position is that it becomes a warrant for doing business as usual without any concern for the theoretical implications of the way practice is pursued. Furthermore, its implacable differentiation between theory and practice ignores what the essays in this collection—some explicitly, others implicitly—make evident: that practice is always a form of theory, is always informed by a set of assumptions that function as theory.[22] Indeed, to pick up on the last of these in relation to historicizing reading, these essays do more than provide histories of response or examine how historical conditions govern the way texts engage audiences. They also strive to redirect the way reader-oriented criticism is pursued by incorporating within it the theoretical principle of the historicity of reading as a discursive practice. Yet if theory and practice are always intertwined, if all our histories are inherently constrained by the principle of textuality, which prevents them from being anything more than products of our contemporary perspective(s), we are still left with the question of why do history at all.

A possible answer—though one I frankly find inadequate—is to accept the argument that history is not a master code for critical practice and that "nothing is to be gained," as Fredric Jameson has pointed out, in substituting "one reified theme"—whether it be History, Textuality, Hermeneutics, Intentionality, or Language/Semiosis—for another.[23] Nonetheless, if history is only one of several codes, that recognition is itself a reason for invoking contextuality as a way to enlarge the scope and texture of critical practice, including the practice of reader-response. What is unsatisfying in this argument, however, is that in justifying the historical as one among several interchangeable options, it provides no specific warrant for history *as* history—that is, as a distinctive practice legitimate in its own right.

A more compelling reason resides in a different trajectory of acceptance. If all histories are textual, constructed by their own historical conditions, so too are all discursive practices, all explanations, all interpretations. But the logic of this principle suggests that there are better or worse constructions, both within historiography and within literary criticism. Whether we are aware of it or not, acknowledge it or not, we cannot do other than construct texts and produce readings from within a particular historical position. What makes a historical study of response a superior activity, therefore, is that it deliberately incorporates that principle within its practice. Indeed, it can be argued that accepting the metacritical principle of the historicity of textuality makes investigation of response as a historical activity our most viable critical strategy. For the goal of historicizing response and the reader's role is not to lead us to some kind of knowledge about the truth of reading in the past, but to render an understanding of what is intelligible about reading as a historically constituted phenomenon. The historical study of response, that is, can function as a discourse of intervention whose value consists of its adequacy for us as subjects embedded in our own histories. .

In this sense, Jameson's well-known injunction to "always historicize" should be viewed not so much as a call to action but as a *fait accompli*. As critics, as readers, as discourse users, we always already historicize because we cannot escape our own historical conditions. The question, then, is not whether we should historicize, since we can never do anything else. The question is whether we will do so consciously, rigorously, and self-consciously—whether we will approach the historicity of reading in a way that recognizes and seeks to address the manner in which that history includes our own discourse practices as historical readers.

Although several essays in this collection seek explicitly to explore reading in this manner, in one sense all the essays share that trait, not so much individually but when taken as a whole. Speaking in different registers, operating from different theoretical perspectives—e.g., intentionalist versus anti-intentionalist principles, realist versus idealist theories regarding the status of the reader, separatist versus conjunctive arguments about the relation between production and reception—these essays indirectly question and comment upon one another's methods and informing assumptions. More like a round-table discussion than a debate, the effect nonetheless is to raise questions and pose problems about the nature, goals, and implications of examining reading as a historical act.

Taken together and juxtaposed to one another, therefore, these eleven essays do not offer final solutions to the questions of historicizing reading and the nature of response in nineteenth-century America so much as they open areas of inquiry and mark out strategies for future debate. But while this volume leaves open—both deliberately and inevitably—the way for further discussion about the purpose, value, and methods of exploring response historically, it also offers some provisional yet spirited answers to the theoretical and practical question of what it means to approach reading as a process constructed through a multiplicity of histories.

Notes

1. Terry Eagleton, *Literary Theory: An Introduction* (Minneapolis: U of Minnesota P, 1983) 74.

2. This term is Elizabeth Freund's in *The Return of the Reader: Reader-Response Criticism* (London: Methuen, 1987).

3. I, of course, am hardly the first to point out the ahistorical tendency of reader-oriented criticism. See, for example, Susan Suleiman, "Introduction: Varieties of Audience-Oriented Criticism," in *The Reader in the Text: Essays in Audience and Interpretation*, ed. Susan Suleiman and Inge Crosman (Princeton: Princeton UP, 1980) 3–45; Frank Lentricchia, *After the New Criticism* (Chicago: U of Chicago P, 1980) 105–12; Robert Holub, *Reception Theory: A Critical Introduction* (London: Methuen, 1984); and Steven Mailloux, *Rhetorical Power* (Ithaca: Cornell UP, 1989).

4. Wolfgang Iser, *The Implied Reader: Patterns of Communication in Prose Fic-

tion from Bunyan to Beckett (Baltimore: Johns Hopkins UP, 1974) xii. This tendency is particularly evident in Iser's theory and analysis of what he calls textual "gaps": see especially *The Act of Reading: A Theory of Aesthetic Response* (Baltimore: Johns Hopkins UP, 1978) 165–79, 198–203. Examples of this erasure of the historical in reader-response criticism of the late 1960s and 1970s include Stanley Fish, *Surprised by Sin: The Reader in "Paradise Lost"* (London: St. Martin's, 1967); Fish, "Literature in the Reader: Affective Stylistics," *New Literary History* 2 (1970–71): 123–62; Fish, *Self-Consuming Artifacts: The Experience of Seventeenth-Century Literature* (Berkeley and Los Angeles: U of California P, 1972); Jonathan Culler, *Structuralist Poetics: Structuralism, Linguistics, and the Study of Literature* (Ithaca: Cornell UP, 1975); Gerald Prince, "Introduction to the Study of the Narratee," *Poetique* 14 (1973): 177–96; Michael Riffaterre, *Semiotics of Poetry* (Bloomington; Indiana UP, 1978); Judith Fetterley, *The Resisting Reader: A Feminist Approach to American Fiction* (Bloomington: Indiana UP, 1978); and Umberto Eco, *The Role of the Reader: Explorations of the Semiotics of Texts* (Bloomington: Indiana UP, 1979). An excellent collection of representative works in reader criticism of the 1970s is Jane P. Tompkins, ed., *Reader-Response Criticism: From Formalism to Post-Structuralism* (Baltimore: Johns Hopkins UP, 1980).

5. For a somewhat different—and perhaps more cynical—etiology of the return to history in literary studies, see David Simpson, "Literary Criticism and the Return to History," *Critical Inquiry* 14 (1987–88): 721–47.

6. See, for example, Jauss's *Aesthetic Experience and Literary Hermeneutics*, trans. Michael Shaw (Minneapolis: U of Minnesota P, 1982) esp. 3–13, 152–88; *Toward an Aesthetic of Reception*, trans. Timothy Bahti (Minneapolis: U of Minnesota P, 1982) esp. 46–75, 139–85; and more recently, *Question and Answer: Forms of Dialogic Understanding*, trans. and ed. Michael Hays (Minneapolis: U of Minnesota P, 1989) esp. 3–50, 95–147.

7. See, for example, Jauss, *Question and Answer* 16, 91–95. For a further critique of Jauss and reception aesthetics see Holub, *Reception Theory*, 134–53; Jonathan Culler, *The Pursuit of Signs: Semiotics, Literature, Deconstruction* (Ithaca: Cornell UP, 1981) 54–57; and Steven Mailloux, *Interpretive Conventions: The Reader in the Study of American Fiction* (Ithaca: Cornell UP, 1982) 167–70. Mailloux, for instance, points out how "in reconstructing the horizon of social norms for a group of French lyrics in 1852 [an analysis contained in *Toward an Aesthetic of Reception*], Jauss discusses the effect of their reception on . . . bourgeois society; but his 'horizon analysis' leaves completely unexplained the interpretive work of readers that would have to be performed *before* such a socialization effect could take place" (170).

8. See Stephen Greenblatt, *Renaissance Self-Fashioning: From More to Shakespeare* (Chicago: U of Chicago P, 1980) 100–104, 119–20.

9. Cathy N. Davidson, *Revolution and the Word: The Rise of the Novel in America* (New York: Oxford UP, 1986); Davidson, ed., *Reading in America: Literature and Social History* (Baltimore: Johns Hopkins UP, 1989); Michael Anesko, *Friction with the Market: Henry James and the Profession of Authorship* (New York: Oxford UP, 1986); William Gilmore, *Reading Becomes a Necessity of Life: Material and Cultural Life in Rural New England, 1780–1835* (Knoxville: U of Tennessee P, 1989); Christopher Wilson, *The Labor of Words: Literary Professionalism in the Progressive Era* (Athens: U of Georgia P, 1985); Robert Darnton, *Literary Underground of the Old Regime* (Cambridge: Harvard UP, 1982); Darnton, *Revolution in Print: The Press in France* (Berkeley: U of California P, 1989).

10. Because of the way it situates itself into the question of history and reading, in other words, *l'histoire du livre* represents not so much a precursor—or competitor—of the kind of historicizing of reading represented by the essays in this collection as a complement to them.

11. David Bleich, *Subjective Criticism* (Baltimore: Johns Hopkins UP, 1978); Norman Holland, *Five Readers Reading* (New Haven: Yale UP, 1975); Holland, *The Dynamics of Literary Response* (New York: Oxford UP, 1968); Janice Radway, *Reading the Romance: Women, Patriarchy, and Popular Literature* (Chapel Hill: U of North Carolina P, 1984).

12. See, for instance, Judith Fetterley, "Reading about Reading: 'A Jury of Her Peers,' 'The Murders in the Rue Morgue,' and 'The Yellow Wallpaper,'" in *Gender and Reading: Essays on Readers, Texts, and Contexts*, ed. Elizabeth A. Flynn and Patrocinio P. Schweickart (Baltimore: Johns Hopkins UP, 1986) 147–64; Mailloux, *Interpretive Conventions*, esp. ch. 3; Peter Rabinowitz, *Before Reading: Narrative Conventions and the Politics of Interpretation* (Ithaca: Cornell UP, 1987); W. Daniel Wilson, "Readers in Texts," *PMLA* 96 (1981): 848–63; and most of the essays in Suleiman and Crosman, *The Reader in the Text*. Even Stanley Fish, despite his assertion in *Is There a Text in This Class?* (Cambridge: Harvard UP, 1980) that accounts of reading always constitute the activity they supposedly report—and thus, by implication, are always grounded in their own specific history—has continued in his practical criticism to engage in what is virtually a reprieve of his earlier affective stylistics. See, for example, "Things and Actions Indifferent: The Temptation of Plot in *Paradise Regained*," *Milton Studies* 17 (1983): 163–85.

13. These appear in Fish, *Surprised by Sin*, and Iser, *The Act of Reading*.

14. Michael Denning, *Mechanic Accents: Dime Novels and Working-Class Culture in America* (London: Verso, 1987); Jauss, *Toward an Aesthetic of Reception* 139–85; Jane Tompkins, *Sensational Designs: The Cultural Work of American Fiction* (New York: Oxford UP, 1985) 122–85. Though not all of these are reader-oriented studies per se, all talk about readers and clearly have been influenced by reader-response criticism.

15. James Wallace, *Early Cooper and His Audience* (New York: Columbia UP, 1986); Nina Baym, *Novels, Readers, and Reviewers: Responses to Fiction in Antebellum America* (Ithaca: Cornell UP, 1984); Mailloux, *Rhetorical Power*; Susan Harris, *Nineteenth-Century American Women's Novels: Interpretive Strategies* (Cambridge: Cambridge UP, 1990).

16. Jonathan Culler, *On Deconstruction* (Ithaca: Cornell UP, 1982) 83.

17. For an informative discussion of the relation between the current crisis in history and these historical antecedents, see Brook Thomas, "The New Historicism and Other Old-Fashioned Topics," in *The New Historicism*, ed. H. Aram Veeser (New York: Routledge, 1989) 182–203.

18. Jacques Derrida, *Limited, Inc.* (Evanston: Northwestern UP, 1988) 131.

19. Derrida, *Writing and Difference*, trans. Alan Bass (Chicago: U of Chicago P, 1978) 279.

20. Stanley Fish, "Commentary: The Young and the Restless," *The New Historicism* 303–16.

21. Ibid. 308.

22. I should note that elsewhere Fish has argued against this position, maintaining that the assumptions underlying practice constitute not theory but belief ("Consequences," in *Against Theory: Literary Studies and the New Pragmatism*, ed. W. J. T. Mitchell [Chicago: U of Chicago P, 1985] 116–18). But precisely what differentiates theory from belief Fish never explains, beyond saying that "theories are something you have" while "beliefs have *you*"—a curious theoretical principle that itself sounds like an article of faith, or a form of belief.

23. Fredric Jameson, *The Political Unconscious: Narrative as a Socially Symbolic Act* (Ithaca: Cornell UP, 1981) 100–101.

PART ONE

Theory and the Historicizing of Reading Practices

Misreading as a Historical Act: Cultural Rhetoric, Bible Politics, and Fuller's 1845 Review of Douglass's *Narrative*

STEVEN MAILLOUX

The poem is the transaction that goes on between reader and text.
LOUISE M. ROSENBLATT (1968)

Every reading is transactional. You run with what you have, and you become something else.
GAYATRI SPIVAK (1989)

As historical acts of reading, interpretations can themselves be read within the rhetorical context of their production and reception. That context might be troped as a cultural conversation of readers, which in this essay will include 1845 readers of several kinds of texts: slaves' songs, the Christian Bible, northeastern U.S. secular and religious newspapers, philosophical treatises on morality, and slave narratives. An act of reading is precisely the historical intersection of the different cultural rhetorics for reading such texts within the social practices of particular historical communities. In analyzing Margaret Fuller's 1845 reading of Frederick Douglass's *Narrative*, I will illustrate this theoretical claim as I simultaneously tell a different story, that of reader-response criticism and reception aesthetics during the last two decades. This second, metacritical narrative will situate my own rhetorical interpretation of Fuller by showing how an earlier reader-response criticism gets transformed into something I call rhetorical hermeneutics.

Reader-response criticism of the 1970s claimed to challenge the formalist theory and practice of New Critical interpretations. Its institutional rhetoric advocated that talk about readers in the process of reading replace talk about literary texts as self-enclosed objects. The Affective Fallacy was declared a fallacy, as several forms of reader talk promoted a range of psychological and social models for interpretation—subjective, transactive, phenomenological, semiotic, affective stylistic, structuralist poetic. Each marked its difference from a text-centered formalism by using a reader vocabulary, but the particular names each gave to "the reader" also distinguished the radically different approaches metacritically lumped together under the name "reader-oriented criticism." Readers were actual, ideal, implied, intended, educated, informed, competent, inscribed; there were mock readers, superreaders, narratees, implied audiences, interpretive communities, literary competencies, reading conventions. As different as their conceptions of reading were, however, the various forms of 1970s reader talk all tended to deemphasize or completely ignore the act of reading as a historical and political activity.[1]

In the 1980s this situation changed. Pressured by various feminist, Marxist, New Historicist, and other sociopolitical criticisms, reader-oriented theory and practice turned more and more to the historical context and the political aspects of readers reading. Also important in this transformation of readerly approaches was the influence of the reception aesthetics proposed by Hans Robert Jauss. Jauss's reception theory had been introduced into the United States during the first wave of the new reader-response criticism, primarily through his "Literary History as a Challenge to Literary Theory," published in *New Literary History* in 1970. But unlike the phenomenological reader criticism of his University of Constance colleague Wolfgang Iser,[2] Jauss's historically oriented reception theory did not receive book-length treatment in English until the 1982 publication of his *Toward an Aesthetic of Reception* and his *Aesthetic Experience and Literary Hermeneutics*, volumes 2 and 3 in the University of Minnesota's widely acclaimed series "Theory and History of Literature."[3]

In contrast to various forms of reader talk that focused on a fictionalized reader represented in the text or an ideal reader implied by the text or an actual reader today reading the text, Jauss's reception aesthetics advocated talking about past historical readers within their specific horizons of expectations. Such talk could develop critical analyses and stories of reading open to a range of factors usually ignored in most reader-oriented criticism, factors constituted by social, political, and economic categories including race, age, gender, ethnicity, nationality, religion, sexuality, and class. This talk about historical acts of reading was strongly encouraged by changes within related institutional practices: the turn to history within theoretical accounts of textual interpretation and the attention to politics within historical analyses of intertextuality. That is, theory talk went historical and historical talk went political. Both combined with reception aesthetics to give reader criticism a more historical orientation—and thus provide a basis for the kinds of essays published in this volume.

There are various ways to trouble the neat narrative I have just told about reader-response criticism. One could point to various places where reader critics of the early seventies did deal with history.[4] Or one could argue that the alleged turns to history and politics in academic criticism and theory were much more complicated than here represented, and of course, they were. Still, I think the story I have told does have a certain heuristic value, making more visible the changes in the rhetorical context (primarily in institutional discourses) that have occurred in the academic talk about readers reading since the heyday of reader-response theory during the seventies.

However we have arrived at our present juncture, the current talk about historical acts of reading provides a welcome opportunity for more explicit consideration of how reading is historically contingent, politically situated, institutionally embedded, and materially conditioned; of how reading any text, literary or nonliterary, relates to a larger cultural politics that goes well beyond some hypothetical private interaction between an autonomous reader and an independent text; and of how our particular views of reading relate to the liberatory potential of literacy and the tranformative power of education. All these questions about the act of reading encouraged reader-response criticism to move more actively in historical and political directions. My own version of this move has led to a focus on the cultural rhetoric in which readings are presented, circulated, adopted, and contested. As I will try to show, this rhetorical focus provides simultaneously a development of reader-oriented criticism, a perspective on recent hermeneutic theory, and an approach within contemporary cultural studies.

Using Rhetoric to Practice Theory by Doing History

Here is one historical act of reading: Margaret Fuller's 1845 review of *The Narrative of the Life of Frederick Douglass, an American Slave*.[5] Fuller begins her review by reading the reception of Douglass's public speaking performances:

> Frederick Douglass has been for some time a prominent member of the Abolition party. He is said to be an excellent speaker—can speak from a thorough personal experience—and has upon the audience, besides, the influence of a strong character and uncommon talents.

Fuller first identifies the radical position of Douglass by placing him as an abolitionist and then describes the rhetorical power of his ethos as an orator: he speaks from the direct knowledge of personal experience, and he conveys the powerful impression of integrity and unusual ability. She then praises Douglass's book for being as "affecting" as his oratory.

> He has had the courage to name the persons, times and places, thus exposing himself to obvious danger, and setting the seal on his deep convictions as to the religious need of speaking the whole truth. Considered merely as a narrative, we have never read one more simple, true, coherent, and warm with genuine feeling. It is an excellent piece of writing, and on that score to be prized as a specimen of the powers of the Black Race, which Prejudice persists in disputing.

By noting the risk Douglass takes as a fugitive slave, Fuller presents the act of publication as itself further proof of the rhetor's strong character and figures this act as officially sealing his narrative with the emblem of an explicitly *religious* motive in "speaking the whole truth."

Fuller then explains why she reads the *Narrative* as an example of literary skills that race prejudice refused to acknowledge. Her argument at this point gets entangled in the ideological rhetoric of what George Fredrickson has called "romantic racialism":[6] the belief, in Fuller's words, that the African Race had in them a peculiar element, which, if it could be assimilated with those imported among us from Europe, would give to genius a development, and to the energies of character a balance and harmony, beyond what has been seen heretofore in the history of the world. Such an element is indicated in their lowest estate by a talent for melody, a ready skill at imitation and adaptation, an almost indestructible elasticity of nature.

Fuller sees these qualities in some black authors' writings that are "glowing with plastic life and fertile in invention," and she claims "the same torrid energy and saccharine fulness may be felt in the writings of this Douglass, though his life, being one of action or resistance, was less favorable to *such* powers than one of a more joyous flow might have been."

Later in her review Fuller takes up Douglass's life of "action or resistance" as it is rhetorically presented in the *Narrative*. Specifically, she reads Douglass's critique of Southern Christianity against the background of the interpretive controversies being widely reported in the secular and religious press. Here is this part of her review in full: In contrast to William Lloyd Garrison, the radical abolitionist whose words introduce the volume,

> Douglass himself seems very just and temperate. We feel that his view, even of those who have injured him most, may be relied upon. He knows how to allow for motives and influences. Upon the subject of Religion, he speaks with great force, and not more than our own sympathies can respond to. The inconsistencies of Slaveholding professors of religion cry to Heaven. We are not disposed to detest, or refuse communion with them. Their blindness is but one form of that prevalent fallacy which substitutes a creed for a faith, a ritual for a life. We have seen too much of this system of atonement not to know that those who adopt it often began with good intentions, and are, at any rate, in their mistakes worthy of the deepest pity. But that is no reason why the truth should not be uttered, trumpet-tongued, about the thing. "Bring no more vain oblations"; sermons must daily be preached anew on that text. Kings, five hundred years ago, built Churches with the spoils of War; Clergymen to-day command Slaves to obey a Gospel which they will not allow them to read, and call themselves Christians amid the curses of their fellow men.

Fuller concludes this part of her reading by asserting, "The Kingdom of Heaven may not at the beginning have dropped seed larger than a mustard-seed, but even from that we had a right to expect a fuller growth than can be believed to exist, when we read such a book as this of Douglass." The review as a whole concludes with a long extract from the *Narrative*, which Fuller introduces as "a suitable answer to the hacknied argument drawn by the defender of Slavery from the songs of the Slave."

Why did Fuller emphasize the religious implications of Douglass's *Narrative* in her review? Why did her historical act of reading argue for this interpretation of Douglass's text? Did Fuller misread Douglass? A psychological reader-response critic might reject the third question as inappropriate and go on to answer the first two questions in terms of a psychobiography of Fuller. A phenomenological or semiotic reader critic might accept all three questions and put forward either an analysis of the implied reader constructed by the *Narrative* or of the codes assumed by it and compare Fuller's review to that reader or those codes. Other seventies forms of reader talk would use related but different notions, such as an intended informed reader or a generally shared literary competence, as a basis for answering the questions.

A rhetorical hermeneutics answers instead with another question: What counts as convincing evidence for addressing these issues? Certainly not a foundationalist theory that first describes a decontextualized model of an idealized reader interacting with a pre-given text and then prescribes comparing this ideal interaction with Fuller's reading of Douglass. But if rhetorical hermeneutics rejects such ahistorical theories of correct interpretation, it does not reject the notion of misreading. Rather, this rhetorical antifoundationalism claims that questions of interpretive validity are rhetorically negotiated in every particular case, not in general through the proscriptions of a foundationalist theory but specifically through particular rhetorical transactions over historically situated topics. In fact, a rhetorical hermeneutics argues that theoretical questions about reading and misreading, about correct interpretations of past and present texts, are never effectively answered in general hermeneutic terms. It advocates instead a turn away from such grand theorizing about interpretation and a turn toward rhetorical histories of specific interpretive acts. Hermeneutic theory becomes rhetorical history.[7]

Such a rhetorical hermeneutics, then, would delay answering the question about Fuller misreading Douglass and begin by addressing the question of why Fuller reads Douglass the way she does. My rhetorical answer to this question presents Fuller's interpretive act as historically located within the cultural conversation of the "Bible politics" of 1845.[8] I will demonstrate my chief theoretical claim in the rest of this essay: rhetorical hermeneutics uses rhetoric to practice theory by doing history.

The *Narrative*'s Rhetoric of Reading

We can begin the rhetorical history of Fuller's interpretation by looking at the long *Narrative* extract she uses to end her review. A part of Douglass's own rhetoric of reading, this extract deals with the way proslavery ideologues misinterpret the songs of slaves. Like many reader-response critics today, Fuller here shows how the text she is reading itself thematizes the problem of reading. The reader-in-the-text strategy appeals to the authority of the text, an appeal prominent in most attempts to argue an interpretation. Such a rhetorical move implies nothing about an ahistorical theory of independent texts, but it does suggest much about historically arguing a case on a particular topic of interpretation.

In the extract Fuller gives, Douglass makes a convincing argument that proslavery ideologues misread the meaning of the slaves' happy-sounding songs when they interpret them as evidence of slave contentment. He puts forward a counterinterpretation which reads the songs as an ironic expression of the slaves' suffering and sadness. In arguing against the racist interpretation of the songs, Douglass's historical act of reading enters into a debate within the ongoing controversy over domestic slavery in the United States. That is, Douglass's interpretation is not simply an interaction with the songs but part of a rhetorical transaction with others engaged in the rancorous struggle over making interested sense of slaves' experiences. Indeed, every act of reading is a reading rhetorically transacted.

Fuller introduces Douglass's reading of slave songs as a "suitable answer" to the "defender of Slavery."[9] But though she also comments on the author's "powers of observation" in the passage, Fuller does not highlight an interesting fact about the rhetorical location of Douglass's "answer" and "observation." Douglass does identify two positions from which the slave songs can be read: from inside the slave's experience and from outside that viewpoint. These are the two reading positions suggested by Fuller's brief introductory comment: Douglass's insider's stance corrects the proslavery outsider's view. However, Douglass actually represents himself as occupying a third position, which is neither insider nor outsider but a combination of the two, and in telling how he reads the songs he suggests additional positions from which historical acts of (mis)reading occur.

Slaves of the out-farms, the extract begins, deemed it a high privilege to be selected as messengers to the "Great House Farm" at the center of the plantation. These slaves would sing "wild songs, revealing at once the highest joy and the deepest sadness." The songs often contained "words which to many would seem unmeaning jargon, but which, nevertheless, were full of meaning to [the slaves] themselves." Later, Douglass voices his astonishment that some people in the North misread these slaves' songs "as evidence of their contentment and happiness." Rather than simply declare himself an insider who reads the songs correctly, however, Douglass complicates what counts as the conditions of correct reading by placing himself first inside and then outside the experience of slavery and suggests that it is precisely that history of changing places that now, in the *Narrative*, gives him the rhetorical authority to correct the misreadings by the defenders of slavery: "I did not, when a slave, understand the deep meaning of those rude and apparently incoherent songs. I was myself within the circle; so that I neither saw nor heard as those without might see and hear. They told a tale of woe which was then altogether beyond my feeble comprehension."[10] Only interpreters occupying the subject position of fugitive slave can correctly read the slaves' songs. Thus, the *Narrative* extract that ends Fuller's review turns back upon her opening comment about Douglass's rhetorical effectiveness and corrects that reading of his speaking performances. It is not, as Fuller implies, that Douglass is an authority simply because he speaks directly "from a thorough personal experience"; for Douglass, it is more important that he also speaks at some distance from the experience of the songs he is reading.[11] In other words, his reading of the songs has authority not simply because he was a slave but because he is now an *escaped* slave, and further he has escaped because of what Fuller calls his "life of action or resistance." It is the very act of resisting that most fully authorizes the rhetoric of Douglass's *Narrative*.

Moreover, the effects of the slave songs first started Douglass on the path to action and resistance. Though he did not understand the full meaning of the songs while a slave, he did respond to them, and their effects on him had consequences: "The hearing of those wild notes always depressed my spirit, and filled me with ineffable sadness. . . . To those songs I trace my first glimmering conception of the dehumanizing character of slavery" (58). Even if Douglass did not fully understand the songs' "deep meaning," his incomplete reading of those songs had specific rhetorical effects that eventually motivated his later acts of resistance. That development took place at least partly through Douglass's growing awareness of literacy's power. His strategic uses of reading and writing constructed a position of agency through which rhetorical effects had political consequences. Douglass reads and writes himself into an act of rebellion.

The story of that rhetorical process has been told quite effectively by several twentieth-century readers of the *Narrative*.[17] I will simply note here that a certain type of reader-response critic would be more interested than most interpreters in the temporal structure of the reader's experience. That is, this critic would discuss not only how Douglass develops as a reader but also how Douglass's reader develops. How, for example, does the *Narrative*'s rhetoric guide the reader in the sequential presentation of Douglass's uses of literacy? How does each episode affect the reading of the next episode? How does the reader make sense of each along the way?

Let me give just one extended example of how a reader-response critic might talk about how the *Narrative* structures the reader's experience through a series of reading episodes leading up to Douglass's achievement of written literacy. After being instructed by the narrator's correction of slave-song misinterpretations at the end of chapter 2, the reader finds in the next chapter's first paragraph an apparently unrelated description of the "large and finely cultivated garden" of Colonel Edward Lloyd, owner of the home plantation where Douglass lived:

> The colonel had to resort to all kinds of stratagems to keep his slaves out of the garden. The last and most successful one was that of tarring his fence all around; after which, if a slave was caught with any tar upon his person, it was deemed sufficient proof that he had either been into the garden, or had tried to get in. In either case, he was severely whipped by the chief gardener. This plan worked well; the slaves became as fearful of tar as of the lash (59).

Here the point is not to correct a misreading, as in the case of the slave songs, but to show the irrelevance of correcting a misreading. It doesn't matter to the slaveholder whether the tar on the slave's body was actually caused by the latter's disobedience; the traces of tar simply signify disobedience, whatever the circumstances. The ploy works because the threat of the lash forces the slaves to accept the master's general interpretation of tarred bodies, even when no act of disobedience occurred. The master's interested reading gets adopted by the slaves because it serves their interests by helping them to avoid a whipping.

At least in this situation the absence or presence of tar is a stable enough sign to read. Not so with the subsequent episode of (mis)reading, which the reader comes upon in the very next paragraph. Colonel Lloyd's horses were a prize possession, and the "slightest inattention to these was unpardonable," resulting in the "severest punishment" for the slaves in charge. But these slaves "never knew when they were safe from punishment. They were frequently whipped when least deserving, and escaped whipping when most deserving it. Every thing depended upon the looks of the horses, and the state of Colonel Lloyd's own mind when his horses were brought to him for use. If a horse did not move fast enough, or hold his head high enough, it was owing to some fault of his keepers" (60). And of course what counts as "fast enough" or "high enough" is what counts as such to Colonel Lloyd. Thus, the slaves are left here with a completely unpredictable act of reading, with the look of the horses dependent on the mind of the master and vice versa.

But if misreadings are correctable in one instance, not correctible but possible to predict in another, and totally unpredictable in a third, it is certainly the position of the reader represented in the text that makes all of the difference: whether slave, master, or escaped slave. This point is brought out clearly in the chapter's final reading episode and concluding comments. Walking along a road, a slave from one of the out-farms fails to recognize his master, Colonel Lloyd, misreading him as a stranger. Colonel Lloyd asks him about his treatment, and the slave, unaware that he is talking to his master, complains. The colonel punishes the slave by selling him without warning, cruelly separating him from his family. Douglass follows this little story with its moral and comments that such incidents partly explain why "slaves, when inquired of as to their condition and the character of their masters, almost universally say they are contented, and that their masters are kind" (62). The reader is not surprised by the consequences of the slave's misreading and has no difficulty supplying the advice behind Douglass's comments: Don't trust the public testimony of *current* slaves.

In transacting the chapter, the reader has seen that in the narrative everything depends on who is doing the reading, from what interested position, within what relationships of power, for what rhetorical purposes, and so forth. More specifically, the question about the reliability of slave testimony has the same answer as the previous chapter's question about slave songs. But here the reader and not the narrator supplies the answer. After engaging chapter 2's rhetorical analysis of reading slave songs and after negotiating chapter 3's sequence of reading episodes, the reader can furnish the hermeneutic guideline: You cannot trust the master or the slave, and therefore it is again, as with the slaves' songs, only the escaped slave, Douglass the author, who speaks from a position of creditable authority. But if the reader contributes this answer, he or she also raises a further question: What are the escaped slave's interests and purposes in writing narratives like the one being read? The answer to this question has been read on almost every page of the tale. Like other versions of the genre, Douglass's slave narrative is explicit about its political interests and rhetorical purposes: to convince readers to support the abolition of slavery.[13]

The reader talk of the last few paragraphs tells us something about Douglass's rhetoric of reading in the *Narrative*, but it only begins to address the historicity of that rhetoric. Before pursuing this point further, I should note that talking about readers reading in texts and about temporal reading experiences are both typical rhetorical strategies practiced by a kind of seventies reader-response criticism associated with Wolfgang Iser, Stanley Fish, and Stephen Booth.[14] It is easy to see that this reader criticism, at least as I have illustrated it here, is in its practice still tied closely to an ahistorical formalism, which prevents development of a more historically rigorous and politically connected form of critical work. Thematizing reading puts the reader in the text and thus enables interpreters to bracket the sociopolitical context of reading. Such reader talk is still only about the text narrowly defined. But so too is most talk about the structure of the ideal reader's response. Is there really a significant difference between describing a sequence of textual episodes and describing the informed reader's reading of those episodes? The reader vocabulary adds very little to the formalist analysis, except the term "reader" and some other readerly descriptors. What the reader vocabulary does do, however, is open up possibilities for different kinds of reading discussions. One could take the reader focus in a psychological direction (as David Bleich and Norman Holland have done) and talk about the specific responses of student readers. Or one could take the reader focus in a semiotic direction (as Jonathan Culler and Umberto Eco have done) and talk about the codes that constitute the conditions of reading. I would like to pursue a different tack here and suggest that reader-oriented criticism can (indeed has already) become more historical and political in talking about both the reader reading in the text and the past reader of the text.

To begin with the reader in the text, we can look briefly at one of the *Narrative*'s most interesting stories of reading: Douglass's interpretation and response to *The Columbian Orator*, Caleb Bingham's popular anthology of speeches and debates. Critics have used *The Columbian Orator* to interpret Douglass's rhetoric, but I want to look more closely at how the narrator's earlier self reads *The Columbian Orator*.[15] Douglass writes:

> Every opportunity I got, I used to read this book. Among much of other interesting matter, I found in it a dialogue between a master and his slave. The slave was represented as having run away from his master three times. The dialogue represented the conversation which took place between them, when the slave was retaken the third time. In this dialogue, the whole argument in behalf of slavery was brought forward by the master, all of which was disposed of by the slave. The slave was made to say some very smart as well as impressive things in reply to his master—things which had the desired though unexpected effect; for the conversation resulted in the voluntary emancipation of the slave on the part of the master. (*Narrative* 83)

Douglass offers this view of why the slave's persuasion worked: "The moral which I gained from the dialogue was the power of truth over the conscience of even a slaveholder" (84).

On this key point Douglas misreads the dialogue in attributing the slave's rhetorical effectiveness to a successful appeal to the master's conscience. The master wants his slave to admit he has been treated well: "Gratitude! I repeat, gratitude! Have I not endeavoured ever since I possessed you to alleviate your misfortunes by kind treatment; and does that confer no obligation?"[16] But the slave counters every example of his master's generosity with a moral argument against the whole system of slavery itself. The master is not looking for ethical justification, however. He desires a show of gratitude for the practical reason that he doesn't want the slave to run away again, and he clearly feels that an internal motive of gratitude would be more effective than an external threat of punishment.

> *Mast.* Is it impossible, then, to hold you by any ties but those of constraint and severity?
> *Slave.* It is impossible to make one, who has felt the value of freedom, acquiesce in being a slave.
> *Mast.* Suppose I were to restore you to your liberty, would you reckon that a favour?
> *Slave.* The greatest; for although it would only be undoing a wrong, I know too well how few among mankind are capable of sacrificing interest to justice not to prize the exertion when it is made.
> *Mast.* I do it, then; be free.
> *Slave.* Now I am indeed your servant, though not your slave.
>   (*Columbian Orator* 242)

The dialogue ends with the slave returning the master's kindness by advising him about the violent threat posed by the slaves: "You are surrounded with implacable foes, who long for a safe opportunity to revenge upon you and the other planters all the miseries they have endured." He concludes: "Superior force alone can give you security. As soon as that fails, you are at the mercy of the merciless. Such is the social bond between master and slave!"

Whatever else is going on in this dialogue, it is certainly not disinterested altruism that motivates the master to emancipate his slave. Perhaps the slave does appeal to his master's conscience, as Douglass suggests, but it is practical exigency, narrow self-interest, that motivates the master's decision. Douglass has misread the dialogue when he interprets its moral as the "power of truth over the conscience of even a slaveholder."

But Douglass has not misread what is most significant about the debate for him. He reads correctly the slave's complete dedication to resisting his bondage, and he later imitates it. This fact returns us to the whole question of what Fuller calls Douglass's "life of action or resistance." As I have said, that life is significantly constituted by the rhetorical effects of Douglass's reading. In the present case, reading *The Columbian Orator* had very concrete effects on Douglass's condition as a slave. On the positive side, he was empowered by adopting pieces of the book's rhetoric: "The reading of these documents enabled me to utter my thoughts, and to meet the arguments brought forward to sustain slavery." On the negative side, his suffering greatly increased because literacy had given him a view of his "wretched condition, without the remedy." "I would at times feel that learning to read had been a curse rather than a blessing" (*Narrative* 84). These rhetorical effects of reading eventually motivated Douglass to find the remedy he required. That remedy, an act of rebellion, develops at least partly through his uses of reading and writing and their rhetorical effects on himself and others.

I say "partly" because Douglass himself represents the initiating moment of rebellion as an act mysterious and inexplicable. Indeed, the *Narrative* resists my attempt to give a rhetorical specificity to the motives for Douglass's initial resistance. He introduces the climactic episode by directly addressing his readers: "You have seen how a man was made a slave; you shall see how a slave was made a man" (107). But when he describes how he physically resisted the slave-breaker Edward Covey, Douglass cannot explain the act of rebellion: "At this moment—from whence came the spirit I don't know—I resolved to fight" (112).[17] Whatever the cause or motive for his resistance, however, Douglass later reads the act as the "turning-point" in his "career as a slave" (113); and by so naming it, he constructs a position of agency, which has been constituted at least partly through his past uses of literacy. Like the slave in *The Columbian Orator*, Douglass would escape from bondage. The battle with Covey, Douglass writes, "rekindled the few expiring embers of freedom, and revived within me a sense of my own manhood. It recalled the departed self-confidence, and inspired me again with a determination to be free" (113).

The Cultural Rhetoric of 1845

Given Douglass's misreading of the master's motivation in the dialogue of *The Columbian Orator* and given the incomplete explanation for his own act of rebellion, one might claim that Fuller has misread the *Narrative* in praising Douglass for knowing "how to allow for motives and influences." But such a criticism of Fuller would be misplaced because she praises Douglass's knowledge of motives and influences not in relation to his own actions but in relation to the ideological practices of slaveholders. Specifically, Fuller centers her review of the *Narrative* on its treatment of "the subject of Religion," upon which Douglass "speaks with great force, and not more than our own sympathies can respond to." For Fuller, the rhetorical power of the *Narrative* resides especially in Douglass's persuasive critique of "the inconsistencies of Slaveholding professors of religion."

Reading the cultural rhetoric through which Fuller reviews Douglass and in which she herself speaks on the subject of religion will allow me to give a final example of how reader criticism can develop beyond formalism and will return me more explicitly to my task of using rhetoric to practice theory by doing history. Fuller's act of interpreting the *Narrative* can best be understood not through a grand hermeneutic theory (whether formalist or intentionalist, phenomenological or semiotic) but by a rhetorical reception study, a historical interpretation of the cultural debates in which Fuller read Douglass. Here I want to emphasize not only that every act of reading is a reading rhetorically transacted but also that rhetorical hermeneutics makes every act of reading an act historically read.

I have already begun a historical interpretation of the 1845 cultural conversation by discussing the rhetorical activity in Douglass's *Narrative*, which is, of course, a participant in that conversation. Fuller reads Douglass as intervening in the contemporary debates over proslavery ideology and its relation to organized religion. There are several ways in which Fuller ties her reading to this debate, and in what follows I will explore only some of these rhetorical connections.

Immediately before Fuller turns to Douglass's critique of slaveowning professors of religion, she compares his rhetoric favorably to that of his sponsor, William Lloyd Garrison, whose introduction opens the volume. Fuller laments Garrison's "over emphatic style. His motives and his course have been noble and generous. We look upon him with high respect, but he has indulged in violent invective and denunciation till he has spoiled the temper of his mind. Like a man who has been in the habit of screaming himself hoarse to make the deaf hear, he can no longer pitch his voice on a key agreeable to common ears." Garrison's well-motivated but fanatical rhetoric has, according to Fuller, turned on its user and affected *his* mind rather than his audience's; and rather than getting the deaf to hear slavery's victims, Garrison has made those who might have heard deaf to his own rhetoric. In contrast, Douglass comes across as "very just and temperate." But Fuller did not reject simply the style of Garrisonian rhetoric; she also had problems with its political arguments for dealing with slaveholders and all those institutionally connected with them.

In 1831 Garrison helped found the New England Anti-Slavery Society and began publication of *The Liberator* in Boston. Garrisonian abolition called for the immediate emancipation of slaves and attacked all forms of compromise with slaveholders, including gradualist anti-slavery and colonization programs. What particularly distinguished the ideological rhetoric of radical abolition was its heavy investment in moral suasion. From the first, Garrisonian abolitionists focused not on the economic or political arguments against slavery but on a religious critique. When the national American Anti-Slavery Society (AASS) was founded in New York City in 1833, its Declaration of Sentiments, written by Garrison, combined an explicitly religious vocabulary with the ideological rhetoric of the American Revolution. "The right to enjoy liberty is inalienable. To invade it is to usurp the prerogative of Jehovah." The declaration goes on to appropriate a biblical trope that appears often in abolitionist rhetoric and figures the economic center of the proslavery argument: "Every American citizen, who detains a human being in involuntary bondage as his property, is, according to Scripture (Ex. xxi, 16,), a man-stealer."[18] The use of this trope of property in 1830s abolitionist literature signals a rhetorical continuity with the earlier American debates over slavery, which were most often framed in terms of political economy.

But a break with earlier discussions also marks the radical abolitionist rhetoric of the 1830s. Larry Tise describes the new rhetorical context after the appearance of Garrisonian abolition: "For the first time since the debate on slavery began in the eighteenth century, every writer who favored its perpetuation found it necessary to discuss the manner in which slavery could be viewed as a moral (at least not immoral) institution."[19] Abolitionist rhetoric was ethical in its appeal and specifically religious in its targets. As the AASS declaration put it, "We shall enlist the pulpit and the press in the cause of the suffering and the dumb. We shall aim at a purification of the churches from all participation in the guilt of slavery."[20] The course of this rhetorical effort at moral suasion has been charted by many historians of Garrisonian abolitionism. Suffice it to say here that abolitionist criticism of the Christian clergy intensified as major religious denominations failed to join the call for immediate emancipation of all slaves and rejection of all support and affiliation with slaveholders. A speech by Wendell Phillips, whose letter follows Garrison's preface and precedes Douglass's narrative, provides an especially useful summary of the radical abolitionist view of organized religion in 1845.

In May of that year, the New York *Observer and Evangelist* reported Phillips's rhetorical performance at the annual meeting of the American Anti-Slavery Society: Phillips gave "a speech of some length, but replete with sentiments, which however repugnant to general opinion, were expressed with a clear and lofty eloquence."[21] The oration focused on the Garrisonian credo that "there must be no union, in either Church or State, with slaveholders." Though Phillips criticized both religious and political institutions, the *Observer and Evangelist* detailed only his attack on Christian churches for their unchristian support of slavery. According to Phillips, abolitionists had for years tried unsuccessfully "to evoke from the Church the voice of Christian remonstrance against the system which the spirit of Christ and of humanity both united to condemn." This focus on the churches emanated from two factors: the rhetorical effectiveness of ministers—"the people have been clay in the hands of those to whom they looked up as religious teachers"—and the current rhetorical context: "All other influences in this land are but the dust of the balance, compared with that which is exerted by the religious feeling of the country. We have no other source of power to which we can appeal." Thus, Phillips applauds recent controversies within some denominations that led to divisions between northern and southern branches: "Two of our great churches are breaking—the Methodist and the Baptist. Thank God!"

Sectional schisms over slavery occurred in the Methodist Episcopal Church in 1844 and in the Baptist Triennial Convention in 1845. In contrast, the Old School Presbyterian General Assembly of 1845, though condemning slavery, voted overwhelmingly that the Bible did not require excluding slaveholders from church fellowship.[22] As other churches also confronted the disunion question 1845, the secular and religious press throughout the country reported extensively on these controversies.

Much of the religious debate over the morality of slavery and Christian union with slaveholders proceeded through radically divergent readings of the Christian Bible. Fuller's review of Douglass enters directly into this multifaceted and highly contested Bible politics of interpretation. When she praises Douglass for his attack on the "inconsistencies of slaveholding professors of religion," she places herself with the forces of Northern antislavery. But when she claims not to be "disposed to detest, or refuse communion with" slaveholders, she just as clearly declares herself not to be a Garrisonian abolitionist. In reviewing the *Narrative*, Fuller stands as an antislavery advocate between radical abolitionists and proslavery ideologues.[23] And from that position she joins in Bible politics herself when she quotes Isaiah 1:13, "Bring no more vain oblations," against proslavery Christians and when she alludes to the Gospel parable of the mustard seed in declaring, "We had a right to expect a fuller growth [in the kingdom of God] than can be believed to exist, when we read such a book as this of Douglass."

But Fuller's entry into the religious debate over slavery includes another aspect of the controversy, an aspect we might call the Bible politics of *literacy*: she condemns those clergy who "to-day command Slaves to obey a Gospel which they will not allow them to read, and call themselves Christians amid the curses of their fellow men." Fuller is referring to the Southern policy of restricting slaves to oral instruction in religion. Taught that Scripture required obedience to their masters, most slaves were unable to read the Bible for themselves. In response to slave insurrections and abolitionist literature, Southern states passed laws making it a crime to teach slaves to read and write, and even in states without such laws, local custom usually discouraged any fostering of slave literacy. Apologists argued that "the teaching of slaves to read and write has a tendency to excite dissatisfaction in their minds, and to produce insurrection and rebellion."[24] In Douglass's case, this argument turned out to be correct. Hugh Auld forbad his wife to teach Douglass to read, claiming that "there would be no keeping him. It would forever unfit him to be a slave. He would at once become unmanageable, and of no value to his master. As to himself, it could do him no good, but a great deal of harm. It would make him discontented and unhappy" (*Narrative* 78). All of these predictions come true as Douglass overhears Auld's warning to his wife and realizes that "the white man's power to enslave the black man" resides in keeping the slave illiterate. He therefore resolves to learn to read on his own. "From that moment, I understood the pathway from slavery to freedom" (78).

Douglass does not mention in the *Narrative* a detail he later notes in a speech given before the Belfast Anti-Slavery Society. As a token of rememberance, the society presented Douglass with an "elegantly bound" and "beautifully gilt" Bible. In his speech he makes use of the Bible to attack slavery but also employs it as a pretext for the following story:

> I remember the first time I ever heard the Bible read, and I tell you the truth when I tell you, that from that time I trace my first desire to learn to read. I was over seven years old. . . . I had crawled under the centre table and had fallen asleep, when my mistress commenced to read the Bible aloud, so loud that she waked me—she waked me to sleep no more! I have found, since I learned to read, that the chapter which she then read was the 1st chapter of Job. I remember my sympathy for the good old man; and my great anxiety to know more about him led me to ask my mistress . . . to teach me to read. She commenced, and would have, but for the opposition of her husband, taught me to read. She ceased to instruct me, but my desire to read continued, and, instead of decreasing, increased.[25]

Thus, Douglass attributes to the Bible the origin of his own desire for written literacy, which enabled him to understand *The Columbian Orator*, fulfill the worst fears of his Southern masters, and eventually rebel against his condition as a slave.

Though Douglass does not include in his *Narrative* this story of biblical influence, he does provide other examples of the Bible politics of literacy: he describes the suppression of a Sabbath school for slaves being taught to read the New Testament (98), and he condemns the man "who proclaims it a religious duty to read the Bible" but "denies me the right of learning to read the name of the God who made me" (154). In her review, Fuller picks up on these powerful complaints against the "professors of religion."

This last phrase refers in Fuller's and Douglass's texts to those defenders of slavery who profess Christianity as they misread Scripture to justify slaveholding practices. Douglass describes the "nigger-breaker" Covey as "a professor of religion—a pious soul—a member and a class-leader in the Methodist Church" (100). Covey's employer and Douglass's master, Captain Thomas Auld, "found religious sanction for his [own] cruelty" and justified whipping a lame young woman by citing the scriptural passage, "He that knoweth his master's will, and doeth it not, shall be beaten with many stripes" (98–99).

This paraphrase of Luke 12:47 appears as an especially ironic misreading when compared with most traditional interpretations. The passage forms part of Jesus' own reading of the parable about a householder surprised by a thief. Peter asks Jesus whether the intended audience for the story is the disciples or everybody. Jesus replies that the parable is directed at the "faithful and wise steward, whom *his* lord" has made "ruler over his household," that is, at the disciples who have been given responsibility for the kingdom of God. The person referred to in Luke 12:47 is this servant, the steward in charge of the household, whose disobedience should be punished with "many stripes."[26] Auld ignores Jesus' reading that focuses on the responsibility of church leaders, and instead he puts himself in God's place so that the passage is turned on the disobedience of *his* slaves rather than on his own responsibility as God's steward.[27]

But a Bible politics of interpretation was employed not just by individual slaveholders to defend slave management techniques nor simply by abolitionist reformers in moral appeals to the consciences of the Christian churches. We might also read "professors of religion" more technically. The debate over Bible politics was indeed a popular lay debate over slavery practices; however, it was also a specifically professional controversy among theologians and philosophers arguing over the morality of slavery. Douglass might have been right (in the Fuller review extract) when he argued that hearing slave songs more effectively revealed the "horrible character of slavery, than the reading of whole volumes of philosophy" (*Narrative* 57); but the reading and debate over such writings by certified experts in ethics often focused the slavery controversy in the 1840s.

One example of professional Bible politics from 1844–45 received wide newspaper coverage during the reception of Douglass's *Narrative*. In a letter to the editor of the Boston *Christian Reflector*, Rev. Richard Fuller of Beaufort, South Carolina, made the usual proslavery arguments that "the Old Testament did sanction slavery" and that "in the Gospels and Epistles, the institution is to say the least tolerated."[28] In the course of his argument, Fuller quotes from *The Elements of Moral Science*, a text frequently used in moral philosophy courses in antebellum colleges, the charge that slavery is a "moral evil."[29] The author of the *Elements*, Francis Wayland, president of Brown University and a fellow Baptist minister, responded to Fuller's defense of slavery in a series of letters to the *Christian Reflector*. In the first he agrees with Fuller "that the tone of the Abolitionists at the North has been ... 'fierce, bitter and abusive.'"[30] Having established his antiabolitionist credententials, he goes on, at very great length, to demonstrate how Fuller has misread or misapplied various biblical references to slavery. Wayland clarifies what he meant by "moral evil" and, of course, quotes the Bible to establish his own overriding principle for condemning slavery: slavery is a "transgression of the law of our Creator, 'Thou should love thy neighbor as thyself.'"[31] Not surprisingly, when Fuller's and Wayland's letters were published as a book in May 1845, the review in Garrison's *Liberator* suggested that both were misreading the Bible. The reviewer especially criticized Wayland and complained that "compromise is the peculiar danger of the Anti-Slavery cause." Abolitionists must never "recognize slaveholders as Christian brethren" and should reject all invitations to do so by answering with the words of Nehemiah, the Old Testament patriarch: "I am doing a great work, so that I cannot come down; why should the work cease, whilst I leave it, and come down to you?"[32]

Bible politics and its interpretive controversies took many forms throughout the 1840s. Professional and popular discussions intersected, as different contestants occupied a wide spectrum of ideological positions: Southern slaveholders, proslavery clergy, Northern antiabolitionist conservatives, Christian (non-Garrisonian) abolitionists, radical Garrisonians, and others. Margaret Fuller explicitly joins these debates as she reads the Bible politics of Douglass's *Narrative* and declares her own non-Garrisonian antislavery views.

One of the most interesting aspects of that reading is Fuller's comment on the "blindness" of proslavery ideology. She compliments Douglass for his just and reliable treatment of even those slaveholders who injured him most. "He knows how to allow for motives and influences." She implies that those "motives and influences" account for the "blindness" of slavery's defenders to the "inconsistencies" of their proslavery ideology. "Their blindness is but one form of that prevalent fallacy which substitutes a creed for a faith, a ritual for a life." Douglass seems to agree with this ideological reading of slaveholders when he charges even Covey less with hypocrisy than with self-deception (*Narrative* 104).[33] Later, in responding to a Southerner's attack on the credibility of his narrative, Douglass develops further his ideological critique of slavery as a self-validating system of belief: "Slavery has its own standard of morality, humanity, justice, and Christianity. Tried by that standard, it is a system of the greatest kindness to the slave—sanctioned by the purest morality—in perfect agreement with justice—and, of course, not inconsistent with Christianity."[34]

No better illustration of Douglass and Fuller's point about ideological blindness can be found than the following passage from A. C. C. Thompson, the critic of the *Narrative* to whose earlier letter Douglass had responded. Thompson writes: "But tell me, is the Southerner to be deprecated because he owns a slave, more than the Northern Abolitionist, who, in defiance of all law and honor, steals a slave from his lawful owner, and will then manufacture an incredible story without the least shadow of truth, to defame the character of slaveholders? If such is your opinion, you have studied some code of morality that I have never seen."[35] No long philosophical argument could make Douglass's point more clearly than these two sentences from his opponent. Thompson apparently cannot even *see* the code of morality that reveals his own slave code ethics as false or even questionable. But, as Douglass argues further, when slavery is "tried by any other" system, "it is doomed to condemnation."[36] And indeed from those other positions slavery *must* be condemned, as Fuller puts it, even if we grant that those supporting the evil of slavery may have at one time had "good intentions" and are now deserving of our "deepest pity." That fact "is no reason why the truth should not be uttered, trumpet-tongued, about the thing."

Both Fuller and Douglass here contribute to what might be called a rhetorical view of ideology: interpretive arguments are produced and read within positions constituted by specific ideologies of particular historical communities. From this perspective, the practices of slavery can be seen as constructing "subjects"—both masters and slaves—within an ideology of proslavery religion. In his later rereading of his own rebellion, Douglass makes explicit how the Bible politics of the slaveholder's ideological rhetoric positions slaves as well as masters. In *My Bondage and My Freedom*, where Douglass retells the story of his fight with Covey, not only does he give himself more agency in choosing to fight; he also identifies his acceptance of proslavery "religious views" as a reason he had not resisted sooner.[37] Thus, both slave and slaveholder are subjects constructed by the cultural rhetoric of proslavery ideology, an ideology consisting significantly of an interested reading of "the African Race" and of the

the Christian Bible. Douglass's and Fuller's readings of the Bible are no less interested, but obviously their interests differ radically from those of slavery's defenders. It is in direct and pointed opposition to the latter that Fuller reads Douglass's *Narrative*, and her review constitutes a rhetorical act within the 1845 debate over biblical interpretation, antislavery politics, and proslavery ideology.

Fuller's reading of Douglass can now be heard as transacting business with the *Narrative* as a participant and topic within the cultural conversation over Bible politics. In reviewing Douglass, Fuller is responding to the current debates over Christianity and slavery; in responding to these debates, she is reading Douglass. Fuller's rhetorical exchanges with the debates and with the *Narrative* cannot be separated, and neither can be isolated from the historically specific, politically charged configuration of cultural rhetoric I have attempted to analyze in this essay. One can talk as a formalist about the rhetoric of the text; but that text is rhetorically constituted by its location and activity within an intertexual space of cultural rhetoric, which includes the subject positions of its author, Frederick Douglass, and its reader, Margaret Fuller. And one can talk as a reader-oriented critic about a specific reader reading; but that transaction, including the agency of the reader and the theme of reading in the text, are constituted by their location and activity within the cultural rhetoric of 1845. Does Fuller misread Douglas? Not within the story I have told about the cultural rhetoric of Bible politics. But my reading is, of course, only as strong as the case I have made. And this rhetorical act of reading will itself be historically read and rhetorically transacted.

Notes

The epigraphs are from Louise M. Rosenblatt, *Literature as Exploration*, 2nd ed. (New York: Noble, 1968) 271, and Gayatri Spivak with Ellen Rooney, "In a Word: Interview," *differences* 1 (1989): 135. I would like to thank Bill Cain and Peter Carafiol for helpful suggestions about an earlier version of this essay.

1. For more on reader-response criticism, especially its inclusions and exclusions, see Peter J. Rabinowitz, "Whirl without End: Audience-Oriented Criticism," in *Contemporary Literary Theory*, ed. G. Douglas Atkins and Laura Morrow (Amherst: U of Massachusetts P, 1989) 81–100; Steven Mailloux, "The Turns of Reader Response Criticism," in *Conversations: Contemporary Critical Theory and the Teaching of Literature*, ed. Charles Moran and Elizabeth F. Penfield

(Urbana: NCTE, 1990) 38–54; and Philip Goldstein, *The Politics of Literary Theory* (Tallahassee: Florida State UP, 1990) 100–146. For the best introduction to reader criticism of the seventies, see Jane P. Tompkins, ed., *Reader-Response Criticism: From Formalism to Post-Structuralism* (Baltimore: Johns Hopkins UP, 1980).

2. See Wolfgang Iser, *The Implied Reader: Patterns of Communication in Prose Fiction from Bunyan to Beckett* (Baltimore: Johns Hopkins UP, 1974); and Iser, *The Act of Reading: A Theory of Aesthetic Response* (Baltimore: Johns Hopkins UP, 1978). Also see Brook Thomas, "Reading Wolfgang Iser or Responding to a Theory of Response," *Comparative Literature Studies* 19 (1982): 54–66, and Steven Mailloux, *Interpretive Conventions: The Reader in the Study of American Fiction* (Ithaca: Cornell UP, 1982), ch. 2.

3. Besides these two books, also see Robert C. Holub, *Reception Theory: A Critical Introduction* (London: Methuen, 1984); and Hans Robert Jauss, *Question and Answer: Forms of Dialogic Understanding*, trans. and ed. Michael Hays (Minneapolis: U of Minnesota P, 1989).

4. See, for example, Stanley Fish's early claim about the "radically historical" nature of his critical method in "Literature in the Reader: Affective Stylistics," *New Literary History*, 2 (1970–71), rpt. in Tompkins, *Reader-Response Criticism* 87. Also see Iser, *Act of Reading* ch.3, on the "pragmatics of literature" and the historical "repertoire" within the text.

5. *New-York Daily Tribune* June 10, 1845: 1. All quotations from Fuller in the text are from this source and this page.

6. George Fredrickson, *The Black Image in the White Mind: The Debate on Afro-American Character and Destiny, 1817–1914* (New York: Harper, 1971) ch. 4. Bell Gale Chevigny applies Fredrickson's term to Fuller's review in *The Woman and the Myth: Margaret Fuller's Life and Writings* (Old Westbury, N.Y.: Feminist, 1976) 340.

7. For a detailed discussion of rhetorical hermeneutics, see Steven Mailloux, *Rhetorical Power* (Ithaca: Cornell UP, 1989), and "Rhetorical Hermeneutics Revisited," *Text and Performance Quarterly* 11 (1991): 233–48.

8. I take this phrase from the title of an 1845 lecture by the Christian abolitionist Gerrit Smith, in which he cited scriptural passages to urge men to vote for antislavery candidates. Since Garrison had concluded by 1845 that the U.S. Constitution was a proslavery document, he rejected any participation in the voting process and thus criticized Smith's citation of the Bible as "useless." See "Bible Politics," *Liberator* November 14, 1845: 183. This is only one of several political controversies over how to interpret and use the Bible, which I will be describing as constitutive of the rhetorical context of Fuller's review. In adapting the phrase "Bible politics" to refer to debates over slave literacy and scriptural defenses of slavery, I am modifying and extending the 1840s usage of the term, which referred primarily to campaigning and voting in national elections and working within

traditional party politics. See Aileen S. Kraditor, *Means and Ends in American Abolitionism: Garrison and His Critics on Strategy and Tactics, 1834–1850* (New York: Pantheon-Random House, 1969); cf. James Brewer Stewart, "Abolitionists, the Bible, and the Challenge of Slavery," in *The Bible and Social Reform*, ed. Ernest R. Sandeen (Philadelphia: Fortress, 1982) 31–57.

9. After having published Garrison's introduction to the *Narrative* the previous week, the *Liberator* printed the slave-songs passage as its first extract from Douglass's story and followed it with the comment: "So much for the songs of the enslaved—so much for their happy and contented lot" (May 23, 1845: 82).

10. Frederick Douglass, *Narrative of the Life of Frederick Douglass, an American Slave*, ed. Houston A. Baker (New York: Penguin, 1982) 57. Subsequent citations of the *Narrative* in the text refer to this edition.

11. Cf. the similar point made by Albert E. Stone, "Identity and Art in Frederick Douglass's *Narrative*," *CLA Journal* 17 (1973): 203. Also see Henry Louis Gates, Jr., "Binary Oppositions in Chapter One of *Narrative of the Life of Frederick Douglass an American Slave Written by Himself*," in *Afro-American Literature: The Reconstruction of Instruction*, ed. Dexter Fisher and Robert B. Stepto (New York: MLA, 1979) 230; and Sterling Stuckey, "'Ironic Tenacity': Frederick Douglass's Seizure of the Dialectic," in *Frederick Douglass: New Literary and Historical Essays*, ed. Eric J. Sundquist (Cambridge: Cambridge UP, 1991) 32–38.

12. For discussions that place Douglass's literacy process within broader histories of literacy, see Janet Cornelius, "'We Slipped and Learned to Read': Slave Accounts of the Literacy Process, 1830–1865," *Phylon*, 44 (1983): 171–86; and Dana Nelson Salvino, "The Word in Black and White: Ideologies of Race and Literacy in Antebellum America," in *Reading in America: Literature and Social History*, ed. Cathy Davidson (Baltimore: Johns Hopkins UP, 1989) 140–56. Also see Henry Louis Gates, Jr., *The Signifying Monkey: A Theory of African-American Literary Criticism* (New York: Oxford UP, 1988) 166–67.

13. Though Douglass and other slave narrators were quite explicit about their rhetorical goals, they often used indirect and subtle strategies in attempting to persuade readers to identify with their interests and accept their purposes. For discussions of these rhetorical strategies and additional bibliography, see Lucinda H. MacKethan, "Metaphors of Mastery in the Slave Narratives," Keith Byerman, "We Wear the Mask: Deceit as Theme and Style in Slave Narratives," and Mary Ellen Doyle, S.C.N., "The Slave Narratives as Rhetorical Art," all in *The Art of the Slave Narrative: Original Essays in Criticism and Theory*, ed. John Secora and Darwin T. Turner (Macomb: Western Illinois UP, 1982) 55–95. Also see Robert B. Stepto, *From Behind the Veil: A Study of Afro-American Narratives* (Urbana: U of Illinois P, 1979), esp. 16–26; William L. Andrews, *To Tell a Free Story: The First Century of Afro-American Autobiography, 1760–1865* (Urbana: U of Illinois P, 1986) 123–38; and Greg-

ory Jay, *America the Scrivener: Deconstruction and the Subject of Literary History* (Ithaca: Cornell UP, 1990) 236–76.

14. For an institutional history and rhetorical analysis of this form of reader-response criticism, see Mailloux, *Rhetorical Power* 29–53.

15. See, for example, John W. Blassingame, Introduction to Series One, *Frederick Douglass Papers*, Series One, *Speeches, Debates, and Interviews*, Volume 1: *1841–1846*, ed. John W. Blassingame (New Haven: Yale UP, 1979) xxii–xxiii; and Joseph Fichtelberg, *The Complex Image: Faith and Method in American Autobiography* (Philadelphia: U of Pennsylvania P, 1989) 120–35.

16. Caleb Bingham, *The Columbian Orator: Containing a Variety of Original and Selected Pieces; Together with Rules; Calculated to Improve Youth and Others in the Ornamental and Useful Art of Eloquence* (Boston: Frost, 1827) 241.

17. The closest Douglass gets to a causal explanation is the magical roots given him by his fellow slave, Sandy Jenkins, but he rejects the claim that his success resulted from the roots' protective powers (119). Later, in his second autobiography, Douglass presents the persuasive case Sandy made for using the roots: "'My book-learning,' he said, 'had not kept Covey off me [in the past]' (a powerful argument just then)" (*My Bondage and My Freedom* [1855; New York: Dover, 1969] 138). For discussion of Douglass's 1855 re-description of his rebellion, see Bernd Ostendorf, "Violence and Freedom: The Covey Episode in Frederick Douglass' Autobiography," in *Myth and Enlightenment in American Literature*, ed. Dieter Meindl and Friedrich W. Horlacher (Erlangen: Universitätsbund Erlangen-Nürnberg, 1985) 257–70; and David Leverenz, *Manhood and the American Renaissance* (Ithaca: Cornell UP, 1989) 108–34.

18. "Declaration of Sentiments of the American Anti-Slavery Society," in *The Abolitionists*, ed. Louis Ruchames (New York: Capricorn, 1964) 80.

19. Larry Tise, *Proslavery: A History of the Defense of Slavery in America, 1701–1840* (Athens: U of Georgia P, 1987) 116. Readers of Tise's important book will no doubt find it ironic that I am using him to support my argument for a change in rhetorical context when one of his main points is to challenge traditional claims about such changes, in particular the claim that "the positive good argument in defense of slavery" was "unique to the Old South" (98). But while Tise does provide evidence for similarities in the available ideological rhetoric over different periods and in different locations of slavery debates, he also asserts that there were differences in the significance given, for example, to moral forms of argumentation in the United States during the 1830s and after. For a rhetorician, such differences in significance are important because they help explain the particular interpretive rhetoric used by a reviewer like Fuller in reading Douglass's *Narrative*. Nevertheless, it is also important for understanding the rhetorical context of Fuller and Douglass to take note of Tise's central thesis. He claims that what makes American

proslavery history truly distinctive is not the content of Southern slaveholders' arguments but their origin. Though Southerners developed a proslavery defense, they did so, Tise claims, by adopting the ideological arguments of Northern anti-abolitionists, who preceded Southerners in formulating a "proslavery republicanism" in response to the abolitionists in the early 1830s (348). These conservative Northern antiabolitionists remained a significant part of the 1845 audience that read Douglass's abolitionist *Narrative* and Fuller's antislavery review. For a general discussion of antebellum readers, see Charles H. Nichols, "Who Read the Slave Narratives?" *Phylon Quarterly*, 20 (1959): 149–62; and Nina Baym, *Novels, Readers, and Reviewers: Responses to Fiction in Antebellum America* (Ithaca: Cornell UP, 1984).

20. "Declaration of Sentiments" 82.

21. "American Anti-Slavery Society," New York *Observer and Evangelist*, rpt. in the *Liberator* May 16, 1845: 79. All quotations that follow are from this page. In these passages the *Observer and Evangelist* appears to be quoting directly from Phillips's speech, though quotation marks are not used.

22. John R. McKivigan, *The War against Proslavery Religion: Abolitionism and the Northern Churches, 1830–1865* (Ithaca: Cornell UP, 1984) 83.

23. Earlier in the year, Fuller had praised the "noble" and "calm" tone of Richard Hildreth's antislavery novel, *The Slave, or, Memoirs of Archy Moore* (5th ed., 1845), concluding her review by saying, "Such productions have results upon the world, such as fierce invective and mechanical arrangements for the expression of opinion never can" (*New-York Daily Tribune*, February 4, 1845: 1). Also see Fuller, *Woman in the Nineteenth Century* (New York: Greeley, 1845). For a more general discussion of Fuller's views, see Francis E. Kearns, "Margaret Fuller and the Abolition Movement," *Journal of the History of Ideas* 25 (1964): 120–27; on antislavery feminism, see Jean Fagan Yellin, *Women and Sisters: The Antislavery Feminists in American Culture* (New Haven: Yale UP, 1989).

24. *Laws of North Carolina, 1830–31*, ch. 6: 11; rpt. in *The Black American and Education*, ed. Earle H. West (Columbus: Merrill, 1972) 21. On Southern laws and policies against teaching slaves to read, see C. G. Woodson, *The Education of the Negro Prior to 1861* (2nd ed. 1919; New York: Arno, 1968), ch. 7. The situation in Douglass's state is discussed by Jeffrey R. Brackett, *The Negro in Maryland: A Study of the Institution of Slavery* (Baltimore: N. Murray, 1889) 197; and Dickson J. Preston, *Young Frederick Douglass: The Maryland Years* (Baltimore: Johns Hopkins UP, 1980) 93–94, 115–16.

25. "The Bible Opposes Oppression, Fraud, and Wrong: An Address Delivered in Belfast, Ireland, on 6 January 1846," *Frederick Douglass Papers*, 1:127. Another version of the incident appears in *My Bondage and My Freedom* 145.

26. *The Interpreter's Bible*, ed. George Buttrick et al. (New York: Abingdon-Cokesbury, 1952) 8:234.

27. Auld's misreading of the passage to justify whipping the woman becomes even more appallingly and directly ironic when one notes Jesus' warning that if the servant left in charge begins "to beat the menservants and maidens . . . the lord of that servant will come" when not expected and "cut him in sunder" (Luke 12: 45–46).

28. "Letter from the Rev. Richard Fuller on the Subject of Slavery," *Christian Reflector*, rpt. in Boston *Christian Watchman* December 6, 1844: 196.

29. Originally published in 1835, *The Elements of Moral Science* went through several editions. An 1859 reprint of the 1837 fourth edition claims 73,000 copies in print (Boston: Gould, 1859).

30. Francis Wayland, "To the Rev. Richard Fuller, D.D.," *Christian Reflector*, rpt. in *Christian Watchman* December 6, 1844: 196.

31. "Dr. Wayland to Dr. Fuller: Letter IV," *Christian Reflector*, rpt. in *Christian Watchman* December 27, 1844: 204.

32. C. K. W., "Drs. Wayland and Fuller," *Liberator* May 16, 1845: 79. This review of Wayland and Fuller's *Domestic Slavery, Considered as a Scriptural Institution* appears on the same page in the *Liberator* as the news report of Wendell Phillips's speech at the AASS meeting discussed above. That report also includes a summary of Douglass' speech at the same meeting. A week earlier the *Liberator* had published Garrison's preface to Douglass's *Narrative* (May 9: 75) and a week later (May 23: 82) began a series of *Narrative* extracts, comments, and review reprints, including on June 20 (97) a reprinting of Fuller's *Daily Tribune* review (without the concluding extract).

33. But cf. Douglass's assertion that "the religion of the south is the mere covering for the most horrid crimes" (117) and his condemnation of the South's "corrupt, slaveholding, woman-whipping, cradle-plundering, partial and hypocritical Christianity" (153).

34. "Letter from Frederick Douglass: Reply to Mr. A. C. C. Thompson," *Liberator* February 27, 1846: 35. Thompson's attack on the *Narrative*, "To the Public: Falsehood Refuted," had been reprinted from the *Delaware Republican* in the *Liberator* December 12, 1845: 197.

35. A. C. C. Thompson, "Narrative of Frederick Douglass," *Albany Patriot*, rpt. in the *Liberator* February 20, 1846: 29. Earlier Thompson wrote, "I do not wish to be understood as advocating slavery, for I am convinced that it is a great evil—but not sinful under ordinary circumstances."

36. "Letter from Frederick Douglass," 35.

37. Douglass, *My Bondage and My Freedom* 241. Douglass does not, however, escape religious ideology, when, by rebelling, he fully rejects the proslavery ver-

sion. Rather, the ideological subject of resistance is constructed as a Christian abolitionist (and later as a specifically Garrisonian lecture agent for the Massachusetts Anti-Slavery Society). In contrast to Douglass's own emphasis on the liberatory powers of literacy, Houston Baker points out the "intriguing restrictions" of the slave's literacy process, which result from the wholesale adoption of a "white, Christian abolitionist framework" (*The Long Journey Back: Issues in Black Literature and Criticism* [Chicago: U of Chicago P, 1980] 36–37). (For further discussion in the Foucauldian terms of an archaeology of knowledge, see Baker, *Blues, Ideology, and Afro-American Literature: A Vernacular Theory* [Chicago: U of Chicago P, 1984], ch. 1; but also cf. Baker, *Modernism and the Harlem Renaissance* [Chicago: U of Chicago P, 1987] 102–3.) The story of Douglass's later break with Garrison is told in many places. See, for example, Douglass, *My Bondage and My Freedom* 395–98; Benjamin Quarles, "The Breach between Douglass and Garrison," *Journal of Negro History* 23 (1938): 144-54; Tyrone Tillery, "The Inevitability of the Douglass-Garrison Conflict," *Phylon* 37 (1976): 137–49; and John R. McKivigan, "The Frederick Douglass–Gerrit Smith Friendship and Political Abolitionism in the 1850s," in Sundquist, *Frederick Douglas: New Literary and Historical Essays* 205-32.

Swept Away: Henry James, Margaret Fuller, and "The Last of the Valerii"

JOHN CARLOS ROWE

Having met Margaret Fuller in 1843, Henry James, Sr., wrote to Emerson, who had introduced him to her: "The dear noble woman! I shall often think of her with joy—and with hope of fuller conferences and sympathies somewhere."[1] The elder Henry James and Margaret Fuller shared interests in Swedenborg's social philosophy (rather than his mysticism) and women's rights, including rights of divorce. In view of the elder James's endorsement of Fourier's socialism and his consistent attacks on private property and the social imposition of institutional limits on the otherwise "infinite" self, his general philosophy agrees with the transcendentalist feminism of Margaret Fuller.

Fuller's famous claim in *Woman in the Nineteenth Century* that "there is no wholly masculine man, no purely feminine woman" follows the logic of transcendentalist philosophy.[2] Yet, her characteristic rejection of any essential sexual difference had obvious consequences for practical social reforms that transcendentalists such as Emerson and Henry James, Sr., were not ready to accept. Emerson's 1855 lecture "Woman" supports women's rights to education, property, and the vote but concludes by urging women to seek more "spiritual" rights by "improving" and "refining" their *men*: "Woman should find in man her guardian."[3] His arguments are perfectly Hegelian, insofar as Hegel insisted upon the maintenance of woman's domestic role and man's role as mediator between family and state. Like Emerson, the elder James was not a radical for women's rights, and he struggled to take what Stuart Culver has termed "a middle ground after the Civil War, . . . between John Stuart Mill, whose *Subjection of Women* was widely recognized as the definitive statement of what Olive Chancellor calls 'the cause,' and Horace Bushnell, whose *Woman's Suffrage: A Reform against Nature* provided a conservative critique of Mill. The elder James reviewed the books in tandem, arguing for divorce while insisting on an irreducible sexual difference."[4] Fuller's application of transcendentalist ideas to women's rights consequently exposed the liberal hypocrisy or mere intellectual temerity of these male transcendentalists.

The elder James and Emerson, together with Hawthorne, are the most influential and complex fathers of the younger Henry James. Their ambivalence toward Margaret Fuller's radicalism is repeated by Henry James, Jr., in his scattered references to Margaret Fuller from such early writings as "The Last of the Valerii" (1874) and *Hawthorne* (1879) to *William Wetmore Story and His Friends* (1903). But James's repetitions are compounded, as all such psychic repetitions are, by the strategic repressions they serve. And in the matter of the "Margaret-ghost," as James was to name his anxiety, the repressions would entangle Oedipal rebellion of the son against the Father, as well as poetic rebellion of the Modern against his romantic and very American precursor, with James's critical reaction to the politics of the New Woman.

Insofar as the younger James's reading of Margaret Fuller's legend fits the psychopoetic model of the strong modern writer overcoming his literary (or actual) fathers, this story of nineteenth-century reading is quite familiar and meets the requirements of the Freudian family romance. If this were all there were to interest us in this bit of literary history, then I would offer it merely as an interpretive "exercise," an *explication de texte* in the new context of psychopoetic reading, valuable for what light it might cast on the Jamesian texts mentioned. However, the larger significance of this history of literary reading begins with the sheer historical coverage suggested by the disturbing legend of Margaret Fuller—that is, a ghost that haunts male New

England transcendentalists (Emerson, Hawthorne, Henry James, Sr.) and major modernists (James, Jr.) in remarkably similar ways. For all their strident rejections of their romantic forebears, male moderns like James, Jr., shared their literary fathers' inabilities to deal with the feminist issues that both transcendentalism (and international romanticism in general) as well as literary modernism helped articulate. The persistence of the uncanny "Margaret-ghost," then, is more than just a footnote in an otherwise complicated and interesting literary history. I intend for it to raise anew the question of Woman—as writer, intellectual, socially constructed gender, and as "literary character"—in the heritage of American modernism.

To rehistoricize reading in nineteenth-century America, we will have to begin with a theory of reading sufficiently broad to encompass both empirical and psychopoetic forces. In the absence of better data on how different Americans read different kinds of literary texts, we should certainly pay more attention to the literary values upheld by literary journals and reviews. By the same token, we should pay special attention to those instances in which nineteenth-century writers read their precedessors and contemporaries not simply for the sake of the usual influences and affinities but also as *models* for what "reading" at its most serious included and excluded—that is, what nineteenth-century reading *involved*. Insofar as Henry James's act of reading Margaret Fuller repeats many of the gestures of his intellectual fathers and insofar as that repetition involves certain obvious distortions, if not downright misinterpretations, of Margaret Fuller, then it may be said to have some exemplary status for us as we attempt to understand the patriarchal assumptions of the conventions for "literary reading" in nineteenth-century America.

In his review of James Elliot Cabot's *A Memoir of Ralph Waldo Emerson* (London, 1887) in *Macmillan's Magazine* in December of 1887 (reprinted in *Partial Portraits*, 1888), James characterizes Emerson's general response to Fuller in the figure of Emerson retreating, "smiling and flattering, on tiptoe, as if he were advancing."[5] James quotes Emerson from the journals—"She ever seems to crave something which I have not, or have not for her"—and concludes that "only between the lines . . . we read that a part of her effect upon him was to bore him" (*American Essays*, 64). Boredom is hardly an emotion we might expect Margaret Fuller to have inspired; her contemporary reputation rested on her sharp intellect, her unabashed egotism, her political convictions, and her physical beauty. Yet James is relying on a judgment he had expressed earlier in *Hawthorne* that Margaret Fuller was finally, fatally, *superficial*: "Her function, her reputation, were singular, and not altogether reassuring: she was a talker; she was *the* talker; she was the genius of talk. . . . She has left the same sort of reputation as a great actress. Some of her writing has extreme beauty, almost all of it has a real interest; but her value, her activity, her sway . . . were personal and practical."[6] James's judgment of Fuller's writings in this context is patronizing, although perhaps no more so than his judgment of Hawthorne's work. In another sense, however, Fuller is represented as Hawthorne's complete opposite. Public and gregarious, "practical" and "personal," James's Fuller casts in shadow Hawthorne's privacy, introspective dreaminess, and hopeless detachment from the urgencies of politics and finances.

This Jamesian description of the Fuller who would become Hawthorne's model for Zenobia in *The Blithedale Romance* comes just before James comments on Hawthorne's account in *The American Notebooks* of his first meeting with Fuller in the woods on his return from Emerson's house:

> It is safe to assume that Hawthorne could not, on the whole, have had a high relish for the very positive personality of this accomplished and argumentative woman, in whose intellect high noon seemed ever to reign, as twilight did in his own. He must have been struck with the glare of her understanding, and, mentally speaking, have scowled and blinked a good deal in conversation with her. . . . We may be sure that in women his taste was conservative.[7]

For each of these transcendentalist "fathers" to Henry James, Fuller is something of a provocation and a riddle, even as each makes his best defensive effort to acknowledge her wit. Knowing what we do of James's vigorous efforts throughout his life and career to replace these fathers with his own authority, we might expect him to find a kindred spirit in Margaret Fuller, who challenged his father's position on women's rights, "bored" Emerson, and caused Hawthorne to scowl and blink "a good deal." The issue here, of course, is neither solely antiquarian nor merely psychopoetic, but the more pressing question of James's own position on women's rights. The divergent critical views on this subject can be summarized by way of the emphases various critics place on the following characters in James's fiction. On the one hand, we have James's Daisy Miller, Isabel Archer, Tina Aspern, Mme. de Vionnet, Milly Theale, and Maggie Verver. Each in her own way is committed to some overt or subtle rebellion that calls into question the patriarchal authority of bourgeois society. On the other hand, we have Henrietta Stackpole, Miss Birdseye, Olive Chancellor, Verena Tarrant, and other "progressives" mocked ruthlessly by James. Those critics intent on defending James as a champion of women's rights stress the first group of characters and the ways they combat the subtler effects of sexism reproduced in the psychological warfare of interpersonal relations. In this view, James's modern "novel of manners" focuses on the more complex fiction of bourgeois patriarchy. Other critics use the second series of characters to deconstruct the first, insofar as James's contempt for overt feminists—ranging from "career" women such as Henrietta to political feminists such as Olive and Verena—suggests his own fears of the New Woman and his preference for the subtler, more manageable "domestic" rebellion of Isabel Archer and Maggie Verver. James's "drawing-room" feminists are most often associated with artistic and imaginative powers missing from the second group of characters, who rant and lecture but rarely write or paint. Having acknowledged the "interest" of Margaret Fuller's writings, James might be expected to identify her with the first group of fictional characters. She wrote one of the politically most influential books of the 1840s; joined the cause of Italian independence; married Count Ossoli, a follower of Mazzini and the Republican cause; and died tragically in a shipwreck off Fire Island on her return to the United States with her *History* of the Risorgimento in hand.

Yet James shows no sympathy for Margaret Fuller, who haunts his writings as the "ghost" of that faded, failed transcendentalism of his father, Emerson, and Hawthorne. Even more clearly than James's Hawthorne, James's Fuller represents just what he feared he himself might become: an adept at intellectual conversation, a cosmopolitan tourist, a naive social reformer and "progressive" (that word James often marked with quotation marks); in short, more Henrietta and Olive than Isabel or Milly. These anxieties surface with a vengeance in James's most sustained treatment of Margaret Fuller in *William Wetmore Story and His Friends*, that curious biography James wrote for the money and at the urging of the Storys' children and published in 1903. The two-volume work is an odd tangle of the sculptor, William Story's romantic Rome from the late 1840s to the Civil War, and

James's own impressionistic recollections of his youth there in 1869 and the winter of 1873. This is the "Italy" so indistinguishable for James in 1903 from the general "ambience" of Hawthorne's *Marble Faun* (1860), the little artistic circle of the Storys, the Bootts, the painter Tilton, traces of the English romantics in Italy, and a cast of James's characters throughout his career—Daisy, Tina, Amerigo, Rowland Mallet, Christina Light, Prince Casamassima. Carl Maves calls it the "sensuous pessimism" of James's romantic, doomed Italy, his early modern equivalent of the romantics' infatuation with ancient ruins.[8]

The volume I am describing is much more than just the biography of William Story; it also configures James's artistic Italy, the daemonic other of Robert Browning's Italy, the prelude to Pound's Italian tone in the Malatesta cantos and to Eliot's "La figlia che piange." Its imaginary frontispiece ought to be Guido Reni's *Beatrice Cenci*, that tourist attraction at the Palazzo Barberini, where the Storys lived. Beatrice Cenci haunted the writings of the Anglo-American romantics, and she returns in the strangest way in James's judgment of Margaret Fuller in the first volume of *William Wetmore Story and His Friends*.[9] James has just described the Storys and Fuller viewing the usual tourist sights: "They do the regular old pleasant things in the regular old confident ways; at the Rospigliosi Casino first, to see Guido's 'Aurora,' and then to the Barberini Palace, unconscious as yet of their long installation there, to guess the strange riddle that the Cenci asks over her shoulder."[10]

Shelley had answered the "riddle" of Beatrice Cenci by helping to turn her into one of the favorite attractions of Victorian tourism and sexism. In *The Cenci* (1819), Beatrice's complicity in the murder of her father, Francesco, represents the rebellion of all those oppressed by tyranny. Even so, Shelley makes *The Cenci* a cautionary tale, in which he warns the reader against impetuous revenge, insisting in his preface: "Revenge, retaliation, atonement, are pernicious mistakes."[11] With his own youthful political radicalism and the "failure" of the French Revolution in mind, Shelley uses Beatrice Cenci to illustrate the tragic fate of those who abandon patience and forebearance even in the face of cruel tyranny. Insofar as *The Cenci* focuses the issue of tyranny in a father's rape of his daughter, Shelley's argument for "stoic, martyr-like forbearance" on the part of the abused accords well with meliorist responses to women's rights like Emerson's and the elder James's.[12] For Shelley, Beatrice's innocence and beauty are defiled by the tyranny of her father and her own will for revenge. Even as her violation reinforces the convention of the chaste, innocent, childlike woman, it also inspires her with the power and mystery of sexual transgression. Her rebellion thus enacts for Shelley a repetition of her father's tyranny.

It is just the sort of argument that would appeal to the subsequent Victorian sensibility that prized woman's patient endurance of oppression and often figured feminist rebellion in terms of perverse sexuality or unnaturalness. In the Victorian imagination, Beatrice Cenci typifies the ambivalent representations of woman that Nina Auerbach analyzes so well in *Woman and the Demon*. Writing of the mermaid, Auerbach notes her "broader spiritual resonance [with] her ancestor the serpent woman. Her hybrid nature, her ambiguous status as creature, typify the mysterious, broadly and evocatively demonic powers of womanhood in general."[13]

This "hybrid nature" applies quite well to what James will call a few lines later in *William Wetmore Story* the "Margaret-Ghost." Guido Reni's portrait of Beatrice Cenci narratively gives birth to James's fullest impression of Margaret Fuller, whom he had "met" only in the whispers of his fathers: "We succeed to generations replete with Guido's tearful turbaned parricide, but are ourselves never honestly to taste of her more, inasmuch as, tearful and turbaned as she is, she is proved, perversely *not* a parricide, or at least not the one we were, in tourist's parlance, 'after.'" In the case of the "tearful turbaned parricide," James is probably thinking of the popularization of Beatrice Cenci as merely abused innocent. Francesco Domenico Guerrazzi's popular romance, *Beatrice Cenci* (1854), sentimentalized her history by transforming her rape by her father into merely the Count's unrealized desire. The event that had been the obsessive focus of romantic treatments of the doomed Cenci family was sentimentalized into an unaccomplished, albeit still profoundly evil, incestuous lust.[14] In his *Italian Notebooks*, Hawthorne noted how contemporary copyists tended to sentimentalize the mysteriously ambivalent look of Guido's Beatrice:

> Its peculiar expression eludes a straightforward glance, and can only be caught by side glimpses, or when the eye falls upon it casually as it were, and without thinking to discover anything, as if the picture had a life and consciousness of its own, and were resolved not to

betray its secret of grief or guilt, though it wears the full expression of it when it imagines itself unseen. . . . The picture never can be copied. Guido himself could not have done it over again. The copyists get all sorts of expression, gay as well as grievous; some copies have a coquettish air, a half-backward glance, thrown alluring at the spectator, but nobody ever did catch, or ever will the vanishing charm of that sorrow. I hated to leave the picture, and yet was glad when I had taken my last glimpse, because it so perplexed and troubled me not to be able to get hold of its secret.[15]

The Jamesian tourist is *after* the Beatrice Cenci who plotted with her lover to murder her evil father in his sleep to avenge the violation of her innocence, and it is on just this reflection that James turns to the most extended reflection on Margaret Fuller in his writings. Beatrice's parricide here must refer to the threat Fuller posed to James's own Boston fathers, unmanned by her refusal to accept their authority: "The unquestionably haunting Margaret-ghost, looking out from her quiet little upper chamber at her lamentable doom, would perhaps be never so much to be caught by us as on some occasion as this. What comes up is the wonderment of *why* she may, to any such degree, be felt as haunting."[16]

James's curious judgment of Margaret Fuller is full of references to Hawthorne, as if James were working to subsume this powerful predecessor. James's "Margaret-ghost" borrows directly from Hawthorne's imaginary portrait of Beatrice Cenci, leaving her cell in the Castello Sant' Angelo for execution: "How ghost-like she must have looked when she came forth! Guido never painted that beautiful picture from her blanched face, as it appeared after this confinement. And how rejoiced she must have been to die at last, having already been in a sepulchre so long!"[17] Placed as she is in that "little upper chamber," James's Fuller recalls quite explicitly the saintly copyist, Hilda, the "Dove in her turret-home," where she copies Guido's mysterious painting in Hawthorne's *Marble Faun*. Of that painting, Hawthorne writes: "It was a sorrow that removed this beautiful girl out of the sphere of humanity, and set her in a far-off region, the remoteness of which—while yet her face is so close before us—makes us shiver as at a spectre."[18] In fact, the entire section of *William Wetmore Story* from which I have been quoting parallels quite minutely Hawthorne's tourist impressions in *The Italian Notebooks*. What James casually terms the "regular old pleasant things" of Italian tourism—a trip to Rospigliosi Casino to see Guido's *Aurora*, a visit to Barberini Palace to see his *Beatrice Cenci*—are just the activities Hawthorne describes in the entries for February 20, 1858.[19] What so perplexes and troubles Hawthorne is his sense of innocence violated, of femininity "unhumanized": "I looked close into its eyes, with a determination to see all that there was in them, and could see nothing that might not have been in any young girl's eyes; and yet, a moment afterwards, there was the expression—seen aside, and vanishing in a moment—of a being unhumanized by some terrible fate, and gazing at me out of a remote and inaccessible region, where she was frightened to be alone, but where no sympathy could reach her."[20] Three times in his notebook entries Hawthorne stresses the unrepresentable quality of this painting: "No artist did it, nor could do it again." Certainly, its "magical" effect has to do with that fact that "we bring all our knowledge of the Cenci tragedy to the interpretation of it."[21] Of course, Hawthorne and James must try their hands at "representing" such an unmasterable mystery, and it is just the mystery of ambivalent sexuality—a young girl's innocence "unhumanized" by some "terrible fate"—that haunts both of them. For Henry James more explicitly than for Hawthorne, however, this "mystery" is implicated in his portrait of Margaret Fuller and nineteenth-century women's rights.

James's Margaret-ghost repeats this Hawthornesque portrait of tragical inhumanity, but not for the sake of emphasizing the violence of rape or incest. Instead, James represents Fuller as exemplary of the very superficiality for which he had sometimes reproached Hawthorne and more regularly criticized the "parlor" reformers of transcendentalist Boston.[22] James reproaches Hawthorne for having written little, and he extends that judgment to Fuller: "It matters only for the amusement of evocation—since she left nothing behind her, her written utterance being naught; but to what would she have corresponded, have 'rhymed,' under categories actually known to us? Would she, in other words, with her appetite for ideas and her genius for conversation, have struck us but as a somewhat formidable bore, one of the worst kind, a culture-seeker without a sense of proportion, or, on the contrary, have affected us as a really attaching, a possibly picturesque New England Corinne?"[23]

James has made it obvious that the "we" of the quotation are "of our own luminous age," and that we moderns are to decide whether or not she is "a candidate . . . for the cosmopolite crown."[24] As James makes so clear in *Hawthorne*, this was the "crown" reserved for him alone, and so it is in these impressions: "Mme. Ossoli's circle represented, after all, a small stage, and . . . there were those on its edges to whom she was not pleasing. This was the case with Lowell and, discoverably, with Hawthorne; the legend of whose having had her in his eye for the figure of Zenobia, while writing 'The Blithedale Romance,' surely never held water."[25] Earlier in this volume, James quotes James Russell Lowell's letter to Story, in which Lowell mocks Margaret Fuller for her political commitments. Here, James can align Hawthorne with Lowell, going so far even as to contradict himself by dismissing the theory that Fuller was the model for Hawthorne's Zenobia—a "theory" to which James had subscribed enthusiastically in *Hawthorne* a quarter of a century before. Here is "poetic repression" on a grand scale, ending with the ugly bathos of James's little joke that the "legend . . . surely never held water," recalling Zenobia's suicide and the drowning of Margaret, Count Ossoli, and their infant son off Fire Island in May of 1850. Woman in the nineteenth century is turned once by Hawthorne, twice by James into Auerbach's "mermaid" through ugly twists of the "facts": "In her Boston days, . . . she had been as a sparkling fountain to other thirsty young. In the Rome of many waters there were doubtless fountains that quenched, collectively, any individual gush."[26] Intellectually drowned in the cosmopolitan Italy only James, the master modern, could navigate, Fuller is thus relegated to the perverse "poetic" justice of her historical end. The extended metaphor of "drowning" is a joke in the poorest taste, of course, and for all its sexism a telling expression of this Boston son's deepest anxieties about the "progressive" woman.

Hawthorne's allegorical "transfiguration" of woman has become James's repression of what Fuller represents to his fathers and to him: woman no longer as the "issue" of patriarchal art, the "character" of its fictions, but woman as Author, as Master. What Hawthorne judged "unhuman" remoteness in the gaze of Guido's *Beatrice Cenci* belongs to Victorian conventions of violated feminine innocence. Just as Melville reflected upon the hideousness of the Polar Bear's ferocity "invested in the fleece of celestial innocence and love" in "The Whiteness of the Whale" chapter of *Moby-Dick*, so Hawthorne dwells upon the incompatibility of good and evil as the essence of what so perplexes him in this representation of Beatrice. As he looks at the feminine innocence of Guido's Beatrice, Hawthorne cannot forget what invests this daughter with sorrow: her father's violation of her. "I wish, however, it were possible for some spectator, of deep sensibility, to see the picture without knowing anything of its subject or history; for, no doubt, we bring all our knowledge of the Cenci tragedy to the interpretation of it," Hawthorne writes in his *Italian Notebooks.*[27] For James, however, Beatrice represents woman secretly contaminated with masculine desire; she is perversely and monstrously full of her father's violence. In fact, the count's unnatural lust has given birth to what for James must seem the ultimate *monstrum horrendum*: a woman with a masculine will. It is just such "unnaturalness" that leads to what this tourist looks for: the crime of *parricide*, rather than the crimes of rape and incest.

This is the threat, I would argue, that surfaces only to be buried again in James's early story from his own Roman days of that winter of 1873, "The Last of the Valerii." (I add parenthetically that my brief reading is intended to provoke new criticism of all the early gothics related to it: "The Madonna of the Future," "Adina," "Travelling Companions," and the like.) Like the other stories from *A Passionate Pilgrim*, "The Last of the Valerii" (1874) is obviously derivative of Hawthorne, and this one in particular a variation on Prosper Merimée's "La Venus d'Ille."[28]

These traditional influences aside, "The Last of the Valerii" is full of the Margaret-ghost. Martha, the American heiress, has married the Italian, Count Camillo Valerio, for love, if we are to believe her godfather, the narrator whose profession is genre painting. Martha has also married the count for his lovely, overgrown, run-down, perfectly *Italian* villa and its "fund" of antiquities. Her mother knows better than the godfather: "It's the Villa she's in love with, quite as much as the Count. She dreams of converting the Count; that's all very well. But she dreams of refurnishing the Villa!"[29] Fuller, together with her husband, Count Ossoli, and Mazzini's followers dreamed of a more encompassing and enduring political conversion of Italy from divided principalities to a unified republic.

The "cause" in "The Last of the Valerii," however, is far more conventional and trivial; it is "conversion" to the domestic authority of the "modern American woman," embodied in Martha as "tinted prettiness, so tender, so appealing, so bewitching" as to make her godfather unable to "believe that [Count Valerio] must, like a good

Italian," also "have taken the exact measure" of "her equally pretty fortune" (260). The desperate financial circumstances of Margaret Fuller, Count Ossoli, and their son in Rome in the winter of 1848 are part of Fuller's "legend," stuff of the scandalous Margaret-ghost, but financial need is merely the conventional touch of James's decadent Italian aristocracy in "The Last of the Valerii."

It is European history in its full antiquity that Martha loves, and it is fetishized in her godfather's description of her lover's very head "as massively round as that of the familiar bust of the Emperor Caracalla, and covered with the same dense sculptural crop of curls." "Bronzed," with eyes like "a pair of polished agates," Count Valerio is already "une morceau de musée" for Martha and her godfather, who makes his own living as "an unscrupulous old painter of ruins and relics" and "plants" his "easel in one of the garden-walks" of the villa early in the narrative (262). At Martha's "urgency," the count begrudgingly "had undertaken a series of systematic excavations" at the villa, on her assumption "that the much-trodden soil of the Villa was as full of buried treasures as a bride-cake of plums, and that it would be a pretty compliment to the ancient house . . . to devote a portion of her dowry to bring its mouldy honours to the light" (265). All this transpires despite the count's protestations, "If you can't believe in them, don't disturb them. Peace be with them!" (266).

What the excavation yields is "a majestic marble image" of Juno: "Her beautiful head, bound with a single band, could have bent only to give the nod of command; her eyes looked straight before her; her mouth was implacably grave; one hand, outstretched, appeared to have held a kind of imperial wand; the arm from which the other had been broken hung at her side with the most queenly majesty" (267–68). However, this "Juno," as the narrator tells us, is of "the great Greek period," "a Juno of Praxiteles at the very least"—or as the count will say with a frown at the very end, "A Greek" (268, 283). Not the Roman Juno, but Hera, sister and wife of Zeus, protectress of women and marriage, and the goddess known to antedate Zeus and the more familiar Olympians in Attica, is thus the unearthed icon. Such primal mythic women are the proper subjects of Fuller's *Woman in the Nineteenth Century*, where she writes: "Certainly the Greeks knew more of real home intercourse and more of Woman than the Americans. . . . The poets, the sculptors, always tell the truth. In proportion as a nation is refined, women *must* have an ascendancy. It is the law of nature." It is a reflection that causes Fuller to relate Beatrice Cenci to her noble Greek precursors: "Beatrice! thou wert not 'fond of life,' either, more than those princesses [Greek women in Euripides and Sophocles]. . . . Thou wert not so happy as to die for thy country or thy brethren, but thou wert worthy of such an occasion."[30] Unlike Shelley or Hawthorne, Fuller equates Beatrice with a true revolutionary, capable of turning her revenge against her father into rebellion against a tyrannical state.

The Greek statue of Juno works mysteriously on Count Valerio, who promptly "steals" the broken fragment of her hand as a private fetish, and then neglects poor American Martha for the "atavism" that seems excavated with this sculpture. The few critical accounts of "The Last of the Valerii" take its romantic allegory at face value; it is an early tale of "the international theme" and thus an unproblematic version of European "evil" purged by the "innocence" and "trust" of American womanhood. Having "shuddered" for her husband's infidelity with a statue, Martha resumes command and orders it reburied. Count Valerio has "learned" something—just what, the critics never tell us—and domestic tranquillity is restored, save for that hand the count keeps hidden in a cabinet of antiquities, "suspended in one of its inner recesses," under lock and key (283).

James himself had seen his own Juno on April 27, 1873, at the Villa Ludovisi: "The sculptures in the little Casino are few, but there are two great ones—the beautiful sitting Mars and the head of a great Juno, the latter thrust into a corner behind a shutter."[31] Like the exotic (and thus orientalized) "turbaned head" of Guido Reni's *Beatrice Cenci*, this "head of a great Juno" has some affinity with the "beautiful head, bound with a single band" of the Juno in "The Last of the Valerii." These tenuous connections return us by various psychic detours to the Margaret-ghost. Most of the critics of the story agree with its conclusion that Martha's reburial of the statue of Juno is the "healthy" thing to do, given the "sickness" of her atavistic husband. But James's conclusions about the "head of the great Juno . . . hidden behind a shutter" casts a different light on the conclusion to "The Last of the Valerii." James reminds us that the Villa Ludovisi is the residence of King Victor Emmanuel and his "morganatic queen," Rosina: "I had an opportunity to reconstruct, from its *milieu* at least, the character of a morganatic queen. I saw nothing to indicate that it was not amiable; but I should have thought more highly of the lady's discrimination if she had had the Juno removed from behind her shutter."[32]

Symbol of a united Italy, of the Risorgimento's long struggle against the Austrians, the Russians (in the Crimean War), and the Papal States, Victor Emmanuel II is represented obliquely by James through his morganatic queen and what presumably the new Italy would do with its ancient heritage: hide it behind a shutter. What is hidden here as well as in "The Last of the Valerii" is the mythic source of feminine power: Juno's "original," the Greek goddess Hera. James seems to answer in his 1873 "Roman Note-Book" and his 1874 story, "The Last of the Valerii," the question he asks of the Margaret-ghost in *William Wetmore Story*. In "our luminous" modern age, the "progressive" new Woman would not only castrate man, but would also cut herself off from her own rich, sexually fertile, mythic heritage. Or so James, coopting Fuller's mythic woman, would like us to believe.

My admittedly tenuous conclusion here gains a bit of solidity when Victor Emmanuel's "morganatic wife," Rosina, is considered. Rosina Vercellana, Countess of Mirafiori, was a drum major's daughter, but she wielded considerable political power through the king and was generally at odds with Cavour. What scandalized the Italian court was hardly the fact that Rosina was the king's mistress (Victor Emmanuel had numerous affairs with ladies at court) but that she wielded significant political power.[33] James's brief reference to Rosina clearly follows the popular gossip that she was a vulgar and ambitious woman intent on using her personal influence for the sake of political gain. In this regard, James's American Martha is a more attractive alternative for the "modern" woman, respecting as she does both history and the hearth.

In his own visit to the Villa Ludovisi, in March of 1858, Hawthorne also commented on "a colossal head of Juno [which] is considered the greatest treasure of the collection, but I did not myself feel it to be so, nor indeed did I receive any strong impression of its excellence. I admired nothing so much, I think, as the face of Penelope (if it be her face) in the group supposed also to represent Electra and Orestes."[34] In keeping with the gendered rhetoric of his age, Hawthorne prefers a figure representing feminine patience and forebearance over the more imperious head of the goddess. What strikes Hawthorne especially, however, serves to conclude his entries for the day: "One of the most striking objects in the first casino was a group by Bernini, —Pluto, an outrageously masculine and strenuous figure, heavily bearded, ravishing away a little, tender Proserpine, whom he holds aloft, while his forcible gripe impresses itself into her soft virgin flesh. It is very disagreeable, but it makes one feel that Bernini was a man of great ability."[35] Close as James's visit matches Hawthorne's twenty-five years earlier, even down to their shared judgment of Guercino's *Aurora* as a "muddy masterpiece," James makes no mention of this group by Bernini. What Hawthorne uncovers in this moment is perhaps too explicit an image of the masculine will-to-power threatened by Hawthorne's Juno and James's Hera and domesticated by their Penelopes and Marthas. Bernini's *Abduction of Proserpine* is the uncanny moment in which Hawthorne's "so puzzled and perplexed" gaze upon Guido's *Beatrice Cenci* may be understood as Hawthorne's own terrified fascination with masculine power—the source of that "unhuman" element in Beatrice's gaze.

What James does not record in his Roman notebook of 1873, however, is recorded in "The Last of the Valerii." Rumors of the unearthed Juno having spread beyond the villa, "a German in blue spectacles, with a portfolio under his arm," visits the villa to inform the count: "Your new Juno, Signor Conte, . . . is, in my opinion, much more likely to be certain Proserpine.'" The count rejects the German's specious expertise, insisting, "T've neither a Juno nor a Proserpine to discuss with you. . . . You're misinformed" (270). Quite clearly, Count Valerio has no interest in modern science, as well as no need to be told what his sculpture represents. "She" is simply the sexual power of myth and history from which this impoverished count has been hitherto alienated.

Like so many of James's tales from these early years, "The Last of the Valerii" is full of images of an anxious, hardly sublimated youthful sexuality. "Yes, by Bacchus, I am superstitious," the count protests during the original excavation. The workers are rewarded with wine when the Juno is discovered, then when it is reburied. The narrator and his god-daughter first sense that the count is cracking up when they watch him pour "a libation" at the foot of the statue (269). They *know* he is nearly lost to them when they find traces of blood on a rough block, with "illegible Greek characters," improvised by the count as a kind of altar before the Juno. James's fantasy of atavistic revival reflects his own troubled fascination with castration. The fetish of the sculpture's hand is all that this hapless count is left, once he has "sold" his birthright for Martha's fortune.

James's nearly comic account of Valerio's love affair with a Greek sculpture is further compounded by the curious transference of the rhetoric of feminine sexuality and birthing from Martha to Valerio. The story is, after all, an account of the *last* of the Valerii line, who retains merely nominal title to his history once he has married an American heiress. In this regard, the story is rather conventionally Jamesian, but the excavation of the long-buried statue, the libation of wine, the blood on the altar, and the hand secreted by the count all suggest some fantasy of his own process of "giving birth" to his family's forgotten past. Juno's "imperial wand," her commanding look, and her "implacably grave" mouth suggest phallic power and masculine legal authority. It is, according to this fantasy, *Juno* who penetrates Valerio, spilling his virginal blood on the altar. Such rhetorical cross-dressing is by no means unusual in James and has obvious relevance for James's ambivalence about his own sexuality. Beyond this biographical significance, however, the violation of Valerio by his Juno suggests a more general masculine fear of nineteenth-century women's bids for economic, legal, and political powers. Valerio is virtually held "in thrall" by his private devotions to this Medusan lover, in keeping with the Victorian rhetoric of the independent woman's "daemonic" powers.

Having uncovered such a threat to masculine authority, James reasserts the more attractive alternative of the domestic wife. Martha may unwittingly initiate this psychodrama by offering to use her fortune to "improve" the villa, but at the end she returns to the drawing room, choosing to exercise a more disguised power over her husband in the familiar interpersonal dynamics of the Jamesian novel of manners. In her final appearance, after she has ordered the Juno reburied, Martha "wandered into the drawing-room and pretended to occupy herself with a bit of embroidery." As if to make sure we catch the classical references to Homer's Penelope and the Greek Parcae, James clumsily describes "the Count lifting the tapestried curtain which masked the door and looking silently at his wife" (283). Unmanned, he surrenders to her: "The Countess kept her eyes fixed on her work, and drew her silken threads like an image of domestic tranquillity. The image seemed to fascinate him." Caught in the modern spell she has woven, the count anticipates Prince Amerigo's surrender thirty years later in *The Golden Bowl*: "At last she raised her eyes and sustained the gaze in which all his returning faith seemed concentrated. He hesitated a moment, as if her very forgiveness kept the gulf open between them, and then he strode forward, fell on his two knees, and buried his head in her lap" (283).

"He never became, if you will, a thoroughly modern man," the narrator begins the concluding paragraph, in which we discover that the count has "kept" his fetish of the Juno's hand, "suspended" in "his cabinet." Whatever sexual passion, Dionysian revel, or imaginative ecstasy of which he and his mythic past might have been capable has been reduced to this "marble hand," the phallic memento. Yet, in Count Valerio's symbolic castration, James has "saved" himself, even as he has sacrificed the Margaret-ghost. I shall not conclude by arguing, as I might, that the "modern" Margaret Fuller would have for James so "unmanned" Count Ossoli by way of her "progressive" feminism as to have reproduced the sentimental "domestic tranquillity" Martha weaves at the end of "The Last of the Valerii." Quite the contrary, James's Margaret-ghost appears best in the law-giving, angular, beautiful figure of Juno— both her head at the Villa Ludovisi and her nearly "restored" form in "The Last of the Valerii." *Restored?* Why, yes, restored to the Attic authority that Fuller's Greek women had (somewhat romantically, no doubt) in myth, sculpture, and classical tragedy.

"She" is just missing a hand, a trivial detail perhaps for this potent authority of Woman buried in the Roman countryside for millennia. Yet, it is a deformed hand that is the singular feature of James's most terrifying ghost in that later story of psychopoetic defense, "The Jolly Corner." What Juno misses, Count Valerio fetishizes, and the Margaret-ghost used too little, it would seem, on the evidence of what James tells us she has left behind. All these failures and lacks, James claims to supplement with his own hand. Even so, the ghostly double for James's literary hand remains that of Spencer Brydon's ghost in "The Jolly Corner," one of whose "hands had lost two fingers, which were reduced to stumps, as if accidentally shot away."[36] The complex weave of references I have traced in James's hand, not all of which I wish to argue belong to James's "consciousness," is James's "tapestried curtain," which he would contend far exceeds the "image of domestic tranquillity" woven by this much reduced modern woman, Martha.

The sexual power that so fascinated Hawthorne in Guido's *Beatrice Cenci* and Bernini's *Abduction of Proserpine* threatens James in the form of the political New Woman, intent upon framing a new mythology beyond that of patriarchal domination. Such mythopoeia is not simply domesticated in the conventional "American Girl," Martha, but is also sublimated in James's own narrative response to and appropriation of sexual power. In "The Last of the Valerii," there is no question of choosing between Juno or Martha; the former is an elusive anachronism, mere token of a lost matriarchy, and the latter is simply a well-intentioned, but sexless, modern wife. The revival of this Juno in the political aims of Margaret Fuller and the New Woman is by no means sublimated in Martha; James makes certain we understand how little she "counts." In this regard, James typifies those high moderns who figured their own literary powers in sexual metaphors, frequently claiming, as T. S. Eliot would for poetry, a certain hermaphroditic productivity. Beyond the hopeless grapple of the typist and young man carbuncular in *The Waste Land*, there is often the promise of the literary transumption of sexuality rather desperately offered by anxious masculine moderns from James to Eliot. If we are to comprehend James's relation to contemporary debates regarding women's rights and his relevance in the current feminist revisions of the literary canon, then we will have to take into account the complex entanglement of his own conception of his modernity and his characterizations of women—both fictional and real. Neither strictly intrinsic nor extrinsic accounts of James's attitudes toward women's rights are satisfactory. All James's ambivalences about sex, the past, woman, and his "fathers" are captured in "The Last of the Valerii" in a "poetic" bid for mastery that could be claimed only by trivializing the "ghostly" women of his fiction: figures liberated in his literature only to bury his own profoundest anxieties.

What, then, may we conclude is the significance of "Henry James" as an example of ultrasophisticated "reading" at the turn of the century—that is, at the moment in which the ghosts of his father's New England had been replaced by the very substantial figures of an international modernism? First, the detours of reading are so wayward as to declare as utterly unreliable the "testimony" of a reader as subtle as Henry James, which is to say a reader who is also a *writer*. Although unreliable, such testimonies are by no means *unreadable*; it is merely a matter of acknowledging that the critical writings of such writers turned readers need to be read as carefully as we read any "literary" text. That may go without saying, but it is equally important to understand that the writer never knows exactly what he or she is "saying," even with the best will in the world. In fact, because of that will—a will to meaning that distorts even as it transforms—the message we are reading will have to be taken at least doubly: as what the writer wants us to hear and as the echo-effect of all that the writer would prefer to keep hidden.

That the reading of the interplay between such expression and repression should involve so fundamentally gender and its construction in and through letters (or "literary reputations") should not surprise us as we look at other accounts of what it means to read in nineteenth-century America. The more determinately Emerson, Hawthorne, James, Sr., and James, Jr., "defined" the "woman writer," the more certainly each in turn revealed his anxieties regarding her indefinite and changing status. James incorporates into his own response to the Margaret-ghost the more general anxieties of his forefathers regarding women in the nineteenth century. Insofar as "art," such as "The Last of the Valerii," is produced out of such anxiety, misreading, and psychic distortion, we must rethink what is meant by "art" as well as "artistic experience."

Has this reading of James reading his nineteenth-century literary past confirmed the "aesthetic value" of such short fiction as "The Last of the Valerii," or has it, quite contrarily, questioned the role played by "aesthetic experience" in maintaining such a caricature as Henry James's portrait of Margaret Fuller? I have argued as if only the latter possibility could be entertained by *my* readers, and that, of course, carries considerable significance for the "rehistoricizing" of nineteenth-century reading. For some, this involves the formidable but nonetheless methodical task of putting together a partial puzzle from the available fragments. For me, it must involve more than such problem solving; it obliges us to inquire into the roles we still play in this game of reading. Is not Margaret Fuller's general reception by those responsible for the various canons of nineteenth-century "American Literature" still very much shaped by this ghostly genealogy stretching from Emerson to James? If we are now able to ask this question, in large part thanks to the work of feminist critics and theorists of the past twenty-five years, then we must also realize that the responsibilities of reading involve far more than merely fidelity to the "facts" of the text or of its history of production and reception. By the same token, the "facts" of historical acts of reading are not simply "factitious," the contrivances of our own free, unfettered wills or whims. The factual and factitious are entangled in every act of reading, and the peculiar way in which they are knotted and woven tells us what we have made of the past and informs others for what we are responsible. It is not a matter of cutting the Gordian knot of others' readings or merely admiring the ingenuity of the one who tied it, but a matter of following the curls of the rope as if we were loosening its grip upon us.

Notes

1. Austin Warren, *The Elder Henry James* (New York: Macmillan, 1934) 48.

2. Margaret Fuller, *Woman in the Nineteenth Century* (New York: Norton, 1971) 116.

3. Ralph Waldo Emerson, "Woman," *The Works of Ralph Waldo Emerson*, Riverside ed., 14 vols. (Boston: Houghton, 1883) 11:356.

4. Stuart Culver, "Divorce and Transcendentalism" (unpublished manuscript, Dept. of English, U of California, Irvine) 5.

5. Henry James, *The American Essays of Henry James*, ed. Leon Edel (New York: Vintage, 1956) 64.

6. Henry James, *Hawthorne*, English Men of Letters Series (New York: Harper, 1879) 76–77.

7. Ibid. 78.

8. See Carl Maves, *Sensuous Pessimism: Italy in the Works of Henry James* (Bloomington: Indiana UP, 1973).

9. Throughout the nineteenth century, the portrait of Beatrice Cenci at the Palazzo Barberini was considered the work of Guido Reni. Twentieth-century art historians have argued that the portrait is probably not his work. It now hangs in the Galleria Nazionale d'Arte Antica in Rome.

10. Henry James, *William Wetmore Story and His Friends*, 2 vols. (London: Thames, 1903) 1:126.

11. Percy Bysshe Shelley, Preface, *The Cenci, Poetical Works*, ed. Thomas Hutchinson, rev. G. M. Matthews (Oxford: Oxford UP, 1970) 276.

12. Earl Wasserman, *Shelley: A Critical Reading* (Baltimore: Johns Hopkins UP, 1971) 95.

13. Nina Auerbach, *Woman and the Demon: The Life of a Victorian Myth* (Cambridge: Harvard UP, 1982) 94.

14. Francesco Domenico Guerrazzi was a follower of Mazzini and was jailed several times for his politics. The political allegory of his romance, *Beatrice Cenci*, is directed at the abuse of power by hereditary aristocrats like Count Cenci, unconstrained by just laws or due process. Money purchases all things in Guerrazzi's

romance. Although Guerrazzi focuses his narrative on the destruction of the Cenci family by the mad count, he emphasizes how such patriarchal rule grows irrational when it is not controlled by civil or religious laws. The themes of incest and parricide so obsessively associated with the Cenci in the nineteenth-century are transformed by Guerrazzi into metaphors for tyrannical power, rather than used for episodes of romantic titillation. Even so, Guerrazzi manages to sentimentalize his subject by turning the actual violation of Beatrice by her father into a merely perverse desire and by assigning Beatrice's lover, Guido, the happy task of dispatching the count. Happening upon the count looking lustfully at his sleeping daughter, Guido stabs him in a rage of jealousy and offended honor. Guerrazzi thus trivializes his political themes by resorting to the melodrama of family conflict.

15. Nathaniel Hawthorne, *Passages from the French and Italian Notebooks*, vol. 10 of *The Complete Works of Nathaniel Hawthorne*, ed. George Parsons Lathrop, Riverside ed., 13 vols. (Boston: Houghton Mifflin, 1899) 504-5.

16. James, *William Wetmore Story* 1:127.

17. Hawthorne, *French and Italian Notebooks* 137.

18. Hawthorne, *The Marble Faun*, vol. 1 of *The Complete Works of Nathaniel Hawthorne* 85.

19. If only to make psychopoetic matters worse, James reverses the order of *his* visits to these Hawthorne shrines!

20. Hawthorne, *French and Italian Notebooks* 505.

21. Ibid. 89, 90.

22. In *Hawthorne*, James writes of the Concord and Boston transcendentalists: "The compiler of these pages, though his recollections date only from a later period, has a memory of a certain number of persons who had been intimately connected, as Hawthorne was not, with the agitations of that interesting time. . . . They appeared unstained by the world, unfamiliar with worldly desires and standards, and with those various forms of human depravity which flourish in some high phases of civilization. . . . This little epoch . . . has three or four drawbacks for the critics. . . . It bore, intellectually, the stamp of provincialism; it was a beginning without fruition, a dawn without a noon; and it produced, with a single exception, no great talents" (81-82). Emerson, of course, is James's exception.

23. James, *William Wetmore Story* 1:128.

24. Ibid. 127.

25. Ibid. 129.

26. Ibid. 128.

27. Hawthorne, *French and Italian Notebooks* 90.

28. Cornelia Kelley, *The Early Development of Henry James* (Urbana: U of Illinois P, 1965) 156ff.

29. Henry James, "The Last of the Valerii," *The Tales of Henry James*, ed. Maqbool Aziz (Oxford: Oxford UP, 1978) 2:259. Hereafter cited by page numbers in the text.

30. Fuller, *Woman in the Nineteenth Century* 210.

31. Henry James, "From a Roman Notebook" (1873), *Italian Hours* (New York: Horizon, 1968) 295.

32. Ibid. 296.

33. D. Mack Smith, *Victor Emmanuel, Cavour, and the Risorgimento* (London: Oxford UP, 1971) 93.

34. Hawthorne, *French and Italian Notebooks* 142.

35. Ibid. 143.

36. Henry James, "The Jolly Corner," *The Novels and Tales of Henry James*, New York ed., 26 vols. (New York: Scribner's, 1909) 17:476.

Historical Hermeneutics and Antebellum Fiction: Gender, Response Theory, and Interpretive Contexts

JAMES L. MACHOR

As feminist criticism has repeatedly demonstrated, reading is a practice invariably coded by gender, a practice now being rethought after centuries of inscribing women within a patriarchal system of interpretive strategies. While this focus on reading and gender has emerged in part from larger feminist concerns about the politics of sexuality and the position of woman as text, it also has been a product of the broader reorientation in criticism effected by reader-response theory—particularly in its attention to the reader's role in the process of signification. This confluence of feminist and reader-oriented approaches has developed from their common awareness that hermeneutical activity is intrinsic to the meaning and canonical status of literary works. Like feminism, reader-directed criticism, as Hans Robert Jauss argues, challenges "the philological metaphysics of tradition" and "the classicism of a view of fiction" which seek to "confer on 'great fiction' its own relation to truth."[1] To combat that metaphysics, some of the most important feminist criticism—particularly by Americanists such as Judith Fetterley, Jane Tompkins, and Janice Radway—has drawn on the methods of reader-oriented criticism to disclose the patriarchal basis of the interpretive conventions that have loaded, and in the process muzzled, the literary canon.[2]

However, despite the attention currently devoted to the role of the reader in literature, there has been a surprising lack of sustained inquiry into the experience of reading as a historically grounded dynamic, marked by substantial differences from one century to another. Although most reader-response and reception theorists have recognized in general terms that "the search for meaning, which at first may appear so natural . . . , is in fact considerably influenced by historical norms"[3]—a premise shared by some of the New Historicists[4]—in practice this recognition usually is sacrificed to a description that obfuscates the status of the reader being invoked. Consequently, the descriptions characterizing the practices of reader-response criticism, reception aesthetics, and the New Historicism tend to move to a common impasse through one of two directions. In the more frequent pattern, readers of reading implicitly privilege their own response by positing themselves as the ideal audience whose experience of the text is shared by all competent readers.[5] The alternative strategy is to make the historical reader a formalistic function of the text itself, thereby neglecting the historicity of interpretive work and, in the process, once again turning the critic into the ideal interpreter.[6] Both practices thus succumb to a temporal solipsism that fixes reading within a single set of interpretive conventions while ignoring the historically constituted conditions of response, including those informing the critics' own activities.[7]

Although the absence of historical reckoning in reader-response practice is significant in itself, it is particularly germane to feminist analysis of the relation between reading strategies and the meaning and status of American literature. Like other reader-response critics, feminists concerned with this relation have tended to present their own accounts of response as the normative paradigm for competent reading by women and thus have paid little attention to female reading as an activity defined by specific historical conditions and interpretive strategies in force for particular reading communities at particular times.[8] To be sure, this ahistorical propensity has begun to change recently, as evidenced in the work of such critics as Jane Tompkins, Cathy N. Davidson, and Susan Harris, who have brought a historical perspective to the relation between American fiction and its audiences. However, these critics have remained largely silent about the historical nexus of interpretive practices and reading experiences and have chosen instead to concentrate on rescuing neglected texts or neglected meanings by establishing the context for a historically specific thematics (Tompkins) or to focus on the way readers treated texts as artifacts and the social significance fiction had in the early Republic (Davidson).[9] Even Susan Harris's recent *Nineteenth-Century American Women's Novels: Interpretive Contexts*, while seeking to identify the assumptions of white women readers at midcentury, devotes most of its discussion to analyses of narratees, narrative strategies, and other factors that define the reader as a function of the literary text itself.[10] Yet if reading as a woman ultimately hinges on the dynamics of female response, the analysis of such reading must entail examining those dynamics in relation to both the ideology of gender and the strategies governing interpretive practices in the past. What it meant to read as a woman, in other words, is a question with a significant hermeneutical history, a history that assumed an especially visible shape in early-nineteenth-century America, when new methods of printing, improved literacy, and changes in women's social roles made female reading an increasingly prominent activity and a pressing topic of inquiry and discussion. Critics therefore need to turn to the question of what it meant to respond to such novels as *Uncle Tom's Cabin*, *The Scarlet Letter*, and *The Lamplighter* in terms of the interpretive strategies characterizing female reading in antebellum America. An examination of those strategies has implications not only for feminist criticism but also for reader-response practice and literary history.

I

To further explain the need for such an approach and the shape it can take—as well as the theoretical implications it entails and the significance it has for analysis of the reading experience—I want to begin with a closer look at the ahistorical propensity in feminist reader-response criticism by examining a particular, though representative example. This tendency is manifested, for instance, in Judith Fetterley's *The Resisting Reader*, which presents a theory of the female reader as both an "immasculated" and a resisting respondent to male American fiction. Encapsulating her approach in her opening chapter on Irving's "Rip Van Winkle," Fetterley points out that "the Americanism of the story's design is the creation of woman as villain: an obstacle to the achievement of the dream of leisure" localized in the male fantasy of unrestrained natural freedom from the need to grow up. In depicting Rip's wife as a harridan who "is seen as the agent of civilization," an embodiment of the values of work and responsibility that Rip seeks to escape, Irving's story encourages a woman reader to identify with its misogynistic values, causing her to become alienated from herself and other women. But even this psychological cross-dressing is stripped away because the fantasy Rip enacts "is thoroughly male and is defined precisely by its opposition to women."[11] Consequently, a female reader finds herself erased from the text by virtue of her gender. Against such erasure, Fetterley advocates—and presents—a resistive reading that restores to women what Robert Scholes calls "textual power," in this case, a power that enables them to decipher and undermine the text's co-optation of women.

What is significant in Fetterley's description of female reading is the way it successfully incorporates what nonfeminist reader-response critics usually omit: the recognition that reading is a political activity characterized by a power struggle over social identity. Yet that struggle, that experience as a whole, for the female reader of Irving's story can take a significantly different shape from the one Fetterley delineates. For Fetterley's description of the reading experience is a particularized re-creation empowered (and constrained) by a historically specific interpretive strategy: the modernist assumption, traceable back to D. H. Lawrence and forward to Leslie Fiedler, that the essence of American fiction is its continual fascination with the male quest for a return to origins, to youth, to nature, away from the female and civilization.[12] What Fetterley's reader resists, in other words, is not Irving's sketch but a particular set of interpretive conventions that have produced the immasculation.[13]

When we consider the experience of Irving's story from the perspective of an antebellum American woman, however, a very different scenario is possible. Bringing an alternate set of reading expectations to the text, that reader might have found herself not at the margins of the story but at its center by experiencing it as a cautionary tale about marriage and wifehood.[14] Reading within a cultural ideology that expected her to attract a man and then nurture his devotion to family life, an antebellum woman could respond to Dame Van Winkle not as an embodiment of womanhood but as a wife whose shrewishness prevents her from being a good spouse. Just as the female characters of domestic fiction from the early Republic onward provided, as Cathy Davidson has shown, a vicarious opportunity for women to experience the institution of marriage and their expected role in the family, Dame Van Winkle could become a warning about traits to avoid for a sound domestic relationship.[15] But for the female reader approaching the text through these middle-class assumptions, the onus for the failure of the family in the story would not fall on Dame Van Winkle alone. In Rip she could find an example of precisely the kind of husband to avoid: one who is so "ready to attend to anybody's business but his own" that he neglects his "family duty." As "one of those happy mortals, of foolish, well-oiled disposition, who takes the world easy," Rip is a loutish father directly responsible for his children's being "as ragged and wild as if they belonged to nobody."[16] From this perspective, Rip's intemperate guzzling of the mountain spirits' intoxicating liquor, which causes his final abandonment, graphically confirms his inadequacy. Unmanned by his intemperance, Rip could be interpreted as a reminder of another middle-class tenet of the period: that a man who drank was no man at all and therefore hardly a suitable spouse. For women responding to the story through these assumptions, Rip's perpetual failure as an adult male, his indulgence and indolence, could even be read as the source of his wife's shrewishness. Far from a figure to be abhorred, Dame Van Winkle would become in such a reading the locus of a more complex response in which her demeanor, though not to be approved, is understandable. Unlike the alienated female reader that Fetterley ascribes to the experience of the story, an antebellum middle-class woman may well have responded critically *and* sympathetically to Dame Van Winkle.

In this version of female reading, the experience of Irving's story, of course, remains anchored in a patriarchal system of values that confines women to concerns about the family, marriage, and proper wifely choices. However, that anchoring is precisely the point. When those values are taken into account, not as a set of invariable, transhistorical assumptions but as part of a reading experience that changes with time, they produce a configuration in which a woman's response to the story need not entail immasculation or resistance. Although Fetterley's renditions of the reading experience are perfectly legitimate recreations for a community of women marginalized by modernist patriarchal reading strategies or for a community of contemporary feminists, that experience is not identical to that of a reader encountering "Rip Van Winkle"—or *Uncle Tom's Cabin*, "Rappaccini's Daughter," or any work of fiction in the period—with a set of codes endemic to her position as a woman in antebellum America. Since reading is mediated by one's historical position, there is no transcendent location that constitutes the essence of female reading.

Because this metacritical principle is acknowledged on a theoretical level by most reader-response critics, my point is not simply that reading is always historical. Rather, the point is that when critics turn from theory to practice, they repeatedly bracket this principle, as Fetterley implicitly does, by producing foundational accounts of reading that fail to describe the relation between the dynamics of a particular response and the historically specific interpretive codes generating it. Nor is this problem avoided by critics who approach reader response by deconstructing it. Admittedly, these critics, in maintaining that "any account of the reading experience is itself a product of a set of interpretive conventions," implicitly assert the historicity of response by exposing any description of the reading experience as a product of historically constituted reading codes. But since this deconstructive principle denies the essential authority of any description, it is then argued that the principle itself can have no impact on critical practice.[17] The argument that we cannot escape our own historical situation thus becomes a warrant for reader-response critics to continue practice as usual by ignoring historical contingencies. Like other approaches, this deconstructive turn, in effect, severs theory from practice by bracketing the issue of history as a purely theoretical concern.

What needs to be emphasized here is that this lack of historical inquiry into the dynamics of response is not unique either to Fetterley's method or to other feminist criticism concerned with the reading of reading but is characteristic of reader-oriented practice as a whole. The problem, that is, lies not with feminist criticism or the interpretations it has produced but with the gap between literary history and the study of the codes underlying the interpretive process. Since the history of what it means to read as a woman is part of the broader question of the historical nature of interpretive work, however, a viable way to begin addressing the latter is through the more specific focus of the former. For if reader-response criticism hopes to move beyond its current limits and meet the challenge of its detractors, at least one of whom has argued that the method, "on the basis of its own premises, suggests that it has a past rather than a future," it must reconceive its practice to confront the historical dynamics of response, including the critic's own.[18]

Such a reorientation needs to integrate response theory, which concentrates on the stages of hermeneutical processing, and the contextual emphasis of reception theory to create a historical hermeneutics that identifies specific reading practices and explores the role of interpretive communities in the way texts were constructed and made meaningful in a given era. For an era other than our own, such a turn would necessitate a close analysis of interpretive traces preserved in the archive, but in doing so, a historical hermeneutics would have to go beyond Jonathan Culler's call for a history of reception that merely surveys the legacy of responses to a particular text to reconstruct the codes that produced its various interpretations.[19] Instead, such an approach would reconstruct the shared patterns of interpretation for a specific historical era to define the reading strategies of particular interpretive communities and to examine the impact of those strategies on the production and consumption of literary texts.

For reader-response criticism concerned with the relation between fiction and gender, an important first step toward a historical hermeneutics for the era of Irving, Stowe, and Hawthorne already exists in Nina Baym's work on antebellum American reviewers, which delineates the poetics of this interpretive community based on shared ideas about plot, character, verisimilitude, and types of readers, as well as the nexus of that poetics and the ideology of gender.[20] A reader-oriented criticism melding response and reception theories, however, needs to go a step further by creating a hermeneutics of reading that addresses the relation among reading codes, the dynamics of response, and ideology. To assert the need for this reconception is not to imply that poetics and hermeneutics are unrelated. Poetics themselves are both a product of hermeneutical activity—i.e., a product of interpretive strategies—and the basis for subsequent hermeneutical practices. What we need to do, therefore, is to examine the interpretive assumptions and conditions underlying and following from that particular poetics. These would include the role this community had—or sought to have—in shaping interpretation, its conceptions of the reading capacity of the audience(s) for fiction, its specific interpretive strategies, and its assumptions about the way reading should proceed. Such analysis, in turn, would provide a historical framework for examining the ideological dimensions of response, particularly through the convergence of reading codes and assumptions about gender.

But a historical hermeneutics, because of its concern with the process of response, would go beyond identifying the codes themselves and their ideological trajectories by invoking that relation to explore the reading dynamic involved in a historically specific pattern of response to particular texts. Doing so would in turn provide a particular context for examining the role of the reader in a text—i.e., the way a text can be said to position its audience within and through formal and thematic patterns. By attending to the latter, I do not mean that historical hermeneutics would return to the assumption of an essential text containing inherent patterns that simply await reader activation. Rather, the underlying premise of this approach would be that any textual configurations which can be said to do work for or on a reader are always a function of that reader's historically specific ideological and interpretive practices. Historical hermeneutics, that is, would focus on the area where reading codes, ideological assumptions—including gender assumptions—and the textual construction of audience intersect.

Such an agenda, however, raises two important questions. The first pertains to the specific focus I am concerned with here: antebellum fiction and response. If a historical approach to reading fiction in pre–Civil War America needs to proceed in relation to a specific interpretive community, what warrants turning to antebellum reviewers rather than "common" readers? Section 2 of this essay addresses this question while fashioning—in part by expanding and modifying several of Baym's points—a profile of female response propounded by the reviewers' interpretive practices. The second question involves more theoretical issues related to reader-response criticism as a whole. Because any description of interpretive codes and reading processes proceeds from the critic's own act of reading—and thus is inherently an interpretive, even a speculative, act—would not a historical analysis of response constitute just one more critical construction no more valid nor valuable than ahistorical examinations? That is, would it not yield just one more reading of reading? In the rest of this section I want to offer a partial answer to this question, but because a satisfactory response ultimately depends upon the way historical hermeneutics is pursued as a practice, I will return to this issue again near the end.

If we agree, then, that the critic is always a reader first, it follows that any attempt to reconstruct a set of historical conventions and integrate them with an analysis of the reading process will itself be mediated by the critic's own interpretive strategies. Hence the critic's role as interpreter, which itself is historically constituted, cannot be eliminated. Yet that mediation is not only inevitable but necessary, since the relation between historical conventions and the reader's role in fiction cannot be pursued solely through the interpretive practices of a work's original audience. To modify one of Jauss's insights, because the interactions between any text, when it first appears, and its audience will involve both fulfillment and reorientation of that readership's interpretive horizons, the critic "must bring his own experience into play, since the past horizon of old and new . . . problems and solutions is only recognizable in its further mediation, within the [critic's] present horizon."[21] Since any text, to some degree, must accommodate and disrupt the conventions of its time if it is to be seen as new and still remain readable, understanding the shape of this process requires a vantage point outside the horizon of expectations governing its contemporary audience.

The inevitability of the critic's role in the reading experience does not mean, however, that a historical hermeneutics must be equally prone to the temporal solipsism of current practice by covertly naturalizing the critic's own historically constituted response. Nor does the fact that any description of reading constitutes the experience it ostensibly describes necessarily mean that an attempt to delineate historical conditions would be just as subjective and unhistorical as the "descriptions" of current methods. A historical hermeneutics would militate against these tendencies by recognizing that the representation of historicized response consists of an intertextual relation between the experience at the work's origin and the reconstitution of that experience by posterity's interpretive practices—practices always (pre)structured by the reader's own position in an interpretive community. While a historical hermeneutics, therefore, cannot eliminate such prestructuring by posterity, what it can do is mitigate it by fashioning an intersubjectivity that counterpoises two different horizons of expectation playing off one another: the set of conventions (re)constructed as the basis of textual response within the historical context formulated and the horizon governing the critic's created account of reading within and against those original strategies. The purpose of such an approach would not be to proscribe other interpretations of reading as unacceptable but, in explicitly confronting the historical nature of reading, to open out and historicize accounts of reading practices.

To do so, such a method would need to turn its practice upon itself in a metacritical move toward examining its own authority while exploring the practical and theoretical implications of such a turn. In the process, however, it could accomplish no less than what reader-response criticism, in theory, continually has sought. Because reader-oriented criticism, as Tompkins has argued, "attack[s] the very foundations of positivism" and its privileging of objectivity by maintaining that "all language . . . is constitutive of the reality it purports to describe," the goal of that criticism is not to reach a transcendent objectivity outside a historical context of interpretive acts.[22] Similarly, the purpose of a historically based reader-response criticism is not to restore the subjective/objective dichotomy but to collapse it by grounding the reading experience of fiction in an awareness of historical conditions, including the critic's own. In its interplay between the historical experience (re)constructed from the archive and the critic's own self-conscious enactment of interpretation, a historical hermeneutics would provide not an objective description of historicized reading so much as a Gadamerian "fusion of horizons" that is always partial, provisional, speculative, and thus open to the flux characterizing interpretation as an intertextual, historical, and gender-based activity.

II

Because literary texts are made meaningful within a field consisting not just of interpretive strategies but also of intersecting ideologies, epistemic frames, and material conditions, the historical study of response must guard against the assumption that interpretive strategies, on their own, determine the dynamics of reading. Nonetheless, because the foremost concern of historical hermeneutics is the specific features of that dynamic, its primary focus must be on the particular codes of reading preserved in the larger historical archive of semiological practices and sociopolitical developments. Such an approach to the relation among gender, fiction, and reading strategies in antebellum America has available two major types of archival material: the responses contained in private letters and diaries and the reading patterns informing reviews and literary essays in popular periodicals. Of the two, the second represents a more justifiable basis for a historical hermeneutics for several reasons.[23] If, as Culler has maintained, "one is to study reading rather than readers"—to fashion, in other words, a sociology of reading grounded in affective practices of shared interpretive codes—the focus must be on "public interpretive practices."[24] Reviews provide such a base for early-nineteenth-century America because they were the primary vehicle for the dissemination and assimilation of ideas about the relation between fiction and ways of reading. Appearing in magazines with circulations that, for the time, were large or in periodicals of national influence, reviews enjoyed a publicly sanctioned authority buttressed by the institutional imprimatur of the publishing industry itself.[25] Despite regional biases and the vested interests of some magazines in particular publishing houses, reviewers, moreover, adhered to a fairly consistent set of interpretive practices. Because reviews were not merely individual assertions of aesthetic values but expressions whose content was corporate and communal, reviewers formed an interpretive community whose assumptions constituted the public forum for the reading and writing of fiction in early-nineteenth-century America.

To say this is not to imply that reviewers controlled or precisely mirrored the reading practices of the mass audience; however, the gap between the two was not as large as it is today because of what James Wallace has called "the peculiar circumstances of intellectual life in early nineteenth-century America." Reviewers and magazine essayists were not professional critics but "moral and intellectual leaders in the community," who shared a common "social standing, education, and opinion" with the novel-reading public.[26] Moreover, that public, residing primarily in cities and small towns, which offered greatest access to fiction through bookstores, reading rooms, and lending libraries, was largely the same middle-class audience that bought and read periodicals.[27]

Because the periodical press recognized that fiction reading was an activity to which Americans were devoting an increasing amount of their leisure time, by the 1840s the vast majority of periodical journalists recognized that this phenomenon could not be addressed, as it had in earlier decades, simply by censuring such reading.[28] Nonetheless, reviewers, editors, and their fellow journalists were not ready to embrace fiction reading without qualification, since they continued to believe that such activity could create "evil and even melancholy effects" that could not be controlled merely by encouraging writers to produce better fiction. Although authors may intend well, "the purity of literature," noted *Graham's Magazine*, "depends on the decency of its readers" (March 1851: 159). Believing, as the *Southern Literary Messenger* announced, that "every step taken by the mass of readers in defiance or disregard of any of the forms of excellence, becomes a stride in the downward pathway that leads to Vandalism and ignorance" (March 1845: 172), reviewers sought to effect a proper relation between the middle class and fiction by acting as surrogates and guides for that readership, directing it not only to read certain types of fiction but also to read fiction *in certain ways*. As one writer for the *North American Review* explained, "Reviewers are supposed to know more than most people about new publications. . . . We are proxies for the public, who now . . . trust to newspapers, magazines, and reviews" for their ideas about fiction (April 1847: 403). Repeatedly, reviewers and editors who addressed this question identified a similar objective. *Godey's Lady's Book* maintained that "it has been our constant duty to guide our . . . readers aright in their choice of literary amusement" and to let them see "that this 'delight' or amusement should be guided by sound principles" (March 1863: 304), while a reviewer in *Graham's* asserted that "the articles in the leading quarterlies and monthlies are among the most valuable portion of modern literature" because of "the important principles that they reinforce" (March 1854: 345). Implicit in these remarks was the idea that reviewers were to act as cultural custodians of the public, its welfare, and its reading—to act as social and, as they sometimes referred to themselves, "literary philanthropists."[29] And *Godey's* made clear that the duty of the "literary philanthropist" was "to strengthen the bands of society by instruction" (September 1857: 275). Such remarks indicate that reviewers, editors, and their fellow columnists, most of whom were male, acted as avatars of the dominant culture, which included traditional ideas about women's status, interests, and reading abilities as well as the assumption that the purpose of reading was to obtain knowledge that facilitated one's ability to contribute to the prevailing social order.[30]

Operating within this ideological frame, reviewers thus sought to exercise their self-appointed roles as cultural custodians by directing and refining the response patterns of the public to bring them in line with a standard of reading epitomized by the reviewers themselves. More specifically, the antebellum periodical press sought to create a wider community of interpretation by promoting specific ideas about the nature of the reader of fiction, the "proper" path along which the reader's engagement with fiction should proceed, and most importantly, particular strategies for readers to follow for responding to novels and tales in a (supposedly) informed manner.

In addressing these issues, reviewers recognized that a substantial portion of their readership, like that of fiction itself, consisted of women. If readers were to be instructed in the proper strategies for consuming fiction, reviewers felt it especially imperative "to impress upon the minds of young women the necessity of reading . . . romances, novels, and tales with great caution," since only through guided reading would a woman "be fitted for the sphere in which she should revolve; be better prepared to discharge her appointed duties in society, and be happier in herself" (*Messenger*, September 1839: 601). Accordingly, when reviewers addressed the relation between the production and consumption of fiction, their remarks frequently were coded in gender-specific assumptions about how readers responded to fiction and how they should read if rightly informed—assumptions that were fashioned, like those characterizing fiction reading in toto, by the ideological and social forces of the time.

For within this period, patriarchal culture was witnessing changes in the social role and significance of women that threatened to destabilize the dominant male order. In an era when industrial and urban growth, transformations in the market economy, a burgeoning women's movement, and an upsurge in female authorship were challenging the traditional status of women, that dominant order was experiencing one of those pivotal moments when it "is obviously obliged," as Luce Irigaray reminds us, "to stake out new boundaries . . . to re-ensure—otherwise and elsewhere—[its] dominance." At such a moment the discourse of male dominance finds that "the serene contemplation of empire must be abandoned in favor of taming those forces which, once unleashed, might explode the very concept of empire. A detour into *strategy, tactics,* and *practice* is called for, at least as long as it takes to [re]gain vision."[31] Such a detour is exactly what antebellum reviewers took through their comments on the relation between fiction and women readers. Indeed, as Baym has argued, reviewers viewed fiction itself, particularly in its depiction of female characters and their social relations, as a way of facilitating such control. What needs to be recognized, however, is that reviewers, presuming that process as bidirectional, conceived the very practice of female response as a means for maintaining patriarchy.[32] Achieving that end meant promulgating interpretive strategies through which women, by the *manner* in which they read, could be resecured within traditional gender boundaries.

At the base of their conception of female reading lay certain assumptions regarding the capacities of women readers and the mass audience for fiction. Reviewers tended to attribute to the latter lower intellectual capacities than those possessed by readers of history or philosophy. As a reviewer for the *Christian Examiner* explained in a kind of Bunyanesque allegory, "It is easier to read a novel than to study political economy or theology, and while there are few who are willing to travel along the hard and difficult path to truth, there are thousands ready to lounge along the broad highway" (November 1855: 355).[33] Besides being prone to laziness in seeking instruction, novel readers were assumed to be guilty too often of consuming fiction indiscriminately without regard for its moral probity and capacity for truth. Reviewers repeatedly bemoaned readers who are "ravenous for fiction" that "deprave[s] the taste, and too often the morals" (*Graham's*, February 1846: 95) and devour it with an indulgence that "is [the] diseased . . . consequence of fever and delirium" (*Messenger*, September 1844: 540). Though rendered as germane to a class of readers not coded by gender, such remarks need to be read in light of the belief that women were the major audience for fiction in this period. If readers of fiction were lazy, indiscriminate, and susceptible to highly wrought, sensationalist narratives, reviewers were implying that women especially were prone to such indulgence. At times, in fact, that connection was explicitly affirmed; a review in *Graham's* warned: "There is something romantic in every inexperienced female mind in the idea of pirates and debauchees. . . . Such gentlemen their imaginations are apt to survey under the light of the picturesque instead of under the light of conscience" (May 1848: 299). The widely read *Godey's* echoed this idea, cautioning that "our most accomplished young women" too often are "weak demented creatures" whose "imagination has been dazzled and their taste corrupted by the frivolous European novels" (May 1842: 286).

Yet a curious inconsistency existed in the way reviewers characterized women readers. Although repeatedly invoking, either tacitly or overtly, the moral weakness of the female mind, reviewers often assumed women were above such appeals to the sensational and unsavory. Citing the presence of uncensured adultery and unpunished murder in Emilie Carlen's *Magic Goblet*, a review in the *North American*, for example, remarked that such passages "are an outrage to all womanly delicacy" (April 1845: 292), while the *Southern Literary Messenger*, in speaking of a class of novelists into which it grouped *Uncle Tom's Cabin*, asked rhetorically whether "the mind of woman," a "stainless mind," could "read such works without a blush of confusion" (June 1853: 322). Instead of such fictions, reviewers recommended "to the fairer portion of our readers" novels that were more appropriate to female sensibilities, either because such works, as the *Messenger* explained, contain "no word or allusion . . . which could . . . suffuse the cheek of female innocence with the blush of outraged modesty (September 1849: 581) or because, as *Graham's* averred, they inculcated "a certain refinement and good taste" that "the ladies . . . will appreciate" (January 1857: 86).

Two conflicting assumptions should be specified in these warnings and recommendations by reviewers. As Baym has noted, reviewers assumed that women were both susceptible and immune to the corruptions of fiction, though she suggests that such assumptions may have embodied an implicit distinction between inexperienced and older women.[34] However, a second contradiction is at work here that cannot be explained by such a distinction. While asserting that the "inexperienced female mind" was highly attracted to romanticized vice, reviewers nonetheless kept claiming that "the mind of woman . . . and her heart" possessed a "native purity" that made moral reserve inherent in the very nature of womanhood (*Messenger*, June 1853: 322). But if women by their nature were refined and moral creatures, horrified by profligacy and vice, it is unclear why they needed the kind of fiction reviewers kept recommending: fiction that taught refinement and probity. The didactic imperative, so central to reviewers' reading strategies, was at odds with their conception of the female reader as a moral agent. But reviewers were unable to see—or perhaps unwilling to admit—that their ideas about female readers rested on incompatible conceptions of womanhood in the culture at large. Masking this ideological inconsistency, reviewers simply enlisted the "female mind" to indict "corrupt" relations between readers and certain types of fiction or invoked the shibboleth of the refined female reader as a "natural" position from which women should censure a story for failing to coordinate its exposition with the moral sensibilities reviewers ascribed to its audience.

Just as reviewers asserted that "a female author puts much of her personal individuality into her books, being more prone to express emotions rather than ideas," so was it assumed that woman readers naturally were inclined to respond emotionally, rather than intellectually, to fiction (*North American Review*, January 1851: 151). "When it relates to taste" in fiction, explained *Graham's*, "the multitude" – which, of course, was assumed to be female – "is of no great authority; but in all that is connected with feeling, they are the highest" (August 1844: 91). Nevertheless, when discussing emotional response, reviewers often criticized it. One writer for the *Messenger* looked forward to the day when the novel-reading public would no longer be deluged "by tears which have fallen from the eyes of every grade of society, from the countess who sobbed herself to sleep . . . over the Children of the Abbey, up to the seamstress in her garret, or down to the scullery maid . . . who wiped her eyes on the duster, at the sorrows of Malvina" (January 1862: 11). Another reviewer similarly complained about the "sentimental propriety which claims . . . the female mind" (*Christian Examiner*, January 1860: 120). Through such remarks, reviewers gave their female audience a contradictory set of codes for reading by calling into question or simply ridiculing the very reactions attributed to women as proper to their nature.

Yet such a conflicting profile no doubt had its advantages for reviewers as a means to devalue female response and thus insulate women further within the confines of patriarchal authority. That goal, and the ideology informing it, is most evident in antebellum comments about fiction's moral obligations to its readers – comments such as the one made by a *Graham's* reviewer, who praised Bulwer's *Last of the Barons* as "a manly English novel" precisely because "it does not contain one passage detracting from the sanctity of marriage, or justify seduction and adultery . . . and exhibits nothing which need call up a blush to the cheek of the chariest maiden" (April 1843: 261). In the calculus of reviewing, good novels were equated to "manly" ones and deserved praise to the degree that they denied women sexual knowledge while championing a system of marriage in which gender roles were fixed and hierarchically encoded.[35] The degree to which reviewers saw the reading of "immoral" fiction as a threat to male power appears in an article from the *Messenger* castigating novels that "render[ed] virtue ridiculous and vice attractive." Warning that "these books have penetrated into the most secluded villages, . . . scattering their seeds of vice broadcast over the land," the writer encouraged "prudent fathers of families" to resist this "deadly incubus" (January 1844: 38). As the metaphors suggest, such fictions for reviewers were tantamount to demon lovers who threatened to symbolically emasculate "prudent fathers" by violating the patriarchal system of bourgeois values and its control over women. Indeed, such control was at the center of the conception of the female reader itself, since reviewers, in defining her as they did, reduced womanhood to a moral barometer for their own reading while establishing the conception as an interpretive convention for women to employ in their own confrontation with fiction. As a result, the practice of reviewers vis-à-vis the act of reading constituted a version of what Irigaray has called the denial of the female as subject and the reduction of women to an object of male reflection.

For in articulating their responses to novels and short stories, whether they spoke about readers or not, reviewers were giving an implicit message to their female audience: that the reviewers' own reactions were to serve as a master code, a kind of metareader or "informed" reader composed of the interpretive strategies that reviewers exercised and that, by implication, readers themselves were to follow.

This informed reader consisted of both a collection of specific aesthetic and moral assumptions and certain requisite capacities for implementing them. These included the belief that fiction always should instruct its audience, display a clear ethical purpose, be consistent in its use of genres, present a controlled narrative voice, and depict characters who reflected real life. More importantly, these premises were to serve as codes for determining the meaning and quality of fictional works. The examples of the reviewers further indicate that the informed reader would recognize the importance of the relation among audience, author, and work, would be capable of differentiating types of readers addressed by fiction, and would possess the ability to decide when a work was establishing a proper role for its readers.

A central conviction was that fiction must be evaluated by how well it balanced instruction and formal control, and whether that balance created a proper role for its audience. A moral purpose itself was not enough, since reviewers, as Baym has demonstrated, distinguished between fictions which activated an appropriate moral stance through the dramatic situation and those that merely layered such instruction on the narrative proper.[36] Though maintaining that an uplifting, tutelary relation, especially for women, was intrinsic and necessary to fiction, reviewers asserted that the relation should be consistent and subtle rather than overt and intermittent. Because the latter was judged a weak form of readerly engagement, the implication was that the informed reader needed to exercise the same interpretive authority and reach the same conclusion. Hence, in commenting on a novel entitled *The Fatalist*, a reviewer for *Graham's* complained, "Neither do we like [notice the plural encompassing the reviewer's audience in this response] the convenient morality of an author in writing a book directly injurious, and then, hoping to atone for it all by a page of morality at the finale" (September 1840: 144). One reason for such objections was that intermittent preaching, particularly at the close of a novel, was inadequate to maintain a proper moral relation with readers whose interest depended on plot and characters—in other words, the weak-minded mass readers, a group that was assumed to consist especially of women. As *Godey's* asserted, "Where we are made to feel interest in a guilty character, and to pardon easily his transgressions, there is a moral fault in the book, no matter how it ends" (April 1860: 368). But why did reviewers also object to overt moralizing in a book that was itself moral—the kind of objection, for instance, *Graham's* made about T. S. Arthur's *Insubordination*: "The morality of the story is no doubt good; but the reasoning by which it is engaged is . . . far too pertinaciously thrust into the reader's face on every page" (June 1841: 296)? Baym has argued that reviewers conceived such intrusions as a "political mistake" because, by placing the writer above the reader, these techniques violated the hierarchy of the "novel-reading situation [in which] power was invested in the reader who had bought the book."[37] I want to suggest, however, that the interpretive logic behind this strategy of informed reading was exactly the opposite of the one Baym offers and that that logic carried strong gender implications.

Given that informed readers were to pay attention to the dynamics of the reader-writer relation, those readers were to view such intrusions as technical gaffs precisely because they prohibited an author from maintaining rightful authority. Since reviewers repeatedly emphasized that good novels united subtle artistry with exemplary ethics—a combination signifying superior accomplishments that informed readers were expected to admire—a novelist who relied on heavy-handed intrusions inadvertently exposed the machinery by which the novel, as aesthetic object, was expected to do its moral work. Maintaining that such intrusions were ineffective in elevating the mass readership—conceived primarily as women who supposedly lacked the mental stamina or patience for dealing with discursive instruction—and aware that such a novel had botched its own principles, the informed reader could rightfully assume a superior position that signaled the author's failure to preserve the proper hierarchy of reader-writer relations. In taking that position, therefore, women readers would read as men by identifying against other women, whose status as members of a purportedly weak-minded mass readership gave to the informed code of reading the capacity to recognize failures in authorial authority in the first place.

In promoting a rather uniform version of informed reading, however, reviewers did not assume it should be practiced in exactly the same way by both sexes. Subscribing to a representational poetics in which fictional value was to be determined by its fidelity to an empirical reality built on sexual difference, the informed code of reading posited that the reader's response to verisimilitude should take a distinct shape for women. Although all readers were to derive instruction from fiction and to judge it by how well it reflected life, its utility for women depended on their ability to extract practical information relevant to their social roles. Thus *Godey's*, in addressing "every lady who wishes to do good," advised its audience to take up Catharine Sedgwick's *Live and Let Live* to learn about the "improvement and ornament" of the "domestic field" (September 1837: 140). Likewise, a reviewer in the *Messenger* recommended *The Image of the Father* because "our lady friends will find in the character of Mrs. Farquhar . . . a bright example of an obedient and *useful wife*" (November 1848: 704). Although such criteria were to guide women's responses to domestic fiction especially, the informed woman reader was expected to glean practical benefits from novels and stories that did not overtly provide them. Historical fiction was especially touted for this advantage, as another reviewer in the *Messenger* asserted: "One of the most beneficial and interesting modes in which fiction can be employed, is that of illustrating historical events" (September 1839: 632). For readers of fiction, and especially women, explained another writer in the same issue, "the advantages of correct knowledge of history must be obvious," primarily because such knowledge can "invigorate the sentiments to virtue." For this reviewer, history in the guise of fiction was important for a woman as a means of cultivating those virtues necessary to her state—a state in which "her vocations are domestic and her duties solitary" (598–99).

When dealing with the question of instruction, as well as such formal and aesthetic features as genre, character, and plot, reviewers nonetheless assumed that diverse types of novels existed and that the audience must adapt. In one sense, this principle of adaptation is implicit in the various classifications reviewers used to discuss fiction, as Baym has pointed out. Because readers needed to know the class to which a work belonged to respond to it properly, poetics and hermeneutics converged in this area. But the criterion of adaptability extended beyond fictional classification. Cognizant that the novel was a changing form, informed readers were expected to approach fiction with an horizon of expectations flexible enough to account for noteworthy artistic accomplishments that might otherwise trouble standard response strategies. "Conformity to academic precepts is now but a negative merit," explained an article entitled "Our Artists" in *Godey's*, which also affirmed that "violation of rules" must be "pardoned" (August 1846: 68). Truly informed readers needed to recognize and give credit to a writer whose work did not fit certain interpretive asumptions, provided that the work offered something in return. A reviewer for *Harper's New Monthly Magazine*, for example, cautioned that while Ann Stephens's *Mary Derwent* made "demands on the faith of the reader which defy all sense of probability," the "incidents are wrought up into a succession of striking scenes . . . which excites both the imagination and the sympathy of the reader" (August 1858: 407). Assuming that new novels might work in different ways, informed readers needed to be flexible enough to allow for meritorious variations in the art of fiction and to adjust to them.

Reviewers did not believe, however, that this strategy of flexibility should take precedence over or even be practiced without other interpretive conventions, particularly those involving identification of the reader addressed in a work. Though generally critical of overtly didactic fiction as unpalatable to the truly informed reader, reviewers implied that such didacticism was another matter when the gender of the reader was at stake. One reviewer for *Graham's*, though complaining of "a consistent intrusion of ethical reflection" in Bulwer's *Harold, the Last of the Saxon Kings*, nevertheless affirmed that such passages "will doubtless much edify all young ladies" (September 1848: 179). The gender-specific assumptions of informed reading underlay another essay in the *Messenger* that offered an ironic bit of advice about how to cope with and avoid heavy-handed passages. Speaking of such moments in the novels of G. P. R. James, the essayist quipped, "We were once greatly assisted in avoiding them by reading one of his books after a lady, who had drawn pencil lines about every such passage as an expression of her sympathy and admiration" (September 1847: 534–35). What is telling about this flippancy is the way it comes at the expense of the very reader whom reviewers identified as an appropriate role for the female audience. As such, it epitomizes the kind of contradictory scripts that were provided ostensibly to educate women but which worked, in effect, to immobilize their responses. Although reviewers maintained that women were to resist fiction that challenged their morality, this "informed" reaction was berated as inferior to the responses of men, who, it was assumed, could more readily appreciate the power and complexity of such challenges. As one article on modern fiction explained, while certain novels, such as those by Bulwer, contained "many highly wrought passages . . . which might shock maiden delicacy," a proper understanding of the relation between the reader and these works must take into account the fact that "Bulwer writes for men," who are best capable of fathoming his "morbid anatomy of the human mind" (*Messenger*, May 1842: 345). And what of the woman who might savor a novel's moral challenge? Like the women who wrote such fictions, she was stigmatized as bold, indelicate, or unfeminine. Such selective use of interpretive strategies indicates that reviewers never really expected women to be truly informed readers capable of making the distinctions advocated as part of the interpretive process. Coded by gender, the informed reader instead served as a means for marginalizing and disempowering women by excluding them from full participation in an ultimately phallocentric system of reading.

Given the way reviewers conceived of themselves as caretakers of culture, such an approach was almost inevitable. Dedicated to preservation, not creation, to replication, not rupture, reviewers did not define female reading as an experience that produces self-revelation in the form that Iser and other reader-response critics have identified as characteristic of reading in general.[38] Nor did they envision it as a means to create new strategies for interpreting texts that challenged old assumptions. Instead, it was to be a form of self-validation and confirmation of the already known. Through a strategy of informed reading that was essentially conservationist and ultimately narcissistic, reviewers sought to multiply their own images, as cultural incarnations, in modified and well-controlled female replicas that could reinforce patriarchal hegemony. The significance of this practice lies not only in the way it defined the patriarchal ideology of antebellum reviewers or in the way it shaped the interpretive codes they encouraged. As a performative model of reading imbibed by middle-class women who came to fiction through the medium of the periodical press, these strategies provide modern criticism with a vehicle for exploring the relation between that fiction and an ideologically weighted version of female response in antebellum America.

III

Although the antebellum objectification of the female reader enacted a restrictive strategy for consuming fiction, it was not a discourse of total impoverishment and confinement, particularly in relation to fictional production. While reviewers effected public paradigms for reading that no doubt limited the way an author could address an audience, those paradigms also established a common ground on which fiction and its readers could meet. In the process, antebellum novelists—both those in the traditional American canon and the larger group of women writers that the canon so often has ignored—were given a set of conventions that they could redefine and challenge to engage their readers and the dominant cultural values in original and dynamic ways.

This question of dynamics, of course, is central to a historical hermeneutics that seeks to unite a history of interpretive strategies with an analysis of the reading process. Yet because we too often forget that the interaction between reading strategies and a text inevitably involves both accommodation and rupture, critics have tended to slight this interplay by focusing on fiction assumed to be most disruptive of conventions, a practice that usually results in championing such male authors as Poe, Hawthorne, and Melville in the antebellum period. Such a focus, unfortunately, neglects texts in which the pattern of accommodation and rupture, particularly in relation to the conventions of female reading, is especially suggestive of the shape reader engagement could take in the early nineteenth century.

One such text is Susan Warner's *The Wide, Wide World* (1850), one of America's first best-selling novels written primarily for women. Recently several feminist critics have sought to redefine the status of Warner's novel by showing how it valorizes female altruism to challenge the patriarchal order or by arguing that it covertly dramatizes dissatisfaction with the degraded status of women.[39] However, the deformations of *The Wide, Wide World* occur on a more fundamental level in that Warner's novel provided its contemporary audience with a vehicle for an informed response that disrupts the reader's ability to activate unambiguously the publicly touted interpretive conventions of female reading.

Although an antebellum woman could have found in *The Wide, Wide World* characters, incidents, and values that accorded with the middle-class assumptions of informed response, including the value of female submission, the experience of reading the novel becomes more problematic at several points. One of these occurs a third of the way into the text, after the reader has witnessed the forced separation of Ellen Montgomery, the narrative's young protagonist, from her consumptive mother and the early stages of her new life with her maiden aunt, Emerson Fortune. In her encounter with the text, the reader repeatedly is urged to view the aunt as an impatient termagant who discourages Ellen from making friends, answers her demand for privacy with "a sharp box on the ear," and denies her access to letters from her beloved mother.[40] Even the aunt's name, Miss Fortune, would curve the antebellum reader's response in this direction, since informed reading included the assumption that such markers could be "indicative of peculiarities of person or character" (*Graham's*, November 1841: 252). When Miss Fortune goes so far as to attack Mrs. Montgomery by telling Ellen that, had her mother "been trained to use her hands and do something useful," she would have "brought you up to know manners," the reader's antagonism toward the aunt would be intense enough to confirm Ellen's own belief that "her aunt was the very most disagreeable person she ever had the misfortune to meet" (139–40). Firmly placing her allegiance with Ellen and her occasional remonstrances against the aunt, the reader would nevertheless have had her secure moral position suddenly undermined by Ellen's halting admission to her friend Alice that "the worst is,—oh the worst is—that I meant—I meant—to be a good child, and I have been worse than I ever was in my life before," primarily because "I have not forgiven Aunt Fortune" (151, 157).

By encountering Ellen's assertion that the ultimate failure is hers, the reader's experience yields a novel in which a traditional Christian message of charity undercuts the reader's own moral stance and, in the process, two conventions of informed reading. Having acquiesced in the unremitting condemnation of Miss Fortune, the reader would now find herself implicated in the same sin that Ellen commits. Yet the situation is such that a simple ethical adjustment could not provide a firm base for response. Does Aunt Fortune deserve the reader's enmity, forgiveness, or both; if "both" is the answer, how should the reader reconcile the two conflicting positions? In the face of such questions, the reader would find herself in a dilemma in which it is difficult to fashion the kind of clear and fixed moral stance expected of informed reading. Instead, she would be obliged to exercise both her analytical powers and her feelings to sort through this ambiguous position. Creating a gap that enables the text's female readers to exercise interpretive power by participating in the creation of meaning, the experience of Warner's novel thus subverts the public assumption that women needed overt moral maxims and ethical closure from fiction. Because the audience is encouraged to learn to be better readers from this experience, *The Wide, Wide World* can be said to accommodate the assumption that fiction should be instructive even as the encounter with the text ruptures expectations about the form didacticism should take for women.

Warner's novel can do so because the work it performs on its reader is a function of the historically specific work that reader does on the text. The antebellum code of informed reading produces a text that manipulates the publicly touted assumption that women were to be active readers of fiction primarily when it challenged standard moral values. Locating in the novel an acceptable message of Christian benevolence, this encounter with the text disarms the need for resistance only to turn the reader's acquiescence into a challenge. As the female reader's "passive" acceptance of the text becomes an occasion of anguish over Ellen's ethical dilemma, the reader may be aroused to active participation in a willed effort to remake her own moral character. In such a response, overt submission becomes a form of power through self-mastery by conforming to, yet significantly diverging from, the patriarchal values of informed female reading. For in the dynamics of their own response to *The Wide, Wide World*, middle-class women could experience the pain and uncertainty accompany-

ing the struggle for the moral purity and submissiveness that reviewers simply assumed were inherent in the nature of womanhood.

Of course, Warner's audience could have resisted such positioning,
and the printed comments by reviewers of the novel in the 1850s indicate that no such disruption accompanied their response. Yet these particular reviews are less a reflection of how the informed code of
response operated during the act of reading by middle-class women
and more a record of holistic interpretations constructed, after the
novel was put down, to conform to the ideological mission of a pre-
dominately male community of respondents. The point, however, is
not whether individual readers responded to *The Wide, Wide World*
precisely in the way just described, since the historical reader exists
not as a category of personhood but as a function: a repertory of strategies enabling a text to become intelligible in a historically specific
way. Both in its original configuration and in its subsequent representation by the critic, any particular configuration of reading is a
paradigm to which real readers may or may not have subscribed, a decision affected by culturally constituted ideological and performative
factors that determine the extent to which the strategies exercise
power and the manner in which they are applied. As an example of historical hermeneutics in action, therefore, the foregoing scenario is not
a reflection of an "actual" reading experience, which can never be
"recaptured," nor is it a definitive description of the relation between
textual signals and the informed strategy of reading in early-nineteenth-century America. Rather, it represents a possible reading experience that indicates the way current interpretations of response can
intersect with past codes to give a historical account of reading characterized by the convergence among past conventions, the textual
engagement of audience, and cultural ideology.

In this sense, the reading strategies of antebellum reviewers, by serving as points of departure for a historical hermeneutics, have as much
value to current reader-response criticism as they may have had for
fiction writers in the early nineteenth century—not because those
strategies provide an unmediated base for historicizing response but
because they can function as a space for constructing a simulacrum of
reading that incorporates the historicity of interpretive conventions.
Although the textual (i.e., constructed) status of such a reading means
that a historicized version of response can disclose only conditions of
possibility for textual significance as a product of two historically me-

diated positions, the admission of this mediated status constitutes the metacritical turn differentiating historical hermeneutics from the ahistorical closure of previous reader-response practice. Such an admission, however, does not invalidate the attempt to approach reading historically any more than it means abandoning the need to "do history." What it does is provide an avenue for uniting the deconstructive principle of the textuality of reading accounts with a functional approach to the historicity of response that takes into account our own historical position as readers of the past and its discourse.

Yet if such an approach to the public strategies of antebellum reading can facilitate a relation among current reading practices, texts from the past, and earlier interpretive codes, those strategies themselves also may have been valuable to women readers in the early nineteenth century. By emphasizing such criteria as authorial authority and the balance between instruction and formal control, reviewers urged women to read beyond plot by focusing on the structures of fiction and their architectonic relationship to content. The informed strategy of reading, even in the reduced version offered to women, reminded them that communication was a dynamic and interactive process that, as the editor of *Godey's* pointed out, required one "in reading any work . . . to make frequent pauses, and trace out the inference, and the particular bearing and tendency of detached portions of it; and upon its completion, to consider the general scope, . . . the correctness of the sentiments advanced, and the character of the style" (April 1838: 191). Through such admonitions, women were encouraged to be more than passive recipients of fictional—and by implication, nonfictional—discourse. According to the interpretive paradigms of reviewers and editors, the reader actively participated in the reading experience by choosing to accept or reject a particular role that a text implied for its audience. Ironically, therefore, the strategies of response promoted by periodicals may have empowered women to approach reading as an intellectual, emotional, and critical activity for controlling the very discourse of public interpretation that sought to control them.

Notes

1. Hans Robert Jauss, *Toward an Aesthetic of Reception*, trans. Timothy Bahti (Minneapolis: U of Minnesota P, 1982) 63.

2. Judith Fetterley, *The Resisting Reader: A Feminist Approach to American Fic-*

tion (Bloomington: Indiana UP, 1978); Jane Tompkins, *Sensational Designs: The Cultural Work of American Fiction, 1790–1860* (New York: Oxford UP, 1985); Janice Radway, *Reading the Romance: Women, Patriarchy, and Popular Culture* (Chapel Hill: U of North Carolina P, 1984).

3. Wolfgang Iser, *The Act of Reading: A Theory of Aesthetic Response* (Baltimore: Johns Hopkins UP, 1978) 3. Besides Iser, critics who have acknowledged the historical nature of reading include Mary Louise Pratt, "Interpretive Strategies/Strategic Interpretations: On Anglo-American Reader-Response Criticism," *Boundary 2* 10 (1982): 201–31; Steven Mailloux, *Rhetorical Power* (Ithaca: Cornell UP, 1989); Jonathan Culler, *The Pursuit of Signs: Semiotics, Literature, Deconstruction* (Ithaca: Cornell UP, 1984); Robert Holub, *Reception Theory: A Critical Introduction* (London: Methuen, 1984); and most reception theorists. Despite their professed historical orientation, however, the last group has displayed little interest in describing the specific interpretive strategies guiding particular historical communities of readers or in examining the impact of those strategies on the process of reading itself. Instead, leading practitioners, such as Jauss, tend to focus on the way authors read other authors (e.g., "Racine und Goethes Iphigenie: Mit einem Nachwort über die Partialitat de rezeptionsasthetischen Methode," *Neue Hefte fur Philosophie* 4 [1973]: 1–46) or on production—i.e., the changing history of major writers' and philosophers' conceptions of the form of aesthetic experience (e.g., Jauss's *Aesthetic Experience and Literary Hermeneutics*, trans. Michael Shaw [Minneapolis: U of Minnesota P, 1982]). By contrast, Culler, Pratt, Holub, and Iser simply leave their recognition of history at the general theoretical level. Only Mailloux has attempted to unite theory and practice by proposing that critics give up trying to forge a general theory of reading and turn instead to "rhetorical hermeneutics," which would "provide histories of how particular theoretical and critical discourses have evolved" to reveal "historical sets of topics, arguments, tropes, ideologies, and so forth" (*Rhetorical Power* 15–17). In taking this turn, however, Mailloux opens up a different gap by failing to explain how such histories would intersect with attempts to describe the specific processes involved in reading particular texts.

4. On the relation between reading and the New Historicism, see Edward Pechter, "The New Historicism and Its Discontents: Politicizing Renaissance Drama," *PMLA* 102 (1987): 292.

5. This phenomenon is prevalent in the practice of virtually every reader-response critic who works from what Steven Mailloux has called the "sociological" model of reading, the model that has had the greatest impact on American criticism (*Interpretive Conventions: The Reader in the Study of American Fiction* [Ithaca: Cornell UP, 1982] 40–43). See, for instance, Iser, *Act of Reading*; Iser, *The Implied Reader: Patterns of Communication in Prose Fiction from Bunyan to Beckett* (Baltimore: Johns Hopkins UP, 1974); Peter Rabinowitz, *Before Reading: Narra-*

tive Conventions and the Politics of Interpretation (Ithaca: Cornell UP, 1987); Stanley Fish, *Surprised by Sin: The Reader in "Paradise Lost"* (London: St. Martin's, 1967); Fish, "Things and Actions Indifferent: The Temptation of Plot in *Paradise Regained*," *Milton Studies* 17 (1983): 163–85; and Mailloux's own *Interpretive Conventions*, particularly the chapter "Practical Criticism: The Reader in American Fiction."

6. This second practice is typical of the New Historicists on those occasions when they address the issue of the reader. See, for instance, Stephen Greenblatt, *Renaissance Self-Fashioning: From More to Shakespeare* (Chicago: U of Chicago P, 1980) 100–104, 119–20. In Greenblatt's *Shakespearean Negotiations: The Circulation of Social Energy in Renaissance England* (Berkeley and Los Angeles: U of California P, 1988), the tactic is different, but the results are much the same. For example, in discussing Thomas Harriot's *Brief and True Report*, Greenblatt argues that the text could have been interpreted as a subversion of Renaissance assumptions about providential sanction—a strategy drawn from Machiavellian anthropology (27). But Greenblatt never explains whether that anthropology formed part of interpretive strategies at the time and whether Renaissance readers actually brought such strategies to the reading of travel reports (or Shakespeare's plays). As a result, his Renaissance reader works out to be an unacknowledged version of Greenblatt himself.

7. To be sure, some recognition of the historical aporia in reader-oriented criticism has appeared (e.g., Holub, *Reception Theory;* Mailloux, *Rhetorical Power;* and Pratt, "Interpretive Strategies"), but that recognition has not been accompanied thus far by any sustained attempts to combine theory and practice in addressing the relation between historically specific interpretive practices and the dynamics of response to individual texts from the literary past.

8. See, for example, Susan Schibanoff, "Taking the Gold out of Egypt: The Art of Reading as a Woman," Kathryn Shevelow, "Fathers and Daughters: Women as Readers of the *Tatler*," and Madonne M. Miner, "Guaranteed to Please: Twentieth-Century American Women's Bestsellers," all in *Gender and Reading: Essays on Readers, Texts, and Contexts*, ed. Elizabeth A. Flynn and Patrocinio P. Schweikart (Baltimore: Johns Hopkins UP, 1986) 83–123, 187–211.

9. See Tompkins, *Sensational Designs,* and Cathy N. Davidson, *Revolution and the Word: The Rise of the Novel in America* (New York: Oxford UP, 1986). A better example of feminist criticism that examines the interplay between the dynamics of response and sociocultural factors is Radway's *Reading the Romance*, but Radway does so by focusing on a contemporary, not a historical, group of texts and its community of readers.

10. Susan Harris, *Nineteenth-Century American Women's Novels: Interpretive Strategies* (Cambridge: Cambridge UP, 1990). Cf., however, Harris's essay below in this collection, which much more directly confronts the specific historical rela-

tion among textual strategies, interpretive assumptions, gender ideology, and female reading.

11. Fetterley, *The Resisting Reader* 3, 5, 9.

12. For a discussion of this strategy as the motor behind patriarchal stories of American literature, see Nina Baym, "Melodramas of Beset Manhood: How Theories of American Fiction Exclude Women Authors," *American Quarterly* 33 (1981): 123–39.

13. By characterizing Fetterley's method in this manner, I am agreeing in part with Rabinowitz, who points out that "Fetterley's 'resisting reader' can come into being only if there is something to resist" (*Before Reading*, 31). But while Rabinowitz uses this point to argue for authorial intention and intrinsic meaning, I would maintain that such resistance – or acquiescence – depends primarily on the reader's position in the network of exchange between the text and the interpretive conventions brought to it.

14. I realize that an alternative description of female reading by a man is susceptible to the charge that it finally subverts the whole thrust of feminism by using its tools to "step in and show the girls how to do it" (Elaine Showalter, "Critical Cross-Dressing: Male Feminists and the Woman of the Year," *Raritan* 3.2 [1983]: 134). But I also believe, with other feminists, that there is a place for men in feminist criticism as a way to prevent it from being ghettoized or becoming an inverted version of the gendered elitism characterizing phallocentric criticism. While feminists probably are correct in arguing that only women can truly experience what it means to read as a woman, a historical inquiry into reading may provide the most productive avenue for male contributions because temporal distance places female and male feminists on more equal footing as outsiders to the particular reading conventions of earlier periods. On this issue of male feminist criticism see Alice Jardine and Paul Smith, eds., *Men in Feminism* (New York: Methuen, 1987); and Jospeh A. Boone and Michael Cadden, eds., *Engendering Men: The Question of Male Feminist Criticism* (New York: Routledge, 1990).

15. Davidson, *Revolution and the Word* 110–50.

16. Washington Irving, "Rip Van Winkle," *The Sketchbook of Geoffrey Crayon, Esq.*, ed. Haskell Springer (Boston: Twayne, 1978) 30–31.

17. Stanley Fish, *Is There a Text in This Class? The Authority of Interpretive Communities* (Cambridge: Harvard UP, 1980) 147, 370–71.

18. Elizabeth Freund, *The Return of the Reader: Reader-Response Criticism* (London: Methuen, 1987) 10.

19. Jonathan Culler, "Prolegomena to a Theory of Reading," in *The Reader in the Text: Essays on Audience and Interpretation*, ed. Susan Suleiman and Inge Crosman (Princeton: Princeton UP, 1980) 56–66.

20. Nina Baym, *Novels, Readers, and Reviewers: Responses to Fiction in Antebellum America* (Ithaca: Cornell UP, 1984).

21. Jauss, *Toward an Aesthetic of Reception* 34–35.

22. Jane Tompkins, "The Reader in History," in *Reader-Response Criticism: From Formalism to Post-Structuralism*, ed. Jane P. Tompkins (Baltimore: Johns Hopkins UP, 1980) 224.

23. In arguing for the superiority of reviews as data, I am not suggesting that letters, diaries, and other private documents cannot be useful in studying reading practices, particularly if one is interested in how "everyday" individuals may have responded to fiction. But this second approach is problematized by the artifactual nature of such texts. Because reviews appear in magazines that are preserved in bulk as public documents, they are representative of a specific interpretive community whose status is defined precisely by general cultural assumptions about what is worth preserving. By contrast, the prolonged survival of letters and diaries depends either on the prominent status of their authors or on the political and economic power of those who seek to ensure the public preservation of such documents. In either case, the representativeness of such artifacts becomes dubious and thus calls into question their use as an index to the interpretive practices of common readers. One also can question whether individuals who self-consciously record their responses to fiction can in any way represent the mass of readers who never do so.

24. Culler, "Prolegomena" 56.

25. Many of the leading periodicals that regularly contained reviews achieved circulations of 5,000 or more, which would be equivalent today to the circulations of the *New Yorker* and the *New York Review of Books* (Baym, *Novels, Readers, and Reviewers* 14). In estimating the readership of these magazines, however, it is important to take into account the common practice of borrowing and the availability of many periodicals in reading rooms, newspaper offices, and libraries for public consumption. Both circumstances contributed materially to an expanded readership for magazines.

26. James Wallace, *Early Cooper and His Audience* (New York: Columbia UP, 1986) 26.

27. Ronald J. Zboray, "Antebellum Reading and the Ironies of Technological Innovation," *American Quarterly* 40 (1988): 79–80.

28. Baym, *Novels, Readers, and Reviewers* 13–43.

29. On this self-conception among antebellum reviewers and its basis in the Americanization of Common Sense philosophy, see William Charvat, *The Origins of American Critical Thought, 1810–1835* (1936; New York: Russell, 1968) 7–26.

30. For a history of this social and utilitarian conception of reading in regard

to literature in general, see Tompkins, "Reader in History"; for its role in America in the early Republic, see Davidson 15–37.

31. Luce Irigaray, *Speculum of the Other Woman*, trans. Gillian C. Gill (Ithaca: Cornell UP, 1985) 136.

32. Baym, *Novels, Readers, and Reviewers* 98, 170, 187–90. To put this matter another way, the difference between Baym's approach and mine in this section is strategic in a way that goes to the heart of an effort to historicize reading. While Baym examines reviewers' conceptions of the work fiction should do on its reader (an approach emphasizing rhetorical poetics), my concern is with reviewers' ideas about the work women readers should do on fiction and on themselves as readers of fiction.

33. Despite the differences in our analyses and purposes, Baym's *Novels, Readers, and Reviewers* has been very helpful in drawing to my attention several reviews and essays, such as this one in the *Christian Examiner*, that have proved useful to this study.

34. Baym, *Novels, Readers, and Reviewers* 53–54.

35. On the relation between reviewers' practices and the suppression of women's sexuality, see also ibid. 181, 189.

36. Ibid. 124–28.

37. Ibid. 126.

38. Iser, *Act of Reading* 150–59; Iser, *Implied Reader* 281–82.

39. Tompkins, *Sensational Designs* 147–85; Joanne Dobson, "The Hidden Hand: Subversion of Cultural Ideology in Three Nineteenth-Century Women's Novels," *American Quarterly* 38 (1986): 228–32.

40. Susan Warner, *The Wide, Wide World* (New York: Feminist, 1987) 159. Subsequent citations are given parenthetically.

Feminism, New Historicism, and the Reader

WAI CHEE DIMOCK

The relation between feminist criticism and New Historicism is a vexed one, having generated not only considerable interest, curiosity, and uneasiness but also, especially in English Renaissance studies, some unusually acrimonious polemics. The acrimony has to do, in part, with the marginal status accorded by one to the other: figuring in each other's discourse at best as a point of departure, and at worst as an *overlooked* point of departure, New Historicists and feminists seem to talk at cross-purposes, keeping their mutual distance, relegating each other to a kind of nonpresence.[1] If the feminist chronicling of women's oppression and celebration of women's difference have appeared misguided to many New Historicists, the New Historicist universalization of power and blurring of genders have struck many feminists as nothing short of reactionary.[2]

In this essay I want to rethink the relation between feminist criticism and New Historicism, using that relation, in turn, as a leverage point, an artificially concocted but no less serviceable juncture, from which and against which both critical enterprises might be evaluated, held up for mutual reflection, and perhaps for mutual realignment.

Eventually I want to challenge not only their supposed disagreement but also their presumed distinction, to show that the discrete identity imputed to each in fact impoverishes both. Still, it is useful, at the outset, to rehearse those presumed distinctions and supposed disagreements, if only to bring into focus some of the tacit premises that have given rise to so much hostility and mistrust. I begin, then, with an imaginary confrontation between New Historicism and feminist criticism, dressed up momentarily as parties at war, and for dramatic effect, I stage the battle over the body of that most familiar and cherished of figures: the figure of the reader.

Or perhaps I should say, familiar and cherished to one side. For feminst critics as different as Nina Baym and Annette Kolodny, Margaret Homans and Louise Rosenblatt, Janice Radway and Cathy Davidson, the figure of the reader has served as a crucial organizing center: a site of contestation, a site of celebration, and a site from which to construct an alternative canon.[3] This is not true of New Historicists, who, preoccupied as they are with the sociocultural field at the text's moment of production (rather than at its moment of reception), have been much less concerned with the reader either as a figure of the past or as a figure of the present moment.[4] Partly to redress the imbalance, and partly to create an occasion for war, I begin with a more or less caricatured appearance of the reader in a more or less caricatured New Historicist exercise, one designed to be uncongenial to feminists.

My starting point, however, is neither a feminist text nor a New Historicist one, but an important (and eminently nonpartisan) essay by Steven Marcus called "Reading the Illegible." Marcus uses the paradigm of reading to describe a cultural phenomenon generated by the complexity of modern life, which, "not perceived as a coherent system of signs," demands to be read—to be organized and interpreted—into some semblance of clarity and order.[5] In the specific example Marcus analyzes, the subject for reading happens to be the urban landscape, but beyond that, he seems also to be giving us a definition of reading in the broadest sense of the word, taking it beyond the generic boundaries of the literary text and using it to include a wide range of activities that have to do with the interpretation of signs, the adjudication of meanings, and the construction of reality. Understood in this nongeneric sense, reading might be said to be a phenomenon peculiar to modernity. Unlike the medieval preoccupation with exegesis and the Puritan preoccupation with typology, reading in its modern guise is not centered on or authorized by one particular text, least of all the Bible. Modern society is a society of interpretation at once deregulated and *de rigueur*[6], for in this world, a world increasingly affected by forces unknown and unseen, and increasingly removed from our immediate comprehension, all of us, whether or not we accept the label, have to become readers of sorts. Indeed, from the mid-nineteenth century onward, reading might be said to be one of the most commonplace cultural activities, an activity dictated by the mysteries of modern life, by the gap, at once titillating and worrisome, between immediate experience and apprehended meaning, between what we see and what we think it signifies.[7]

Still, if all of us are readers, and if reading is what we do every minute of our lives, the phenomenon cannot be very interesting. What makes it interesting, a subject worthy of historical analysis, is its emergence, in its modern, nongeneric form, as a field that sustains and indeed requires special knowledge, a field where the recession of meaning goes hand in hand with the concentration of expertise, and where standards of competence are erected over and against an illiteracy that is, paradoxically, the rule rather than the exception. The rise of the medical profession is a dramatic case in point. As we learn from Paul Starr's magisterial study, *The Social Transformation of American Medicine*, the spectacular ascent of this group both in social status and in economic power had everything to do with their ability to institute a new set of reading conventions, conventions that established not only their own expertise but also the lack of it in those they served. From being a more or less marginal, more or less disreputable group until the mid-nineteenth century, medical practitioners effectively solidified their identity—by regulating certification and licensing and by building an elaborate system of specialized knowledge, technical procedures, and rules of behavior—so that, by the second half of the nineteenth century, the profession had come to occupy a central place in American society. Their success was reflected, according to Starr, not only in their authority over the "construction of reality," the "interpretation of experience," and the "meaning of things," but also in the medical illiteracy of those they served, ordinary people who were incapable of reading their own symptoms and who had to defer to the judgment of these more qualified, or at least more certified, experts.[8]

The American Medical Association was not alone in its triumph.

The same half-century also saw the rise of other professional groups, most notably the American Bar Association, as well as other organizations less powerful and less prosperous, such as the American Historical Association, the American Economic Association, and, of course, the Modern Language Association.[9] As the names of these august institutions suggest, the rise of professional communities has everything to do with the redistribution of social authority. And whether we call such authority "professional sovereignty" (as Paul Starr does) or "professional jurisdiction" (as Andrew Abbott does), it would seem to be predicated on a set of reading conventions, on the authority of expert readers, and conversely, on the dependency of the illiterate.[10] Indeed, the rise of professionalism, a phenomenon that has fascinated sociologists from Emile Durkheim to Daniel Bell,[11] might also be described as the rise of a new way of reading, with a new way of organizing knowledge and a new way of structuring authority.

Given the centrality of reading in a culture of professionalism, one obvious way to historicize the literary reader is ask whether this figure inhabits a structure of authority comparable to that inhabited by its nonfictive counterparts, by the professionals who also happen to be expert readers. Along those lines, a New Historicist might be tempted to pursue a set of interrelated questions: In a culture more generally governed by the ideal of interpretive competence, what sort of *literary* reading conventions might we expect to find? If interpretation is itself a valuable social asset, an asset whose usefulness extends far beyond the domain of the literary, how might it, in turn, shape the literary domain? Do reading conventions in texts generate structures of authority in the same way that reading conventions in the social realm do? And are we prepared to argue that such structures are historically specific, that there might be a textual structure that would answer to the structure of authority underwritten by professionalism?

Charlotte Perkins Gilman's "The Yellow Wallpaper," a story that has inspired numerous feminist readings,[12] turns out, from this perspective, also to be an ideal text for an imaginary New Historicist exercise, ideal not only because this is a story told by a mad narrator, and therefore one that foregrounds the question of interpretive authority, and not only because there is actually a doctor in the story, but also because, by a happy coincidence, Gilman herself was a paragon of professionalism in the late nineteenth century. Supporting herself for nearly thirteen years, from 1887 to 1900—between the time she left her first husband and the time she married her second—Gilman made a living as an editor of magazines (the *Impress* and the *Forerunner*), a veteran on the lecture circuit, and a respected authority on the economics of housework.[13] Between 1898 and 1904, she published four books on the subject—*Women and Economics* (1898), *Concerning Children* (1900), *The Home: Its Work and Influence* (1903), and *Human Work* (1904). In her best known book, *Women and Economics*, she made an impassioned plea for professionalizing housework, arguing that it would secure not only gender equality for women but, just as important, managerial efficiency for the home. Her lifelong interest in architectural design reflects the same faith in professionalism.[14] For her, ideal apartment houses should provide "trained professional service" for "professional women with families": they should have no kitchens, so that cooking would be done not by women but by professional cooks; and they should provide supervised cleaning by "efficient workers" hired by "the manager of the establishment," as well as day care administered by "well-trained professional nurses."[15] Indeed, for her, the goals of feminism can be achieved only through the agency of professionalism, only by bringing specialized knowledge, rational authority, and administrative expertise to the home.

In itself, Gilman's commitment to professionalism is hardly remarkable. What is remarkable, however, is the apparent discrepancy between *Women and Economics* (1898) and "The Yellow Wallpaper" (1892), written just six years before. In this story about mental collapse, a story that ends with the narrator crawling on all fours, where is the redeeming hand of professionalism? And when we witness the terrible mistakes of the husband (who, of course, is a doctor), and when we see what befalls him at the end, are we not supposed to lose faith in the very ground of professional authority?

These questions, perplexing as they might seem, are actually not impossible to answer, especially if we are willing to entertain the possibility that the husband might not be the only model of professional authority, and that another, more commendable figure might be lurking behind the scene. In any case, it is surely significant that the husband is not just a doctor but an emphatically bad one. This means, of course, that he is a bad reader, who, when confronted with a set of symptoms, repeatedly fails to come up with the right interpretation. As his wife becomes more insane, he becomes more optimistic in his diagnosis. Indeed he tells her: "But you really are better, dear, whether you can see it or not. I am a doctor, dear, and I know." And he adds, "Can you not trust me as a physician when I tell you so?"[16]

Repeatedly the husband urges his wife to trust the soundness of his judgment by reminding her that, as a doctor, he has an interpretive authority over her life. But the point, of course, is that he really has no such authority because, being a bad reader, he should never have been a doctor in the first place.[17] What makes him a villain of sorts, then, is not so much that he is a cruel husband as that he is an incompetent doctor. But if he is giving professionalism a bad name here, there is no reason why that bad name should be the last word on the subject. Indeed, the very fact that he is such a noticeably unworthy specimen should alert us to the possibility that there might be a worthier example somewhere else, a professional who not only occupies a position of authority, but actually has a legitimate claim to it.

Where might such an alternative position be found, what would be its structure of authority, and who would be the privileged figure within that structure? If we look for it merely within the actualized fictional world of "The Yellow Wallpaper," only within that immanent structure where every available position is occupied by a particular character, we are bound to be disappointed, I think, because neither the mad narrator, nor her husband the doctor, nor the sister-in-law, can claim to be a figure of authority. However, if we were to think of "The Yellow Wallpaper" as a compositional structure—as a structure generated by a mode of rhetorical address—we might indeed argue for an alternative position, a position that is invisible, unembodied, and yet existing as an object of inference or perhaps even as a structural predicate. Such a position, we might further argue, can indeed function as a virtual repository where the absent attributes of professionalism—rational authority, expert knowledge, and interpretive competence—can be securely lodged.

As must be obvious by now, such a virtual position can be occupied only by one figure. In the absence of any competent reader inside the story, it is the outside reader or, I should say, the implied reader who is called upon to occupy the position of interpretive authority, functioning both as the text's ideal recipient and its necessary coordinate. As my vocabulary suggests, what is being invoked here is the model of reading associated with Wolfgang Iser, a model invoked to provide a supplement to the more familiar model of positionality, and to suggest an opening, a point of exit from the closed system of the text.

Such a procedure, of course, runs the risk of conjuring up an idealized reader. Even more dangerously, it also runs the opposite risk—of turning the reader into a strictly textual phenomenon, immanent within the text and ontologically dependent upon its functions, and so returning once again to a textual system of absolute closure.[18]

To reduce such risks, it is helpful to supplement Iser, in turn, with Tony Bennett's concept of the "reading formation." By this Bennett means a set of determinations which "mediate the relation between text and context, connecting the two and providing the mechanisms . . . , [the] intertextual and discursive relations which produce readers for texts and texts for readers."[19] Bennett's concept is especially important here because, in speaking of reading as a "formation," a reciprocal process by which readers and texts are mutually produced and mutually productive, he also restores a dialectical agency to the reading process, claiming for it a larger operating field as well as a larger instrumental effect.

This emphasis—on the dialectical agency of reading, on the interplay between production and reception—seems to me crucial in any attempt to historicize the reader. It is also crucial, I think, to any historical criticism (including New Historicism, though not confined to it) that, for various political or philosophical reasons, might wish not to reduce subject positions merely to structural effects, merely to something that is given or entailed. Unlike Iser's model, which remains hostage to a system of textual immanence, Bennett's model is structurally contingent but not necessarily structurally determinate. It constitutes the reader not only as a figure of structural dictate but also as a figure of structural potential.

Of course, in "The Yellow Wallpaper," the subject position we are trying to imagine happens to be not a critical position but an authoritative one, which, as we have seen, none of the characters can occupy. But as we have also seen, there is nonetheless a virtual position, commanded by a virtual figure. After all, quite aside from the meager cast of three characters, is not someone else there as well, invisible to the others, but necessary to the unfolding of the text, someone who can do what the others seem incapable of doing for themselves—that is, interpret their story for them? When we come to the end of the story, when the husband is lying on the floor and the wife is crawling around, is not someone else still sitting, still sane and still rational, whose sanity and whose rationality are the very credentials by which she can diagnose the ailments of these characters? Against the pathetic benightedness of all the characters in the story, who hardly can tell what is delusion or hallucination and what is "real," is not someone else always there with open eyes, always granted a clear knowledge, both of the "reality" of the wife's madness and of the "reality" of the marital situation? And against the husband's less than professional expertise, is not someone else always making a competent judgment, or, should we say, a competent reading?

The position of authority in "The Yellow Wallpaper" is occupied by the reader, and we might add, not just any reader, but a reader with a specific and historically recognizable profile, created in the image of professionalism at its most idealized, endowed with the sacred attributes of specialized knowledge and interpretive competence. To return, then, to my initial question, about whether or not there might be a textual structure that would answer to the structure of authority underwritten by professionalism, the answer would seem to be yes. Indeed, one is almost obligated here to argue that, in the literary domain, what is professionalized is not just the careers of authors but also, less tangibly though no less significantly, the literary form itself, which, in the case of "The Yellow Wallpaper," comprises a network of knowledge between author and reader, a network maintained largely at the expense of the characters in the story. Along those lines, one would have to argue that the literary domain is not really distinct from the social domain, that, by a homologous process, professionalism would seem also to have inscribed a differential structure here, a structure of authority and dependency. Within the text, the characters are "professionalized," in the sense that they are organized into fields of subjectivities, which is also to say, fields of knowledge. They become subjects for the reader to know. And presiding over the text, administering to its interpretation, is this reader professionalized in the more familiar sense of the word, in that she is assigned a privileged position, a position of readerly expertise and readerly knowledge.

Here, then, is the New Historicist reading—much simplified, to be sure, but still recognizable as such in its Foucauldian grid of power, knowledge, and subjectivity and in its view of subjectivity as the determinate effect of discursive formations, whose structural totality generates, saturates, and circumscribes all individual practices.[20] Such a reading would argue that "The Yellow Wallpaper" is a text embedded in and structured by the culture of professionalism, a text in which the unequal distribution of knowledge and the unequal distribution of authority are reproduced in its very literary form. Along those lines, such an argument would also have theorized about the homologous genesis of social and literary forms, about the power relations inscribed in such forms, and about the permeable boundary, or perhaps even the lack of boundary, between the literary and the social.[21]

This is an argument I have made when teaching the story, but it is also an argument I now want to resist making.[22] Or rather, it is an argument I want both to make and to unmake, both to set forth and to destabilize. One way to destabilize that argument, I think, is to consider the gender of the reader. I have been referring to the reader as a "she"; this is not so much a polemical posture on my part as a deferential gesture to Gilman, because this is the pronoun she herself would have used.

In an essay entitled "Why I Wrote 'The Yellow Wallpaper,'" Gilman explained that she herself had been subjected to the "rest cure" administered by Dr. S. Weir Mitchell, the same treatment the narrator in the story is subjected to, and it had left her "so near the borderline of utter mental ruin that I could see over." What saved her, and what restored to her "some measure of power," was her decision to defy the doctor and to go back to work—"work, the normal life of every human being; work, in which is joy and growth and service, without which one is a pauper and a parasite." And it was in the spirit of work that she wrote "The Yellow Wallpaper." She wrote it, she said, "to save people from being driven crazy, and it worked."[23] In a later essay, she also explained for whose benefit all this work was being done: "One girl reads this, and takes fire! Her life is changed. She becomes a power—a mover of others—I write for her."[24]

What difference does it make to recognize that Gilman was writing specifically for a female readership, or, to put the question more generally, what difference does it make to introduce the category of gender into the paradigm of reading? A big difference, I think. If we are going to acknowledge that the implied reader in "The Yellow Wallpaper" is not just a professional but also a woman, we will also have to ask whether such a conjunction was actually in place when the story was being written, whether gender and occupational identity did indeed coincide and coalesce at that particular historical moment. Once we put the question that way, it becomes clear that there is in fact an interesting mismatch between the two defining attributes of the implied reader. At the turn of the century, the professional who was also a woman was a rare breed indeed. Professionalism was something denied to women and something they were trying to attain. No women practiced law before the 1870s, and as late as 1873, the Supreme Court still upheld a decision by the Illinois Supreme Court to refuse Myra Bradwell admission to the Illinois bar simply because she was a woman.[25] Meanwhile, women made up no more than 2.8 percent of the medical profession in 1880, and even by 1900, the figure was a mere 5.6 percent.[26] The reader in "The Yellow Wallpaper" who is both a woman and a professional is very much an ideal reader, not only in the sense that she is the right reader but also in the sense that she is not quite real yet, not quite there in the flesh.

It is in this gap—in the non-identity between the ideal reader invoked by the story and the actual women reading it—that we can speak of the dialectical agency of the text or, to use a more familiar phrase, of its cultural work. For, given such a gap, a gap between the putative and the actual, does not the story have its work cut out? Is that gap not the space within which the story labors and the space that it labors to narrow, even to eliminate? As Gilman's own repeated celebration of "work" suggests, the idea is hardly foreign to her. "The Yellow Wallpaper," then, is not just the product of a culture of professionalism, not just an inert index; it is also a transformative agency, with the power to produce effects of its own. It has that power because, within a gendered paradigm, the structure of professional authority it ostensibly relies upon is actually something it is in the process of bringing into being. Its supposed ground turns out to be its desired consequence. A feminist reading of the story would focus on the reader, not as a site of homologous formation, not as the locus from which we can see a line of continuity between the text and the culture of professionalism, but as a figure constituted by a deliberate and enabling gap, a gap that, even as it shadows forth the temporal distance between what the female reader is and what she might become, also restores to the text the possibility of agency in the world.

I have dramatized the disagreement between a New Historicist and a feminist reading, not to show that one is victorious over the other, but to make a different—and somewhat paradoxical—point: namely, that the two readings are not at odds. In fact, they are not even adjacent, since the two phenomena that they describe turn out to be non-adjacent in the first place. This nonadjacency comes about because, even granting the primacy of a culture of professionalism, we must still point to a temporal discrepancy—a noncoincidence between what Raymond Williams calls the dominant, the residual, and the emergent—within that historical formation.[27] To the extent that "The Yellow Wallpaper" is conditioned by history, this "history" must itself be seen not as a field of synchronized unity, but as a field of uneven development. The professionalism that prevails in one account as a normative standard can figure in the other only as a deferred potential.[28] Given this structure of delays and relays—this nonadjacency between the dominant and the emergent—professionalism and feminism might be said to be in contact only through the mediated space of a temporal lag.

Even if we are to focus on a figure that seems common to both—the figure of the reader—we are still bound to encounter, not a unified entity, but a sedimented construct, a figure traversed by time and dispersed in time, making its staggered appearances in its residual, established, and emergent forms, and through its inflections by class, gender, and race.[29] There are readers and readers, it would seem, and when we meditate on their points of divergence as well as their points of coincidence, when we think about their uneven genesis, conflicting identities, and multiple points of reception, "history" itself will have to be reconceived as something less than homogeneous, something less than synchronized.

This, at least to my mind, is one way to understand that well-known phrase "the textuality of history."[30] By this phrase, we usually refer to the idea that the past is transmitted by texts, that it can never be recovered or apprehended as a lived totality. Here, I want to use the phrase in a somewhat different sense, focusing not on the process of textual transmission, but on the dynamics of historical development, on its sedimented, non-uniform, and therefore untotalizable *texture.* History itself has a texture, I argue, because at any given moment there is a precarious conjunction of the "has been" and the "not yet," the "already" and the "probably," a conjunction brought into play by the very passage of time, by the uneven velocities and shifting densities of social change. To historicize a text, then, is also to recover those uneven velocities and shifting densities, to deconstruct its spatial unity into a virtual (and uncharted) sequence, a momentary conjunction of temporal traces, with no particular center of gravity and no particular teleology. Any reading that tries to lock the text into a single posture—to impute to it a center and a teleology—can do so only through an act of historical repression, only by turning a temporal relation of multiple sedimentation into a spatial relation of either opposition or containment.[31]

But—and this is a "but" that needs to be rendered in large print—if we are indeed committed to the idea of multiple sedimentation, as a practical program rather than a polemical statement, what we must then proceed to challenge, it would seem, is not just the model of containment associated with New Historicism, but also the model of opposition associated with feminism. After all, it is not just New Historicism that threatens to lock the text into a single posture. Feminism (or, I should say, a certain brand of feminism, what its critics call essentialist feminism) threatens to do much the same thing, though obviously from the other direction. In celebrating gender as the ground of difference, and in identifying the female as the positive term within this topography of difference, feminism also comes dangerously close to reifying gender into a binary opposition and reifying opposition itself into a unitary term.

The shortcomings of essentialist feminism have been pointed out, most emphatically by Toril Moi, and they are indeed such as to deserve emphasis.[32] Still, the phrase "essentialist feminism" might be guilty of doing some essentializing of its own, since the so-called essentialist feminists are by no means as rigid or ossified as their critics claim.[33] What concerns me, then, is not the merit or demerit of individual practitioners so much as the general term "feminism" itself, and it is this that I want to interrogate and unsettle. I want to bring a kind of heuristic weight to bear on the meaning of this word, to test its contents and its contours, and to ask to what extent a "feminist" project can be understood as a self-sufficient and autonomous enterprise.

Indeed, playing the devil's advocate now, I want to deconstruct the neat opposition I have so far relied upon—the opposition between New Historicism and feminist criticism—and, with that in mind, I return to the second reading with the question, What is so "feminist" about it? Such a question, I hope, is not without its shock effect. Most people, it is safe to say, will immediately label the second reading "feminist," not only because it has indicated both Gilman and "The Yellow Wallpaper," but also because, in singling out the female reader as the text's privileged reader and in locating the text's agency in the trajectory of that figure, it has claimed for gender a centrally determinative (and indeed centrally redemptive) status. In all these respects, it is identifiably feminist, tracing its genealogy most directly to Annette Kolodny's essay "A Map for Rereading: Gender and the Interpretation of Literary Texts," an essay instrumental in forging a new critical paradigm, the paradigm of gender and reading. Within this paradigm, the relation between two terms once considered separate—gender and reading—is now understood to be neither fortuitous nor incidental, but primary and constitutive. Gender, that is to say, enters into the reading process not as an external or even secondary consideration, but as an organizing principle, as the perceptual coordinates by which details are selected and meaning imposed—in short, as the cognitive ground shaping an entire field of vision.

Kolodny's essay has inspired and informed an entire generation of feminist critics. And yet, to those of us sensitized to the dangers of essentialist feminism, the essay also comes very close to embodying just those dangers. In introducing the category of gender into the reading process, Kolodny not only dismantles an older model, one that universalizes reading, but she also puts a new one in its place, one that foregrounds gender specificity and proceeds, on that basis, to separate reading into two distinct and distinctive modes, using gender, of course, as the line of division. What she emphasizes, accordingly, is the mutual illegibility between genders, and, more particularly, the illegibility of a female text to male readers. Summing up "The Yellow Wallpaper" and "A Jury of Her Peers" (a story by Susan Keating Glaspell), Kolodny suggests that, while neither story "necessarily excludes the male as reader—indeed, both in a way are directed specifically at educating him to become a better reader—they do nonetheless insist that, however inadvertently, he is a *different kind* of reader and that, where women are concerned, he is often an inadequate reader."[34]

"A different kind of reader": the phrase is resounding but also problematic because, in positing gender simply as a category of *difference*— simply as the ground of distinction between two discrete terms— Kolodny has put herself on the edge (and, some would say, over the edge) of a binary opposition, opposing male to female and, in so doing, constituting each into a stable and unified identity. Gender, in short, operates as a principle of reification here, and it is within this reified landscape that Kolodny can speak of "male texts" and "female meaning" as if they were discrete and substantive terms.

All the same, it is a mistake simply to find fault with Kolodny or to critique her on absolute grounds. Rather, her critical practice must

itself be contextualized, must be seen, that is, against the background
of its inception, in 1980, when feminist theory was just beginning to
emerge as a newly articulated and not fully legitimized form of discourse, one that had to struggle not just for visibility but also for a
kind of internal coherence. If Kolodny's differential map of gender
came close to being a binary opposition and if her appeal to female
unity came close to reifying female identity, those dangers were nonetheless necessary, and perhaps even beneficial, in an emerging discourse that was still struggling to be heard, still struggling to claim for
itself a recognizable voice and a recognizable profile. Within this context, the traditional feminist appeal to "female experience" or to "the
women's tradition" bespeaks not a theoretical naiveté, but a tactical
wisdom.[35] By the same token, however, it is also understandable why
a new generation of feminists writing today should feel the urgent
need *not* to think about the female simply as a category of identity
(which is also to say, not to think about gender simply as a category
of difference): why Eve Sedgwick, for instance, would want to invoke
the notion of the "continuum" to analyze the mobile distribution of
sexual identities and the asymmetrical structuring of gender relations;
why Alice Jardine would choose to analyze "woman" as signifying
effect rather than as originary subject; why Judith Butler would argue
for a feminism that deconstructs the very concept of "identity" itself;
and why Mary Poovey would seize upon the idea of "uneven development" to emphasize the unstable ideological work of gender, its non-
uniform institutional articulations, and hence its inability, at any
given moment, to achieve anything like a totalization of the social
field.[36]

I hope that, by now, I have contextualized my own reading of "The
Yellow Wallpaper" as well. Indebted to the paradigm of gender and
reading, but mindful of its potentially reifying hazards, I have tried
not to posit a binary opposition between male and female reader, not
to homogenize difference within the field of gender.[37] I have tried
instead to mobilize and multiply the sites of difference, to analyze it
as a relational and sequential (rather than substantive) phenomenon,
and hence not a phenomenon that can be imputed to any single gen-
erative site or fixed along any single line of demarcation. What I have
come up with, then, is a figure of internal difference,[38] who, in this
case, happens to be the female reader, a figure not quite professionalized yet not quite what she is supposed to be, and mobilized, there-

fore, by the very force of incipience, by the discrepency which both constitutes and destabilizes her temporal being. Suspended between the dominant and the dormant, lagging behind the male reader but not willing to remain there for good, such an internally divided figure also collapses the binary opposition between genders into a complexly imbricated and complexly sequential play of identity and difference.

And yet, to what extent is this female reader a *feminist* construct? It is a figure that pleases feminists, to be sure, one that is heartwarming and edifying to conjure up. Still, if this figure embodies an internal gap, as I have tried to argue, a gap that redeems both the text and the author, this redeeming feature is nonetheless not the effect of gender organization, but the effect of temporal discrepancy. In other words, what makes the female reader the locus of "not yet"—what suspends her between the "not" and the "yet" and preserves her as an indeterminate and therefore untotalized quantum—is not the agency of gender, but the agency of history. Or, to be more precise, we might say the agency of gender is itself historical, because it is history—understood as the medium of sequence, succession, and sedimentation—that produces the space between the "not" and the "yet," within which gender can operate as a field of difference.

To put it this way is also to see how symbiotic "gender" and "history" are and how unfruitful it is to oppose a "feminist" reading to a "historicist" reading. Indeed, in order not to reify gender into an unvarying category of difference, and in order not to limit difference to an unvarying site of production, a feminist reading must also be a historical reading. It must try, that is, not just to describe or taxonomize difference, but also to trace its shifting contexts, modalities, and operative axes. It must study the changing pattern, throughout history, of what functions as difference and what counts as difference. In short, gender is most useful as an analytic category when it is seen as a temporal (and temporary) construct, when it is understood to be constituted in time and constrained by time, mobilized by temporal necessity and subject to temporal reconfiguration.

Does that mean, then, that gender is completely subsumed by history and that a feminist reading is really no more than a historicist reading? This is a formulation I want to resist as well. If the relation between feminism and historicism is not one of categoric opposition, neither is it one of categoric subordination. For just as a vigorous historicizing of gender reorients the entire concept, so a vigorous engendering of history transforms the very meaning of what it is to be historical. Gender, that is, is to be understood not as an incidental addition to a stable historical field, but as a principle productive of uneven textures, productive of the discrepency between the dominant and the emergent—a principle inflecting and disturbing the shape of historical time, challenging not only normative temporality but also its spatial disposition of margins and limits. Since I have labored thus far to show that history is crucial as a category of gender studies, I want to turn my attention now to the other side of the argument—which also happens to echo the title of an important essay by Joan Wallach Scott—namely, that gender is equally crucial as a category of historical analysis.[39]

It is helpful here, in fact, to return to the New Historicist reading offered earlier in the essay, the reading that was inspected, found wanting, and set aside. What is it that makes that reading so unsatisfactory? The problem, I submit, is not that it is too historical, but that it is not historical enough. Indeed, the charge of essentialism, so often levelled at feminism, can be directed against this reading as well, against its tendency to reify power relations within the literary *form* itself, as if power could inhere in a form and be ontological to that form, independent of the contexts in which it figures, the uses to which it is put, and the audiences it speaks to and for. This essentializing tendency in New Historicism reinstates the very timelessness that it sets out to critique. The text, that is, is imagined here as an atemporal circulating medium, ceaselessly negotiating with its synchronic social forms, but otherwise untempered by diachronic inflections, untempered by the destabilizing effects of time passage.

The absence of the diachronic in New Historicism is regrettable but also forgivable, since a truly historical understanding—one based not on the knowledge of particular events, but on the ability to generalize about continuity and change, to discern the shape of temporal movement and the facilitating conditions for that shape—is a gift rare not only among critics but (if I might say so) among historians as well. But it is precisely here, against this incapacity or impasse, that gender can intervene as a category of historical analysis, as a conceptual vehicle that propels us towards a version of the diachronic, more local and more modest, perhaps, but no less vital. For if gender is indeed to be understood as a principle of unevenness, as a fault line along which normative temporality is broken up, decentered, and dispersed into various stages of the residual, dominant, and emergent, any historical inquiry that takes gender as its analytic coordinate will also come to grips with that fractured temporality. Such an inquiry, in other words, will be diachronic, with the diachronicity being generated not so much by the subject itself as by the analytic frame, which breaks up the seeming unity of time into its multiple sediments and infinite relays. In the case of "The Yellow Wallpaper," it is the gendered reader, understood both as a historical figure and as a historied figure, that provides the point of entry for this radically destabilized sense of time. But speaking more generally, we might also say that gender, as a principle of unevenness, will be important for any attempt to conceptualize history, not as a homologous or synchronized formation, but as a field of endless mutations and permutations, a field where the temporal nonidentity between cause and effect and the structural nonidentity between system and subject quite literally open up a space for alternatives, however visionary and unsustained. History, thus engendered and thus decentered, is anything but a totalizing category, anything but an injunction to closure. In fact, it is not even something over and done with, but a realm of unexhausted and inexhaustible possibility.

Notes

This essay appeared, in slightly altered form, in *American Literature* (December 1991).

1. This is a crude generalization, needless to say, but at least to my mind, it describes the work of leading New Historicists such as Stephen Greenblatt and Walter Benn Michaels, and the work of leading feminists such as Sandra Gilbert and Susan Gubar. However, there are important exceptions here. For New Historicist work in American Studies that addresses gender, see Richard Brodhead, "Sparing the Rod: Discipline and Fiction in Antebellum America," *Representations* 21 (1988): 67–96; Gillian Brown, "The Empire of Agoraphobia," *Representations* 20 (1987): 134–57; T. Walter Herbert, "Nathaniel Hawthorne, Una Hawthorne, and *The Scarlet Letter:* Interactive Selfhoods and the Cultural Construction of Gender," *PMLA* 103 (1988): 285–97; Myra Jehlen, "The Ties That Bind: Race and Sex in *Pudd'nhead Wilson*," *American Literary History* 2 (1990): 39–55; and David Leverenz, *Manhood and the American Renaissance* (Ithaca: Cornell UP, 1989).

2. For an implicit New Historicist critique of feminists, see Walter Benn Michaels, *The Gold Standard and the Logic of Naturalism* (Berkeley and Los Angeles: U of California P, 1987) 3–28, 217–44. A more explicit critique is offered in Jonathan Goldberg, "Shakespearean Inscriptions: The Voicing of Power," in

Shakespeare and the Question of Theory, ed. Patricia Parker and Geoffrey Hartman (New York: Methuen, 1985) 116–37. For feminist critiques of New Historicists, see Lynda E. Boose, "The Family in Shakespeare Studies; or, Studies in the Family of Shakespeareans; or, The Politics of Politics," *Renaissance Quarterly* 40 (1987): 707–42, esp. 727–42; Marguerite Waller, "Academic Tootsie: The Denial of Difference and the Difference It Makes," *Diacritics* 17 (1987): 2–20; Carol Thomas Neely, "Constructing the Subject: Feminist Practice and New Renaissance Discourses," *English Literary Renaissance* 18 (1988): 5–18; and Judith Lowder Newton, "History as Usual? Feminism and the 'New Historicism,'" in *The New Historicism*, ed. H. Aram Veeser (New York: Routledge, 1989) 152–67.

3. Nina Baym, "Melodramas of Beset Manhood: How Theories of American Fiction Exclude Women Authors," *American Quarterly* 33 (1981): 123–39; Annette Kolodny, "A Map for Rereading; or, Gender and the Interpretation of Literary Texts," *New Literary History* 11 (1980): 451–67, rpt. in *The New Feminist Criticism*, ed. Elaine Showalter (New York: Pantheon, 1985) 46–62; Kolodny, "Dancing through the Minefield: Some Observations on the Theory, Practice, and Politics of a Feminist Literary Criticism," *Feminist Studies* 6 (1980): 1–25, rpt. in Showalter, *The New Feminist Criticism* 144–67; Margaret Homans, "Eliot, Wordsworth, and the Scenes of the Sister's Instruction," *Critical Inquiry* 8 (1981): 223–41; Louise Rosenblatt, *The Reader, the Text, the Poem: The Transactional Theory of the Literary Work* (Carbondale: Southern Illinois UP, 1978); Janice Radway, *Reading the Romance: Women, Patriarchy, and Popular Literature* (Chapel Hill: U of North Carolina P, 1984); Cathy Davidson, *Revolution and the Word* (New York: Oxford UP, 1986). See also a useful collection, Elizabeth A. Flynn and Patrocinio P. Schweickart, eds., *Gender and Reading* (Baltimore: Johns Hopkins UP, 1986).

4. On this point, see Brook Thomas, *The New Historicism and Other Old Fashioned Topics* (Princeton: Princeton UP, 1991). Significantly, this omission is *not* true of feminist New Historicists, who have been very attentive indeed to the figure of the reader. See, for example, Nancy Armstrong, *Desire and Domestic Fiction* (New York: Oxford UP, 1987); Jane P. Tompkins, *Sensational Designs: The Cultural Work of American Fiction* (New York: Oxford UP, 1985); and Davidson, *Revolution and the Word*.

5. Steven Marcus, "Reading the Illegible," in *The Victorian City: Images and Realities*, ed. H. J. Dyos and Michael Wolff, 2 vols. (London: Routledge, 1973) 1: 257–76.

6. See Sacvan Bercovitch, *The Office of "The Scarlet Letter"* (Baltimore: Johns Hopkins UP, 1991). Bercovitch will not be among the figures I discuss, since his work, though historical, does not strike me as New Historicist.

7. Most American historians have pointed to the second half of the nineteenth century as a cultural divide, when modern habits of perception and interpretation came into being. See, for instance, Thomas Haskell, *The Emergence of Professional Social Science* (Urbana: U of Illinois P, 1977); John Higham, "The Reorientation

of American Culture in the 1890s," in *Writing American History: Essays on Modern Scholarship* (Bloomington: Indiana UP, 1970) 73–102; Samuel P. Hays, *The Response to Industrialism: 1885–1914* (Chicago: U of Chicago P, 1957); and Robert Wiebe, *The Search for Order, 1877–1920* (New York: Hill, 1967).

8. Paul Starr, *The Social Transformation of American Medicine* (New York: Basic, 1982) 13, 19. See esp. 3–29, on the "social origins of professional sovereignty." For related arguments, see Eliot Freidson, *Profession of Medicine: A Study of the Sociology of Applied Knowledge* (New York: Dodd, 1970); Freidson, *Professional Dominance: The Social Structure of Medical Care* (New York: Atherton, 1970); and John Harley Warner, *The Therapeutic Perspective: Medical Practice, Knowledge, and Identity in America, 1820–1885* (Cambridge: Harvard UP, 1986).

9. The American Bar Association was founded in 1878, the MLA in 1883, the AHA in 1884, and the AEA in 1885. For the rise of professionalism, see Burton J. Bledstein, *Culture of Professionalism: The Middle Class and the Formation of Higher Education in America* (New York: Norton, 1976); Anton-Hermann Chroust, *The Rise of the Legal Profession in America* (Norman: U of Oklahoma P, 1965); Mary Furner, *Advocacy and Objectivity: A Crisis in the Professionalization of American Social Science, 1865–1905* (Lexington: U of Kentucky P, 1975); Haskell, *The Emergence of Professional Social Science;* and Magali Sarfatti Larson, *The Rise of Professionalism* (Berkeley and Los Angeles: U of California P, 1977). See also a valuable collection, Thomas Haskell, ed., *The Authority of Experts* (Bloomington: Indiana UP, 1984).

10. Andrew Abbott, *The System of Professions* (Chicago: U of Chicago P, 1988).

11. Daniel Bell, *The Coming of Post-Industrial Society* (New York: Basic, 1973); Emile Durkheim, *Professional Ethics and Civic Morals,* trans. Cornelia Brookfield (Glencoe: Free, 1958). Durkheim's highly favorable account of professionalism was first delivered as lectures at Bordeaux in the 1890s. In *The Acquisitive Society* (1922), R. H. Tawney also praises the professions as a fortress of disinterestedness in a rapacious society. The first critical view of professionalism was Talcott Parsons's seminal essay, "The Professions and Social Structure" (1939), *Essays in Sociological Theory* (Glencoe: Free, 1954) 34–49. For recent accounts of professionalism besides Bell's, see Alvin Gouldner, *The Future of Intellectuals and the Rise of the New Class* (New York: Seabury, 1979); Ivan Illich, *Medical Nemesis: The Expropriation of Health* (New York: Pantheon, 1976); and Illich, *Disabling Professions* (London: Boyars, 1977).

12. See Sandra Gilbert and Susan Gubar, *The Madwoman in the Attic: The Woman Writer and the Nineteenth-Century Literary Imagination* (New Haven: Yale UP, 1979) 89–92; Kolodny, "A Map for Rereading"; Jean Kennard, "Convention Coverage; or, How to Read Your Own Life," *New Literary History* 13 (1981): 69–88; Paula Treichler, "Escaping the Sentence," *Tulsa Studies in Women's Literature* 3 (1984): 61–77; and Judith Fetterley, "Reading about Reading," in Flynn and

Schweickart, *Gender and Reading* 147–64. For critiques of this feminist orthodoxy, see Janice Haney-Peritz, "Monumental Feminism and Literature's Ancestral House," *Women's Studies* 12 (1986): 113–28; and Mary Jacobus, "An Unnecessary Maze of Sign-Reading," *Reading Woman: Essays in Feminist Criticism* (New York: Columbia UP, 1986) 229–48.

13. Polly Wynn Allen, *Building Domestic Liberty: Charlotte Perkins Gilman's Architectural Feminism* (Amherst: U of Massachusetts P, 1988); Mary A. Hill, *Charlotte Perkins Gilman: The Making of a Radical Feminist, 1860–1896* (Philadelphia: Temple UP, 1980).

14. See Dolores Hayden, *The Grand Domestic Revolution: A History of Feminist Designs for American Homes, Neighborhoods, and Cities* (Cambridge: MIT P, 1981).

15. Charlotte Perkins Gilman, *Women and Economics* (Boston: Small, 1898) 241–42.

16. Gilman, "The Yellow Wallpaper," *New England Magazine*, May 1892. Citations are from the Feminist Press edition (Old Westbury: Feminist, 1973) 23–24.

17. A diagnosis is usually taken to be more scientific or more objective than a reading. Here, though, I emphasize the degree to which it is governed by interpretive conventions.

18. See Wolfgang Iser, *The Implied Reader* (Baltimore: Johns Hopkins UP, 1974); and Iser, *The Act of Reading* (Baltimore: Johns Hopkins UP, 1978). My critique of Iser parallels that of Robert Holub, *Reception Theory* (London: Methuen, 1984). For a different critique (challenging Iser's distinction between the determinate and the indeterminate), see Stanley Fish, "Why No One Is Afraid of Wolfgang Iser," *Diacritics* 11 (March 1981): 2–13.

19. Tony Bennett, "Texts in History: The Determinations of Readings and Their Texts," in *Post-Structuralism and the Question of History*, ed. Derek Attridge, Geoff Bennington, and Robert Young (New York: Cambridge UP, 1987) 74. For a helpful discussion of Iser and Bennett in the context of Bakhtin, see David Shepherd, "Bakhtin and the Reader," in *Bakhtin and Cultural Theory*, ed. Ken Hirschkop and David Shepherd (Manchester: Manchester UP, 1989) 91–108.

20. This is, of course, the paradigm in Foucault's *Discipline and Punish*, trans. Alan Sheridan (New York: Pantheon, 1979). For critiques of the structural determinism in Foucault and in New Historicism, see Frank Lentricchia, "Foucault's Legacy: A New Historicism?" in *Ariel and the Police* (Madison: U of Wisconsin P, 1988) 86–102; Louis Montrose, "Texts and Histories," in *Redrawing the Boundaries of Literary Studies in English*, ed. Giles Gunn and Stephen Greenblatt (New York: MLA, 1991); Carolyn Porter, "Are We Being Historical Yet?" *South Atlantic Quarterly* 87 (1988): 743–86; and Edward Said, *The World, the Text, and the Critic* (Cambridge: Harvard UP, 1983).

21. For a succinct summary of this model, see Stephen Greenblatt, Introduc-

tion to *The Forms of Power and the Power of Forms in the Renaissance*, special issue of *Genre* 15.1–2 (1982): 3–6.

22. Here I thank my former students at Rutgers University for their spirited (and skeptical) response to my New Historicist reading.

23. "Why I Wrote 'The Yellow Wallpaper,'" *The Charlotte Perkins Gilman Reader*, ed. Ann J. Lane (New York: Pantheon, 1980) 20.

24. Quoted in Allen 145.

25. Bradwell v. Illinois, 83 U.S. 130. See Lawrence Friedman, *A History of American Law* (New York: Simon, 1985) 639; and Nadine Taub and Elizabeth M. Schneider, "Perspectives on Women's Subordination and the Role of Law," in *The Politics of Law*, ed. David Kairys (New York: Pantheon, 1982) 125.

26. Starr, *Social Transformation of American Medicine* 117.

27. See Raymond Williams, "Dominant, Residual, and Emergent," in *Marxism and Literature* (Oxford: Oxford UP, 1977) 121–27.

28. For a suggestive account of the genesis of agency through the noncoherence of discursive formations, see Anthony Appiah, "Tolerable Falsehoods: Agency and the Interests of Theory," in *The Consequences of Theory: Selected Papers from the English Institute, 1987–88*, ed. Jonathan Arac and Barbara Johnson (Baltimore: Johns Hopkins UP, 1991) 63–90.

29. There is no occasion to discuss race in this paper. But for a stimulating analysis, see Susan S. Lanser, "Feminist Criticism, 'The Yellow Wallpaper,' and the Politics of Color in America," *Feminist Studies* 15 (1989): 415–41.

30. See Louis Montrose, "Renaissance Literary Studies and the Subject of History," *English Literary Renaissance* 16 (1986): 5–12; and Montrose, "Professing the Renaissance: The Poetics and Politics of Culture," in Veeser, *The New Historicism* 15–36.

31. The "containment" position is most forcefully articulated by Stephen Greenblatt, in "Invisible Bullets: Renaissance Authority and Its Subversion," in *Political Shakespeare*, ed. Jonathan Dollimore and Alan Sinfield (Ithaca: Cornell UP, 1985) 18–47. For a critique of Greenblatt, see Donald Pease, "Toward a Sociology of Literary Knowledge: Greenblatt, Colonialism, and the New Historicism," in Arac and Johnson, *Consequences of Theory* 108–53.

32. Toril Moi, *Sexual/Textual Politics* (London: Methuen, 1985). Moi's blanket condemnation of Anglo-American feminists (and her inattention to their positionings within the larger critical discourse) seems to me both unhelpful and unjust. For more thoughtful meditations, see Diana Fuss, *Essentially Speaking* (New York: Routledge, 1989); and Rita Felski, *Beyond Feminst Aesthetics* (Cambridge: Harvard UP, 1989). See also *The Essential Difference: Another Look at Essentialism*, special issue of *Differences* 1 (Summer 1989).

33. See, for example, the considerable difference between Elaine Showalter's

earlier book, *A Literature of Their Own* (Princeton: Princeton UP, 1977), and her more recent work, *The Female Malady* (New York: Pantheon, 1985), or between her "Feminist Criticism in the Wilderness," *Critical Inquiry* 8 (1981): 179–206, and her "Critical Cross-Dressing: Male Feminists and the Woman of the Year," *Raritan* 3.2 (1983): 130–49.

34. Kolodny, "A Map for Rereading" 57.

35. For a persuasive defense of essentialist feminism on the ground of tactical necessity, see Paul Smith, *Discerning the Subject* (Minneapolis: U of Minnesota P, 1988) 132–51. In a different context, Gayatri Spivak has also argued for a *strategic* alliance with essentialism to recover the subjectivity written out of conventional historiography ("Subaltern Studies: Deconstructing Historiography," in *In Other Worlds* [New York: Methuen, 1988] 197–221, esp. 206–7).

36. Eve Sedgwick, *Between Men: English Literature and Male Homosocial Desire* (New York: Columbia UP, 1985); Alice Jardine, *Gynesis: Configurations of Woman and Modernity* (Ithaca: Cornell UP, 1985); Judith Butler, *Gender Trouble: Feminism and the Subversion of Identity* (New York: Routledge, 1990); Mary Poovey, *Uneven Developments: The Ideological Work of Gender in Mid-Victorian England* (Chicago: U of Chicago P, 1988).

37. For an interesting critique of *l'Ecriture feminine* as the metaphorization of difference (and linking metaphoricity to binarism), see Domna C. Stanton, "Difference on Trial," in *The Poetics of Gender*, ed. Nancy K. Miller (New York: Columbia UP, 1986) 157–82.

38. The figure of "internal difference" is of course a central poststructuralist postulate. For a feminist deployment of this figure (emphasizing class but addressing the same problems of binarism), see Jane Gallop, "Annie Leclerc Writing a Letter, with Vermeer," in Miller, *Poetics of Gender* 137–56.

39. Joan Wallach Scott, "Gender: A Useful Category of Historical Analysis," *American Historical Review* 81 (1986): 1053–75. See also Joan Kelly, "The Social Relations of the Sexes," *Women, History, and Theory* (Chicago: U of Chicago P, 1984) 1–18.

PART TWO

Reading Communities and the Contexts of Inscribed Audience

Cooper's Allegories of Reading and "the Wreck of the Past"

ROBERT DALY

Allegories of Reading started out as a historical study and ended up as a theory of reading.

PAUL DE MAN

In sum, this rhetorical perspective attempts to describe the historical circumstances of various rhetorical exchanges rather than address questions about whether texts or readers determine interpretations. Rhetorical histories thus replace Foundationalist Theory.

STEVEN MAILLOUX

Cooper now appears to have been our best bad writer. For the last century, discussions of Cooper have followed a familiar paradigm: indirect praise through marshaling of other readers who have thought well of him is followed either by direct attack or by qualified apology. The most familiar early example is, of course, Twain's. "Fenimore Cooper's Literary Offenses" opens with praise from Lounsbury, Matthews, and Collins, then suggests that "it was far from right" of them "to deliver opinions on Cooper's literature without having read some of it," and goes on to a masterful demolition of *The Deerslayer*, as judged by the standards of Twain's own time and place. In Twain's view, for example, it was simply a blunder for Cooper to let Deerslayer "talk the showiest kind of book-talk sometimes, and at other times the basest of base dialects." It just is not realistic. Twain argues that people invariably stay within the community defined by their dialect and that Cooper simply "failed to notice that a man who talks corrupt English six days in the week must and will talk it on the seventh, and can't help himself."[1] Questions of occasion, audience, and performance do not arise in Twain. Although others have noticed that Natty is nomadic and bears in his speech elements of several linguistic communities, and though several of Cooper's characters move easily among American, British, Delaware, French, and Dutch linguistic communities—all save the British, and in Twain's view middle-class Americans, arguably members in good standing of the "corrupt English" community—Twain sees only a failure of mimesis, not an attempt to find a linguistic correlative for the character's nobility, class, and level of excitement or for the importance of what is being said. Given the standards of late-nineteenth-century American realism, this conclusion is not surprising.

What is surprising is how thoroughly Twain's view defines the terms of later analyses. Most later writers think Cooper's work worthy of attention, and their tone is far removed from the wonderful ironies and magisterial dismissal of Twain, but a few examples will suggest that his paradigm is still common even in contemporary criticism.

Arvid Shulenberger notes that "Cooper has been praised by such diverse novelists as Balzac, Thackeray, Conrad, Melville, and D. H. Lawrence" but quickly admits that the "virtues of Cooper's novels, in style, substance, and form, are in general not the virtues recognized in the best modern fiction." He concludes that, to appreciate Cooper, one must share or at least sympathize with what he takes to be Cooper's "belief that the most important elements in fiction were the moral principles it illustrated."[2] William Charvat begins with the extraordinary worldwide popularity of *The Last of the Mohicans* and the praise of Tolstoy, Balzac, Goethe, and Thackeray before finding that "Cooper's prose is pompous, and . . . his pomposity was the product both of his militant sense of status and of his defensiveness about status at a time when egalitarianism was the reigning social mood."[3] Donald Ringe notes the approval of Marius Bewley and Howard Mumford Jones, then argues that we "should not minimize Cooper's real and annoying faults" but should attempt "to see the novels in their own terms, and to seek the meaning that they, like all works of literary art, will yield if carefully read for themselves alone."⁴ This New Critical notion that one mode of reading will do for "all works of literary art" and that the act of reading is clearly separable from other forms of life tends, when applied to Cooper, to yield annoyance with an author whose work is both attractive and disappointing. In the fifties and sixties, then, New Critical readers added to our understanding of Cooper but still tended to return to the formula Twain set forth in 1895.

Although our modes of reading have changed in recent decades, the new emphases on history, on the social embeddedness and social consequences of literature, and on the activity and agency of both generalized and historically specific readers have so far occasioned little change in our view of Cooper. Emily Budick, for example, acknowledges that Cooper adumbrates one of her central concerns, "the story of an America that attempts to secure for itself a special covenant with God through an act of sacrifice like the *akedah* [specifically, the binding of Isaac, more generally the sacrifice of a son by a patriarchal father]." She even notes that "Cooper confronts the failure of American historical consciousness that will occupy historical romancers throughout the nineteenth and twentieth centuries" and carefully phrases her acknowledgement that he "also hits on the scene of the akedah that will be the medium of their investigation." Yet once again, even viewed from this perspective, Cooper disappoints her expectations: "He stages this scene curiously and obliquely, not deciphering its relevance to the problems of American history and American historical consciousness that he himself recognizes. Cooper's failure to follow through on his own insights contributes to a perpetuation of the ahistorical, mythic imagination that troubles his inheritors in the literary tradition."⁵ This apparent failure of Cooper to operate within what Jauss calls our "horizon of expectations" might lead us to reconsider our expectations or at least to interrogate the old notion of Cooper as perpetuator of American myth.⁶ Yet so far, it has not done so.

Even the latest, though probably not the last, such depiction of Cooper is set in terms that have by now a certain familiar resonance. Kenneth Dauber begins with acknowledgements of Cooper's importance from Bryant, Parkman, Simms, Longfellow, Melville, and Whitman, then assays the familiar turn: "And yet, is there not something more than a little odd in this unanimity about Cooper's speaking for us?" From this question Dauber moves to an informed and cogent demonstration that Cooper's themes and politics share little enough with those of the writers who admired him and thought him, in some sense, an important American writer. He goes on to argue that "Cooper has always seemed a not especially acute intelligence whose writing yet defines the dilemmas of his nation more fully and more sharply than anyone else in his age." In explicating the second part of this conclusion, Dauber adverts to "Cooper's myth," this time a rather deconstructive myth in which the representative self can be preserved only by being abandoned. But in explicating the first part, he returns to Twain's categories and tone. Twain wrote that *The Deerslayer* "is just simply a literary *delirium tremens*," that "its humor is pathetic; its pathos is funny; its conversations are—oh! indescribable; its love-scenes odious; its English a crime against the language." Dauber echoes Twain with a similar dismissal: "His neoclassicism is too English, his picturesqueness too international to take very seriously, and his style proper is notoriously awkward and muddy, too simply incompetent to be national, international, or anything but dismissible." Like Twain, Dauber concludes that Cooper "was particularly slack about detail." Despite significant changes in our modes of reading, then, the taxonomy of Cooper dismissal has remained remarkably consistent, and Dauber can remark, after ninety-five years of intervening analysis, that "Twain is not after all wrong in faulting Cooper for what he sees as mimetic inadequacy."[7]

Rare and potentially heartening as such critical unanimity is, it does leave some questions unaddressed. Without repeating yet again the long and varied list of Cooper's admirers, major authors among them, we might wonder how they could not see then what we so clearly see now. What occasioned their apparent blindness to a clear case of "mimetic inadequacy"? Did they see something in Cooper that we have not? Twain alone addresses such questions directly, and his explanation is not likely to be universally applicable. He picks for his Cooper admirers two professors and a minor writer, easy targets all, and he concludes that they praised Cooper's writing only because they had not read it.

One way of advancing beyond this explanation is to expand our view of the reading of Cooper, to consider how other readers read him before Twain and how recent developments in literary theory might offer us new ways of reading him now. It is important to note that this mode of address is not merely a variation on the old subtext, evident in many dismissals of Cooper, that modes of reading improve with time and that earlier readers admired Cooper simply because they were less advanced than we are. This superstition is yet another version of the Whig myth of progress that Cooper cordially loathed and that Hawthorne satirized in "Earth's Holocaust": "The truth was, that the human race had now reached a stage of progress, so far beyond what the wisest and wittiest men of former ages had ever dreamed of, that it would have been a manifest absurdity to allow the earth to be any longer encumbered with their poor achievements in the literary line."[8]

My intention, slightly humbler, is not to sublate all previous analysis of Cooper but to continue that conversation in a new vein, one more appropriate to current developments in literary and cultural theory. Cooper has not fared well with the dominant mode of perception and discourse organized as the New Criticism. Quite apart from the question of whether the New Criticism's "formalist legacy has remained virulent in contemporary theory," it is at least arguable that we are moving, in Carolyn Porter's words, from a formalist mode, with "the canonical author as unknowable genius, and the reader as passive and awestruck worshipper of literature," to a more historical mode that calls "attention to the problems posed by the relation between the . . . historical conditions of a particular text's production and reception at a moment in the past and the historical conditions of the present out of which our concern with that text arises."[9] As Porter suggests, this concern with history is not coterminous with the New Historicism, a movement she criticizes for what she sees as its formalist subtext.

Nevertheless, the New Historicism is part of a much larger concern with history, culture, and the activity of reading, all formerly marginalized as background but now foregrounded as central to our concerns. So, for example, Wolfgang Iser moves, as the subtitle of his recent book suggests, "from reader response to literary anthropology."[10] Stanley Fish, who differs from and with Iser on other matters, is also concerned with the social embeddedness of both literature and criticism: "Being embedded means just that, being embedded always, and one does not escape embeddedness by acknowledging, as I do, that it is itself a fractured, fissured, volatile condition."[11] The fact of embeddedness may remain constant, but the nature of that embeddedness changes over space and time.

Indeed, those changes within and among societies have become central to interpretive anthropology, which has become more literary even as literary criticism has become more anthropological. Recent definitions of "culture" suggest the importance of reading and interpretation. Clifford Geertz has written that "it denotes an historically transmitted pattern of meanings embodied in symbols, a system of inherited conceptions expressed in symbolic forms by means of which men communicate, perpetuate, and develop their knowledge about and attitudes toward life."[12] Anthony F. C. Wallace specifies the epistemological implications of such a definition:

> "Culture" refers to a system of ideas about the nature of the world and how people should behave in it that is shared, and shared uniquely, by members of a community. The system is learned by children and forms a template, as it were, for the underlying conceptions of self, society and human nature that guide all behavior in that community. Because these ideas are encoded in public symbols such as literary texts, art, the dance, drama and religious ritual, they are accessible to anthropological observation and inquiry.[13]

If literary texts enact the epistemological templates through which a culture makes sense of the world, reads the world and life within it, the question arises of whether such texts might alter that habitual epistemology and so alter the communal culture—whether they might help to determine what determines them.

Giles Gunn addresses the question of the cultural agency of literary texts in considering "a significant modern alternative to all theories of art and culture that attempt to isolate them from the practical contexts that give them life—either as the old New Critics did, through their definition of the self-interpreting text, or, to employ Geoffrey Hartmann's phrase, as the 'new New Critics' do, through their notion of the self-deconstructing text." Gunn delineates one mode of reciprocity between art and the larger culture: "Art not only imitates life but equally influences it, by providing, often for the first time, a significant form for those very aspects of subjective human experience it purports only to reflect."[14] This argument is some distance both from Shelley's notion that "poets are the unacknowledged legislators of the World" and from Auden's statement that "poetry makes nothing happen."[15] Rather than either of these extremes, it expresses the possibility that art and literature can both affect and be affected by other elements of a community's culture. This reciprocal interaction need not posit any hierarchy, need not imagine some single economic, political, linguistic, or psychological first cause from which all other social codes and media of exchange necessarily follow. Instead, it can be simply a way of acknowledging, as Barbara Herrnstein Smith does, that "those with cultural power and commonly other forms of power as well" tend to be those who have developed "competence in a large number of cultural codes."[16] In our time, such power tends to accrue from being conversant with a large number of modes of perception and discourse, not merely from mastering the one master code.

This movement from the competent or informed reader, who was presumably able to read anything well, to some attention to particular readers obtains in Steven Mailloux's *Rhetorical Power*, which moves away from an essentialized theory of reader response, away from a general theory of reading, toward a "rhetorical hermeneutics" that considers "the political effectivity of trope and argument in culture." Where de Man began with literary history and ended up with a theory of reading, Mailloux argues that "interpretive theory must become rhetorical history" and places his own argument in the context of other recent writings that "share a suspicion of Theory and a preoccupation with history." Mailloux's work joins theirs in attempting to "place theory, criticism, and literature itself within a cultural conversation," to "interpret the rhetoric of a text as participating in the cultural debates of a specific historical period and place," an attempt that not only considers that authors have some influence on their times, but also grants them an awareness of the ways in which their literary strategies are likely to become, or at least to influence, larger cultural strategies.[17]

Mailloux's treatment of rhetoric as social praxis significantly advances our own cultural conversation. It suggests that writing is itself an interpretation likely to influence other interpretations, that since all writing is rhetorical, our interpretations should also be rhetorical, and that since both rhetoric and hermeneutics change over space and time, we must inquire into the specific cultural matrix in which a work of literature was produced and received. His arguments move beyond the autotelic work of art, tidily separated from the rest of life and from such considerations as its modes of production and reception. Though he does not use the term, Mailloux's historicization of reader response encourages us to listen for what Stephen Greenblatt calls "resonance": "By resonance I mean the power of the object displayed to reach out beyond its formal boundaries to a larger world, to evoke in the viewer the complex, dynamic cultural forces from which it has emerged and for which as metaphor or more simply as synecdoche it may be taken by a viewer to stand."[18] A sensitivity to such resonance would enable us to read not merely Cooper's reflection or portrayal of the cultural debates of his times, but rather his participation in them.

The gulf between these current general theories and their possible application in Cooper criticism can now be specified. Where Mailloux emphasizes that "the rhetoric of a text does not simply 'reflect' these social practices and circumstances" but rather that "discursive rhetorical practices are modified extensions and varied repetitions of nondiscursive practices," Kenneth Dauber insists on the separation of Cooper as writer from the world in which he lives: "The writer is removed from any active role in creating democracy. He does not make his world *in* writing, for writing, now, is but the reporting of a world as it were already made, a world constituted as something of which the writer as writer is no longer a part."[19] This juxtaposition is not intended as a critique of the work that Dauber has done and done well. It is instead an illustration that our theory has run well ahead of our practice, and that the critical conversations of our own time, taken collectively, may now suggest taxonomies more appropriate to Cooper than those carried over from Twain, the New Criticism, and deconstruction.

The final two voices in those critical conversations take us beyond the isolated consciousness of the writer to considerations of what Pierre Bourdieu has called "habitus" and "field." One critique of Mailloux's work is that it makes the author far too conscious and calculating. Forrest Robinson suggests that "Mailloux's Mark Twain is an implausibly deliberate rhetorician" whose work is a "rhetorical performance, conceived on purpose to draw the reader toward a properly critical view of white supremacist ideology."[20] This critique, however, seems extreme. To recognize rhetorical performance and literary strategy, it is not necessary to enshrine either a completely conscious and explicit authorial intention or a fully specifiable social determinism. Indeed, a more moderate recognition that author and society influence and, to some extent, constitute each other tends to validate Mailloux's larger theory that literature participates in the cultural debates of its time and place and that a "rhetorical hermeneutics" will enable us to attend to that participation.

One way of doing so is suggested by Bourdieu, whose notion of habitus "came from the desire to recall that beside the express, explicit norm, or the rational calculation, there are other principles that generate action." This habitus, a set of dispositions that one learns from one's social field, Bourdieu compares to a "feel for the game" that one develops as a result of long practice. The rules of the game and various strategies within them need not be conscious at the time of play or creation. Yet a scholar may, in retrospect, specify such patterns easily enough.[21] In his explicit statements, Cooper tends toward pictorial explanations, writing that he simply sees that something is true. He rarely explains the line of reasoning that stands behind, for example, his reevaluation of Jefferson, but we may now delineate his choice of social alternatives—Jeffersonian democracy as preferable to aristocracy, Whig reform, and Jacksonian democracy—and the literary strategies informed by that choice.

Bourdieu's habitus, a complex set of dispositions, is "the product of social conditionings" and "becomes active only *in the relation* to a field," but the agent whose actions are informed by that habitus affects the field, with the result that neither habitus nor field is dominant: each exists in reciprocal interaction with the other. For that reason, the habitus "contributes to determining what determines it."[22] Bourdieu's work, in conjunction with the other works just described, affords a view of culture that is local, contingent, and specific; that is based on the epistemological templates through which a community interprets the world; and that is open to literary study. In fact, as Evan Watkins has recently argued in contrasting current theories of reading with those of the New Criticism, "Post-New-Critical reading practices, however, find a guarantee of the primacy of reading as the conceptual angle of entry into understanding the effectivity of any set of cultural codes."[23]

Instead of merely judging Cooper by Twain's standard of verisimilitude, we can now take Carolyn Porter's advice to consider the relation between the historical conditions of our own reading and those of reading in Cooper's time. From this admittedly selective and interested overview of current reading practices, we may infer that we are interested in the relations between a literary text and what Robert

Scholes calls "a larger cultural text, which is the matrix or master code that the literary text both depends upon and modifies."[24] We may consider that cultural text to be constituted as a repertoire of epistemological templates and interpretive strategies that can both inform and be affected by literature. And we can use, as an apt metaphor or synecdoche for these cultural practices, the local and various act of reading. Having moved forward from Twain to the reading practices of our own times, we can move back from him to reading practices of Cooper's times. In doing so, we may find in Cooper certain literary and cultural strategies that we value still, may see his work as more than a period piece, and may be able to address a recurrent problem delineated by H. Daniel Peck: "Although many readers find Cooper's novels compelling, they are often hard pressed to locate the source of his power."[25]

In his own time, Cooper was criticized for mimetic excess, not mimetic insufficiency. Where reviewers assumed that readers wanted adventure and incident, Cooper gave them too much detail. Early and late, as Nina Baym's research makes clear, reviewers wondered at Cooper's focus on specific detail. In the *North American* for July 1822, a reviewer wrote of *The Spy*: "One capital defect is that excessive minuteness which leaves nothing for the imagination to supply. The enumeration of little unimportant actions . . . and full length descriptions . . . are prodigious weakeners of style." And in October of 1844, a reviewer in *Graham's* wrote that "at times his attention to minutiae is so close, that, although it does not fatigue, it is still calculated to irritate a reader who is clamorous for incident, and desirous of being borne onward quickly to the completion of the story."[26] If Cooper's works were mere adventure stories, as some critics have claimed, such an intrusion of detail would be merely a defect, a gratuitous deferral of the next exciting incident. But if they are enactments of reading within a specific cultural matrix that the work both depends upon and alters, then such criticism gives us important clues to a significant difference between our cultural situation and Cooper's, and it suggests one of his strategies for dealing with a cultural matrix of which he clearly disapproved.

As we have seen, we are moving away from an essentialized model of reading, one that assumed the interaction between reader and text to change little from one time and place to another. This model of an informed reader competent to read any text with one mode of interpretation derives from what Wittgenstein called "our craving for generality" and "contemptuous attitude toward the individual case."[27]

Cooper faced a similar problem among his contemporaries, the coexistence of rapid change with the general perception that no change had taken place and that the present order of things was sanctified by tradition and history, neither of which, of course, required any detailed investigation, since they were simply early forms of the present. In such a view, the synchronic tends to efface the diachronic. The present culture and mode of reading become naturalized. Such a reader might well be irritated on reading a selection of details that resisted easy reading from his or her present perspective, a selection of details that seemed to require, for their interpretation, some knowledge of nautical terms, or French language, or American Indian, Dutch, and British culture. From the perspective of Cooper's readers, these things were mere history, and Americans had progressed beyond them.

For such readers, Cooper noted in *Home as Found*, "'always' means eighteen months, and . . . 'time immemorial' is only since the last general crisis in the money market."[28] If history is merely the backward extension of the present moment, then there can be no thresholds, ruptures, or discontinuities within it. Whatever is must always have been. Should a Cooper leave Three-Mile Point on Lake Otsego to his heirs and should they open it to public use on sufferance for even a short time, the public would not only encroach but would also claim, and some believe, that it had been public land from "time immemorial," a choice of words that seems to preserve not memory, but precisely its absence.

Through such effacement of memory, more was at stake than some acres of land, the last will and testament of Judge Cooper, or even the honor of the Cooper name. Eric Sundquist notes that "the gap between experiment and sacrament in America has often been slight."[29] Cooper's work suggests that, in the sanctification of the present moment and of individual whim, certain cultural codes and possibilities, enacted in the past and still potentially valuable, were being irretrievably effaced. American culture was narrowing down, coming to be read by a single code that Cooper repeatedly satirized, notably in the figure of Jason Newcome in the Littlepage trilogy. Newcome is a Yankee schoolmaster who believes that the present customs of his Connecticut village constitute all culture and that everything else is barbarism and irrelevance. He wishes to reform the American language and, with it, all cultural practices, and he simply does not see alternatives to his own mode of reading. For him, the practices of his native town are culture and always have been.

In Cooper there are great thresholds between one culture and another, one generation and another. For that reason, the past as a totality is an irrecoverable wreck, and Cooper's work evinces remarkably little nostalgia for the complete resurrection of any one past culture. The past, like Crusoe's ship, cannot be restored. Nevertheless, Cooper argues that "something surely is worthy to be saved from the wreck of the past."[30] Cooper chooses to save, or to recreate, what the Newcomes (and for Cooper both reformist Whigs and Jacksonian democrats fell into this category) had taken and were taking away. His works are alive with cultural multiplicity and its attendant modes of reading. In his recreation of American culture during the French and Indian Wars, for example, French, Dutch, Iroquois, African, English, and other languages, monies, and cultures mingle and compete on the great palimpsest of the American past. In this world, success comes not from mastering a single hegemonic discourse and clinging to it like a limpet, but from being conversant with a variety of discourses, having a repertoire of possible strategies for recognition and response. However problematic the historicity of this view of the past, it operates well as a fictional world that enables Cooper to stage modes of reading that he considered superior to those of his contemporaries. In such a world, the great mass of detail is intended to give both dramatized readers and the undramatized reader of Cooper's work an opportunity to complicate and enlarge their own modes of reading. A reader who wants only a fast pace and adventurous incidents may well become as irritated as the reviewer for *Graham's*. A reader who wants verisimilitude in each detail and who assumes that this pointillist realism is the goal of all fiction may well see only authorial ineptitude and, if he writes as well as Twain does, may well convince *his* readers that Cooper was trying to write like Twain and failing. But if we consider that reading is the activity under examination rather than merely a given that we all take for granted in exactly the same way, we may see Cooper's elaborate settings and plots as ways to stage dramatized readings and to influence the interpretive codes of his own readers.

This recognition enables us to specify in a new way a general point made well by James Wallace in his analysis of Cooper's early career, from *Precaution* to *The Spy*. In these early works, Wallace argues, Cooper was attempting to cultivate a community of readers for American fiction, to lead "them by easy steps away from the popular fiction of British origin into an indigenous fiction."[31] Reading this indigenous fiction would require attention to an America that was culturally various and vocally polyphonic. It would require a good deal of what Clifford Geertz calls "local knowledge," knowledge of separate times, languages, and cultures that cannot be sublated into a single synthesis or subsumed under a global idea. Cooper's America is, as Geertz says of the world, "a various place . . . and much is to be gained, scientifically and otherwise, by confronting that grand actuality rather than wishing it away in a haze of forceless generalities and false comforts."[32] Cooper would have his dramatized readers, audience figures all, confront that variety and enact modes of reading to deal with it. In his romances, then, the central focus is less on the particular facts of history or the presentation of realistic detail than on the interpretive process itself, on the ways in which his characters read the signs, and on the ways in which their readings affect their chances for survival.

To stage this new mode of reading, however, Cooper must first efface the old one by returning to times and places in which the grip of his own cultural moment will be weakened. For that reason, he sets *The Spy* in the "neutral" ground of Westchester County, New York, between the British and American camps, during the Revolution. He sets *The Pilot* off the coast of England and *Lionel Lincoln* in Boston, both during the Revolution. During this time, America is no longer British, not yet American, poised on one of those thresholds in American history. He sets *The Last of the Mohicans* in the area around Lake George in 1757, during the last French and Indian War. After this war, in the Treaty of Paris, France ceded to England her colonial empire along the St. Lawrence Valley and all her land claims west to the Mississippi; the language of America gradually became English, her culture and coinage more uniform. But during that war, as in Cooper's book, the nation stood on a threshold, with Delaware, Iroquois, English, and French cultures mixing and contesting for the future of America. In *The Prairie*, "the trapper" has followed the frontier west; in *The Wept of Wish-ton-Wish*, Puritans and the Indians allied under the Wamponoag chief, Metacom, contest, mingle, and even intermarry on the Connecticut frontier. *The Deerslayer* is set near Lake Otsego when that was on the frontier; *Wyandotté* is set on a frontier land patent in upstate New York at the time of the Revolution; *Satanstoe* is narrated by Cornelius Littlepage, and the story told in his pages is set in 1758, when the nation, Cooper tells us in his own metaphor, was in its adolescence: "This period in the history of a country, may be likened to the hobbledehoy condition in ourselves, when we have lost the graces of childhood, without having attained the finished forms of men."[33] In such places and at such times, the country is like an adolescent, not yet fixed or even fully defined, no longer a child, not yet an adult, still able to learn and change, liminal.

The concept of liminality has been fairly well imported from interpretive anthropology into literary and cultural criticism, and it will not need extended explanation. Suffice it to say that, for Arnold Van Gennep, Victor Turner, and many others, liminars stand on a threshold, "betwixt and between the positions assigned and arrayed by law, custom, convention, and ceremonial"; that in "this interim of 'liminality,' the possibility exists of standing aside not only from one's own social position but from all social positions and of formulating a potentially unlimited series of alternative social arrangements"; that "'liminars' . . . may be initiands or novices in passage from one sociocultural state and status to another, or even whole populations undergoing transition"; and that "the essence of liminality is to be found in its release from normal constraints, making possible the deconstruction of . . . common sense . . . into cultural units which may then be, reconstructed in novel ways," a freedom from the past that enables the future to be constructed from the "cultural units" of the past.[34] Of course, such freedom may be more apparent than real, and it is important to remember that it is freedom *within* a particular culture rather than freedom *from* all culture. "Liminality" is a synthetic abstraction from cultural practices that ritualize social transition and thereby enable a culture to accommodate change. A liminar may, for a time, be free to choose among the social positions in culture but is never able to transcend culture completely. That Turner and contemporary Americans make so much of liminality suggests that it is an important part of the culture of our time and place, not an escape from that or from any other culture. Moreover, Turner is right to note that since liminality as a metaphor for transition enables persons and cultures to survive by changing over time, its long-range function is conservative. Cooper's texts work to preserve American culture by enacting modes of reading through which it can grow. In the adolescence of persons and entire cultures, on the sea, and on the frontier, Cooper found the freedom from the common sense of America in his own time that he would need to imagine America anew, and to teach Americans the better modes of reading that would not merely reflect but would, in large part, constitute that new culture.

However problematic the historicity of the actual frontier, a retrospective and fictive view of it offered Cooper, as an unconsciously romantic view of it would later offer Frederick Jackson Turner, an image of freedom and cultural possibility, a rich text from which Americans could learn more varied modes of reading. Turner argued that, "for a moment, at the frontier, the bonds of custom are broken and unrestraint is triumphant. There is not *tabula rasa*. The stubborn American environment is there with its imperious summons to accept its conditions; the inherited ways of doing things are also there; and yet, in spite of environment, and in spite of custom, each frontier did indeed furnish a new field of opportunity, a gate of escape from the bondage of the past." Cooper locates that freedom from historical and hermeneutical determinism on the frontier and on the sea, and Turner follows him in recognizing the similarity between the two: "What the Mediterranean Sea was to the Greeks, breaking the bond of custom, offering new experiences, calling out new institutions and activities, that, and more, the ever retreating frontier has been to the United States directly, and to the nations of Europe more remotely."[35] In Cooper's view, the country clearly was in need of such a liminal field. Noah Webster was undertaking to reform the American language according to his own New England model, much as Jason Newcome had dreamed of doing, making it narrower and more monological than it had been. A commercial aristocracy interested primarily in extending its own hegemony was reenacting the selfishness and recreating the class divisions that a hereditary aristocracy had enacted in Europe. New Englanders were fashioning homegrown titles for themselves, both proclaiming their cultural uniqueness and fawning over European marks of distinction. Though Cooper had at first supported both Jackson and Van Buren, Jacksonian democrats were disappointing his hopes by enshrining individual whim as the only motive for action, while Whig reformers were aiming for cultural uniformity. In short, the Newcomes had won and were winning still, in the field of historical fact. In fiction, however, Cooper could advert to various forms of the liminal field and clear away the Newcomes and their teachings in order to replace them with his own paradoxical view of what an American writer could add to the palimpsest.

What Cooper added was a fiction based not only on history and imagination, but also on the interpretive process that unites these two in the act of making sense. His books center on enactments of interpretation, and for his dramatized readers, interpretive skill is a matter of life and death. In *The Spy*, Harvey Birch's readings of British military strategy are necessary for Washington's prosecution of the war. If a separate nation is to be born, Birch must know both British and American culture and read them aright. As a double agent, moreover, Birch serves a loyalty higher than himself but serves it precisely through cultural and interpretive multiplicity, knowing the codes of both British and American combatants.

In *The Pilot*, another romance of cultural struggle set during the Revolution, John Paul Jones is the best on board at reading the dangerous shoal waters. So important is this ability that it overrides all other forms of distinction. Military rank, social class, and wealth are temporarily set aside, and all on board obey Jones, from Captain Munson on down. It is important to note that Jones is not revealed to have been the king all along and that he does not claim to have ruled the ship "from time immemorial." The shifting patterns of deference attest both to the importance of reading the shoals and to the ease with which a sense of cultural multiplicity enables even a rigidly organized ship's company to adapt to change. The nautical language in the book, so annoying to the same critics who chide Cooper for a lack of realistic detail in other matters, suggests that his contemporary readers, too, are culturally narrow and are therefore perplexed by a code that other people find clear and useful.

The importance of reading and the survival value of cultural multiplicity are more fully developed in *The Last of the Mohicans*. For shooting, all defer to Hawk-eye; for tracking, all to Uncas; for strategy, all to whoever seems to have the best idea, even to Cora Munro, when she suggests that the men take to the river and leave the women to fend for themselves. Once they are captured, Cora Munro knows enough of the American wilderness to leave signs: she breaks twigs upward to signify that a human being, an animal with an opposable thumb, has passed this way. One of her captors quickly breaks them downward to simulate the passing of another animal, but Uncas is a good reader and follows the trail. Cora is, moreover, an interesting enactment of cultural multiplicity, mingling two bloods and knowledge of several cultures, including British and French. Though her death is usually interpreted as evidence of Cooper's obsessive fear of miscegenation (a theme he deals with bravely enough in *The Wept of Wish-ton-Wish*) and passive repetition of the romancer's convention that brunettes die and blondes live, it is also likely that her passing, mourned at length by British and Mohicans alike, represents the passing of a cultural multiplicity that had in fact been effaced and that might have saved America from the reductions of Cooper's time. Certainly his characterization of the two sisters suggests that Cora is far more worthwhile than her passive and infantile sister, Alice.

Evidence for this reading is found in specific literary strategies informing the actions of Hawk-eye and Heyward. In the course of the romance, it gradually becomes clear that survival in this new world will depend only in part on keenness of eye, fleetness of foot, and strength of arms: it will also depend on reading and understanding, on powers of recognition and response. Heyward's blunders early on stem not from any inherent weakness of mind or body, but only from cultural misprision. At first he simply attempts to apply his British categories to a world in which they are inappropriate. Though Hawk-eye dismisses many of Heyward's cultural readings and imperatives as childish, Hawk-eye's view is also partial.

He reads most signs well, using English and Indian codes, and he faces impending death with a stoic calm bordering on ennui, but when he cannot make sense of an unfamiliar sound (the screaming of horses in their distress), a dimly remembered lesson about the nature and culture of heaven, or a challenge in a language he does not understand, he forgets his surroundings and comes dangerously close to panic. In these instances, Heyward comes to the rescue with information and action based on his knowledge of other cultures. The most extended of these incidents is occasioned by the challenge of the French sentinel:

> "Qui vive?" demanded a stern, quick voice, which sounded like a challenge from another world, issuing out of that solitary and solemn place.
> "What says it?" whispered the scout. "It speaks neither Indian nor English!"[36]

Hawk-eye thinks at first that it might be a ghost, and given his linguistic and cultural limitations, it might as well be, a revenant of a vanished and forgotten time. For Hawk-eye, the sentinel is so completely *outré* that he hardly seems human, as the scout's use of the neuter pronoun suggests. Though Cooper, moreover, has riddled this book with explanatory footnotes, stories within stories, and parallel stories, also in footnotes, for careless readers who might otherwise miss the point of a particular episode in the main tale, he does not translate any of his French. Readers unfamiliar with the language simply confront it as landlubbers confront the nautical language in *The Pilot*. If they cannot understand it, their puzzlement reenacts Hawk-eye's and stands as one more evidence of what America has lost as a culture and what Cooper's fiction will save for it from the wreck of the past.

Heyward does not share in that puzzlement. He answers the sentinel, converses with him, and convinces him that the source of this pleasant and familiar voice is human, French, and of a social class and authority superior to the sentinel's own. When the sentinel asks, "Etes-vous officier du roi?" Heyward intentionally misreads the obvious emphasis on loyalty to the king for a more useful emphasis on rank as an officer and replies, "Sans doute, mon camarade; me prends-tu pour un provincial! Je suis capitaine de chasseurs (Heyward well knew that the other was of a regiment in the line)" (137). Heyward knows and the sentinel does not need to be told that officer outranks sentinel, that Paris outranks the provinces, and that cavalry outranks infantry.

In his work on social class and distinction, Bourdieu observes that any social code—language, drinks, clothing—"provides the small number of distinctive features which, functioning as a system of differences, differential deviations, allow the most fundamental social differences to be expressed almost as completely as through the most complex and refined systems available in the legitimate arts." Heyward and the sentinel are not merely conversing; they are both reading the subtext of their conversation, and Heyward, more than the sentinel, is authoring it. Heyward knows not only the French language, but also the class structure and social codes in which the language is implicated. Knowledge of such codes imparts power, and Heyward uses that power to mislead the sentinel and to save his group. The conversation illustrates Bourdieu's argument that the "classificatory systems" of society "are not so much means of knowledge as means of power, harnessed to social functions and overtly or covertly aimed at satisfying the interests of a group."[37]

Heyward's knowledge of French language and culture enables him to so overawe the sentinel that even when Cora, a clearly identified and acknowledged member of the English enemy, also speaks French to him, he does not infer that one can know French without being French and that Heyward may not be what he represents. Instead, the French sentinel has been so lured by the enchantment of language and so lulled by his own monolingualism into the belief that he is in his own familiar world among friends that he walks off carelessly, singing in French of wine and love, only to be killed by Chingachgook.

Like Heyward and Cooper's other characters, he has been an audience figure, caught in the act of interpretation, in a test of reading skill played for high stakes. Heyward reads well and lives; the sentinel reads poorly and dies. The focus of Cooper's mimesis, then, is less on the world observed or even on the subjective observer than it is on the act of observation and interpretation itself, on the characters' abilities to read well as a prelude to informed action.

It is clear, moreover, that this reading ability is not a pure skill but an activity dependent upon knowledge.[38] One does not interpret French simply by virtue of one's intellectual power: one has to know the language and something of the culture that informs it. And this knowledge that makes skilled reading possible lies in the wreck of the past, in both history and story. In *The Last of the Mohicans*, Cooper's characters draw this knowledge largely from their own histories. In *The Prairie*, however, there is another source. Ellen Wade can draw both on her own experience of life and on the stories she knows.

How she can do so is made clear in recent work by Wolfgang Iser and Baruch Hochman. Iser argues that fiction is not merely opposed to fact in a simple binary antithesis. It is a third term mediating between the world of fact and the world of imagination. It draws from both and fashions them into a shaped construction that gives to fact a human significance (making it matter to us) and to imagination an apprehensible form (making it make sense to us). Fiction, then, is not a subset of either fact or imagination: "This act of fictionalizing cannot be deduced from the repeated reality and so clearly brings into play an imaginary quality which links up with the reality reproduced in the text." But neither is fiction "identical to this protean potential of the imaginary," since it is a construction in public language that "endows the imaginary with an articulate gestalt—a gestalt that is quite different from the fantasies, projections, daydreams and other reveries that ordinarily give the imaginary a direct route into our experience."[39] As Iser makes clear, then, fiction is formed from both fact and imagination. It requires both for its reading and, though distinct from both, is linked to both.

The nature of this linkage is explored by Baruch Hochman, who argues that persons in life and characters in literature are ontologically distinct and even quite different in the modes in which they are presented to us. They are, nevertheless, epistemologically congruous, since we bring to bear the same interpretive skills in making sense of both: there is, Hochman argues, a "full congruity between the way we perceive people in literature and the way we perceive them in life, with all the possibilities of disjunction and synthesis that are available in one domain being possible in the other." One can, of course, argue that people are much more than mere texts, mere occasions for interpretation, and Hochman recognizes a signal difference, that "characters in literature, as opposed to people in life, intrinsically mean something." The link, then, is not ontological but interpretive, since "we bring to the interpretation of characters in literature the skills we use in 'reading' characters in life."[40] One implication of this argument is that those skills can be developed and their range expanded through attention both to literature and to life. Skills formed through our interaction with either are useful in our interactions with both.

In *The Prairie*, Ellen Wade enacts this kind of reading. Left in charge of the shabby fort and fearless children of Ishmael Bush, she looks out to see a party of armed men headed straight for them: "It was a fearful moment for Ellen." She reacts by recalling stories in which other women have faced such fearful moments with both courage and strategy. In attempting to read her situation and her options, "she endeavored to recall to her confused faculties some one of the many tales of female heroism, with which the history of the western frontier abounded." Three come to mind. She selects "the case most nearly assimilated to the situation in which Ellen now found herself, and with flushing cheeks and kindling eyes, the girl began to consider, and to prepare her slender means of defense."[41] Since the story she selects is already an interpretation, already "assimilated" to her characteristic modes of perception and discourse, she can see the patterns in it and apply them quite quickly to her defense.

Her skill in this kind of reading is reconfirmed when Dr. Obed Battius attempts to overawe her with a great deal of legalistic and latinate balderdash. She sees quite through him and is "as little moved by his rhetoric as her companions. At those passages, which he intended should be tender and affecting, the intelligent girl, though tortured by painful feelings, had even manifested a disposition to laugh, while to the threats she turned an utterly insensible ear" (149). Young Ellen, neither noble nor rich, has learned to read well, to take the measure of her multicultural world and then to take measures.

Ruth Heathcote, in *The Wept of Wish-ton-Wish*, is less able to do so. Donald Ringe argues cogently that earlier critics have tended to concentrate on merely one of the several cultures represented in the book. They focus only on the displaced English Puritans, or on the Indians, or on the latter part of the book.[42] These reactions all tend to reduce the cultural multiplicity that the book enacts. The book, however, also enacts cultural reductions and concomitant misreadings.

More radically than in his earlier works, Cooper centers on the variety of cultures that interact on the Connecticut frontier. The Heathcotes are English, to be sure, but they are English Puritans in America, who harbor in their blockhouse one of the regicide judges of Charles I. The Indians are an alliance of Wamponoags and Narragansetts in conflict not only with the English but also with the Mohicans. In this work, the vicissitudes and complications of history are reduced and misread by all sides, with tragic results. After an alliance of English and Indians has killed his father, the Narragansett chief Miantonimoh, young Conanchet assumes that all English are his enemy and comes into the settlement bent on revenge. The Heathcotes treat him kindly, and he revises his view. But other Indians do not.

They attack the settlement, free Conanchet, take Ruth Heathcote prisoner, and burn the blockhouse where the rest of the family have sheltered. They read the destroyed blockhouse as evidence that the family are dead, but the Heathcotes have preserved themselves in a deep well unknown to the Indians. The Heathcotes and the colony survive. After twelve years, in another Indian attack, Conanchet recognizes the Heathcotes, spares them, and returns their daughter to them. He recognizes that a binary opposition of English and Indian is too simple a taxonomy for reading people.

Others in the tale read more simply and destructively. The Reverend Mr. Meek Wolfe, rather better described by his family name than by his Christian name, sees only savage Indians and a convenient opportunity for gain. Dr. Ergot asserts that science and rationality form the master code for reading all, and it is telling that Cooper has named him for a hallucinogenic fungus. In the tale, as in American history, these modes of reading win.

Conanchet is captured by the English, turned over to his enemies, the Mohicans, and killed. The Heathcotes adopt the child of Conanchet that Ruth has borne in the forest, but Ruth herself cannot survive the transition back to English culture. The Rev. Mr. Wolfe and company use a narrow and handy reading of Christianity as cause to murder the Indians and take over their lands. Wish-ton-wish is a valley full of wishes for cultural multiplicity, but the narrow readers win out, and the tale ends in weeping, both for Ruth and for what might have been.

In this respect it resembles Cooper's later career. In *Notions of the Americans*, written at the request of Lafayette, Cooper attempts to correct misreadings in over forty books that Europeans have written about America. Cooper warns Americans against the development of any dominant class based on money or on any other single criterion. In *The Bravo*, *The Heidenmauer*, and *The Headsman*, he dramatizes the destruction wrought by the hegemony of any one class—hereditary aristocracy, plutocracy, or oligarchy—in Europe. In *A Letter to His Countrymen*, he argues, with some justice, that these European novels have affirmed the best of American principles. He also pleads for American intellectual independence from Europe. Finally, having lost much of his readership (perhaps because he has taxed them too severely, perhaps because they are no longer interested in any culture outside their own), he writes that he is giving up his profession as a writer.

This renunciation lasts about a year before Cooper is back with *The Monikins*, a social satire on the kind of cultural imitation appropriate to monkeys and manikins. In this work, neither English nor American culture is adequate by itself. In *The American Democrat* he warns against simple domination by the majority, a monarch, or an aristocracy, and in *Homeward Bound* and *Home as Found*, he explores yet again the ways in which Jacksonian democracy can reenact the class dominance and social reductions of Europe. Steadfast Dodge, an American newspaper editor, forgets the past, enshrines present whim, and uses democratic principles, much as Meek Wolfe used Christianity, as a handy and slippery rationale for the next move in his ceaseless struggle for gain and approval. He hopes to invoke democracy to get the land, then announce that the land grab has been sanctified by tradition from "time immemorial." Though he fails in Cooper's fiction, Cooper worried that others of his ilk were succeeding in America.

Americans were not giving up on the marks of distinction appropriate to a class system. They were simply basing their class system on money and power instead of on heredity. As Cooper noted, they proclaimed themselves different from and better than Europe, indeed historically unique, while aping the cultural narrowness and intolerance characteristic of the European class systems at their worst. In this cultural narrowing, both the Jacksonian sanctifiers of present moment and present whim and the reductive Whig reformers represented cultural dead ends.

Alternatives to these are explored in Cooper's last works. In *The Pathfinder*, we are back on the frontier, trying to find a proper marriage for Mabel Dunham. In this world, natural classes are determined by function, and there is enough tolerance and mobility for Jefferson's natural aristoi of talent and merit to rise to an appropriate level. Mabel will choose Jasper Western, who captains the *Scud* on Lake Ontario, and they will eventually move into the merchant class in New York.

The world of *The Deerslayer* is at first pastoral and innocent, almost childlike. The Deerslayer is Natty Bumpo at his youngest, uneducated and, most of the time, unthinking. Hetty Hutter is simple-minded from birth, and the Delawares share with them a certain innocence. But in this pastoral idyll familiar forces are already hastening the cultural decline of Cooper's own day. Hurry Harry March is bent on profit; Tom Hutter has built his "castle" on pilings in the lake, and Judith Hutter is vain and acquisitive. In this book, such complications are simply expelled. Tom is scalped alive and left to die, Hetty is killed accidentally in the final fight, and a dying Indian gives Deerslayer the name Hawk-eye. The book is a haunting reverie, as Daniel Peck suggests, of childhood, in which "the full force of history is never allowed to break in."[43]

That force breaks in repeatedly in *Wyandotté*, where again the focus is on the necessity of reading well in the context of cultural multiplicity. In a liminal setting, on a land patent in upstate New York at the time of the Revolution, many cultures and most religious sects, including Catholics, read each other well or badly. The Willoughby patent is a microcosm, in which African, Indian, Dutch, New England, New York, and British cultures must understand each other if the settlement is to survive. As Donald Ringe observes, "the problems of this little colony are those of the world at large."[44]

But Captain Willoughby, retired from the British army and sympathetic to the American cause, tends to read only from the perspective of the British army and white America, and he does not read well. Reading peace from the evidence of war, he neglects to hang the gates that would guard his property. Reading a friend where he has an enemy, he does not suspect the duplicity of his overseer, Joel Strides. Finally, he misreads Wyandotté, a Tuscarora Indian who served with him and helped him found the settlement. Wyandotté is both noble and drunken, both a Christian convert and a chief who holds to his tribal code of vengeance. Indeed, the best description of Wyandotté is that given by Willoughby's son, Robert: "he never forgot a favor, or forgave an injury." While not morally a better man than his father, Robert is a much better reader.

Willoughby forgets that he had Wyandotté flogged long ago and that the Indian has not forgotten it. Nor has Wyandotté forgotten that Willoughby's family saved his life during an epidemic of smallpox. Willoughby, however, forgets that he is not in the British army now, forgets that an Indian may not dismiss scars on his back, the mark in his culture of a coward, and as a result of reading from a narrow perspective and only in the present, misreads the loyalty of Wyandotté, "feeling an uneasiness, on the subject of the Tuscarora's fidelity, that he could not entirely conquer." We learn Willoughby's remarkable way of dealing with his unease a little later in Wyandotté's soliloquy: "Why tell Wyandotté he flog ag'in, just as go to enemy's camp?"[45]

It is a good question. In the British army, such a threat would have been thought, by officers at least, an appropriate way of securing the loyalty of a subordinate. In this situation, however, it elicits a somewhat different response. Wyandotté, enraged beyond all reason, plunges his knife into Willoughby's heart, a lesson for ahistorical and careless readers everywhere.

Yet Cooper enables his audience to read *Wyandotté* better than Willoughby reads Wyandotté. He explicitly links the narrow tribalism of the Indians with that of the whites: "To own the truth, one of the great failings of the savages of the American forests, was to think of the neighboring tribes, as the Englishman is known to think of the

Frenchman, and vice versa, as the German thinks of both, and all think of the Yankee. In a word, his own tribe contains everything that is excellent," and is therefore sufficient (338). There is no need to learn of other tribes who are at all separated from us by space or time.

Wyandotté plays out the effects of this kind of reading. It is important to note that Captain Willoughby dies and his son, Robert, survives, only because Robert is a better reader, not in any way morally better. Robert has returned home both to see his father and to spy for the British. As soon as he is among the American regulars, he realizes that this second motive for his errand will be suspected, persuades the fair Maud to marry him, and declares that the only motive for his return was true love. His father had much purer intentions but poorer interpretive skills because of less knowledge of the past and of cultures other than his own.

That knowledge comes from history and from story, however problematic the theoretical distinctions between the two. And Cooper conserves both in his works. The past is gone and irrecoverable, its traces being effaced and forgotten. As Cooper's dramatized reader and writer, Cornelius Littlepage, writes in the opening pages of *Satanstoe*: "I see scarcely a mode by which the next generation can preserve any memorials of the distinctive usages and thoughts of this." To preserve some memory of those "usages and thoughts," ignored in the wash of history and unrecorded in the histories of the time, Cornelius puts pen to paper, writing a tale that falls between accustomed categories: "I shall not attempt the historical mode at all" or make his narrative "a silly attempt to write a more silly fiction." Convinced that "something surely is worthy to be saved from the wreck of the past," Littlepage elects to save precisely the cultural multiplicity that existed before Jason Newcome and Company reduced the language to Webster, culture to Connecticut, and history to the present moment.[46] In that world, the British Major Bulstrode, the Dutch Dirck Van Valkenburgh, the New England Jason Newcome, and Cornelius Littlepage (whose mother is Dutch and father English) contest for the hand of Anneke Mordaunt, a nice synecdoche for America. In fact, Cooper believed that America had made a bad match in choosing Jason, and in his fiction he had her read better and choose Littlepage, the cultural hybrid, author, and text. David Simpson has argued that Cooper did the same in his language, enriching American English far beyond the bounds of Webster by bringing in words from many other cultures and making them American. As Simpson points out, many American words were printed for the first time in Cooper: he did not simply settle for a substitute from England or New England.[47]

It is clear, then, that Cooper does not enact these allegories of reading to assert the superiority or sufficiency of any single cultural code. Many modes of reading work well in some circumstances (i.e., have pragmatic value in preserving the reader's life) and badly in others. It is the multiplicity of cultural codes that saves. And these codes remain forever incommensurable, neither able to be translated into a single master code nor able to substitute for each other. In our time belief in the social effectiveness of cultural codes and in the need to know several is increasing. Bruce Lincoln argues that discourse "can be used in the construction and reconstruction of social groups and hierarchies" and that "the only alternative to comparison is one brand of parochialism or another: That is, the stance of those who privilege the data with which they happen to be familiar while ignoring, and thus remaining ignorant of, the rest."[48] In Cooper's time such parochialism was dominant, and Cooper's fiction preserved what was being lost in fact.

In our own time, we are developing again a multiplicity of modes of reading. Each new formalism begins as a replacement for intellectual history and becomes a chapter in intellectual history. Each new historicism begins as a textualized frame of reference for reading and becomes a theory of reading. These antinomies are neither temporary glitches, mere problems to be solved so that we can soar aloft to more thoroughly commanding views, nor final aporetic barriers to further interpretation. They are among the engines of discourse, and they take us on—not up into the perspective of God or the sun, not down into anomie and silence—just on to increased understanding of the books we read and write.

Now that our modes of reading are becoming more historically informed, perhaps it is time to read Cooper again, less as a maker of timeless American myth than as a historian of American epistemologies, a writer who attracted an enormous community of readers, then lost some of them in trying to alter the way they read. He never found a single term for his works, but it might be useful to regard them as the kind of texts we still call readers. They still offer us, from a particular time and place, a series of reading lessons, interrogations of cultural orthodoxy in the context of codes layered many deep on the palimpsest of America.

Notes

1. Mark Twain, "Fenimore Cooper's Literary Offenses," *The Portable Mark Twain*, ed. Bernard DeVoto (New York: Viking, 1968) 541, 553.

2. Arvid Shulenberger, *Cooper's Theory of Fiction: His Prefaces and Their Relation to His Novels* (Lawrence: U of Kansas P, 1955) 3, 92.

3. William Charvat, Introduction, *The Last of the Mohicans*, by James Fenimore Cooper (Boston: Riverside, 1958) v, xvii.

4. Donald Ringe, *James Fenimore Cooper* (New York: Twayne, 1962) 19, 62, 7–8, 20. In his updated edition of 1988, Ringe drops the New Critical language of his preface.

5. Emily Budick, *Fiction and Historical Consciousness: The American Romance Tradition* (New Haven: Yale UP, 1989) 19–20.

6. Hans Robert Jauss, *Toward an Aesthetic of Reception*, trans. Timothy Bahti (Minneapolis: U of Minnesota P, 1982) 25–26; Jauss, *Aesthetic Experience and Literary Hermeneutics*, trans. Michael Shaw (Minneapolis: U of Minnesota P, 1982) 14, 17, 28, 270.

7. Kenneth Dauber, *The Idea of Authorship in America: Democratic Poetics from Franklin to Melville* (Madison: U of Wisconsin P, 1990) 81–84, 103, 86, 94; Twain, "Fenimore Cooper's Literary Offenses" 556.

8. Nathaniel Hawthorne, "Earth's Holocaust," *Nathaniel Hawthorne's Tales*, ed. James McIntosh (New York: Norton, 1987) 153.

9. Carolyn Porter, "History and Literature: 'After the New Historicism,'" *New Literary History* 21 (1990): 254; Porter, "Are We Being Historical Yet?" *South Atlantic Quarterly* 87 (1988): 749.

10. Wolfgang Iser, *Prospecting: From Reader Response to Literary Anthropology* (Baltimore: Johns Hopkins UP, 1989).

11. Stanely Fish, *Doing What Comes Naturally: Change, Rhetoric, and the Practice of Theory in Literary and Legal Studies* (Durham: Duke UP, 1989) 32.

12. Clifford Geertz, *The Interpretation of Cultures* (New York: Basic, 1973) 89.

13. Anthony F. C. Wallace, review of *Culture Theory*, ed. Richard A. Shweder and Robert A. LeVine, *New York Times Book Review* 10 Mar. 1985: 36.

14. Giles Gunn, *The Culture of Criticism and the Criticism of Culture* (New York: Oxford UP, 1987) 99, 105.

15. Shelley, "A Defense of Poetry," *Norton Anthology of English Literature*, ed. M. H. Abrams et al., 4th ed. (New York: Norton, 1979) 2:794; Auden, "In Memory of W. B. Yeats," *Selected Poetry of W. H. Auden* (New York: Modern Library, 1958) 53.

16. Barbara Herrnstein Smith, *Contingencies of Value: Alternative Perspectives for Critical Theory* (Cambridge: Harvard UP, 1988) 51.

17. Steven Mailloux, *Rhetorical Power* (Ithaca: Cornell UP, 1989) xii, 104.

18. Stephen Greenblatt, "Resonance and Wonder," in *Literary Theory Today*, ed. Peter Collier and Helga Geyer-Ryan (Ithaca: Cornell UP, 1990) 79.

19. Mailloux, *Rhetorical Power* 104; Dauber, *The Idea of Authorship in America* 92.

20. Forrest Robinson, review of *Rhetorical Power*, by Steven Mailloux, *American Literature* 62 (1990): 511.

21. Pierre Bourdieu, *In Other Words: Essays towards a Reflexive Sociology* (Stanford: Stanford UP, 1990) 76.

22. Ibid. 116, 195.

23. Evan Watkins, "Reproduction, Reading, and Resistance," *American Literary History* 2 (1990): 555.

24. Robert Scholes, *Textual Power: Literary Theory and the Teaching of English* (New Haven: Yale UP, 1985) 33.

25. H. Daniel Peck, *A World by Itself: The Pastoral Moment in Cooper's Fiction* (New Haven: Yale UP, 1977) ix.

26. Quoted in Nina Baym, *Novels, Readers, and Reviewers: Responses to Fiction in Antebellum America* (Ithaca: Cornell UP, 1984) 110.

27. Ludwig Wittgenstein, *The Blue and Brown Books* (Oxford: Blackwell, 1972) 18.

28. James Fenimore Cooper, *Home as Found* (New York: Capricorn, 1961) 212.

29. Eric Sundquist, *Home as Found: Authority and Genealogy in Nineteenth-Century American Literature* (Baltimore: Johns Hopkins UP, 1979) xi.

30. Cooper, *Satanstoe; or, The Littlepage Manuscripts: A Tale of the Colony*, ed. Robert L. Hough (Lincoln: U of Nebraska P, 1962) 419.

31. James Wallace, "Cultivating an Audience: From *Precaution* to *The Spy*," in *James Fenimore Cooper: New Critical Essays*, ed. Robert Clark (Totowa, N.J.: Barnes, 1985) 52.

32. Clifford Geertz, *Local Knowledge: Further Essays in Interpretive Anthropology* (New York: Basic, 1983) 234.

33. Cooper, *Satanstoe* 368.

34. Victor Turner, *The Ritual Process: Structure and Anti-Structure* (New York: Aldine, 1969) 95; Turner, *Dramas, Fields, and Metaphors: Symbolic Action in Human Society* (Ithaca: Cornell UP, 1974) 13–14; Turner, *On the Edge of the Bush: Anthropology as Experience*, ed. Edith L. B. Turner (Tucson: U of Arizona P, 1985) 159–60.

35. Frederick Jackson Turner, *The Significance of the Frontier in American History*, ed. Harold P. Simonson (New York: Ungar, 1963) 57–58.

36. Cooper, *The Last of the Mohicans: A Narrative of 1757*, ed. James Franklin

Beard et al. (Albany: State U of New York P, 1983) 137. Subsequent citations appear in the text parenthetically.

37. Pierre Bourdieu, *Distinction: A Social Critique of the Judgement of Taste*, trans. Richard Nice (Cambridge: Harvard UP, 1984) 226, 477.

38. Robert Scholes makes this point about reading in general in *Textual Power* 33.

39. Wolfgang Iser, "Feigning in Fiction," in *Identity of the Literary Text*, ed. Mario J. Valdes and Owen Miller (Toronto: U of Toronto P, 1985) 205.

40. Baruch Hochman, *Character in Literature* (Ithaca: Cornell UP, 1985) 44, 65–66.

41. Cooper, *The Prairie: A Tale*, ed. James P. Elliott (Albany: State U of New York P, 1985) 146. Subsequent citations are given parenthetically in the text.

42. Donal Ringe, *James Fenimore Cooper*, updated edition (New York: Twayne, 1988) 32.

43. Peck, *A World by Itself* 160.

44. Ringe, *James Fenimore Cooper* (1988) 80.

45. Cooper, *Wyandotté; or, The Hutted Knoll: A Tale*, ed. Thomas Philbrick and Marianne Philbrick (Albany: State U of New York P, 1982) 375, 310, 319. Subsequent citations are given parenthetically in the text.

46. Cooper, *Satanstoe* 5–6, 419.

47. David Simpson, *The Politics of American English, 1776–1850* (New York: Oxford UP, 1986) 158–67.

48. Bruce Lincoln, *Discourse and the Construction of Society: Comparative Studies of Myth, Ritual, and Classification* (New York: Oxford UP, 1989) 172.

The Address of *The Scarlet Letter*

STEPHEN RAILTON

Reader-response critics often use "reader" and "audience" as synonymous terms, but it is worthwhile preserving a distinction between them. We could use the term "reader" for anyone who at any time opens a book and begins processing a text. "Audience," on the other hand, could be reserved to designate the specific group, the contemporary reading public, to whom an author originally addresses the text. All readers, of course, can be identified with larger groups, which Stanley Fish has taught us to call "interpretive communities."[1] But as an author writes a text, there is one particular group for whom he or she is writing; let us call that group the author's "audience." Thus, the readers of *The Scarlet Letter* have all come into existence after the novel was written. The novel's audience, though, was there before Hawthorne sat down to write it. As reader-response criticism shows, any reader's ideological allegiances as a member of a particular community play a crucial role in determining the way that reader produces meaning from a work of literature. But only the "audience," as I am suggesting we define it, can play a role in the creation of the work itself. The reader responds to the text, but first, in the very act of literary conception, there is the response of the text to its audience: the way the text is shaped by the author's ambitions and anxieties about performing for a particular group.

Because the role that this audience plays in the text is a subjective one, we have to make further distinctions. The contemporary audience for *The Scarlet Letter* was there, both sociologically and psychologically, before Hawthorne sat down to write his novel: it was "there" in America in 1850 as the actual reading public available to him as a professional writer and "there" in Hawthorne's mind as his internalized construct of the people he hoped would buy, read, and understand his novel. As Walter J. Ong has pointed out, any writer's sense of audience is an imaginative abstraction, a "fiction."[2] But Ong's emphasis needs to be qualified and historicized. For Hawthorne, or for any writer who hopes to perform successfully for his or her audience, this "fiction" is dialectically constructed by inescapable cultural facts. How Hawthorne conceptualized his audience had to start with his sense of the readers, real rather than ideal, who constituted the reading public in mid-nineteenth-century America.[3] Thus, it was this historically given audience, as I shall try to show in the first half of my essay, that inhabited his imagination and that presided over the fiction that he wrote as *The Scarlet Letter*.

In the second part of this essay, I will focus on the difference between the way a text originally responds to its audience and the way readers subsequently respond to a text. Because a text's audience and its readers are constructed in historically different ways, there is necessarily a distance between their potentialities as responders.[4] Secure in our chronological place as the latest arrivals on the literary historical scene, we are likely to think that we are better equipped to understand or appreciate a text than its original audience, that we know better. This seems especially true of our attitude toward the Victorian Americans for whom Hawthorne wrote. As readers, after all, we have rescued *Moby-Dick*, *Walden*, and *Leaves of Grass* from their benighted failure as an audience. It is certainly true that we know differently. *The Scarlet Letter* was the first novel to use a woman's sexuality to explore and challenge the structures of society; in the hundred and forty years since, many other writers have followed Hawthorne's lead. We could say that we have the benefit of this additional experience, but we should also acknowledge what we have lost. Just as it is apparently impossible for anyone these days to read Hawthorne's book without already knowing that Dimmesdale had been Hester's lover—a fact that even the most perceptive contemporary reader could not have suspected until the book's third chapter,[5] and would not know for sure until the middle—so it is almost impossible for us to imagine how those contemporary readers would have initially reacted to Hester Prynne. We know otherwise than the readers of 1850. We cannot help but bring to the novel a very different set of preconceptions—about someone like Hester, about adultery, about Christianity.

And we should admit that we often know less. At Petroglyph Point in Mesa Verde National Park is a rock covered with signs scratched by the Anasazi who lived there 700 years ago. No one now can interpret them. They communicated without ambiguity to the people for whom they were "written" but are perfectly opaque to us. As itself a hieroglyphic emblem, *The Scarlet Letter* looks like a much more accessible sign. That it works for and speaks so powerfully to modern readers is a measure of its achievement. But Hawthorne was not writing for us or for the theoretical reader of much reader-response criticism. Every reader's responses are relevant to any attempt to determine the ultimate significance of the text. We can, however, gain a lot by trying to reconstruct the way Hawthorne wrote it for his contemporary audience, by trying to understand how it was meant to speak to and work on the readers of his day.

There is no question about the force of his concern with the response of his contemporary audience. In the letters he wrote as he was finishing the novel, the emphasis is not on whether his novel had succeeded on its own terms—he seemed to know he'd written a great book, though a "dark and dismal" one. For him the question was whether it would succeed with its audience.[6] He was urgently worried about material success: he had lost his job at the Custom House; he was broke with a family to support. He was, however, equally anxious about rhetorical success. He and his publisher arranged with Melville's friend Duyckinck to publish an excerpt from the book in *The Literary World* as a kind of promotional device. Hawthorne's one stipulation was that the excerpt come from "The Custom-House," not from *The Scarlet Letter*: "I don't think it advisable to give any thing from the story itself; because I know of no passage that would not throw too much light on the plan of the book."[7] He says "plan," not "plot," which suggests that he had organized the novel strategically to work on its contemporary audience in a specific way. Given his concern here with a kind of secrecy, we could even say that the novel's deepest "plot" was somehow against its audience. That leads to the question I want to try to answer first: how did *The Scarlet Letter* address its audience? That question in turn leads to a more theoretical one. *The Scarlet Letter* reaches us a century and a half after it was addressed. Can readers in the 1990s respond according to plan, when the plan was worked out in 1850?

I

There is in fact an aboriginal audience inscribed into the text. Before Hester appears in the marketplace, the narrative puts in place the throng of Puritan men and women for whom the scarlet letter is first "published." Putting a "crowd of spectators" (54) in place before the story itself begins is Hawthorne's acknowledgment of the point that the audience precedes the text. His preoccupation with audience response is signaled by the way he puts those Puritans at the center of his stage: both chapter 1 *and* chapter 2 begin by drawing our attention to them. How historical *The Scarlet Letter* is, how much it is "about" the Puritan culture that provides its occasion, is a question that has long been debated by the commentators.[8] But the main role the "Puritans" play in the text is that of audience to its drama: they exist chiefly as an interpretive community.[9] Hawthorne regularly pauses the narrative to elaborate on how the people of Boston react to a new development in the story, how they "see" Hester and the other central characters, how they interpret the scarlet letter. And as an audience, the "Puritans" are not very historical. Although they dress like seventeenth-century colonists, their reactions, and the assumptions behind those reactions, are those of the genteel readers who formed Hawthorne's mid-nineteenth-century audience. The first step in appreciating Hawthorne's "plan" is to recognize the way he writes into the novel a version of his reading public, disguised in period costumes.

The "Puritans'" understanding of human nature is hardly Calvinist. Rather, it reflects the polarizations of the moral melodramas that were the most popular works of Hawthorne's time. *Uncle Tom's Cabin*, usually considered the best-selling book of this period, began appearing a year after *The Scarlet Letter*.[10] One characteristic Stowe's novel shares with the more conventional genteel best-sellers is its distribution of characters into the fixed patterns of melodramatic allegory: little Eva St. Clare is wholly angelic, Simon Legree is the incarnation of evil. These are also the patterns into which the Puritans of Hawthorne's novel keep trying to fit the central characters. To them, in that first scene, the *A* Hester wears "seemed to derive its scarlet hue from the flames of the infernal pit" (69). To them Dimmesdale appears as if robed in the spotless white Eva invariably wears: "They deemed the young clergyman a miracle of holiness. . . . In their eyes, the very ground on which he trod was sanctified" (142). When in the penultimate chapter they realize Dimmesdale is about to die, "it [would not] have seemed a miracle too high to be wrought for one so holy, had he ascended before their eyes, waxing dimmer and brighter, and fading at last into the light of heaven!" (252). Such an image would have been inconceivable to a Calvinist. It was, however, a very familiar one to Hawthorne's contemporaries: the first staged version of *Uncle Tom's Cabin*, which opened to eager throngs of spectators in 1852, actually ended with little Eva rising up from the stage into heaven.[11] The Puritans cannot settle on an interpretation of Chillingworth—to some he has been sent miraculously by "Heaven" to cure their saintly minister's body (121); to others, he is either "Satan himself, or Satan's emissary," come to plot against the saintly minister's soul (128)—but in either case their reading of his character relies on the type of moral dichotomies found in genteel fiction.

Why Hawthorne felt he had to plan carefully for his own audience becomes clear when we realize that the Puritans are a terrible audience. Their responses, and the assumptions behind them, are wholly inadequate to either the moral or the interpretive demands of his story. In that opening scene the novel explicitly condemns them for their failure of sympathy: they see Hester as an Other and cast her out of their society, even though the novel shows us that she is still essentially governed by their values: "She knew that her deed had been evil" (89). In the second half, they take "Another View of Hester." Since she quietly goes about her charitable duties as "a Sister of Mercy" to the poor and sick (161), they see her as "our Hester,—the town's own Hester" (162). But when the chapter titled "Another View of Hester" goes on to show us still *another* view of Hester,[12] we see how profoundly estranged from the town she has become: "She cast away the fragments of a broken chain. The world's law was no law for her mind" (164). The Puritans' utter failure as "readers" of the story is brought home to them dramatically at the climax, which depicts another public-ation of the scarlet letter while again they stand around the scaffold as a literal audience. Hawthorne, as he does throughout the novel, divides his focus in this scene between the action and their reaction. As we noted, they expect to see Dimmesdale ascend in glory to heaven. Instead, he goes up the steps of the scaffold to take his shame upon him. This not only explodes their predictions about the plot of Dimmesdale's life; it also razes the structure of assumptions by which they have understood reality. When Hester "published" her letter at the start, they stood in self-righteous certainty of their judgment on her. When Dimmesdale reveals his letter at the end, however, they are thrown into the "tumult" of interpretive chaos, "so taken by surprise, and so perplexed as to the purport of what they saw, — unable to receive the explanation which most readily presented itself, or to imagine any other, — that they remained silent and inactive spectators of the judgment which Providence seemed about to work." (253)

Hawthorne put this surrogate audience into the text to guide his own audience's responses. His readers could watch them watching the story, and learn from them how not to read *The Scarlet Letter*. That explains why those Puritans are disguised Victorian Americans, for the assumptions that Hawthorne plots against are those that he identifies with his contemporary readers. He valued fiction for the truth that it could tell, but also said he wrote "to open up an intercourse with the world."[13] He summed up his thematic project as a writer by referring to himself as "a person, who has been burrowing, to his utmost ability, into the depths of our common nature, for the purposes of psychological romance."[14] But inseparable from this was his rhetorical project, the "apostolic errand" he refers to obliquely in "The Custom-House" (7). His "plan" for *The Scarlet Letter* was to communicate as well as to explore the depths of our common nature, the truths of the human heart. What he felt standing between him and the achievement of that plan were just the kind of moral and psychological simplifications that the book's Puritans accept as true. Their superficial judgments cut them off from the depths of our common nature.

When Dimmesdale gets back to his study after the breathtaking reunion with Hester in the woods, the narrative provides a final gloss on what has happened to him: "Another man had returned out of the forest; a wiser one; with a knowledge of hidden mysteries which the simplicity of the former never could have reached" (223). This characterization links Dimmesdale with such earlier figures in Hawthorne's fiction as Young Goodman Brown and Ethan Brand, both of whom also learn the dark secrets of the heart (Brown in the forest). By their knowledge Brown and Brand are estranged from the world. In the first paragraph of "The Custom-House," however, Hawthorne announces his desire as a "speaker" to "stand in some true relation with his audience" (4). It is this desire to publish the truth—about himself, about the hidden mysteries his own experience has taught him—that carries Dimmesdale at the end up the scaffold's steps. There he becomes, at last, a true preacher, trying to stand in a true relation with *his* audience, and his text (like Hawthorne's) is "The Revelation of the Scarlet Letter." But Dimmesdale's revelation falls on blind eyes as his audience proves unwilling to abandon the "simplicities" of their former interpretation. To sum up the Puritans' failure even in this scene, we can invoke the novel's tersest paragraph: "The scarlet letter had not done its office" (166). As a sign of the truth of the human heart, the letter remains opaque to its aboriginal audience. By letting his audience see this other audience's blindness, however, Hawthorne is looking for a way to enable the scarlet letter to perform its office as a letter: to communicate.

For we are meant to consider the reason for the Puritans' failure. It is not simply their lack of sympathy for Hester as a sinner; that is but the symptom of a deeper cause: their failure to be honest with themselves and each other about the truths of their own nature. By means of the "sympathetic knowledge of the hidden sin in other hearts" that Hester's letter gives her, we see the people of Boston in much the same light that reveals Salem to Goodman Brown in the wilderness, as a brotherhood of shame and guilt: "If truth were everywhere to be shown, a scarlet letter would blaze forth on many a bosom besides Hester Prynne's" (86). Like Brown, however, the Puritans self-righteously reject this community: he exiles himself from society; they project their hidden sinfulness onto Hester and then, as a kind of repression, banish her and her *A* from their knowledge of themselves. In this unwillingness to "Be true" (260) to the truth of their common nature lies the source of their inadequacies as "spectators." They see the world in the simplistic terms on which the repression of self-knowledge depends. Their reading of Dimmesdale's character is the obverse side of their repression of Hester. Onto the minister they project their image of the pure, angelic self, the self-gratulatory image that is fostered by their denial of the sinful self. Their misreading of Dimmesdale is as egregious as their inability to sympathize or identify with Hester, and it is treated even more explicitly as their failure as an audience. The minister achieves "a brilliant popularity in his sacred office," but "the people knew not the power that moved them thus." On the other hand, we're told exactly what that power consists of—the burden of guilty self-knowledge: "This very burden it was, that gave him sympathies so intimate with the sinful brotherhood of mankind: so that his heart vibrated in unison with theirs, and received their pain into itself, and sent its own throb of pain through a thousand other hearts, in gushes of sad, persuasive eloquence" (142).

What Hawthorne is describing here is the basis of the "true relation" in which, as the "speaker" of *The Scarlet Letter*, he hopes to "stand with his audience": a fellowship of seekers for the truth of the heart, united by a knowledge of their mutual human frailties.[15] It is this way of "reading" the scarlet letter that he models for every reader in "The Custom-House," when he depicts himself taking up the *A* and placing it on his own breast (31–32). This is exactly the opposite of what the Puritans do, when they condemn an Other to wear the letter as their scapegoat. This, though, is what Dimmesdale himself will finally do, when he reveals his letter to them. And this is the lesson Hester ultimately learns from Dimmesdale, when at the very end she voluntarily puts the *A* back on. It is, we learn in "The Custom-House," and learn author-itatively, the true way to interpret the novel: we must not merely pick up *The Scarlet Letter*—we must wear it, must admit the truth it tells us about ourselves. In terms of Hawthorne's "plan," this means he must lead his audience beyond the psychological "simplicities" reflected in their conventional, melodramatic moral categories. In this sense, the whole rhetorical problem of the novel is summed up, anxiously, in the last three sentences of chapter 22, the chapter that precedes "The Revelation of the Scarlet Letter": "The sainted minister in the church! The woman of the scarlet letter in the market-place! What imagination would have been irreverent enough to surmise that the same scorching stigma was on them both?" (260). The answer, of course, is Hawthorne's imagination. But that answer only locates the point from which, as a Victorian American author, he felt he had to begin. The end toward which he worked depended upon his audience's willingness to accept the terms of his imagination.

Given the pieties of his genteel audience, "irreverent" is a good term for those terms. He wants to unite those aspects of human nature which his culture kept asunder—the most saintly and the most debased, the best and worst.

Among the culture's most devout pieties was the idea of true womanhood, which insisted on the segregation of heroines from sin, especially from sinful sexuality.[16] Thus, Hawthorne knew, his audience was likely to put almost as much distance as the Puritans do between themselves and Hester as a convicted adulteress. The literary type to which contemporary readers would have referred her was not the one that probably comes first to the modern reader's mind—the feminist protagonist, whom they had never met—but rather the Dark Heroine, a figure familiar from other books. Victorian American preconceptions about such a figure define the second step in Hawthorne's rhetorical plan: to create sympathy for Hester. The first eight chapters of the novel are largely devoted to this task. When Hester enters the story through the prison door, before describing her, before describing the *A* to which all the Puritans' eyes are drawn, Hawthorne describes the baby in her arms. His audience meets her first as "the mother of this child" (52). Stowe, who had her own rhetorical design on the same reading public, and knew as much as Hawthorne about how to achieve it, relies on exactly the same strategy. To that audience, a male black slave was as much an Other as a convicted adulteress. To close the gap between her hero and her readers, Stowe lets them meet for the first time in Tom's cabin, where he is meekly learning how to write from the master's child while his wife cooks in the foreground and his children play in the background. As if these domestic emanations weren't enough, Stowe allows only a few pages to pass before Tom too has a baby in his arms.[17] Both Hester's and Tom's babies are intended as passports to admit their bearers into the region where genteel readers and their sympathies were already at home.

By continually referring to Hester as a "mother"—as sacred a category to contemporary readers as minister was to the Puritans—and by developing in detail her struggles both to make her way as a woman in the wider world and to raise a daughter (the focus of chapters 5 and 6), Hawthorne seeks to complicate his readers' response to "this poor victim of her own frailty, and man's hard law" (87). This strategy culminates in chapters 7 and 8, the most dramatic episode of the novel's first half. Hester, "a lonely woman, backed by the sympathies of nature" (101), goes to the Governor's Hall to argue "a mother's rights" (113) before the men who intend to take Pearl from her. This scene goes after the sympathies of contemporary readers as directly and as shrewdly as Stowe does in her novel, where the forced separation of mothers and children is restaged again and again as the surest way to get white women readers to identify with the sufferings of slaves. The brilliantly plotted intention of this episode in which Hester fights "the public" (101) to keep her child is once and for all to split Hawthorne's audience's responses from the Puritans' admonitory attitude: Victorian readers can only take Hester's side *against* the Puritans, and thus have been compelled to identify with her. Thematically, this means that they have been forced to include the Dark Heroine inside their sense of what it is to be human, even to be a mother.

Hawthorne works toward the same end in other ways. A major component of his plan could be called his strategy of narrative delay. Perhaps the most remarkable trait of the book's opening is the way it stalls and stutters before allowing the story proper to begin. We have already seen how chapter 2 restates the opening of chapter 1, by redescribing the audience before the prison door. Then chapter 2 goes on for about 300 words to wonder what this waiting throng "might be" assembled to see (49–50). Who is about to emerge from the prison? The narrative actually offers eight different answers to this question, none of which is accurate. It then keeps its audience waiting eight paragraphs more before Hester herself appears. This pattern of asking questions but delaying the answers recurs in many different contexts. Hawthorne leaves open such trivial questions as whether Hester cut her hair off, or just confined it under her cap (163), and such crucial questions as "where was [Dimmesdale's] mind" as he marches forward to give the Election Sermon after having agreed to run away with Hester (239). In a sense this pattern organizes the whole novel. In the opening scene, both Chillingworth privately and the Puritans publicly ask who is the father of Hester's infant (62, 65); the answer to this question is withheld—from Chillingworth (and the reader) until the middle, from the Puritans until the end.

Much more is at stake here than narrative suspense. One part of the reputation Puritanism had in the nineteenth century was its intolerance. Hawthorne's concern, as I have said, was with his contemporaries' assumptions, but as a means of addressing his concern he exploits the association of Puritanism with intolerance for all it is worth to him as a writer trying to complicate and enlarge those assumptions. At the heart of the Puritans' failure as interpreters of the scarlet letter is their inability to tolerate any kind of ambiguity. They cannot profit from the delay the narrative provides at the start: they "know" who is coming out of jail and how they should respond to her. When they see her—pointedly, they see only the letter she wears—Hester's appearance simply reconfirms their preconceptions. On the other hand, what Hawthorne's own audience is meant to learn from the narrative's habit of postponing answers to the questions it raises is how to suspend judgment—how, for example, to take another view of Hester. Hawthorne models this too in "The Custom-House," when he recounts how, after finding the *A*, he tried many different ways to solve the "riddle" of what it might mean (see 31–32).

Closely allied to this pattern of narrative delay are the novel's stylistic or syntactic habits. In the book's second paragraph we are told that "it may safely be assumed that" the Puritans picked a site for their prison early in Boston's history (47). Such a point, we might think, could easily have been determined; his use of this construction (I mean the syntactic one, not the jail) indicates again how much more interested he is in his contemporary audience than in New England history. Indeed, the syntactic construction stands in opposition to the jail: it opens up rather than locks in possibility. By emphasizing the uncertainty of even so factual a matter as a date, Hawthorne is calling attention to the problematic relationship between "assumption" and truth. Just as his narrative delays answers, his style withholds certainties. "We shall not take it upon us to determine," he writes in the last paragraph of chapter 1, "whether" the rose beside the prison door is merely natural, "or whether, as there is fair authority for believing," it supernaturally symbolizes Ann Hutchinson's antinomianism (48). In the first paragraph of chapter 2, he has no sooner suggested that "some noted culprit" might be about to emerge from the prison than he qualifies himself: "An inference of this kind could not so indubitably be drawn" (49). Instances of this stylistic indefiniteness could be multiplied almost indefinitely. Very little in *The Scarlet Letter* is stated as unequivocal fact. "It may be," "it might be," "perchance," "perhaps," "it seemed," "according to some," "it was reported"—these or similar locutions appear in almost every paragraph. While the Puritans cannot tolerate ambiguity, Hawthorne requires his audience to live with it. What "may safely be assumed" or what "kind of inference" should be drawn remains much of the time an explicitly open question, which is how this stylistic trait echoes the narrative one we looked at. The audience, forced in this way to abandon any privileged position as mere spectators, must become an active part of Hawthorne's interpretive community. Hawthorne separates his audience from the "simplicity" of the Puritans' responses and from the black-and-white terms of contemporary moral melodrama, and initiates them instead into the problematic realm of the "hidden mysteries" that is his subject.

"Simplicity" versus "hidden mysteries"—these are the antitheses he uses to measure the difference between the assumptions Dimmesdale takes into the woods and the knowledge which, after meeting Hester, he brings back. In terms of his "plan," the great scene between the lovers is the one for which Hawthorne has been carefully preparing his audience all along. Structurally, it occupies the same position in the novel's second half that Hester's confrontation in the Governor's Hall occupies in the first; thematically, it completes the project that he began by enabling the audience to sympathize, and thus identify, with Hester. Now he is ready dramatically to expose them to what meeting Hester in the wilderness can reveal about the truths of their own hearts.

Like the scene in which Hester fights to keep her child, her meeting with Dimmesdale in the forest evokes a paradigm readers would have met frequently in the period's best-selling melodramas. According to the biblical archetypes on which those stories relied, it is a temptation in the wilderness. *Uncle Tom's Cabin* offers a parallel scene at Simon Legree's, when Cassie, Stowe's version of the Dark Heroine and Hester's sister in passion and despair, exhorts Tom to choose a better life. With "a wild and peculiar glare" in her "large, black eyes," with "a flash of sudden energy," Cassie urges him to murder Legree and be free.[18] When Hester uses "her own energy" to exhort Dimmesdale to break with "these iron men" who "have kept thy better part in bondage too long already," she too "fix[es] her deep eyes on the minister's, and instinctively exercis[es] a magnetic power" over his spirit (197–98). "Any life is better than this," cries Cassie; Hester exclaims, "Do any thing, save to lie down and die!" (198)

There is, of course, an apparently crucial difference between these two exhortations. Cassie, full of hate, tempts Tom to murder, but Hester's voice, which sounds so full of love, seems to summon Dimmesdale toward a "new life" of "human affection and sympathy" (200). It might seem beside any point Hawthorne had in mind to note that the Decalogue equally forbids killing and committing adultery. Yet Hawthorne's novel goes on to show decisively, in its own terms, which are psychological rather than Mosaic, that the passions Hester arouses in the woods are just as destructive as Cassie's murderous rage at Legree's. Hawthorne takes his audience into the woods with Hester, but he brings them back out with Dimmesdale. Chapter 20, "The Minister in a Maze," follows him homeward, which allows Hawthorne carefully to explore the "revolution in the sphere of [his] thought and feeling" that breaks loose after he yields his "will" to "Hester's will" (217). Chapter 20 also forces a sudden change in the text's representation of the Puritans. Hawthorne abruptly individualizes them. Instead of an aggregate, admonitory audience or an iron-visaged, repressive society, they are converted into men and women, as Dimmesdale meets an aged, venerable deacon, a "poor, widowed, lonely" old mother, and a maiden "fair and pure" (217–20). In the woods Hester rejects society as scornfully as it originally exiled her, but when Dimmesdale comes out of the woods society is portrayed as individuals with sympathetically human faces. And in each encounter with these members of his congregation, Dimmesdale feels "incited to do some strange, wild, wicked thing or other" (217)—not premeditated murder, certainly, but something equally destructive of "human affection and sympathy." Dimmesdale, horrified to discover the anarchic violence of his own desires, wonders if he has somehow sold his soul to Satan in the woods. In the passage that follows, Hawthorne offers his own interpretive gloss on the meeting with Hester and states conclusively that indeed it was a temptation in the wilderness:

> The wretched minister! He had made a bargain very like it! Tempted by a dream of happiness, he had yielded himself with deliberate choice, as he had never done before, to what he knew was deadly sin. And the infectious poison of that sin had been thus rapidly diffused throughout his moral system. It had stupified all blessed impulses, and awakened into vivid life the whole brotherhood of bad ones. Scorn, bitterness, unprovoked malignity, gratuitous desire of ill, ridicule of whatever was good and holy, all awoke, to tempt, even while they frightened him. (222)

We have yet to note the real distinction between Stowe's and Hawthorne's versions of this temptation scene. If there is not finally much
difference in the kind of lawless, selfish, violent energies that fuel
Cassie's and Hester's exhortations, there is nonetheless a vast difference in the larger role that meeting the Dark Heroine plays in the novels' thematic economies. Despite Cassie's attractiveness, Tom is never
really tempted, nor is Stowe's audience. When she comes with her murderous scheme and Tom hastily replies, "Don't sell your precious soul
to the devil, that way!" Stowe's audience is reminded of what evil is;
when a few seconds later Tom asks God to "help us follow in His steps,
and love our enemies," Stowe's audience is reminded what good is. At
no point during Tom's temptation in Legree's wilderness does the narrative challenge that audience's preconceptions. Hawthorne, though,
in keeping with his pattern of openness and delay, withholds his definitive interpretation of what transpired in the woods until three chapters after Hester seduces Dimmesdale with that "dream of happiness."
Because Dimmesdale at first succumbs to the temptation, he is forced
to realize firsthand the "hidden mysteries" of his own heart: that is the
maze he gets lost in, and at the center of it is "a profounder self" (217)
than he had previously suspected.

Within this pattern—and we had better be explicit about this—Hawthorne allows Hester to seduce the audience as well. Probably every
reader's hopes for her and Dimmesdale's happiness, and something
fiercer and profounder too, are aroused when she lets down her magnificent hair in the woods. By letting desire loose inside the narrative,
Hawthorne attempts a radical challenge to the Victorian audience's
self-image. At the very start of the scene he quietly insinuates what
meeting Hester in the woods should mean: "The soul beheld its features in the mirror of the passing moment" (190). By withholding his
authoritative reading of the scene for twenty pages, he gives his audience an opportunity to follow Dimmesdale through the maze; for
when he realizes what has been let loose *in himself*, "the Reverend Mr.
Dimmesdale thus communed with himself" (221), and it is by thus
communing with his self, with his own previously hidden impulses,
that Dimmesdale discovers his "profounder self" and becomes
"another man," and "a wiser one." The conventional temptation-in-
the-wilderness scene of popular fiction, by signaling itself as such,
allowed readers to shield themselves against any disturbing response.
In Stowe's novel, the true way depends on rejecting the Dark Hero-

ine—and so remaining safe from any self-knowledge her character might reveal. Evil remains an abstraction to be resisted; Cassie is allowed to learn from Tom, but not to teach him anything. In Hawthorne's novel, though, the truth depends on communing first with Hester and then with oneself. The encounter in the woods is ultimately a *self*-recognition scene. The way it works on its audience makes lawless desire a fact of human nature that, as a fact of human nature, cannot be denied. In place of the straight lines and neat polarities of moral melodrama, Hawthorne has led his audience deep into the maze of their own hearts.[19]

II

We know who the first "reader" of *The Scarlet Letter* was, and as it happens, we also know a bit about her response. The day Hawthorne finished writing the manuscript, he finished reading it aloud to his wife. "It broke her heart," he wrote a friend, "and sent her to bed with a grievous headache—which I look upon as triumphant success!"[20] Signs of her distress are still evident in a letter she wrote to a friend a week later: "I do not know what you will think of the Romance. It is most powerful, & contains a moral as terrific & stunning as a thunderbolt. It shows that the Law cannot be broken."[21] As modern readers we may be tempted to smile here and congratulate ourselves on our increased sophistication. Despite Sophia Hawthorne's credentials— both as an intimate of the author, and as a reader herself (Melville, for example, was very impressed with her response to *Moby-Dick*)[22]—we are likely to dismiss her reading as naive. Her insistence on "the Law" sounds too much like the narrow-minded reading the "Puritans" try to impose on the story. And we have outgrown her quaint Victorian reductiveness, which values a work of art for the "moral" it supplies— as if literature, Ezra Pound wrote contemptuously in 1918, were merely "the ox-cart and post-chaise for transmitting thoughts poetic or otherwise."[23]

I want to end this essay by considering the gap between the way *The Scarlet Letter* addressed its contemporary audience and the way it seems to speak to us at the end of the twentieth century. Let me start with a reconsideration of Sophia Hawthorne's response. Behind her assertion of "the Law" is nothing like the Puritans' self-righteous smugness. They take the law for granted, but it is clear from her reactions—

the grief, the headache, the mixed emotions she betrays even a week later with words like "terrific" and "stunning"—that as a reader she has been fully open to the experience of the text. As far as the Law goes, she is clearly right about the values Hawthorne's novel ultimately privileges. It was post-Victorian writers like Henry James and Pound who taught us to look for the meaning of form in works of literature; when we approach *The Scarlet Letter* from that perspective, it seems even more inexorably, less ambiguously to affirm the Law. At the start, in the absolute middle, and again at the end the novel returns to the scaffold that represents the Law. From a strictly formal point of view, we should never have been tempted in the wilderness; the structural placement of that scene, given the logic of returning to the scaffold that the narrative has already established, is enough to indicate that in the "wild, heathen Nature of the forest" (203), we have gone astray. Of course, it is by vicariously going astray with Hester in "the mystery of the primeval forest" (183) that readers can discover the truth of their hearts—but it is from Dimmesdale, whose attempt to come home from the woods leads him too to return to the scaffold, that Hawthorne expects his audience to learn how to live with that knowledge. Even Hester eventually agrees, as we can tell from her decision to resume the letter that Dimmesdale has taught her must be revealed.

One reason to value Sophia's response is that it registers Hawthorne's radical achievement even as an apostle of the moral law. The law must be obeyed—this, in one form or another, is the moral of every genteel fiction of his time. But Hawthorne's exploration of this truth in *The Scarlet Letter* more closely resembles (and anticipates) the severe wisdom of Freud's *Civilization and Its Discontents*: the law must be obeyed, and therein lies the tragedy of our instinctual lives. Sophia's broken heart indicates that she too was seduced by Hester's "dream of happiness" in the woods. The novel's deepest power flows from the way it enacts, not simply moralizes on, its theme. When the anarchic desires that the forest represents get let loose in the novel, we want to live there. To the palpable promise of erotic fulfillment that Hester's lawless energy summons up in us we are prepared to sacrifice everything—even, to take the human fact with which the narrative immediately daunts the lovers in the woods, to sacrifice Pearl. Amidst the imperious claims of their re-aroused passion, Hester and Dimmesdale, and probably even the Victorian audience, forgot about this child. But if in the first half Hawthorne uses Pearl's presence to encourage his audience to sympathize with Hester, here he uses her absence to keep a kind of moral distance from Hester's exhortation. When Pearl comes back into view, which happens even before the lovers leave the woods, she points the way that Dimmesdale later realizes he must take. When he climbs up to the scaffold, he sacrifices his own desires to the claims of his relationships as an adult to other people: to Pearl as her father, to his parishioners as their minister, even to Hester as her partner in shame. But embracing the Law instead of Hester is hard, even tragic, as *The Scarlet Letter* almost alone among the period's fictions acknowledges. Like most best-selling novels, including *Uncle Tom's Cabin*, it ends with a recovered family: on the scaffold at the end are Dimmesdale, Hester, Pearl, and Chillingworth, finally united in public. But unlike all those other endings, Hawthorne's fully reckons the cost, in terms of an individual's instinctual desires, by which a family is achieved and maintained.

The law must be obeyed, but this is a terrific truth, not a conventional truism: Mrs. Hawthorne's reading seems both critically and emotionally sound. Yet because the terms it relies on—a moral, the Law—seem so distant from those that modern readers bring to a text, such terms also establish the cultural gap across which the novel speaks to us. For example, published modern readings of it often regret or more often simply ignore the moral that Hawthorne himself provides. We know he was pleased with his wife's reaction as an audience. We cannot say exactly how he felt about her conclusions as a critic. Presumably he knew literature could not do police work, could not lay down or enforce laws. But we also know that he wanted his work to explore and express truths. The moral he offers his audience exhorts them to the same project: "Be true! Be true! Be true! Show freely to the world, if not your worst, yet some trait whereby the worst may be inferred" (260). It is true that he offers this as only one among the "many morals" that may be drawn from the tale he has told, but this is one of those points in the text where he abandons his technique of narrative and stylistic ambiguity. Instead of offering us a number of morals to choose from, he insists, with all the unequivocality of the imperative mood, on this one. This moral does bring toward a conclusion the rhetorical project that governs Hawthorne's intentions throughout the book: to initiate contemporary readers into the truths about themselves that their culture has repressed. But in our time there remains our distrust, not to say positive distaste, for a moral. Do readers have the right of re-vision? Can we ignore or reject the author's own reading, offered inside the text itself?

Well, we could say that this enjoinment is not addressed to "us." Given the way our century began, for instance, with Freud's revelations about the truths of the human psyche, we do not approach Hawthorne's "drama of guilt and sorrow" (253) with anything like the self-image of his Victorian American readers. Since we do not share their pieties, we cannot easily appreciate the "irreverence" of the burden he puts on his imagination by tasking it to show that the scarlet woman and the saintly minister both wear the "same scorching stigma." It is analogous to the way that every modern reader already knows that Dimmesdale is Hester's lover: the "hidden mysteries" into which Hawthorne felt obliged to guide his audience so carefully are not hidden for us. The "profounder self" that Dimmesdale is a-mazed to discover, and that Hawthorne's contemporaries did not consciously recognize either, is a fact of human nature that our culture largely takes for granted. Or think how differently a Victorian and a modern reader are apt to react to Hester in that first scene. In both cases the reflexes are conditioned by cultural experience. But whereas Hawthorne's culture had conditioned his audience, as they valued the image of themselves that the genteel culture sanctioned, to reject any identification with so dark a heroine, our own cultural experience, including the high ideological status accorded the dissatisfied wife, leads today's readers to prejudge Hester, so passionate a victim of a bad marriage and a repressive society, almost antithetically.

We need not judge such differences as either for better or for worse. But we should take account of them. Americans going to Latin America have to be warned not to use their thumb and forefinger to signal "OK"—because in Mexico or Brazil that friendly sign stands for something very different. Similarly, the gestures Hawthorne uses to communicate his vision to his contemporaries speak to postmodern readers in ways he could not have anticipated. The context in which he wrote was defined by his audience's mid-nineteenth-century faiths; for our part, we cannot help but read from within the context of late-twentieth-century doubts. Thus to post-deconstructionist critics, the various maneuvers by which Hawthorne sought to recondition the responses of Victorian readers—delay, withholding, equivocation, ambiguity—may look definitive. What for Hawthorne was a means—a strategy to change his audience's preconceptions—now seems, given our preconceptions, to be an end. Within the past ten years, as could have been expected, have appeared critical readings that argue the "indeterminacy," the "illegibility," the "pervasive ambiguity" of the novel.[24] That ambiguity was a means for Hawthorne seems clear from the care he takes eventually to provide interpretive closure, as in that sequence we examined where, twenty pages after Hester's urging instinctual fulfillment in the wilderness has had a chance to work on Dimmesdale (and on us), the narrator tells us unambiguously that Dimmesdale (and we) have been seduced by our own profoundest self. But such authoritative passages, though written in the language that spoke most authoritatively to his contemporaries, fall deafly on our modern ears. Satanic bargain, deadly sin, whatever was good and holy—post-deconstructionist readers can ignore such locutions or dismiss them as inauthentic. It is an irony of literary history that Hawthorne begins by acknowledging the problem of trying to speak the truth to a culture of euphemism, which means there are many words he cannot use without "startl[ing]" his "present day" readers (51). He manages to solve that problem brilliantly, writing one of the nineteenth century's most mature explorations of adult sexuality so tactfully that only a few extremists were upset. But he could not have anticipated the problem of trying to define the truth for a culture of doubt, and so the novel cannot defend itself from the postmodern emptiness of the words it ultimately relies on to make its truths persuasive to its audience.

Feminist readings of the novel are also likely to confuse Hawthorne's means with ends. The strategic care he takes in the first third to nurture his Victorian audience's sympathy for Hester can similarly seem definitive, so that the passions she arouses in the forest can seem exemplary, the novel's ultimate act of visionary witness. Modern readers, unlike Victorian ones, are prepared to go as deep into the wilderness as Hester can take them, but are often simply unwilling to follow Dimmesdale back from the woods to the scaffold, although that is the ground, the ground of moral duty, that Victorian readers were most familiar with.[25] Never mind that the narrative decisively defines the "dream of happiness" in the woods as a "temptation"; to such recent readers, Dimmesdale's decision to stand with Hester in "shame" rather than live with her in "joy," his decision to "reveal" the scarlet letter, does not look like moral heroism, but rather psychological cowardice or emotional betrayal. When Hawthorne makes Dimmesdale Christlike in this scene of "triumphant ignominy before the people" (257)—

he submits to "the will which God hath granted [him]"; he forgives his enemy; he stands (in fact, we are told explicitly that though he tottered on the way to the scaffold, he "did not fall!") "as one who, in the crisis of acutest pain, had won a victory" (251-55)—the novel again relies on the most definitive terms available at the time to convince a contemporary audience. Uncle Tom dies a similarly Christ-like death when he wins his "victory" at the end of Stowe's novel. But the Christian scaffolding with which Hawthorne props up Dimmesdale's actions no longer resonates with us. For many modern readers, Dimmesdale dies—and publishes the truth—in vain.

Certainly for most readers, in Hawthorne's time and ours, the tragic waste of Hester's powers and passions is what resonates most deeply as we close the tale. Doubtless it was this that broke Mrs. Hawthorne's heart. The novel redeems this loss, however, in two ways. Neither is the redemption that contemporary readers may have been looking for. When Sambo and Quimbo witness Tom's martyrdom at Legree's, we are told explicitly that by this means their souls are saved.[26] Yet we are not told about the eternal fate of Hester's soul. (Indeed, Hawthorne leaves out this detail so conspicuously that we seem warranted in thinking that his use of Christian iconography at Dimmesdale's death is largely a means too: his means of giving Dimmesdale's act of "being true" the highest possible stature in his audience's eyes.) Rather, the most immediate event that redeems Hester's, Dimmesdale's, and our anguish at being on the scaffold instead of in the woods is the earthly fate of Pearl's self. By living up to his responsibilities as her father, Dimmesdale frees her from her "errand as a messenger of anguish" to "grow up amid human joy and sorrow" (256). This is probably the one place where the novel backs down from its commitment to tell the truth, however tragic—for the notion that parents, by doing the right thing, can somehow spare their children from the tragedies of their own lives is hopelessly naive, however attractive. The happy ending permitted Pearl is another place where the novel would have spoken more convincingly to Victorian than to modern readers.

The novel, though, does not quite end with the prospect of Pearl as "married, and happy, and mindful of her mother" (262). It goes on to describe Hester's earthly fate as well. Having learned from Dimmesdale how to "be true," Hester settles permanently in Boston and puts on the letter "of her own free will" (263). To modern readers who see the letter as "illegible" or as only the badge of Hester's "victimization by patriarchy,"[27] this ending must seem absurd or grotesque. But in terms of the novel's rhetorical project, the most redemptive thing that happens when Hester resumes the *A* is the growth of a new interpretive community around it. As we noted, Dimmesdale's revelation of the scarlet letter confounds rather than communicates to the Puritans who make up the novel's internal audience. At the very end, however, another group of viewers emerges to see the *A* in a wholly new way: "The scarlet letter ceased to be a stigma which attracted the world's scorn and bitterness, and became a type of something to be sorrowed over, and looked upon with awe, yet with reverence too" (263).

Like the first time we see someone seeing the letter—when Hawthorne puts it on his own breast in "The Custom-House"—this last time is exemplary. This is how to read the scarlet letter: with sorrow for human frailty, awe at the hidden mysteries of the heart, reverence for another soul as equally human. By interpeting the letter in this spirit, the community that gathers around Hester at the end forms a third term to mediate between the repressive injustices of society and the lawless desires of the wilderness. The bases for this community's interpretation are sympathy and self-knowledge, and in their sensitivity as interpreters we see the basis for the belief that Hester prophetically embodies at the end: that "a new truth would be revealed, in order to establish the whole relation between man and woman on a surer ground of mutual happiness" (263). Is not this "new truth" the truth that Hawthorne has tried to express in *The Scarlet Letter*? If the profounder self he reveals in the wilderness had been recognized and rightly understood, the Puritans never would have banished Hester. In fact, if we think about it, is it not likely that if the needs and desires of that profounder self had been acknowledged, Hester and Chillingworth never would have married? Hester, we have to remember, had to repress the truth about herself and her own desires to marry Chillingworth in the first place, and in a sense it is from that first act of repression that the tragedy of her life follows.

But if the novel reaches interpretive closure at the end, in this sympathetic community's reading of the *A*, it does not reach stasis. Restoring the status quo is not the end of Hawthorne's rhetorical project. For just as the ultimate interpretive community in the novel has been brought into existence by the experience of the tale itself, so Hawthorne hopes to change his audience by the "new truth" he has revealed and carefully enabled them to experience by reading the tale. The novel's very last line leaves his readers staring at the *A*. It leaves them, that is, with a project of their own: to join the community that sees the letter as the sign that speaks to all of us about our own profounder self. What Mrs. Hawthorne read in the novel—that life is tragic, but redeemed by moral significance—would qualify her, I think, for membership in that community. Self-knowledge and sympathy are not outdated virtues, but it is legitimate to ask whether many modern readers are interested in belonging to the particular interpretive community into which Hawthorne sought to turn his contemporary audience. He addresses himself to their nineteenth-century assumptions and leads them to the new truths revealed at the end, in the woods and on the scaffold. We start with different assumptions. His novel is bound to lead us to other, different ends.

Notes

Parts of this essay are derived from my chapter on Hawthorne and *The Scarlet Letter* in *Authorship and Audience: Literary Performance and the American Renaissance* (Princeton: Princeton UP, 1991).

1. See Stanley Fish, "Interpreting the *Variorum*," *Critical Inquiry* 2 (1976): 465–85; also Fish, *Is There a Text in This Class? The Authority of Interpretive Communities* (Cambridge: Harvard UP, 1980).

2. Walter J. Ong, "The Writer's Audience Is Always a Fiction," *PMLA* 90 (1975): 9–21.

3. More than one kind of reading public was available to Hawthorne. Henry Nash Smith has suggested distinguishing the readers of the early 1850s by "brow levels"—i.e., high-, middle-, and lowbrow audiences (*Democracy and the Novel* [New York: Oxford UP, 1978] 6–10). And David S. Reynolds's *Beneath the American Renaissance* (New York: Knopf, 1988) shows us how the literary expectations and appetites of the type of audience that Smith would call "lowbrow" differed from the values we associate with the genteel culture. I am assuming that Hawthorne wrote *The Scarlet Letter* for the same kind of audience that had read his tales and sketches for twenty-five years in such "middlebrow" publications as *Godey's*; in "The Custom-House," for instance, when he describes the place where his imagination works, the environment is that of an unmistakably genteel parlor.

4. See Hans Robert Jauss, "Literary History as a Challenge to Literary Theory," in *Toward an Aesthetic of Reception*, trans. Timothy Bahti (Minneapolis: U Minnesota P, 1982). Jauss's great contribution is to remind us that at any given literary-

historical moment, readers approach a new text from within a certain "horizon of expectations," which will determine their response to a work of art; once read, a text can in turn begin to reshape or expand that horizon, so that at subsequent literary-historical moments it can be read in previously unthought of ways (see 21–25).

5. Chapter 3 is called "The Recognition." Since it begins by describing Chillingworth's deformed appearance as he emerges from the forest to see Hester on the scaffold, while chapter 2 ended by describing the man Hester had married as "slightly deformed" (*The Scarlet Letter*, ed. William Charvat et al. [Columbus: Ohio State UP, 1962] 58), the novel tempts its reader to jump to the conclusion that *this* is the recognition. For Hester and Chillingworth to see each other after two years in such a setting is a dramatic recognition, but *the* recognition occurs much later in the chapter: when Dimmesdale speaks to Hester, and Pearl somehow recognizes her father's voice: "The poor baby . . . directed its hitherto vacant gaze towards Mr. Dimmesdale, and held up its little arms, with a half pleased, half plaintive murmur" (67). Since the immediate question of the chapter—for Chillingworth, for the Puritans, and for the uninitiated reader—is who is Pearl's father, Hawthorne is thus very subtly rewarding readers who do not jump to interpretive conclusions, who keep open a question like "What does the recognition mean?" Of course, readers who cannot delay interpretive closure will not recognize the recognition. Throughout my essay, references to *The Scarlet Letter* will be to the Ohio State edition and will be cited in parentheses in my text.

6. See his letters to J. T. Fields, January 20, 1850, and to Horatio Bridge, February 4, 1850, in *Nathaniel Hawthorne: The Letters, 1843–1853*, ed. Thomas Woodson et al. (Columbus: Ohio State UP, 1985) 307–8, 311–12.

7. *Letters, 1843–1853* 322.

8. The most ingenious recent advocate for reading the novel as an examination of colonial Puritanism is Michael J. Colacurcio; see his "Footsteps of Ann Hutchinson: The Context of *The Scarlet Letter*," *ELH* 39 (1972): 459–94, and "'The Woman's Own Choice': Sex, Metaphor, and the Puritan 'Sources' of *The Scarlet Letter*," in *New Essays on "The Scarlet Letter,"* ed. Michael J. Colacurcio (Cambridge: Cambridge UP, 1985) 101–36.

9. I am not so much borrowing Fish's idea of "interpretive communities" here as trying to co-opt it. Hawthorne would have liked Fish's phrase but not his relativism. For him there is a right and a wrong interpretive community. The Puritans' reading of the scarlet letter defines the wrong one. Yet his faith in the possibility of a definitive interpretation—one that finds, not makes meaning—is announced at the very start of "The Custom-House," where he says he writes for "the few who will understand him, better than most of his school-mates and life-

mates" (35). The community adumbrated here eventually emerges, as we will see, within the text itself.

10. To develop my analysis of how Hawthorne's novel addresses his audience's preoccupations, I will be comparing *The Scarlet Letter* to *Uncle Tom's Cabin.* Because my emphasis is on the way Hawthorne's vision of human nature set him outside and at odds with those preconceptions, the comparison may seem an invidious one, a mere reformulation of what Jane Tompkins refers to as a "long tradition of academic parochialism" that "assigns Hawthorne and Melville the role of heroes, the sentimental novelists the role of villains" (*Sensational Designs: The Cultural Work of American Fiction* [New York: Oxford UP, 1985] 125, 149). That is not my intention. The contempt Hawthorne could at moments feel for the contemporary audience that made "sentimental novels" the best-selling fiction of his time and place is notorious these days and certainly has to be included in our understanding of his hypostatization of his audience. But comparing Hawthorne's and Stowe's novel does not require one to assent to his frustrated vilification of "that damned mob of scribbling women." I am in complete agreement with what Tompkins says elsewhere, that "the work of the sentimental writers is complex and significant in ways *other than* those that characterize the established masterpieces" such as *The Scarlet Letter* (126). (I have registered my own appreciation for the greatness of Stowe's novel in "Mothers, Husbands and *Uncle Tom,*" *Georgia Review* 38 [1984]: 129–44.) "Conventionality" is also a term with many possible referents: if we were to focus on the politics of Hawthorne's and Stowe's novels rather than on what Hawthorne defined as his central thematic concern, the truth of the human heart, I could be comparing the radicalism of *Uncle Tom's Cabin* to the conventionality of *The Scarlet Letter* (see, for example, Sacvan Bercovitch, "The A-Politics of Ambiguity in *The Scarlet Letter,*" *New Literary History* 19 [1988]: 629–54). What my comparison does depend on, however, is the cultural-historical legitimacy of Hawthorne's belief that his conception of the human self was in conflict with the genteel self-image that Stowe's readers found reflected and confirmed in her novel. While Stowe brilliantly challenges her audience's assumptions about a social evil, Hawthorne is trying to complicate and change that audience's assumptions about themselves.

11. The dramatization was written by George L. Aikens. The ascent into heaven was an impressive piece of stagecraft—and an impressive instance of Victorian faith, which did not require wires and a winch to make the trick believable. Even in Stowe's novel, Tom twice has a vision of Eva being directly translated, in a radiant cloud of glory, into heaven (*Uncle Tom's Cabin* [New York: Library of America, 1982] 368 and 406–7).

12. This chapter's title is another instance of the kind of punning in which

Hawthorne engages in "The Recognition"; once again, the reader who suspends closure is rewarded.

13. Hawthorne, Preface to the 1851 edition of *Twice-Told Tales*, ed. Roy Harvey Pearce et al. (Columbus: Ohio State UP, 1974) 6. That Hawthorne felt fiction had to tell the truth is an idea that appears in many places throughout his work. In the preface to *The House of the Seven Gables*, for instance, he writes that even fiction that claims the "latitude" of Romance "sins unpardonably" if it "swerve[s] aside from the truth of the human heart" (*The House of the Seven Gables*, ed. William Charvat et al. [Columbus: Ohio State UP, 1965] 1).

14. Hawthorne, Preface, *The Snow-Image* (1852), in *The Snow-Image and Uncollected Tales*, ed. Roy Harvey Pearce et al. (Columbus: Ohio State UP, 1974) 4.

15. Hawthorne repeats this passage at the end, when he describes the source of Dimmesdale's oratorical power in the Election Day sermon: "If the auditor listened intently, and for the purpose, he could detect the same cry of pain. What was it? The complaint of a human heart, sorrow-laden, perchance guilty, telling its secret, whether of guilt or sorrow, to the great heart of mankind; beseeching its sympathy or forgiveness,—at every moment,—in each accent,—and never in vain! It was this profound and continual undertone that gave the clergyman his most appropriate power" (243-44). Hawthorne's repetition of this idea, not to mention the evident earnestness of the passage itself, indicates how crucial to him was the ideal of sympathy for mutual human frailty as the basis of the bond between author and audience. I do not have space in this essay to contrast this with the basis on which Emerson put the relation between himself as speaker and his American audience; suffice it to say that it was diametrically opposed. To Emerson, every heart vibrates, not to human frailty, but to godlike self-reliance; the power of the Emersonian orator flows from the way he addresses himself to "the better part" of every auditor, not the worst. I point this out just to indicate that if one draws a wider circle around Hawthorne's available audience than I limit myself to—if one were to include the people who listened so enthusiastically to Emerson in 1850 as well as those who read genteel fiction—one would still be staring at the problem Hawthorne knew he was up against: that his truths of the human heart were at odds with the popular assumptions of his culture.

16. See Barbara Welter, "The Cult of True Womanhood: 1820-1860," *American Quarterly* 18 (1966): 151-74.

17. See *Uncle Tom's Cabin*, ch. 4, "An Evening in Uncle Tom's Cabin" 32-44.

18. *Uncle Tom's Cabin* 461-63.

19. Chillingworth is vouchsafed such a chance as well. Just before she seeks out Dimmesdale in the woods, Hester goes to talk with Chillingworth at the seashore. Here, too, meeting Hester represents an opportunity to see one's self: "The unfortunate physician . . . lifted his hands with a look of horror, as if he had beheld

some frightful shape, which he could not recognize, usurping the place of his own image in a glass. It was one of those moments—which sometimes occur only at the interval of years—when a man's moral aspect is faithfully revealed to his mind's eye. Not improbably, he had never before viewed himself as he did now" (172). Hawthorne's emphases here underscore the centrality of this kind of self-recognition scene to his project in the novel.

20. Hawthorne to Horatio Bridge, February 4, 1850, *Letters, 1843–1853* 311.

21. Sophia Hawthorne to Mary Mann, February 12, 1850, quoted ibid. 313.

22. See Melville's letter to Sophia Hawthorne, January 8, 1852, *The Letters of Herman Melville*, ed. M. R. Davis and W. H. Gilman (New Haven: Yale UP, 1960) 145–47.

23. Ezra Pound, "A Retrospect," rpt. in *Literary Essays of Ezra Pound*, ed. T. S. Eliot (New York: New Directions, 1968) 11.

24. These epithets are from, respectively, Millicent Bell's "The Obliquity of Signs: *The Scarlet Letter*," *Massachusetts Review* 23 (1982): 9–26; Norman Bryson's "Hawthorne's Illegible Letter," in *Teaching the Text*, ed. Susanne Kappeler and Norman Bryson (London: Routledge, 1983) 92–108, rpt. in *Nathaniel Hawthorne's "The Scarlet Letter,"* ed. Harold Bloom (New York: Chelsea, 1986) 81–95; and Evan Carton's *The Rhetoric of American Romance* (Baltimore: Johns Hopkins UP, 1985) 191–227.

25. Recent critics who find the book's imaginative center with Hester in the woods or who reject Dimmesdale's revelation on the scaffold include Nina Baym, *The Shape of Hawthorne's Career* (Ithaca: Cornell UP, 1976) 123–51; and David Leverenz, "Mrs. Hawthorne's Headache: Reading *The Scarlet Letter*," *Nineteenth-Century Fiction* 37 (1983): 552–75.

26. Stowe, *Uncle Tom's Cabin* 481–82.

27. This is the feminist reading offered by Cynthia S. Jordan, *Second Stories: The Politics of Language, Form, and Gender in Early American Fictions* (Chapel Hill: U of North Carolina P, 1989) 152–72.

Poetry Readers and Reading in the 1890s: Emily Dickinson's First Reception

WILLIS BUCKINGHAM

When Emily Dickinson's *Poems* first appeared in 1890, her reluctant Boston publisher, Thomas Niles of Roberts Brothers, wondered whether his firm could afford to underwrite even a small edition of 500 copies.[1] Within three months the book had elicited well over 100 reviews, and Roberts Brothers was shipping its sixth printing. By decade's end, sales of that first volume alone had reached 10,000; two additional collections of poems and one of letters accounted for another 10,000 books sold. The 600 notices her books received are recently collected in my *Emily Dickinson's Reception in the 1890s: A Documentary History*.[2] These reviews demonstrate that Dickinson's *Poems* occasioned an immediate and remarkable response from magazinists and journalists of the day. During that first decade of publication the Amherst poet was brought and held in prominence by a community of some 500 commentators who contributed reviews, book trade news, and literary gossip to papers and journals throughout the country. Hers was distinctly a "reviewers' book," a case of readers dictating to the book trade led by professional readers.[3]

Having the early reviews in hand corrects the long-standing belief that Dickinson could not find an appreciative audience until the twentieth century.[4] These readers' reports also tell us how end-of-the-century reviewers formulate norms of valuation and define poet-reader relations. In so doing, they illuminate the readership to which Dickinson herself belonged. Those who write about her in the nineties are only, on average, about fifteen years her junior. Nor are the reviewers all male; forty percent of the signed reviews are by women, a percentage that probably held overall.

The focus of this study is not on ways Dickinson was first taught or studied or on how these documents reveal schools of criticism. Rather, in drawing on all known writing about the poet from the decade, it seeks what is common among poetry audiences as their fulfillment conditions for the reading of verse. The attention here is to Dickinson's first reviewers less in their roles as arbiters than as describers (and interpreters) of the social experience of poetry available to readers of their time. In their extent and diversity, these documents provide a broadly based perspective on nineties' poetry users and their shared interests and satisfactions.

More particularly, this essay highlights an often unrecognized feature of nineteenth-century literary activity: the way in which poetry reading, though taking place in solitude, joined itself to other social activities, especially communion between like-minded persons. According to the interpretive logic of these documents, poetry reading at its best creates an intimacy between the reader and the poet, a sacramentalized society of two. Verse reading also defines (and in the eyes of some reviewers, may slightly redefine) a larger community: those persons already loosely bonded as the "poetry lovers" for whom the reviewers speak. Nineties' descriptions of these dynamics between reader and writer and among readers underscore the processes by which literature enters people's lives and by which reading communities and their values are shaped with the help of texts.[5]

It is not as easy as it might seem, a century later, to give these voices from the nineties a well-considered hearing. Their statements have long struck modern readers as quaint critical baby-talk, threaded through with analytically useless terms like "genius" and "sympathy." As Joyce Carol Oates observes, we are more profoundly separated from the Victorians than from earlier literary communities. This disjunction, she notes, is especially acute in language: "We presumably share a common language with our [Victorian] ancestors but much of our vocabulary—such words as 'soul,' 'eternity,' 'subservience,' 'dependence'—even 'lady'—even 'sin'—is irrevocably altered."[6] Opaque as "genius" and "sympathy" seem today, they encode the normative satisfactions of a historically distinct and influential group of professional poetry readers.[7] By means of such terms as these, nineties commentators intend to reveal and shape the poetry desires of their generation.[8]

"Genius" and "sympathy" are the two most frequent and powerful words in Dickinson's first readers' vocabulary of praise. They refer to the mind and to the heart, the centers of enjoyment most often referenced in these documents. Reviewers also prominently mention aesthetic pleasure. But their admiration for technique is only as an adjunct to inspired thought and feeling. The true poet, says the Springfield (Mass.) *Sunday Republican*, will use a technical device such as rhythm "as an instrument and not as an object of attainment" (178).[9] The desired poetical goals remain thought and feeling, to the poetic expression of which some critics believe song and sound are indispensable. Indeed, when Dickinson is faulted, it is almost always for her technical irregularities.[10] However, form for her reviewers is ancillary satisfaction, of mind and heart, rather than a sufficient pleasure in itself.

Interest in "affect" holds as true for those critics praising Dickinson's "genius" as for those commending her "sympathy." "Genius" occurs in nearly one hundred notices, often in their first paragraph. The *Boston Saturday Evening Gazette* writes of Dickinson's verses that they "are the outcome of the genius of an accomplished woman" (33). Phrases suggestive of originality and enthrallment accompany the appearance of this word: "witchery of genius," "rare and original genius," "so singular a genius," "the erratic and unconfinable genius," "wonderful and strange genius," "the surprises of genius," and a genius whose trait is the "startling abruptness of the seer." For one writer she has "too much genius and too little flesh and blood," and to another she is a "genius without talent," but on no characterization of the new poet is there greater accord than on this. And in Dickinson's case "genius" is not a term reviewers wait for her second or third book to validate, for the word appears with equal frequency throughout the decade. With her first slim book she skips *cum* and *magna* and goes right to *summa*.[11]

T. W. Higginson, throughout the nineties, praises Dickinson above all for her "high thoughts." Many follow his lead but not in the sense of ideas as arguable propositions or mere opinion. As Arlo Bates says, "Her theology is of a sort to puzzle metaphysicians, and yet one finds it often most suggestive and stimulating" (32). It is a "high sort of seeing" and contains elements of excitement, risk, surprise, intensity, awe, and even suggestions of the occult. For nineties reviewers, Dickinson's ideas are fresh, original, intense, condensed, oracular, and unhackneyed.[12] Innumerable references to "power" appear in this context, as do indicators of strangeness and suddenness ("barbaric," "startling,") and words that combine the two in ignition imagery: the "fire" and "sparks" of genius (243, 391).

This sense of "truth" as "superb surprise" parallels Dickinson's own delight in poetic discourse as revelation "at a slant" and tallies with her description of poetry as untranslatable experience, as "Sumptuous destitution," and as those moments "when abroad seems close." It derives from Transcendentalist ideas of genius and theories of inspiration. The proof of genius is that suggestive, even extravagant statement can occasion illumination and profound inner affect. Nineties reviewers steadily apply this model to Dickinson, describing her poems ballistically as the "swift revelations" of "lyrical projectiles" (348, 336), frequently comparing her to other American sages and seers: to Thoreau in fourteen notices, to Whitman in twenty, and to Emerson in fifty-six. The *Boston Sunday Herald* begins its review, "Madder rhymes one has seldom seen—scornful disregard of poetic technique could hardly go farther—and yet there is about the book a fascination, a power, a vision that enthralls you, and draws you back to it again and again" (34).

Startling originality, strangeness, and vision are some of the reviewers' most frequent terms for Dickinson's attractiveness to them. A related cluster contains words associated with masculinity: strength, power, vigor, and magnetism. In her study of antebellum fiction reviewing, Nina Baym remarks that on the subject of style

> the most common word of praise was "vigorous," and along with it came such related terms as animated, powerful, terse, bold, nervous, vivid, vivacious, spirited, warm, elastic, impassioned, salient, racy, energetic, original, direct, expressive, sprightly. The second most common operative concept was most often expressed by the word "graceful," along with its relatives: melodious, fluent, flowing, harmonious, sweet, cadenced.

She points out that "vigor in style was associated with the masculine, grace with the feminine" and that when fiction reviewers had to choose between the two they preferred vigor.[13] Nineties reviewers are intensely aware of Dickinson writing as a woman, yet most of the adjectives of praise for her thought and oracular manner suggest that the poet's genius has masculine components. As the *Philadelphia Evening Bulletin* put it, "Her verse . . . was epigrammatic in quality and almost masculine in the vigor of its underlying thought" (385).

Not surprisingly, critics relate the other central interest of Dickinson's poems, their emotional expressiveness, to her womanhood. "They are the poems," said the *Christian Inquirer*, "of a woman, in that their inspiration is that of subtle feeling rather than philosophic thought." Especially disclosing Dickinson's heart is her "comprehending sympathy" (127, 128). "Sympathy" is a frequent word in reviews of the nineties, one fundamental to the friendship ethos of nineteenth-century literary culture. It reflects a deep sense of bonding, of inner sharing, and of spiritual knowing and kindredness discovered with nature, between persons, and as between friends, between author and reader.

When the nineties reviewers give so much attention to their subject author's personal traits, as they do with Dickinson's sympathy, they are not substituting shallow filiopietism for the critic's job of work. They are sketching the poet's implied character, and in so doing they are talking about their experience of intimacy with the speaker of the poems and the "best self" in themselves that that experience brings forth. When reviewers remark on the Amherst poet's "sympathy," whether the immediate context is her empathy with nature or with those who suffer, the implied larger reference is to readers' pleasure in like responding to like, their spirits vibrating with the soul of the writer.

In other words, reviewers feel themselves "supposed." Dickinson evokes for them pleasures similar to those produced by delineation of character in nineteenth-century fiction with its demand for psychological characterization wherein "human passions respond to their own description." "For every man recognizing in himself the elements of character delineated," *Harper's* had declared in 1860, "recognizes also the fidelity of the picture of their inevitable operation in life—sees himself openly revealed—his secret sympathies, impulses, ambitions—his vices, his virtues, his temptations; and follows with terrible fascination the course of his undeveloped future – passes thoughtful and alarmed, and hangs back upon the very edge of sorrow and destruction."[14] Dickinson's "very great power," reports the Chicago *Figaro*, "thus concentrated, has laid bare many emotions that we all hide deep down in our hearts, thoughts . . . we hardly are conscious of thinking until these vivid words light up with flashes here and there that deep, dark undercurrent of life from which arise, almost unbidden, the best and the worst that is in us" (118).

In associating poetry that "breathes" with human presence, these Dickinson readers mirror the affectivist aesthetic of Matthew Arnold, who valued poetry because of its direct appeal, in his words, "to the great primary human affections: to those elementary feelings which subsist permanently in the race, and which are independent of time."[15] These responses also reflect one of the chief pleasures associated with novel reading, in which "deep emotion called up on another's behalf was morally uplifting."[16]

At least provisionally, Dickinson's reviewers tend to keep mental and emotional responses to poetry distinct, as if they are separate poles of experience, as different as male and female. Thus, the issue of Dickinson's femininity is never far from their minds. Reviewers are sure Dickinson is a genius, and there is no doubt about her womanliness, yet with many models of male genius they had but few of undoubted female genius. They had Sappho, but among modern examples there were George Sand, George Eliot, Harriet Beecher Stowe, and Charlotte Brontë, all of whom were strong in thought and all of whose work was regarded as thematically unfeminine. Poetry commentators of the 1890s speak of Dickinson as fiction reviewers had of George Sand in the 1840s: "Next to the pleasure of talking about one's-self to a sympathizing listener, is the expression of one's secret thoughts by another and a superior mind."[17] The omnipresence of words of power and their contiguity with the word "genius" suggest that the stunning epigrammatic force of Dickinson's thought fits easily into the male model of genius foremost in readers' minds. The *Figaro*'s review of the first volume begins: "Strange product of heredity, environment and climate are these profound, far-reaching, often unmusical 'poems' of Emily Dickinson's. They are instinct with a woman's sensitiveness, and yet are strong with the fearlessness of a man. With sudden flashes of genius," it continues, "she touches the very heart of things" (118).

If these readers enjoy the almost masculine flash and force of her thought, Dickinson also provokes in them constantly heightening sympathies, leading to uplifting communion with her. Realizing Dickinson spiritually is indistinct from appreciating what they believe her presence is founded in, her female "nature." Her poems, they readily admit, lack feminine grace and finish in their forms of expression. But everywhere they have womanly feeling, as the *Independent* claims about her poem on her second baptism into maturity, "I'm ceded, I stopped being theirs" (53). *Godey's Magazine* notes that the poems are not only womanly and feminine; they have "housewifeliness" (502). This strong sense of gender derives partly from Dickinson's focus on themes common to female verse, such as womanhood, home, human relationships, melancholy, and death. For this community of readers, she is the very model of retiring womanhood, strong in endurance and fortitude, capable of intense feeling for nature, able to discriminate among and tellingly render the various states of the human soul. With the precision of a woman genius (ten critics compare her to Emily Brontë in this respect), her poetry expresses, at its best, what the nineties assume is a characteristically feminine sensitivity to human feeling.

Some reviewers also respond to her as a "type" of woman in a more restricted sense. William Dean Howells's influential nineties review describes the new poet in terms of local color portraiture: her native themes and her "heart of full womanhood" derive from "tendencies inherent in the New England, or the Puritan, spirit" (77, 74).[18] Henry Lyman Koopman, writing for the magazine of Brown University, argues that qualities that appear now as only idiosyncratic to Dickinson will, as the race advances, emerge as general characteristics of womankind. Dickinson prefigures, Koopman continues, what women in literature would soon make plainer: "Woman is at once more conservative and more lawless than man; more abandoned both to love and to hate; more intense in imagination and sympathy, but narrower; capable of an apparently intellectual enthusiasm that really springs from the affections" (512).

Others find Dickinson hauntingly expressive of feminine repression. The New York *Commercial Advertiser* attributes her poems' "strange visions" and their "extreme hunger" for "human companionship" to "her woman nature" (85). Gertrude Meredith, writing a poem in tribute, confesses:

I hold her volume in my hand,
With half my mind I snatch its words:
(The other half enough affords
For listening and answer bland).

She was a woman, too, it seems,
Whom life not wholly satisfied;
She loved: more heartily, she died;
To die's the keener in her dreams.

And I, who flagged, my zeal renew:
The trivial's phantom-terrors flee
This witness of reality.
I can live more since death's so true. (129)

Caroline Healey Dall, prominent in the women's rights movement, is among a dozen nineties reviewers who connect Dickinson with Marie Bashkirtseff, a cosmopolitan Russian painter whose posthumous diary had just been published, candidly revealing her experience of gender repression. Bashkirtseff's *Journal*, the moment-to-moment record of feelings and impulses, read like a novel and (according to its 1890 translator) described a woman "at odds with destiny, as such a soul must needs be, when endowed with great powers and possibilities ... continually thwarted by the impediments and restrictions of sex."[19] "Quite as remarkable a revelation" as Bashkirtseff's, writes Caroline Dall, "is to be found in the poems of Emily Dickinson." Like Gertrude Meredith, Dall finds Dickinson a catalyst for thinking about women's roles and women's fate. It is necessary to know more "of the poet's history," she says in her review, because "face to face with life and love, but above all with death and disappointment has this woman come. Nothing of human experience has she scorned, nothing evaded, and so critically has she tested what she has endured that few people will understand what they find in her alembic. Every line challenges much thinking. . . . The women who have this book in their hands have a good deal to think of" (121, 122).

This reading of the new poet as specifically revelatory for women unites admiration for both emotional and intellectual—and what corresponded in the logic of the period to female and male—sources of power. There is no question to reviewers that Dickinson speaks as a woman—in her style, which had reserve and (some dared to maintain) inner harmony; in her subjects, the domestic and the private; and in her tone, exalted, piquant, and pure. She also has spontaneity, "the birthright gift," according to the New York *Critic*, "of the lyric poet and of woman" (416). She has, above all, a woman's passions and sensitivity. But her words also carry rough, stunning, epigrammatic directness, just as her thought has the attraction, freshness, intelligence, and orphic force of assured genius.[20]

By the nineties, in other words, whatever strengths poets draw from, whether those of mind or heart, their office is to exert affective force. Poetry is a "hotted up" medium; when it works, something within reels and stumbles. As Dickinson herself puts it, describing the mysterious power of honest passionate language:

By homely gift and hindered Words
The human heart is told
Of Nothing—
"Nothing" is the force
That renovates the World.[21]

For her first commentators as well, even at its most visionary and cerebral, poetic expression remains ontologically separate from textuality, from words as impersonal objects. Arlo Bates describes the Amherst poet's "high muse" as an ability to express, androgynously, "real emotional thought" (29). Delineation of affect, not meaning, is her reviewers' goal.[22] When both genius and sympathy are affectively felt, reading becomes a series of pleasing aftermaths: on the genius side, a kinetic push of forceful mental presence; on the sympathy side, a warmth or bonding response to personal presence. Writing as a craft can be studied and criticized, but these professional readers place distinctively literary experience, with poetry as it highest form, well beyond scientific analysis; one cannot parse while reeling from a blow or opening to love.

These nineties readers also isolate poetry from science by insisting on its mysteriousness. Dickinson's "high sort of seeing" contains elements of excitement, risk, surprise, intensity, awe, all with suggestions of the occult. Lilian Whiting, a frequent reviewer of Dickinson and a woman with a lifelong interest in spiritualism, remarks on mediumship when she finds the poems "profound in thought and full of almost startling divination and insight" (26). There is in Dickinson's poems, says the *Boston Evening Transcript*, "a strange magic of meaning so ethereal that one must apprehend rather than comprehend it"

(61). Her poems seem an enactment of breathed-forth fervor and passion within the affiliatory presence of moved spectators. For H. P. Schauffler in the *Amherst Literary Monthly*, it is not insights but "hope, remorse, anger, patriotism; these all seem to live and breathe out their various lights and shadows under the guiding influence of her magnetic touch" (226). This prospect of achieving "inner room" companionship with the poet is similarly imagined by the *Boston Transcript*: "Having been allowed by Mrs. Todd to enter into the outer chambers of knowledge of this poet in the first and second volumes, the door is opened in the third into an inner, a sacred room, whose air is the very breath of a human spirit" (458). The vestal, temple imagery elsewhere associated with her oracular thought here expresses expectations for personalized devotional experience, yearnings for deepened human relationships, modeled on that between Christ and the individual.[23] The reader and poet become secret friends. Louise Chandler Moulton confesses to her *Boston Herald* readers, "With every page I turn and return I grow more and more in love" (37).

Reflecting this intimate friendship ethos, Dickinson's publisher, Roberts Brothers, regularly issued her 1890 *Poems* in delicate gift-book bindings. By sacramentalizing poetry reading (the best selves of "devoted" readers enjoying heart-to-heart communication with nearly divine poet-friends and preceptors), reviewers situate the reading experience at the farthest remove from rational explanation. This extreme subjectivizing of imaginative experience claims for poetry reading a world apart from Darwin and Spencer. Facing the supposedly superior objectivity of science and its increasing demands for objectivity and verifiability, critics move poetry to the sanctuary, hoping the temple doors will close behind them. Dickinson's gnomic accents accord well with this need to mystify the office of poetry. It is with the free spirits—the brilliant, untrammeled, and the enigmatical, like Blake and Emerson, Whitman and Browning—that the strength and originality of her thought reminds her first readers.[24] She is a refreshingly aboriginal presence in a literary world that already has as many "excellent formalists" as it needs (182). The *Christian Register*, which begins its review comparing Dickinson to an Aeolian harp, concludes that just as Browning and Emerson finally elude us, so "we cannot parse or analyze [her poems]." They "usher us into the deeper mysteries" (134, 135).

This strategy for dealing with the threat of science italicizes an ambivalence implicit in these reviews: that poetry, in a democratic age, is increasingly an elitist diversion. In terms of readership percentages, poetry during the century had steadily given way to fiction. But the review columns show little egalitarian interest in teaching poetry appreciation. As the poetry-reading life becomes increasingly personalized and sacralized, the less amenable to direct instruction (through explication) it becomes. The ability to take poetic pleasures becomes an unearned grace; one has it or does not. Though Dickinson's "odd" life draws attention, her typical notice primarily delineates the responses of the reviewer as a qualified reader. Reviews consist of brief excerpts from poems, each tagged with such impressionistic comment as "noble and inspiring" (107). Readers learn not how to read but whether they belong among "poetry Lovers." When their responses tally with the reviewers', they are confirmed as sensitive readers. The *Amherst Literary Monthly* is typical in phrasing its remarks as polite exclamations: "Note the dainty touch" and "Mark the power of naturalness both in thought and expression. Why you feel perfectly at home when that thought, clad in its simple, unadorned attire, greets your mind" (150). The way to write a review in the nineties is to identify the various affects a new volume of verse evokes, illustrating each through brief quotation.

Literary litmus tests cannot enlarge poetry's potential audience; they serve, rather, to confirm the reading fitness and practice of those who consult reviews, a community already presumably experienced and confident as readers of verse. Reviewers assume alliance with their readers on the basis of mutual love of good poetry, and almost none of them, at the outset of Dickinson's debut, predict a wide readership for the new poet. Her intellect seems too bold and sibylline and her sentiments too rare and delicate ("too little flesh and blood") to attract the common reader. When, to everyone's surprise, she achieves popularity, many express relief, as if her booming sales are unlooked for but welcome evidence that poetry still functions in an egalitarian culture. The democratic ethos apparent here also finds expression in her reviewers' disinclination, overtly at least, to base their judgments on learning and taste. But as Dickinson's reception develops, her popularity begins to be held against her, especially by the most influential high-culture arbiters.[25] Critics express their impressions as if certain of their universality, but their exclusive reliance on subjectivity demonstrates little confidence that her poetry can appeal to those outside the steadily decreasing circle of persons like themselves. The *Boston Tran-*

script's insistence (noted earlier) that Dickinson must be apprehended, not comprehended, implies a self-selected community of qualified readers who, in perusing reviews, expect the pleasures of self-confirmation and the "social" reward (union with the reviewer) of sharing "high-minded" and like-minded felicities. Reading poems and reading reviews have much in common. "Those who are fit," says the *Springfield Republican* of Dickinson, "will read and know themselves divined" (21).

Taken as a whole, these notices demonstrate how social constructions of femininity and masculinity worked on Dickinson's behalf when her first book entered the literary marketplace. As reading expectations for fiction and especially for poetry moved toward increased intimacy, mystery, and sacred personalism, her voice and the way it constructed the writer-reader relationship ("These are my letters to the world") found ready acceptance. Dickinson, herself an avid fiction reader, reflected that crossover of sacred tears from fiction to poetry when she exclaimed to Susan Gilbert in the fifties: "I would paint a portrait which would bring the tears, had I canvass for it, and the scene should be—*solitude,* and the figures—solitude—and the lights and shades, each a solitude. I could fill a chamber with landscapes so lone, men should pause and weep there."[26]

In fiction of worth, said the *Christian Examiner* in the same decade (when the poet was in her twenties), there must be "some ingenuity of contrivance to keep the mind of the reader suspended and engaged, and swept forward, while it is swayed to and fro, by curiosity and emotion, and a constantly heightening sympathy."[27] Nineties readers respond to Dickinson (as the poet did to her favorite authors) as a friend and correspondent, bold, brilliant, attractive, and passionate, a loved presence evoking uplifting feelings. For her first reviewers, Dickinson's half-veiled verses have the power to engage and sweep them forward, in comprehending sympathy. When fulfilled, these expectations constitute poetry's special exhilaration and expanse. But it is an expanse perceived only by a coterie of knowing respondents, whose sympathies testify to the mysterious power of poetry even as their reading strategies rarefy that power.

Notes

This essay is dedicated to David Porter, organizer of the Emily Dickinson International Conference entitled "Emily Dickinson in Public," held in Amherst,

Mass., October 27–28, 1989, at which an earlier version of this paper was presented.

1. Before publication Niles confessed, "It has always seemed to me that it would be unwise to perpetuate Miss Dickinson's poems" (quoted in Millicent Todd Bingham, *Ancestors' Brocades: The Literary Debut of Emily Dickinson* [New York: Harper's, 1945] 53).

2. Willis Buckingham, ed., *Emily Dickinson's Reception in the 1890s: A Documentary History* (Pittsburgh: Pittsburgh UP, 1989). An appendix summarizes sales records, printing by printing, of each Dickinson volume published in the nineties (557–58). All page references in the text are to reviews collected in this volume. In subsequent note references this volume is cited as *EDR*.

3. The writers largely responsible for Dickinson's emergence, especially during the first weeks, were contributors to dailies and weeklies in New England. She was a "Boston fad" before the national monthlies had a chance to comment. On the phenomenon of the "reviewers' book" see Cathy N. Davidson, "Toward a History of Books and Readers," in *Reading in America: Literature and Social History*, ed. Cathy N. Davidson (Baltimore: Johns Hopkins UP, 1989) 20–21.

4. It has been a commonplace of twentieth-century Dickinson scholarship that the poet was poorly received and understood when first published. A "war-of-the-critics" approach to her reception caused this impression in part; by treating opposed views equally, this method overrepresented the handful of critics who cleverly savaged Dickinson's verse. For example, Caesar R. Blake and Carlton J. Wells reprinted sixteen 1890s reviews in their *Recognition of Emily Dickinson* (Ann Arbor: U of Michigan P, 1964) 3–68. Among them, six were strongly positive, three ambivalent, and seven strongly negative. The 600 items assembled in *EDR* indicate a largely favorable early response.

5. Of course, using reviews as cultural evidence is itself an interpretive act and does not substitute for reading the reviews themselves.

6. Oates continues: "We can analyze our [Victorian] ancestors' stated beliefs, and the philosophical, sociological, political, and psychological foundations of those beliefs, but it is virtually impossible for us to believe: we read their musical notations but we can't hear them. . . . Hamlet is our contemporary, Emma Bovary is our contemporary, even Swift's Gulliver is our contemporary, but what of the numberless heroines of the best-selling novels of 1850–1950?" ("Pleasure, Duty, Redemption Then and Now: Susan Warner's *Diana*," *American Literature* 59 [1987]: 423). Fred Kaplan makes a similar point in *Sacred Tears: Sentimentality in Victorian Literature* (Princeton: Princeton UP, 1987) 4–5.

7. Among nineties reviewers different and overlapping subgroups can be identified—principally by the specific readerships they implicitly and explicitly address: well- or less-educated readers, regional audiences, college students, housewives, those interested in book trade news or literary gossip, those choosing books

as special occasion gifts, etc. Nevertheless, nineties commentators seldom show interest, on the surface at least, in identifying themselves as a special kind of poetry reader, nor do they reflect differences among their presumed auditors, except when they comment on the difficulty of Dickinson's poetry and its accessibility to the general as opposed to the "discerning" reader. Some of those who stress the poet's thought are concerned, especially in the first weeks and months of her reception, that her work is too oracular to appeal to the common reader. Those who respond primarily to Dickinson's power of character usually have no such worries; they assume that the force of her personal presence will be transparent to all.

8. The intended audience of these professional reviewers, of course, consists of persons curious about new poetry books, a "literary class" of readers. However, professional critics and journalists may constitute a "high culture" community, or they may reflect what they believe their readers *ought* to appreciate rather than what they honestly enjoy themselves. *EDR*, attempting as it does to collect all known comment on the poet, includes representation from the humbler magazines and papers (such as religious and home weeklies and smaller city dailies). Even so, we need to be aware of an unvoiced readership in the nineties, just as today inexpensive editions in bookstores and cardshops testify to a Dickinson constituency not represented in the academic community.

9. Dickinson's poems occasioned fierce debate between those who believed poetry could dispense with traditional form and finish and those who believed it could not. For example, T. W. Higginson claimed on the poet's behalf that "when a thought takes one's breath away, a lesson on grammar seems an impertinence" (*EDR* 14). T. B. Aldrich countered: "But an ungrammatical thought does not, as a general thing, take one's breath away, except in a sense the reverse of flattering" (284).

10. A surprising number of nineties reviewers, admitting the absence of conventional metrics in Dickinson, nevertheless rejoiced in her "wilding" music; see *EDR* items 27, 44, 51, 64, 135, 145, 263, 334, 419, 441, 495, 557. For a recent study of the poet's sound as it relates to meaning, see Judy Jo Small, *Positive as Sound: Emily Dickinson's Rhyme* (Athens: U of Georgia P, 1990).

11. Interestingly, neither Mabel Loomis Todd nor Thomas Wentworth Higginson, co-editors of the 1890 *Poems*, used "genius" in their prepublication promotional articles on the new poet. However, they were quick to use the term once others had applied it.

12. The nineties reception reinforces a model of reading which is active and engaged rather than merely passive. See Cathy N. Davidson's discussion of Rolf Engelsing's theory that as books became mass-produced, readers read extensively rather than intensively ("Towards a History of Books and Readers" 14–18).

13. Nina Baym, *Novels, Readers, and Reviewers: Responses to Fiction in Antebellum America* (Ithaca: Cornell UP, 1984) 131.

14. Ibid. 107, 55; *Harper's* quoted in ibid. 55.

15. *The Complete Prose Works of Matthew Arnold*, ed. R. H. Super (Ann Arbor: U of Michigan P, 1960) 1:4.

16. Baym, *Novels, Readers, and Reviewers* 141.

17. Quoted in ibid. 52. Higginson once wrote to Dickinson, "It is hard to understand how you can live so alone, with thoughts of such a quality coming up in you" (quoted in Thomas H. Johnson, ed., *The Letters of Emily Dickinson* [Cambridge: Harvard UP, 1958] 2:461).

18. Howells's "Editor's Study" review drew notice because of his fame and the literary heft of *Harper's Monthly*. His essay resonated as late as 1896, when the *Boston Transcript* observed, "This New England woman was a type of her race" (*EDR* 505). Howells's comments may also have been notable to *Harper's* subscribers because his "Editor's Study" infrequently devoted itself to poetry, especially to new poets; see James W. Simpson, ed., Introduction, *Editor's Study by William Dean Howells* (Troy: Whitston, 1983) xxxviii.

19. Mathilde Blind, trans., Introduction, *The Journal of Marie Bashkirtseff* (London: Cassell, 1890) 1:[vii]–viii.

20. In her study of antebellum fiction reviewing, Nina Baym stresses the tendency of critics to place restrictions on individuality for female characters and for women authors. Though many of those writing about Dickinson in the nineties enjoy her feminine presence, in general she is admired for some "womanly virtues" (freshness, charm, naturalness) more than others Baym mentions (unselfishness, inexperience, grace). The poet's most appealing personal quality for both male and female critics appears to be the freedom and individuality (at the level of genius) which Baym feels was specifically denied women novelists before the war: "Where the novel, generally speaking, was defined as a field for the expression of the individual author, possibly rising to genius, it was defined in the case of the woman author as a field for the expression of the sex, in which case genius in the large sense is out of the question, since the most she can do is lose herself in gender and hence sacrifice the individuality that is the foundation of genius" (*Novels, Readers, and Reviewers* 103, 257).

21. *The Poems of Emily Dickinson*, ed. Thomas H. Johnson (Cambridge: Harvard UP, 1955) 3:1077 (as numbered in this edition, poem 1563).

22. See Jane P. Tompkins's discussion of the importance of personal experience in nineteenth- and twentieth-century literary interpretation, "The Reader in History," in *Reader-Response Criticism: From Formalism to Post-Structuralism*, ed. Jane P. Tompkins (Baltimore: Johns Hopkins UP, 1980) esp. 216–19, 224–26.

23. See Richard Rabinowitz, *The Spiritual Self in Everyday Life: The Transfor-*

mation of Personal Religious Experience in Nineteenth-Century New England (Boston: Northeastern UP, 1989) 180.

24. For nineties comparisons of Dickinson to particular authors and artists see "Index and Finding List," *EDR*.

25. See Introduction, *EDR* xviii–xix.

26. Johnson, *Letters* 1:310. Barton St. Armand finds parallels between Dickinson's vision here and "nineteenth-century emblem books and other folk works, especially popular 'sandpaper' drawings" (*Emily Dickinson and Her Culture: The Soul's Society* [Cambridge: Cambridge UP, 1984] 222).

27. Quoted in Baym, *Novels, Readers, and Reviewers* 78.

Probable Readers, Possible Stories: The Limits of Nineteenth-Century Black Narrative

RAYMOND HEDIN

Children, the saying goes, should be seen and not heard. The situation of angry and assertive black characters in nineteenth-century African American narrative reveals an interesting variation on this bit of folk wisdom. Throughout the century, angry black characters could be heard only under certain well-defined circumstances. They could be seen hardly at all, and then only under even more stringent circumstances. The felt restrictions on voice and physical presence— "Body" as it is sometimes called, or "physicality," as I shall call it— ultimately derived from a white audience outside the texts. That audience, however, exerted such pressure that it all but forced itself onto the very pages of black texts. There, as listeners and observers, the white intruders simultaneously validated and confined the black characters they perceived. Yet once on the page, they became objects of manipulation as well as intimidating presences; there on the page, at least, black writers could exercise some degree of control over an audience which they could not keep at bay.

The complex intersection of black writers and the white presences within their texts is the point where the question posed by New His-

toricists and others before them—is genuine opposition to the dominant culture possible on the terrain controlled by that culture?—
merges with the audience-related question of how the teller of tales
shapes his listeners while being shaped by them. For black writers in
the nineteenth century, what was the relationship between the seemingly desirable end of being listened to and recognized by whites and
the danger of being contained, controlled, or diminished by them as
the price of attention? Conversely, to what extent did the very survival of black stories depend on their central voices not quite being
heard accurately or their central characters not quite being seen for
what they were to their authors?

These questions are central to an understanding of the African
American narrative tradition because they reveal the conditions under
which black narratives were produced and the strategies by which
black writers made the most of those conditions. Those strategies, in
turn, would themselves become defining characteristics of African
American narrative well into this century.

I want to address these questions by looking closely at several texts
dealing with black revolt or revolution, starting with Nat Turner's
1831 *Confessions* and ending with Sutton Griggs's 1899 *Imperium in
Imperio*. Such texts, as we shall see, inevitably bring issues of voice and
physicality into sharp focus: their protagonists must be forceful to suggest the depth of black resistance, yet they must also avoid any suggestion of uncontrolled savagery in order to be tolerated by a white
audience. But I will also include a discussion of Charles Chesnutt's
fiction to suggest that, at the end of the century, issues of intratextual
audience and assertive storytelling had broadened out well beyond the
specific issue of revolt. In the context of social Darwinism, the issue
for black writers took on a stark clarity: how can a black story become "fit"—or how can it be fitted—to survive the hostile audience of
its day?

I intend to look closely at these texts in full awareness that literary
theorists today have made the inside of texts uncomfortable territory
for critics to investigate at length. But even if a critic ultimately hopes,
as I do, to reach past specific texts to describe and account for the
contours of the African American tradition itself, he has good reason
to spend considerable time on textual description. Precisely because
black texts—at least until very recently—have been peculiarly im-
bedded in and sensitive to their complex and defining relationship to

mainstream (white) American culture, they often present within themselves, in the form of white listeners/observers, a sensitive register of
that relationship. Within their texts are encoded the very cultural relationships which, outside the texts, serve to shape them. In the intratextual relationship of black character and story to these white presences,
black texts reveal both their sense of restriction and their strategies for
coping with it. To put this in more historical terms, over the course
of the nineteenth century the initial stances of these white listeners
and observers toward the particular black characters they encounter
change from overt hostility to smug inattention, with a number of variations along the way. Because those stances reflect in each case the
anticipated initial response of white readers outside the text, the history of such stances encodes, in summary form, the history of the relationship between black writers and a white readership that underwent
changes – or showed various faces – while remaining consistently problematic. Furthermore, because these anticipated responses draw forth
a series of strategies from black writers, many of which build upon
one another, a consideration of those strategies offers a summary history of black narrative approaches to their inescapable white readership. Hence, black texts are narrative and metanarrative at the same
time. Hence also, when I refer in this essay to "the reader," I am using
a shorthand term to refer in each case not to a reified, timeless abstraction but to those particular readers whose specific features are suggested by the white observers and listeners inside the text.

I

The 1831 *Confessions of Nat Turner* is not, strictly speaking, a black
narrative at all, since it was written by Thomas Gray, a white Southern lawyer and slaveowner who interviewed Turner for three days
after his capture and then published the *Confessions* (Gray's title) complete with Gray's introduction, conclusion, and intermittent commentary. But precisely because of Turner's status as captive interviewee
entirely at the mercy of a hostile interviewer, the *Confessions* reveal in
clearest form the starting point for black voices attempting to speak in
the nineteenth century and the negative potential inherent in a black
character's full physical presence.

Gray is no patron, but he enjoys the patron's ability to define for his
readers in advance the nature of the story they are about to read and

of the black revolutionary they are about to meet. The last thing that Gray wants to do, as self-appointed ideal reader of the *Confessions*, is to validate in any way the stature of a man in whose presence "my blood curdled in my veins."[1] Quite the contrary: Gray offers the *Confessions* to the public as a horrific lesson in the twisted operations of a mind "endeavoring to grapple with things beyond its reach" (40). William Andrews, for instance, has pointed out the ways in which Gray's introduction undermines Turner's claims to prophecy by labeling him a "gloomy fanatic" who had led a "fiendish band" of murderers (39); thus, Turner becomes fixed as satanic even before he has had a chance to claim a divine calling.[2] Gray concludes the interview by reminding his readers of Turner's innocent victims and near victims, and he interjects at will during Turner's own narrative account.

Not content to usher Turner on and off stage with such billing, Gray reaches out directly to do violence to Turner's *voice*, gracing the basically straightforward Turner with a florid, Latinate style suspiciously akin to Gray's ("I wondered greatly at these miracles, and prayed to be informed of a certainty of the meaning thereof" [44]). Gray also attributes to the openly unrepentant Turner the unlikely perspective suggested in such statements as "We found no more victims to gratify our thirst for blood" (49). Ironically, by such methods the nineteenth-century reader gained confidence that he was listening to Turner himself precisely because Gray conveniently provided a false style and voice to highlight the genuine; partial editing undercut itself.

The central battle enacted within the text is a battle of voices; Gray seems to need Turner's voice to demonstrate the power of his own. During their exchanges, however, Gray, like Richard Nixon in the 1960 debates, seems to be speaking directly to his opponent—"Do you not find yourself mistaken now?"—whereas Turner in reply, like Kennedy in those same debates, seems to be speaking past his local opponent toward a different audience entirely: "Was not Christ crucified?" (45). And because Gray does allow Turner to speak instead of merely summarizing his claims, Turner's story emerges, if not unscathed by Gray, nonetheless surprisingly intact.

But it is through Gray's response—or rather his silence—as much as through any claims on Turner's part that the power of Turner's voice and presence is established. The question-and-answer format all but disappears halfway through the interview, and for the last several pages

Turner holds sway relatively unchecked; Gray's earlier intrusions turn his later silence into testimony. For the receptive reader of the period, whose very status was problematic given the overwhelmingly negative public response to the revolt, the impression of Turner's power over Gray is strengthened in Gray's summary paragraph, where, in a more reflective voice, he lapses into an unguarded, relatively balanced assessment of Turner. He acknowledges Turner's truthfulness, the decisiveness of his character, and the consistency of his personal ethic ("He was never known to have a dollar in his life; to swear an oath, or drink a drop of spirits" [51]). He even acknowledges Turner's "natural intelligence and quickness of apprehension" (51). Thus Gray validates precisely the qualities of rationality and morality which Turner's violence had called into question. For a moment the adversary has turned patron; his careful if not obsessive listening to Turner seems to have led him to question, however briefly, his own reading of his text. His resulting confusion suggests that it was he, more than Turner, who was "endeavoring to grapple with things beyond his reach." Thus Gray provides the most eloquent validation Turner could have hoped for; he becomes part of Turner's testimony, a hostile witness whose very hostility underscores the credibility of his reluctant admissions.

But why would Gray, as editor, leave that momentary acknowledgment intact inside a text which is evidently intended to turn its audience completely against Turner? I can only conclude that he left it in as a show of his own strength, the way a speaker utterly confident of himself and of his audience often acknowledges a qualm or two, a conflicting viewpoint not without power, before reasserting what he knows is an essentially ironclad argument.

For Gray's ultimate recourse is to change the rules of the contest itself. Recovering from his moment of hesitation, he abandons the battle of words, his against Turner's, in which Turner had proven formidable, and simply conjures up a frightening physical image of Turner:

He is below the ordinary stature, though strong and active, having the true negro face, every feature of which is strongly marked. . . . The calm, deliberate composure with which he spoke of his late deeds and intentions, the expression of his fiend-like face when excited by enthusiasm, still bearing the stains of the blood of helpless innocence about him; clothed with rags and covered with chains; yet daring to raise his manacled hands to heaven, with a spirit soaring above the attributes of man; I looked on him and my blood curdled in my veins. (51)

Winthrop Jordan has shown that even in the eighteenth century, whites had already begun to suspect what they did not yet fully articulate: that blacks were not merely biologically inferior but were in fact uncontrollable savages.[3] The proslavery argument for the physical inferiority of blacks, however, did not take clear shape until the three decades before the Civil War, when, partly in response to Turner's violent rebellion, the nature of blacks became a central item in the slavery debate. It was during this period that the claim that blacks were *biological* beasts, mere animals, became overtly overlaid with a strident insistence on, if not an obsession with, the nightmare vision of blacks as *metaphorical* beasts, inherently wild, amoral agents of destruction rendered all the more threatening by "typical" physical characteristics which revealed their inherent barbarity.

Turner's *Confessions* were central to this change. That Gray felt no need to specify the markings of Turner's "true Negro face" suggests that the image was well established; Gray had only to inscribe that face with "fiend-like" passion to transform black physicality from a sign of mere inferiority to a sign of dangerous savagery. In linking Turner's "true negro face" to inherent violence, Gray played his trump card, crystallizing the fears of his audience and giving shape to a strategy with which black writers would have to contend for a long time. "*I looked on him* [my emphasis]," Gray writes, "and my blood curdled in my veins" (51). From Thomas Gray to Thomas Dixon, beyond them to the *Chicago Tribune* descriptions of Robert Nixon which Richard Wright drew on in *Native Son*, and most recently to campaign ads picturing Willie Horton, hostile whites have invited their readers or viewers to contemplate images of black physicality— whether those images be a generalized face which assumes a broad cultural consensus or whether they take on the graphic specificity of writers such as Dixon, who in times of social stress reactivate the details—to perpetuate the notion of frenzied black savagery.

Several critics, including myself, have written about the constrictions of voice felt by slave narrators and signaled by the presence of white patrons who introduced the narratives and often provided approving postscripts.[4] Paradoxically, these empowering white readers imposed greater restraints on slave narrators than the hostile Gray imposed on Turner. For Gray welcomed and highlighted any signs of barbarity he could evoke from Turner, whereas slave narrators were compelled to present themselves positively to justify their patrons' support. Like Ellison's narrator before the powerful whites of his home town—a section of *Invisible Man* which is itself a comment on the entire tradition of stultifying "support"—they were free to speak only so long as what they said was consistent with the words of praise which made their speech possible in the first place.

But if the slave narrators were limited in voice, they were even more constrained in their depiction of their own bodies. For after the *Confessions*, the physicality of blacks became a distinct liability. In this context, the first-person voice and outward focus of the abolitionist-era slave narratives had the useful side-effect of keeping the narrators themselves more or less out of sight, at least as concrete, physical agents. A body rarely described except in the posture of suffering victim—being whipped, for instance, or feeling the pangs of hunger and thirst—could not readily suggest a dangerous savage.[5] The slave narrators became the black narrative tradition's first invisible men. Their most obvious successor—though by no means the only one—is Ellison's unnamed, unseen, and undescribed narrator, who in this too, as in so many other ways, provides a gloss on the whole narrative tradition: the impact of his accumulated anger is muted for the reader by his lack of threatening physical presence.

II

In his 1853 short story "The Heroic Slave," Frederick Douglass became the first black writer to draw on the model of frame narration in fiction, turning the white presences which circumscribed slave narratives—including his own—into a chosen and therefore manipulable strategy. "The Heroic Slave" was based on an 1841 uprising of 105 slaves aboard the slave ship *Creole*. Led by Madison Washington, the slaves killed one owner, took command of the ship, and led it to the British port of Nassau, where the governor, in spite of American protests, released all but 19 of the insurgents.

The structure of the story reveals Douglass's finely calibrated sense of where a black voice could and could not speak on its own authority. Douglass introduces the story in a confident third-person voice ("The State of Virginia is famous in American annals for the multitudinous array of her statesmen and heroes") and then reintroduces each section of the story in that same voice.[6] He speaks with calm, unaided assurance about whites ("A more brutal set of creatures [than the whites in a Virginia tavern] perhaps, never congregated" [213]) and about the morality of slavery ("what a world of inconsistency, as well as of wickedness, is suggested by the smooth and gliding phrase, AMERICAN SLAVE TRADE" [225]).

But in establishing Washington's character and the nature of the revolt—issues touching directly on the humanity of blacks themselves— Douglass relies on the views of mediating white presences.[7] Everything Washington does and says in the story is either heard or seen by one of two white participants/observers, who in turn interpret Washington for the reader. Washington cannot speak without them; Douglass cannot interpret without them. Thus, they stand between Douglass and his hero, simultaneously empowering and limiting both of them.

Douglass carefully orchestrates his white observers to validate both Washington's private emotions and his public actions. The story consists of four "glimpses" (I will return to this visual term later) of Washington at crucial points in his life. The first three events—Washington's impassioned soliloquy on freedom in a Virginia pine forest in 1835, his escape through Ohio in 1841, and his forced march toward the *Creole* in 1847 after he was captured trying to free his wife—emphasize his private character and elicit a correspondingly personal admiration from a man named Listwell, who is conveniently situated to witness each occurrence. Listwell, previously indifferent to slavery issues, is transformed by overhearing the soliloquy: "From this hour I am an abolitionist" (182). He gives Washington refuge during his flight and finally slips him three files during his forced march, thus contributing, though from a comfortable distance, to the revolt.

The fourth event is the revolt itself, which is interpreted for white readers neither already committed to abolition nor unalterably antipathetic to blacks—that is, for readers similar to Listwell in his initial stance. The interpretation of this public act occurs after the fact in the public setting of a Virginia coffee house, where an old sailor named Jack Williams taunts a Southerner, Tom Grant, who had served aboard the *Creole*, forcing him to explain how members of such a patently inferior race could have succeeded in the revolt. The only possible explanation, according to Williams, is that the whites involved were cowards. To defend himself, Grant has no choice but to argue that the blacks proved *not* to be inferior.

As if to acknowledge that it will be hard to convince his readers that a violent uprising of blacks was an act of principled heroism, Douglass portrays Grant as a much less willing convert than Listwell. Grant is no sympathizer with blacks in general even now, bristles at the "insult" of being called an abolitionist, and admits how grating it was finally to acknowledge the character of "one whom I deemed my inferior" (230, 238). And yet the reader is shown the process, in Grant's own words, by which he came to acknowledge that Washington was in fact "a superior man" (237). Through Grant's testimony readers similar to Grant are given access to Washington's bravery, intelligence, and self-control. They learn especially that the revolt was a principled assertion of freedom rather than an act of savagery or vengeance. For Grant owes his life, he admits, to Washington's intervention in the interests of keeping the revolt untainted by unnecessary bloodshed: "God is my witness," Washington tells Grant in the act of sparing him, "that LIBERTY, not *malice*, is the motive for this night's work" (234–35).

In each of these four sections, Washington speaks at length in his own voice—even, as we have just seen, conversing with Grant, however implausibly, in the midst of the revolt. In the second section, Washington in fact recounts his own concentrated slave narrative, prompting immediate approval from Listwell. In one sense, then, Washington's voice exists primarily to elicit an ideal audience response, first from the indifferent Listwell, then from the more hostile Grant; their conversions are the point of the story and constitute them as born-again, fictional cousins of Thomas Gray.

Yet the framework of the story conveys not only Douglass's dependence on his white observers but his considerable power over them. For in another sense, Listwell, Grant, and Williams exist solely to allow Douglass to give surprisingly full voice to the philosophy of an angry black revolutionary. On the level of character, they are all shown to be lesser men than Washington. As fictional presences, they are conjured and dismissed as needed. Listwell simply disappears after the third section, his auxiliary role completed. Williams, the skeptic who prodded Grant to speak, does the same in the fourth section, implicitly silenced—Douglass's equivalent to erasure—not so much by Grant's speech as by the force of Washington's character as revealed by Grant. "The Heroic Slave" thus captures nicely the essentially double-edged quality of fictionalized white frame narration in the nineteenth century and of the larger cultural relationship it suggests of black speaker/writer to his audience: on the one hand, whites are indispensable spokesmen and supporters; on the other, they are mere scaffolding.

The interplay between being in control and being controlled is replicated in the domain of physicality. It is immediately clear that Douglass is reluctant to linger over the physical image of Madison Washington: "*Glimpses* [my emphasis] of this great character are all that can now be presented," the narrator tells his readers in the opening pages, though they are not told why this is so (175). Although "anxiously we peer into the dark, and wish even for the blinding flash, or the light of northern skies to reveal him," Washington will remain "enveloped in darkness" and "brought to view by a few transient incidents" which "afford but partial satisfaction" (175).

Although this propensity for veiled revelation no doubt reflects Douglass's desire to romanticize his hero—"like a guiding star on a stormy night, he is seen through the parted clouds and the howling tempest" (175)—it is equally clear that Douglass wants his readers to respond primarily, as Listwell does, to "the man whose *voice* had arrested his attention" (176, my emphasis). Thus the structure of the opening scene locates Douglass's audience first in the presence of Washington's elevated speech, uncluttered by the body which utters it. Pulling up his horse near the edge of a dark pine forest, Listwell "caught the sound of a human voice"; anxious to know "what thoughts and feelings, or, it might be, high aspirations, guided these rich and mellow accents," he drew near enough to listen, without being seen, to the "soliloquy" (176). That soliloquy—no mad rant here, no Turneresque enthusiasm for violence—is an impassioned lament over the speaker's enslavement. It expresses his determination, not to draw blood against his oppressors, but simply to seek the "inalienable birth-right of every man" (178). It is a speech whose every note insists on a humanity denied by slavery: "Here I am a man,— yes, a *man*!— with thoughts and wishes, with powers and faculties as far as angel's flight above that hated reptile [which had just slunk across his path]— yet he is my superior, and scorns to own me as his master, or to stop and take my blows" (177). Only after this speech does Douglass allow Listwell to catch a "full view of the unsuspecting speaker" (178). Even then, his description of Washington's stature circles around Washington's physicality and, after the fact, mutes its disturbing power:

Madison was of manly form. Tall, symmetrical, round, and strong. In his movements he seemed to combine, with the strength of the lion, a lion's elasticity. His torn sleeves disclosed arms like polished iron. His face was "black, but comely." His eye, lit with emotion, kept guard under a brow as dark and as glossy as the raven's wing. His whole appearance betokened Herculean strength; yet there was nothing savage or forbidding in his aspect. A child might play in his arms, or dance on his shoulders. A giant's strength, but not a giant's heart was in him. (179)

It is not surprising, then, that in the more volatile posture of revolt, Washington—already once removed from the reader through the mediation of Grant's retrospective voice—becomes even more of a speaker, even less of a physical presence. Washington's voice obliterates any suggestions of a "true negro face." "The fellow loomed up before me," says Grant. "[But] I forgot his blackness in the dignity of his manner, and the eloquence of his speech" (235). Even in the very midst of the revolt, Washington seems more bent on explaining its rationale than he does in getting on with business: "We have struck for our freedom," he tells Grant; "We have done that which you applaud your fathers for doing" (235). As if further to counter the memory of Nat Turner, he emphasizes his control over his men and his aversion to unnecessary bloodshed: "When you lay helpless on deck, my men were about to kill you. I held them in check" (236).

It is worth noting that Douglass turns these defensive strategies around, just as he did for his dependence on white observers. For in Grant's retelling of the revolt, only he and Washington are given the dignity of speech; the "terror-stricken" sailors are rendered mute under stress and are *seen* by Grant in the posture of "so many monkeys" clinging to the rigging (236). For the white sailors to be seen and not heard is to be put in the position of the vulnerable, the childish, or—of course—the subhuman. But to speak without being seen—the imposed yet paradoxically intimidating position of the black protagonist—is to be in a position of power enhanced by mystery. Like the offstage voices and shrouded presences of melodrama, Washington's disembodied voice keeps the audience's emotions on edge—for the threat of revolt lies beneath all such stories of revolt, however rationalized—even while refusing to disturb those emotions gratuitously. As careful as he is not to activate fears of the "true negro face,"

Douglass is willing to insist that Washington's voice, "that unfailing index of the soul, though full and melodious, had that in it which could terrify as well as charm" (179). And left to its own devices, such a voice, far from putting the fears of the audience entirely to rest, puts them instead to work—for the black writer instead of against him.

The move from the situation of Nat Turner to that of Madison Washington is one of the crucial moments in the African-American literary tradition. There is a surface similarity within the texts as well as outside: both black speakers and their stories depend on white listeners for their existence; for both men, to be at all is to be perceived by whites. Yet the similarity masks a fundamental difference, a central though by no means total reversal of the flow of power. In the *Confessions*, Gray, as listener, observer, and master of ceremonies, has Turner literally in chains before him and figuratively under his complete power. Yet by producing on the page the very source of subversion which he sought to contain, Gray ceased to contain it. As a result, the *Confessions* became exemplary as well as cautionary for later black writers. In "The Heroic Slave," Gray's successors are still so powerful, still so unavoidable, that Douglass is driven to bring them into his text. Yet once they are there, they are at his beck and call. They are—in ways which suggest both the limits and potential of voice and story for African American writers yet to come—simultaneously indispensable and subservient.

III

Between the Civil War and the turn of the century, I have been able to find no further instance of white frame narrators/observers; the relatively unassertive gentile black fiction of the reconstruction period did not require them. It was only when blacks began to write again with an angry voice that they again sought mediation—and faced again the issues of voice and presence inherent in such mediation.

Frame narration reappears in Charles Chesnutt's *The Conjure Woman* (1899), a collection of stories in which the problematic relation of frame to tale reflects the difficult situation of the black writer at the turn of the century. *The Conjure Woman* has often been read as little more than a stereotypical plantation novel extolling the benign relationship of white patron to black retainer, that had become so dear to Reconstruction-era readers. It is not hard to see the basis for that view. The frame narrator is a middle-aged white man named John who has come south with his wife, Annie, in deference to her fragile health. They buy an old plantation and in the process inherit Uncle Julius, an ex-slave who purports to be an expert in grape culture but whose real specialty is recounting tales of slave experience, one of which constitutes the center of each story of the book. John finds these tales mildly amusing and, with considerable condescension, grants Julius a series of small favors, the desire for which has seemed to motivate Julius's storytelling. Both listener and storyteller get what they want: Julius is rewarded, while John is convinced he sees through the trickery, merely pretending not to see Julius's self-interested motives because it pleases him to satisfy his more sentimental, less cynical wife, who always wants to give Julius what he wants. According to this reading, Chesnutt acquiesces in the comic reduction of black storyteller into a transparent semibuffoon and of his black folk tale into genial anecdotes whose cutting edge is entirely blunted.[8]

In assessing *The Conjure Woman*, however, it is important to remember just how hostile the post-Reconstruction white audience of Chesnutt's day had become to anything which suggested black aggression. The dominant black voice of the period was Booker T. Washington's; there was no market, as there had been in the abolitionist era, for overt expressions of black anger. As early as 1880, for instance, in *Uncle Remus: His Songs and Sayings*, Joel Chandler Harris had shown an awareness that aggressive black folk tales could not reach print unbuffered. Harris was able to leave the tales themselves intact only by creating a sentimental framework for them in the figure of the loyal Uncle Remus and his young white listener, who finds the tales amusing and renders them, by implication, fit for a child. It is Remus's seeming distance from the harsh world of the tales—his not *openly* endorsing their ethic of cunning and self-interest—along with the boy's inability to understand the tales fully, that allows the tales to stand unmodified. The tales depend for their survival on the approval of an uncomprehending, internal audience, *past* which rather than *to* which the aging, grandfatherly Remus—no threatening black male here—directs his voice.

Chesnutt adopts a similar strategy in *The Conjure Woman*. There is no overt anger in the Remus-like Uncle Julius, a "venerable-looking old man" first seen by John in the act of "smacking his lips with great gusto" over a hatful of grapes.[9] Julius, John says, "respectfully rose as we drew near"; and although John describes him as a "tall man . . . apparently quite vigorous," he is also "slightly bowed with the weight of years" (9). Correspondingly, the tales told by this muted teller are themselves muted by his light touch in telling them, and their diminished nature seems confirmed by John's amused response.

I see no reason to conclude, however, that Chesnutt himself embraced this reduction of teller and tale. For the implicit or at least potential anger in these tales remains. They deal, for instance, with the brutal process of slavebreaking, the anguished separation of mother from child and husband from wife at the owner's merest whim. Moreover, while the slaves neither revolt nor escape, the satisfaction of limited but real revenge against the master is one of the recurring themes of the tales.

That Chesnutt uses a white framework at all suggests his awareness that the tales retain an angry core which required buffering. His publication two years later of *The Marrow of Tradition*, a novel whose subject is brutal mob violence against blacks, further suggests that Chesnutt had not yet lost or muted his own racial anger. Rather, John's failure to see the tales as anything but amusing implies that Chesnutt cannot imagine at this time a white audience capable of responding with sensitivity to what the tales convey.[10] *The Conjure Woman* contains an implicit critique of a post-Reconstruction white audience so locked into its comfortable view of slavery that it cannot hear any other version; instead of the tales converting their listener, the listener converts both teller and tale into the nonthreatening presences he is able to accept.

And yet Chesnutt turns the impregnability of his audience to his advantage, manipulating John's impregnable comfort to slip past him a number of subversive tales that are wounded but not dead. Because John is totally unmoved by the tales' darker side, even while he gives it lip service, he is both an inadequate audience and precisely the audience Chesnutt needed, the best possible reader he could imagine. In the post-Reconstruction era, a white listener cannot plausibly be asked to embrace the full implication of such tales; but he can become their strategically placed misreader, a genteel Thomas Gray through whose gaps in perception the tales can seep, damaged but recoverable. The Darwinian equation had two sides: the tales became fit to survive by being fitted to their audience; at the same time, they could only survive an audience unfit to hear them.

The Wife of His Youth and Other Stories of the Color Line, also published in 1899, contains several stories which further reveal Chesnutt's concern with the tension between potentially disturbing black stories and audiences not eager to be disturbed. None of them does this more tellingly than the second story of the collection, "Her Virginia Mammy." There are three central characters here, two of whom become storytellers and all three of whom alternate as audience. The first story is told by a dance teacher, Clara Hohlfelder, whose uncertain parentage renders her reluctant to marry her aristocratic lover, John Winthrop. One evening, after leading a class of black students, with whom, to her own surprise, she feels "perfectly at home," she discovers a light-skinned black woman, Mrs. Harper, waiting in her dressing room.[11] Immediately sensing a sympathetic bond without asking herself why it might be there, Clara tells this apparent stranger of her love for Winthrop, acknowledging that "the circumstance which prevents us from marrying is my story" (44). With Mrs. Harper's sympathy increasing—"Ah, yes . . . I have known of such a case" (44)—Clara recounts how, years ago, she had asked her father to explain a mysterious inscription on a piece of paper she had found. Then "for the first time I learned my real story," the story of her discovery aboard a wrecked ship and her subsequent adoption by the man and woman she had thought to be her parents (45).

The reader soon realizes what Clara does not and cannot allow herself to realize: that Mrs. Harper is her mother, who has been longing for years to find her lost daughter. Seemingly a white woman in the presence of a black, female listener, Clara has no reason to hedge her narrative of self-revelation. But when Mrs. Harper reciprocates with a story, she must equivocate, for she knows that there is more to Clara's story. She knows that her own story will register only insofar as it serves to complete Clara's story; the black woman's story is at best a narrative middle which must serve Clara's desired, happy "end," her marriage to Winthrop. So Mrs. Harper—a black storyteller characteristically placing the sensitivities of her audience foremost—tells her story accurately but ambiguously, allowing Clara to misread it for her own purposes. She too was on that ship, she says; she can assure Clara that her father was indeed a Virginia gentleman, that her mother "*belonged* [my emphasis] to one of the first families of Virginia, and in her veins flowed some of the best blood of the Old Dominion" (53). "You were the colored nurse?—my 'mammy,'" Clara exclaims, to which

Mrs. Harper replies, "Yes, child, I was—your mammy. Upon my bosom you have rested; my breasts once gave you nourishment" (55).

Clara can now turn to Winthrop and exult, "Listen, John, I have a wonderful story to tell you" (58). Winthrop, who has entered during Mrs. Harper's story and has realized who Mrs. Harper is, does not contradict Clara's version, for seeming to misread it serves his purposes too, allowing him at last, as a Winthrop and a lover, to put his arm around her "with an air of assured possession" in which the power of race, class, and gender merge suggestively (59). Thus Winthrop and Clara get the story they need; Mrs. Harper, like Uncle Julius, is left with only as much of the story as her immediate audience can accept. Clara's deep need to reduce Mrs. Harper's story to something which will "fit" her own story signals the extent to which she has indeed become white.

In the atmosphere of turn-of-the-century social Darwinism, survival of the fittest was an intense social concern for the light-skinned blacks who provided Chesnutt with much of his material. Light-skinned blacks faced opportunities of rising—often through "passing"—which were not available to darker members of their race; they also faced the acute fear of falling back into the pit of racial "regression." "We must do the best we can for ourselves and for those who are to follow us," says Mr. Ryder in "The Wife of His Youth," because "self-preservation is the first law of nature" (7).

Self-preservation was the central issue for black stories at the time as well. Becoming fit to survive often involved the narrative equivalent of "passing," with similarly inherent ambiguities. The black story had to look like a white story; it had to at least look like a story which was fully acceptable to the whites who heard it inside the text. If it became fully and unequivocally acceptable, however, it ran the risk of losing its own identity; it would become a white story—as *The Conjure Woman*, for instance, is often taken to be.

To prevent that occurrence, the white reader outside the text became crucial. For if the white listener inside Chesnutt's stories has the seeming power to reduce the black story to what he finds acceptable, the reader outside the text—a reader Chesnutt hopes for but cannot imagine plausibly enough to insert into the story—has access to more; in "Her Virginia Mammy," he has access to the story narrated fully neither by Clara nor Mrs. Harper but available in the intersection between the two. The readers Chesnutt feared and realistically expected are inside his tales; the readers he desired were outside the stories and—such was his implicit fantasy—outside the world of racial assumptions which permeated them.

In Chesnutt's incorporation into his tales of the complex, unspoken negotiations between teller and audience, and in his use of those negotiations to suggest the relationship between race and relative narrative possibilities, his fiction provides a relevant gloss on the status of black story and voice at the turn of the century. His stories are experiments in finding or creating a readership whose existence he had no reason to suppose: is there, they ask, someone out there who can see and accept more than the characters in here, in the America I know too well?

Chesnutt's experiment had mixed results at best. During his lifetime, he never found the audience he needed, at least not an audience who could respond with more than condescending appreciation for what Howells called his "artistic reticence";[12] and even today, many critics remain convinced that his stories passed over the color line irretrievably. The long-term fate of Turner's *Confessions*, however, suggests that such experiments had at least a chance of succeeding. For although the mainstream image of Turner for the last century and a half has remained that of a crazed fanatic, Turner's efforts to project his sense of himself past his hostile warden found fruit with at least some readers throughout the nineteenth century and beyond. In 1856, Harriet Beecher Stowe attached Turner's *Confessions* to her novel *Dred* as a supporting appendix for her relatively sympathetic treatment of slave insurrection. In 1861 William Wells Brown published a favorable essay on Turner, based largely on the *Confessions;* Brown felt the essay important enough to include two years later in *The Black Man: His Antecedents, His Genius, and His Achievements* and then again, in abridged form, in his most significant work, *The Negro in the American Rebellion* (1867). George Washington Williams took a similarly positive view of Turner in his 1883 *History of the Negro Race in America*. To Brown, Turner was a "martyr to the freedom of his race"; to Williams he was simply a "martyr to freedom."[13] Both writers were expanding on the image of himself that Turner had emphasized in the *Confessions*: "Was not Christ crucified?" he had replied to Gray's taunt that the revolt had failed completely.

The more aggressive versions of Turner that emerged in the 1960s also took Turner's text as their starting point. Robert Hayden based his 1966 "Ballad of Nat Turner" on the vision of "angels in dazzling combat" described in the *Confessions*; Daniel Panger's *Ol' Prophet Nat* (1967) reveals its debt to the *Confessions* in the title itself, a debt which the rest of the novel expands. And the widely publicized outrage with which many critics, white as well as black, greeted William Styron's 1967 *Confessions of Nat Turner* derived in part from their conviction that Styron's first-person narrative all but ignored the long-standing sense of Turner which I have just described. They were offended that Styron had in effect informed Turner's voice and character with a perspective closer to that of Thomas Gray than to Turner's; they resented the fact that the popularity of Styron's version undermined the force of Turner's own voice and story more effectively than Gray had.

By examining the power of established, mainstream myths to overpower competing, black narratives, Chesnutt's *The House behind the Cedars* (1900) reveals a concern relevant both to his other stories and to Styron's appropriation of Turner. In this novel, the light-skinned Rowena Walden, attempting to pass for white, moves from North Carolina to South Carolina and falls in love with a white man, George Tryon. The two of them attend the medieval tournament held yearly in the South Carolina town in which Tryon lives and to which Rowena has moved. When Tryon wins the tournament and chooses Rowena as his "Queen of Love and Beauty," she imagines that "I am Cinderella," that she has fallen in love with a prince, and that her past will be rendered irrelevant by the strength of their love.[14]

But to Tryon and to the entire town, the tournament retells a far different story. They perceive not a fairy tale that obliterates the past but a chivalric romance which reaffirms their version of the South's glorious history and of its continuing traditions. In the act of clinging to the old ways, Tryon and his friends cling of necessity to the old racial prejudices, for their Anglo-Saxon pride of race was part of the romance, and they cannot abandon the former without destroying the latter. When Tryon learns that Rowena is black, he is torn but succumbs to the dominant myth of his culture: the radical fairy tale of transforming love is destroyed by the conservative romance of white dominance.

House behind the Cedars dovetails with Chesnutt's other fiction in emphasizing the pitfalls awaiting blacks who step into the dominant culture's sense of story. It reveals Chesnutt's awareness of how tenacious the presiding racial myths of the mainstream culture had become, how difficult it was for whites immersed in that culture to enter into other stories or scripts. At the same time, the power of established stories or myths made it all the more essential for a black writer to try to preserve his own sense of story, at least to slip into print—as Nat Turner had done—the beginnings of a countermyth, in the hope that it would somehow begin to exercise its subversive power.

IV

The Conjure Woman marks the last appearance of white frame narrators/observers until they are conjured up again in the 1960s as objects of irony; if their inclusion led to such severe restriction on teller and tale, better perhaps to step outside the frame altogether. That move was taken first by Chesnutt's contemporary, Sutton Griggs, whose *Imperium in Imperio*, published the same year as *The Conjure Woman*, strikes a hesitant but nonetheless new note in black fiction. For Griggs's narrator, Beryl Trout, is the first free-standing, first-person black narrator in black fiction; he is the first black narrator of an angry work who does not depend for his existence on internal white observers. Ironically, however, precisely because he has no white framework to validate him, Beryl Trout is also one of the most restricted narrators in all of black fiction.

Imperium in Imperio is a novel about a secret organization plotting a nationwide rebellion of blacks angered by America's failure to treat them according to the country's stated principles of equality. Griggs needs a black narrator, since a white observer of a radical black organization would not be plausible. However, because an impassioned, partisan black narrator was equally impossible for such a story at the turn of the century, Griggs creates a black narrator who had once been the "warm personal friend" of the Imperium's two principal leaders and had served as the organization's secretary of state.[15] Yet by the time of his narration, as he explains in his introduction, he has exposed and thus destroyed the Imperium; he has, in his own words, "betrayed the immediate plans of the race to which I belong . . . in the interests of the whole human family" (2). He admits even in the telling that his race has indeed suffered injustice; nonetheless, he did what he did to avert cataclysmic violence which would have threatened "mankind," "humanity," and "civilization" itself (264).

Trout's role is precise if difficult: he must be black to know the story and to convey its legitimate impulses, yet he must be as unblack as possible to tell the story. Or to put it differently, Griggs has side-stepped the protection available through the white narrator/observer but only by creating a black narrator who has internalized the very restrictions usually imposed by such presences. And yet paradoxically, it is because Trout does internalize those restrictions that he is able to give voice to a story that is far more aggressive than he is. For having framed the story by both his own introductory disavowal of it and a concluding reaffirmation of his disenchantment, he is sufficiently cre-dentialed as "civilized" to let the story emerge unscathed, its inher-ently angry force relatively intact. In Beryl Trout, the first-person black narrator—no longer under intratextual monitoring by whites—becomes the kind of narrator who would monitor himself, who would distance himself from his own tale, to be licensed to tell it. If, in *The Conjure Woman*, Chesnutt created tales that could pass for white, Griggs now creates a black storyteller who can pass for white in order to keep the tale black.

His narrative stance thus anticipates by four years the dilemma expressed in DuBois's famous comment that "one ever feels his twoness—an American, a Negro; two souls, two thoughts, two unrec-onciled strivings."[16] But it anticipates it in a particular way that might cause us to rethink the nature of the double vision so often imputed to blacks. For Trout is not so much divided against himself as he is, in effect, Griggs's double agent, serving the story's ends by seeming to play himself off against them at the same time.

A significant development is taking place here. When the narra-tors/observers of black narrative were white, the object of black story-tellers had been to *narrow* the gap between black story and both internal and external audiences to gain validation. Now that the nar-rator is black, the object of the author becomes rather to *emphasize* the gap between the black narrator and his story to convey the emo-tions of the angry story and the rationality of the narrator at the same time. Beryl Trout was the first but by no means the last double-agent narrator in black fiction. In fact, for five decades, from the intermit-tent narrator of *Cane* through the nameless (and invisible) narrator of *The Autobiography of an Ex-Coloured Man* up to and including *Invis-ible Man*, the double agent would remain virtually the only kind of black first-person narrator to reach print when the story to be told was potentially threatening or disconcerting to white readers. This double-agent narrator made it possible for black writers in the first half of this century to present to white readers subjects as volatile as anger, violence, and sex without tainting the individual narrator with the irrational implications of those themes.

The seeming distance from black physicality which characterizes *Imperium in Imperio* serves similarly double ends. For much of the novel, Bernard Belgrave, the eventual voice of revolt, and Belton Piedmont, the eventual voice of nonviolence, remain partially hidden, seen in misleading ways through the filter of white observers, whose pervasive power implicitly dictates the black characters' physical muting. But in the final scene, with no whites nearby, these two men take on undiminished physical stature; their ability to emerge on the page only in the presence of other blacks highlights both the power and the blindness of the whites who consistently have refused to see them as the men they are.

In a manner that reflects his economic dependence, Bernard initially is described derivatively, through his resemblance to his white father, who is "tall and of a commanding appearance . . . [whose] whole noble looking head and handsome face bore a striking resemblance to Bernard's own" (86). Defined along similarly economic lines, Belton fares worse. That his poverty initially drains this "pure and lofty soul" of his masculinity is suggested by the reader's first view of him, dressed only in ragtag, patchwork clothes, the most telling of which is a "worn-out slipper from the dainty foot of some young woman" (116, 2). He is further unmanned later, when, driven to learn for himself what whites were thinking about blacks, he disguises himself as a black maid, travels to New York, and there becomes the object of several seduction attempts by white males whose remarkable capacity to misperceive blacks is thus comically underscored. The lesson Belton learns through this experience—a lesson reinforced by a crazed white physician who treats him like a cadaver before his time—is both the implicit message of the novel itself and the starting point for much of what I have argued thus far in this essay: that "the white man was utterly ignorant of the nature of the Negro of today" (133).

Yet since they are not as diminished, emasculated, and deadened as whites would have them, Bernard and Belton reveal themselves in full force in the climactic scene of the novel, which reveals as well the true nature of the Imperium and of all the black men who compose it. In Bernard's call to revolt, "the whole man was to speak that day," a man of "noble brow," dressed in a Prince Albert suit with a standing collar and necktie (205). With his civilized nature thus certified, however, Bernard also displays a "fierce, determined glance [in which] you could discover that latent fires . . . had been aroused" (205).

In his courageous, solitary resistance to Bernard's incendiary speech, Belton too becomes physically whole for the first time: "Belton stood with his massive, intellectual head thrown back and a look of determined defiance shone forth from his eyes" (227). Just as Bernard had been civilized in his call for revolt, Belton "cried out in impassioned tones" as he counseled restraint (229). Reason and passion, soul and body, can unite in black men speaking before other blacks. The mind-body completeness granted to both men is fitting, for Griggs, aware of a white readership hovering beyond the all-black audience in the Imperium's chamber, wants to give equal recognition to the rationality which characterizes angry blacks and to the passion (rather than docility) which informs even blacks who counsel restraint.

Nonetheless, after the restorative descriptions of Belton and Belgrave, Griggs, through the still effaced narration of Beryl Trout, turns away from his brief acknowledgment of the "whole man" and presents an uninterrupted but entirely verbal record of the debate itself; as it did in "The Heroic Slave," the more denotative aural ultimately dominates the more suggestive visual. And just as Douglass presented his chosen strategy of mere "glimpses" as if he had no choice, Griggs's narrator leads into Bernard's speech with a seeming complaint that the reader will get but a "faint idea of his masterly effort," since "words can portray the form of speech, but the spirit, the life, are missing" (205–6).

This seeming lament notwithstanding, it was precisely the strategy of many early black writers to give a muted idea of their angry character's masterly efforts. In a novel, one of the available strategies for raising mere words to the emotional intensity of human speech is to provide the reader with a photograph of the speech act, of the speaker in the very act of speech. By contrast, black writers from Douglass to Griggs—and well beyond, I would argue—have tended to withdraw the camera at the moment of greatest intensity to keep the spirit and life of assertive speech from being dragged back to earth by association with a physicality that is even more suspect and threatening.[17]

This pattern of deflected, diminished, or carefully hedged physicality however, has been as two-edged as the voice of black narrators. If it has reassured the anxious reader that he is not in the presence of an uncontrolled beast or savage, it has also served as a channel for aggression, a strategic concession which, far from denying the validity or the force of black anger, allows its expression. In this way, voice and image have developed in complex tandem throughout the black literary tradition as markers of a white audience's power over black writers and of the power of black writers to counter with strategies of their own.

V

This subject is not without its historical ironies, and since my acute awareness of those ironies is the fuel behind this essay, I want to acknowledge them. For as a white critic of black literature, I have come to realize that the literary situation of the white observer-critic of black writing today is an interesting inversion of the situation of the white critic-observer who framed, inhabited, validated, and restricted the nineteenth-century black narrative; where whites once ruled, we are now dependent and hesitant.

Or to put it differently, white critics—we, I—find ourselves now in a position not unlike that of the black writer in the nineteenth century: we cannot confidently validate our own statements, our own posture, without the support of established black critics. For although the relationship of whites to blacks in the culture at large regrettably has not changed radically, it has reversed itself within the (still separate?) realm of black studies. For white critics now require validation instead of dispensing it; we must be as careful in what we say today as black writers had to be in the nineteenth century. We are as aware as they were of a powerful and unavoidable audience which has much more cultural weight than we do in the area of our interest. Although some white critics have begun to resist these pressures, on the whole it is still all but impossible for a white critic not to defer to and draw on the authority of black critics, or to feel comfortable offering a negative assessment of black writing.

I would have to be extraordinarily naive not to understand the reasons for this reversal nor, on one level, to see its appropriateness. Furthermore, the reverse equation I offer requires considerable qualification, more than I can offer briefly. Of course, white, often tenured academics of the late twentieth century cannot claim vulnerability to their audience/censors to the same extent that black writers of the nineteenth century (and later) experienced it—we can get published without any more difficulty than black critics, for instance—nor, by a long shot, is there as much at stake. In the rest of our lives, we go back to being white and enjoying the relative immunity from racial stress which that status still confers; we are vulnerable only in the well-defined, freely chosen realm of our professional activities.

The issue now is voice and authority, not survival. White critics are often thought to lack authority, so the argument goes, because we are inherently outsiders to black culture or black experience. That argument, once an understandable cornerstone of the Black Aesthetic movement, is rarely made in public any more. But it has filtered into mainstream assumptions and is voiced nowadays—the ironies multiply—more by white colleagues outside the field than among blacks who are within it; its most overt manifestation is in the pervasive unwillingness of department chairs to hire entry-level white Ph.D.'s as specialists in black literature.

The relative validity of the assumption that white critics are inherently deficient is a large subject for another essay; my point here is simply that white critics have been on the defensive for the last thirty years, even though we often protest, as black writers once did, that we are not on the defensive, that we are not intimidated in any way by the black audience we seek and need nor by the mainstream assumption—an ironic, derivative internalizing of what the mainstream assumes is the black perspective—that we are poaching.

As I have tried to show, black writers have consistently found ways to turn their vulnerability to their audience to good use, or at least to make the best of the situation. Similarly, I think, being a white critic has its advantages, not in spite of its discomforts but because of them. For the historical reversal I have just sketched out gives us at the present moment a peculiar connection to the situation of early black writers; it provides us, whether we like it or not, with a heightened appreciation of the pressures of audience and the way those pressures can shape what we write. That does not make us black, but it confirms for me at least the conviction which I originally brought to the enterprise, that there are legitimate points of entry into the world of black writing other than racial similarity, that there are ways for a white critic to feel a genuine affinity with the literature he studies. The feeling of defensiveness is now one of those ways. If awareness of audience has diminished as a shaping force behind African American writing in the last two or three decades, it has transferred its force to the field of African American criticism.

Notes

1. *The Confessions of Nat Turner, the Leader of the Late Insurrection in Southampton, Va. As Fully and Voluntarily Made to Thomas Gray* (Baltimore, 1831), rpt. in *Nat Turner*, ed. Eric Foner (Englewood Cliffs: Prentice, 1971) 51. Subsequent references are to this edition.

2. William Andrews, *To Tell a Free Story* (Urbana: U of Illinois P, 1986) 73–75. Andrews provides the first extended discussion of Turner's *Confessions* and the only one I have found that addresses the verbal contest between Gray and Turner.

3. Winthrop D. Jordan, *White over Black* (Chapel Hill: U of North Carolina P, 1968), esp. ch. 6. Long before literary critics discovered the concept of an embattled "body," historians had begun investigating in specific terms how racial fears, politics, and pseudoscience combined to place the physicality of American blacks under duress. Jordan provides a more comprehensive discussion of issues already raised by David Brion Davis, *The Problem of Slavery in Western Culture* (Ithaca: Cornell UP, 1966), esp. ch. 15. In *The Black Image in the White Mind* (New York: Harper, 1971), ch. 3, George M. Fredrickson extended Jordan's and Davis's investigations of racial pseudobiology into the nineteenth century.

4. Cf. Raymond Hedin, "Strategies of Form in the American Slave Narrative," in *The Art of Slave Narrative*, ed. John Sekora and Darwin Turner (Macomb: Western Illinois UP, 1982) 23–34. Robert Stepto was the first critic to discuss the "authenticating frameworks" of the slave narrative in *From Behind the Veil* (Urbana: U of Illinois P, 1979), esp. 3–31. For comprehensive discussions of the issue, see John Sekora, "Black Message/White Envelope," *Callaloo* 32 (1987): 482–515; and Andrews, *To Tell a Free Story.*

5. Occasionally a slave narrator will describe a fight between himself and an owner or slave driver; the most famous of these descriptions is Douglass's fight with Covey in his 1845 narrative. But even this description focuses on the action rather than the actor and is itself preceded by Douglass's extended, unsuccessful plea with his owner, Thomas Auld, for relief from Covey's brutality. Thus Douglass's body, through his fight, is the agent of his last, *rational* recourse rather than a sign of his bestiality.

6. Fredrick Douglass, "The Heroic Slave," in *Autographs for Freedom*, ed. Julia Griffiths (Rochester, 1852) 1:174. Subsequent references are to this edition.

7. For a seminal study of "The Heroic Slave," see Robert Stepto, "Storytelling in Early Afro-American Fiction: Frederick Douglass' 'The Heroic Slave,'" *Georgia Review* 36 (1982): 355–69.

8. I see no point in citing critics to suggest their deficiencies. Suffice it to say that critical reconsideration of Chesnutt in the last two decades has taken as its starting point his seeming similarity to plantation writers. For recent views of the relationship of John to Julius and of Julius to his tales, see Lorne Fienberg, "Charles W. Chesnutt and Uncle Julius: Black Storytellers at the Crossroads," *Studies in American Fiction* 15 (1987): 161–73; and R. V. Burnette, "The Conjure Woman Revisited," *College Language Association Journal* 30 (1987): 438–53.

9. Charles W. Chesnutt, *The Conjure Woman* (Boston: Houghton, 1899) 8–9. Subsequent references are to this edition.

10. John's wife, Annie, does respond sympathetically to Julius, but the validity of her response is called into question by her failure to recognize Julius's manipulations. She is more sentimental than perceptive, and her gushings do not convert her husband, even though he grants Julius his favors partly to keep her content. On the whole, although slave narrators such as Harriet Jacobs made overt appeals to women readers, I postulate that the crucial audience for threatening black stories in the nineteenth century was male as well as white. The problematic issue was not whether the stories and their tellers were powerful enough to move their readers but whether they were controlled or muted enough to be acceptable. In the conventional gender divisions which held them, that requirement meant that the judgment of white males—putative bastions of rationality in the midst of "mere" female sentiment—was central. Consistent with this division, all the important internal validators/observers of black stories are male.

11. Charles W. Chesnutt, *The Wife of His Youth and Other Stories of the Color Line* (Boston: Houghton, 1899) 40. Subsequent references are to this edition.

12. William Dean Howells, *Atlantic* May 1900: 700. Chesnutt's problems with finding and keeping an audience have been described by several critics, most tellingly by William Andrews, *The Literary Career of Charles W. Chesnutt* (Baton Rouge: Louisiana State UP, 1980).

13. William Wells Brown, *The Black Man: His Antecedents, His Genius, and His Achievements* (Boston: Wallcut, 1865) 71; George Washington Williams, *History of the Negro Race in America* (New York: Putnam's, 1883) 2:91.

14. Charles W. Chesnutt, *The House behind the Cedars* (Boston: Houghton, 1900) 55, 62.

15. Sutton Griggs, *Imperium in Imperio* (Cincinnati: Editor, 1899) 1. Subsequent references are to this edition.

16. W. E. B. DuBois, *The Souls of Black Folks* (Chicago: McClurg, 1903) 3.

17. Chester Himes's *If He Hollers Let Him Go* (1945) marks a notable change from this strategy, though that change was not elaborated until the 1960s.

PART THREE

Reading and Writing against the Grain: Race, Gender, and Response

Uncle Tom's Cabin and
Antebellum Black Response

MARVA BANKS

Writers, critics, and scholars alike have tended to speculate about the theoretical implications of reader responses, and contemporary reader-response theorists are aware of the broad range these responses now encompass. Though response-oriented criticism has expanded to include several nontraditional reading communities, few of its practitioners have devoted much attention to the black audience. In fact, until recently, the black interpretive community has been one of the most neglected elements in the framework of literary criticism. The responses to the publication of *Uncle Tom's Cabin* corroborate this.

When Stowe's novel appeared in book form in March 1852, the responses of white readers in Europe and the United States—North and South—were carefully recorded and commented upon. These comments became part of a substantial history of reader response. However, this rather extensive history has virtually ignored black readers' responses to *Uncle Tom's Cabin*. It is as if the black reader did not exist or was a mere phantom who could say with Ralph Ellison's protagonist, "I am invisible, understand, simply because people refuse to see me." Though ignored historically, however, the antebellum black audience did exist and had opinions regarding Stowe and her novel. Between 1852, when *Uncle Tom's Cabin* was published in book form, and 1855, when comments about the novel began to diminish, over two hundred articles containing comments by black readers appeared in the antebellum black press. Seven black papers regularly printed these comments. Of the seven, *Frederick Douglass' Paper* carried most of these responses.

To understand the responses of nineteenth-century African Americans to the publication of *Uncle Tom's Cabin*, we need to understand the historical moment in which they came to the novel. The critical issue is what blacks had to say about *Uncle Tom's Cabin* and how the times in which they lived shaped their responses. The purpose of this essay, then, is to analyze surviving black responses to Stowe's novel, recorded in the antebellum black press, as products of the specific historical conditions blacks faced in America between 1852 and 1855, and to show how those responses embody an awareness among black readers of the connections between Stowe's novel and their peculiar historical moment.

The historical moment for blacks at midcentury encompassed a society in which political, economic, and social oppression was rampant in the South *and* in the North. From the time blacks arrived in this country as bond servants of white Americans, they had been accorded inferior status. Indeed, as historian Eric Foner points out, "Racial prejudice . . . was part of the cultural heritage which English colonists brought to the New World, and white supremacy has been a feature of American society from the very beginning."[1] This view of black inferiority crystallized in the mid-nineteenth century as the prevailing racial ideology of whites in both North and South. Though the attention of the nation and of the world was focused on Southern slavery as the most dramatic manifestation of the oppression blacks suffered, the 220,000 blacks residing in the North during the 1850s also were victimized daily by racism. The most telling sign of Northern white views of black inferiority was the enactment of numerous antiblack laws. These laws clearly defined black inferiority while entrenching white power through an exclusionary practice that restricted and degraded blacks.

Specifically, these antiblack codes denied African Americans citizenship, refused to issue them passports, and withheld from them homestead benefits.[2] These laws segregated blacks in public schools and confined blacks in cities to the most depressed neighborhoods; statutes restricted blacks to baggage and cattle compartments on trains and boats and assigned them to black pews, balconies, and lofts in churches and theaters. In most Northern cities blacks were prohibited from serving on juries and from testifying against whites.[3] And although blacks were not legally disenfranchised in any Northern states during the nineteenth century, biased requirements often discouraged them from going to the polls.[4] For example, although property requirements for white male voters were eliminated in New York State in 1821, a prohibitive requirement that blacks own $250 in property to vote was still in effect in the 1850s.[5]

As if these deplorable laws did not degrade blacks severely enough, two more racist forces conspired to announce unequivocally a doctrine of black subjugation. The more overtly heinous of these forces, the New Fugitive Slave Law, enacted by the federal government on September 18, 1850, sought to ensure a speedier return of fugitive slaves by denying the alleged runaway the rights to testify and be tried by a jury, thus assuming his or her guilt rather then innocence.[6] However, the second force, the revitalized American Colonization Society, arguably was as dangerous, in part because its more subtly invidious racism masked its complicity with the Fugitive Slave Law. Like that law, the society had as its major strategy the assertion of white supremacy by proclaiming the innate inferiority of African Americans.[7] Its stated objective—"to aid in the emigration of blacks with their consent to Africa or such places as Congress deemed most expedient"—concealed its real motives, which were later revealed to include the following: (1) to rid the country of undesirable free blacks, and (2) to hasten the emancipation of Southern slaves by providing them a place to go where they would not threaten white safety and well-being.[8] The complex motives of the American Colonization Society embodied a racist ideology, whose chief aim was to export blacks to Africa (or elsewhere) to protect white supremacy in the United States.

Under such conditions, blacks could not devote their full attention to a novel. Of necessity, therefore, *Uncle Tom's Cabin*—despite its phenomenal sales and popularity among whites—was a secondary issue for most antebellum blacks. In fact, when references to the novel appeared in the black press, they were often appended to discussions of more pressing concerns such as politics, education, and employment. Consequently, comments on the novel were concerned less with its artistic merit than with the social and political issues it raised.

As an avenue into the particular character of the mid-nineteenth-century black responses to *Uncle Tom's Cabin*, I want to turn briefly to James Baldwin's 1949 essay "Everybody's Protest Novel," which, I would argue, provides retrospectively a kind of preparatory gloss on the responses by blacks almost a hundred years earlier. Epitomizing the reactions of twentieth-century black critics to Stowe's novel, Baldwin argues that *Uncle Tom's Cabin* was not intended to do anything more than announce that slavery is wrong by "slapping the wrists" of slaveholders. Noting how the novel became something like the "alabaster missionaries to Africa [who] cover the nakedness of the natives,"[9] Baldwin treats (albeit indirectly) the role of black colonization in the novel. Baldwin attacks most forcefully Stowe's denial of the individual humanity of blacks, as evidenced by her reducing all of her black characters to "stock" personalities. "Apart from her . . . procession of field hands [and] house niggers," notes Baldwin, "she has only three other Negroes, only one of which is truly negroid." For Baldwin, the mixture of these stereotypes with Stowe's "self-righteous, virtuous sentimentalizing" creates a dangerous element in the novel.[10] Indeed, Baldwin emphasizes Stowe's racism as it emerges in both *Uncle Tom's Cabin* and in her personal behavior after publishing the novel. What is significant here is that all four of the concerns found in some degree in Baldwin's essay also characterize antebellum black responses: (1) *Uncle Tom's Cabin* as antislavery propaganda, (2) *Uncle Tom's Cabin* as promulgator of colonizationist ideas, (3) *Uncle Tom's Cabin* as a catalogue of sentimental racism, and (4) Stowe's personality as confirmation of blacks' generally ambivalent opinions of the novel. But whereas Baldwin emphasizes the novel's racist stereotyping and treats only obliquely the issue of colonization, it was the latter that eventually constituted the major focus through which antebellum blacks responded to *Uncle Tom's Cabin*.

While these four categories demarcate the general character of mid-nineteenth-century black responses, it should be noted that that response was not monolithic; rather, it encompassed several strains. For even among the prevailing reactions, there were distinct ones. Some of these responses remained constant; others changed over time.

The initial perception blacks had of *Uncle Tom's Cabin* was that it served as an important antislavery weapon. And indeed it was a powerful piece of propaganda that exposed the horrible evils of slavery and advanced a forceful argument against it. Naturally, the early black reaction to Stowe's novel was enthusiastic. In fact, as early as April 8, 1852, less than a month after the book's publication, Frederick Douglass eagerly announced in his *Paper* that "Uncle Tom's Cabin, the thrilling story from the pen of Mrs. Stowe would soon be on sale."[11] Douglass's enthusiasm was repeated at the May 11, 1852, meeting of the American and Foreign Anti-Slavery Society in Rochester, New York, where prominent black physician and abolitionist Dr. James McCune Smith led a delegation of blacks in proposing a resolution that praised *Uncle Tom's Cabin*. The proceedings of the meeting were published in *Frederick Douglass' Paper* on May 27, 1852:

> Dr. James McCune Smith moved the following resolution: Resolved, That the warm thanks of this meeting be presented to Mrs. Harriet Beecher Stowe, for writing the inimitably beautiful and truthful story called *Uncle Tom's Cabin*, and that we rejoice that the Almighty is awakening the finest literary talent of the country to lay their best offering on the altar of human freedom. Dr. Smith eulogized "*Uncle Tom's Cabin*" and said its success—unexampled as it was—proved the depth and breadth of the anti-slavery feeling in this country. The writer touched a vein richer than California gold. (3)

Black shoemaker William J. Wilson, the Brooklyn correspondent for *Frederick Douglass' Paper*, added his praise to *Uncle Tom's Cabin* in his June 17, 1852, column, published over his name "Ethiop":

> "Uncle Tom's Cabin" is all the topic here, aside from the vulgar theme of politics, which is being eclipsed by its greater rival, my "Uncle Tom's Cabin," since its entry into Gotham. Mrs. Beecher Stowe has deserved well of her country, in thus bringing Uncle Tom's Cabin, and all its associations . . . into these Northern regions, and placing it upon the Northern track, and thence round the land. This species of abolitionism finds its way into quarters here hitherto so faced with . . . pro-slavery politics, unionism, churchism, and every other shade of "ism." (3)[12]

William Still, famous black conductor of the Philadelphia underground railroad, wrote a letter in the May 6, 1854, issue of the *Provincial Freeman* extolling the tremendous antislavery assistance *Uncle Tom's Cabin* gave to the underground railroad:

The number of fugitives had doubled the last year's figures. *Uncle Tom's Cabin* had aided in this respect. . . . [T]hat mischievous book *Uncle Tom's Cabin* may be charged with helping the underground railroad largely: for few of the intelligent "articles" that are in the South, have not read, or heard it read, and consequently have at once "fired up" to strike for Canada. By the way, quite recently I had the pleasure of an interview with a very intelligent "piece" of property from the South, who had Uncle Tom with him thinking as much of the old fellow as any other friend living. (2)

For the fugitive slave, or "passenger," on the underground railroad—the "articles" and "piece" in Still's letter—the characters and the story were believable. In fact, we may assume that the story, in many ways, was for them motivation for action in the real world, for Still maintained that the reading of the novel inspired some slaves to "strike for Canada." Hence, as Charles H. Foster observed, "One slave after another, [was] fleeing, fleeing . . . the cruel bondage."[13]

Black expatriates who had read *Uncle Tom's Cabin* also were impressed with its antislavery strength. William Wells Brown, a fugitive slave who had emigrated to England and who, because of the passage of the New Fugitive Slave Law, was still in England at the time of the publication of Stowe's novel, wrote a glowing letter to William Lloyd Garrison, which was printed in *Frederick Douglass's Paper* on December 10, 1852. The letter reported the wide acclaim accorded *Uncle Tom's Cabin* in London:

Dear Mr. Garrison: —I forward to you, by this day's mail, the papers containing accounts of the great meeting held in Exeter Hall last night. No meeting during this anniversary has caused so much talk and excitement as this gathering. "Uncle Tom's Cabin" has come down like a morning's sunlight, unfolding all eyes upon the "peculiar institution," and awakening sympathy in hearts that never before felt for the slave. (2)

William Craft, another black emigrant to England, wrote a letter to Garrison that was printed in the *Liberator* on December 10, 1852, crediting to *Uncle Tom's Cabin* the tremendous rise in antislavery sentiment in England. "Uncle Tom's Cabin," he wrote, "is arousing a great feeling of indignation in the English mind against America's peculiar institution" (5). And Henry Bibb, editor of the Canadian black antislavery journal, the *Voice of the Fugitive*, used *Uncle Tom's Cabin* to bolster his appeal to his Northern U.S. brothers to do what they could to alleviate the suffering of their brothers still in bondage. In an editorial of July 29, 1852, he wrote:

> What can I do? is the question which comes home to every heart. We cannot go unloose their bonds. We cannot change the cruel laws which keep them in slavery, nor the still more cruel one which returns them to it. The heart sickens at the thought that there are multitudes in our free country, suffering in the same way that "Uncle Tom" did and multitudes more enduring all Cassy's wrongs and wretchedness. . . . But if we in the North may not do all we would, let us do what we can. (2)

Although many blacks were understandably excited by the astounding antislavery power of Stowe's novel, as evidenced by the number of changed opinions regarding slavery, they soon discovered that *Uncle Tom's Cabin* possessed an equivalent capacity to promulgate certain racist images. As Charles Foster points out, while Stowe's novel "is written from an essentially abolitionist perspective, it does not challenge racism, but to a degree, encourages it."[14] According to J. C. Furnas, *Uncle Tom's Cabin* "provided numbers of whites who had only vague notions of an innate black inferiority with an apparently authoritative racist creed to plump up their previously inchoate notions."[15] Indeed, Stowe's sympathy for African colonization and her proclivity to racial stereotypes reinforced, in important ways, the dominant argument of proslavery advocates: white supremacy.

The African colonization scheme posed a real danger to free blacks. Proof of that danger is the fact that approximately 30,000 blacks had been deported involuntarily since the founding of the American Colonization Society in 1816.[16] Consequently, many blacks fought the scheme vigorously. As early as January 1817, they mobilized to combat the dangerous tenets of the society through conventions, petitions, speeches, resolutions, and editorials.[17]

During the 1850s Frederick Douglass led the attack against African emigration. The columns of his *Paper* were dominated by the numerous discussions opposing the emigration of black Americans. In a July 31, 1851, editorial headed "African Colonization," Douglass lashed out against colonization and admonished black expatriates in England and Canada to return to the United States and lend their support to the antislavery crusade:

Taking advantage of the depressed, disheartened and anguish-smitten state of our people, our inveterate persecutors and destroyers are vigorously plying all their hellish enginery [*sic*] for our removal and expatriation. Colored Americans, Come Home! If ever there was a time when every intelligent colored American was needed at home, now is such a time. We need the men who can wield pen and tongue. Whose character can bring commendation even from the stony hearted oppressor. . . . We beg them. . . . Come home and help Samuel B. Ward, C. L. Redmond and Amos Beman rouse the slumbering conscience of the nation to our wrongs. Of course you must judge for yourselves what is best for you to do. (1)

What Douglass's final sentence says, in effect, is that only the expatriates themselves, because many of them were fugitive slaves, know whether or not it would be safe for them to return to the United States. *Douglass' Paper* shared this opposition to African colonization with the other black abolitionist newspapers. Virtually no issue of any anti-slavery black journal was without some objection to colonization.

To show how deeply entrenched the tenets of the American Colonization Society were in the national political tradition, Douglass unearthed a striking correlation between nineteenth-century African colonization propaganda and Thomas Jefferson's famous *Notes on the State of Virginia* (1787). In 1853, Douglass wrote an editorial based on his interpretation of this excerpt from Jefferson's book:

For one, I am prepared and ready now to give my voice unhesitatingly in favor of any feasible plan to send every negro far away [to Africa] from our land, with all possible dispatch—This must be done in the Spirit of kindness and christian philanthropy toward the blacks, and from the pressing motive of self preservation on the part of whites.[18]

Douglass's editorial on April 22, 1853, entitled "Thomas Jefferson and Slavery," analyzes the close ideological link between Jefferson's views and the views of nineteenth-century advocates of African colonization. Douglass concludes that Jefferson's pronouncement lay at the heart of the polemic of the society, thus proving Jefferson's efficacious influence on African colonization doctrine. Douglass commends Jefferson's honesty and says that he wishes that the contemporary colonizationists "would throw off their mask of hypocrisy, for we are tired of the syren song of the colonizationists, 'with their consent'" (2). An excerpt taken from the *Greenville* (S.C.) *Mountaineer* and printed in *Douglass' Paper* does precisely that: "We regard every free Negro as the vilest enemy. . . . We believe that S. C. would advance her interests . . . if she were to ship her free Negroes to another land" (April 8, 1852: 2). The South Carolinian, at least, had taken off his mask.

Black educator and abolitionist William G. Allen joined the attack on African colonization when he wrote a letter published in *Douglass' Paper* on April 19, 1852, charging that "colonizationists have recently dug up Thomas Jefferson, for a two-fold purpose of helping them berate African intellect, and thus make out that the race is not fit to live among white folks; and to aid colonization" (3). Allen, too, observed the practice of African colonizationists in invoking Jefferson's racial creed to justify their colonization scheme.

Free black Martin Cross deviated from the standard prose expression of opposition when he articulated his disapproval poetically in the March 25, 1853, issue of *Douglass' Paper*:

> Talk not to me of colonization
> For I'm a free man of this native land
> Not of Africa's burning sun and sand
> We hereby make our proclamation
> That we're opposed to emigration
> This is the land which gave us birth—
> Our father's graves are freedom's earth. (2)

The African colonization threat reached a new intensity in 1852 when the book version of *Uncle Tom's Cabin* appeared and was interpreted as showing Stowe's favorable opinion toward colonization. To be sure, the novel presents at least two dramatic expressions of procolonization sympathy. We see the first example when George Harris, despairing of ever achieving success in America or in Canada, seeks an alternative homeland. Where will we go, he wonders. The answer is Africa. In a letter to his friend detailing his future plans, Harris writes:

> It is with the oppressed, enslaved African race that I cast my lot; . . .
> the desire and yearning of my soul is for an African nationality. . . .
> I grant that this Liberia may have subserved all sorts of purposes, by
> being played off, in the hands of our oppressors, against us. Doubt-
> less the scheme may have been used in unjustifiable ways, as a means
> of retarding our emancipation. . . . But the question . . . is, Is there

not a God above all man's schemes? May he not have overruled their designs, and found for us a nation by them?[19]

According to Leon Litwack, "Harris is clearly aware of the complex dynamics of the colonization plan and the multiple motivations of the organization. And although he knows that Liberia has been used by the colonizationists to 'retard emancipation,' Harris maintains that such sinister and self-serving schemes should not obstruct its value as the foundation of a new independent black nation."[20] "I want a country, a nation of my own," Harris says. "I think the African race has peculiarities, yet to be unfolded in the light of civilization and Christianity" (610). Although Harris recognizes the sinister machinations impelling white support of colonization, he cannot overlook the opportunity Liberia offers blacks to build their own independent nation. Thus determined to establish his own nation, George Harris departs with his family for Africa.

The second example—and the one that antebellum blacks focused on as the more telling index to the novel's and Stowe's personal views on the expatriation of blacks to Africa—appears in the chapter entitled "Concluding Remarks." Having disposed of her major black characters in Africa, Stowe presents her solution to the problem of what to do with free blacks in nineteenth-century America. According to Jean Yellin, "Stowe mixed antislavery sentiment with white supremacy" when she suggests emigration for black Americans as a means of ameliorating the race problem instead of immediate emancipation and recognition of the rights of free blacks.[21] Stowe recommends emigration for blacks and gives explicit instructions as to how blacks should be prepared for their exportation to Africa: "Let the church of the north receive these poor sufferers in the spirit of Christ: receive them to the educating advantages of Christian republican society and intellectual maturity and then assist them in their passage to those shores, where they may put into practice what they have learned in America" (626).

Although the majority of Stowe's black characters accept her remedy for the race problem and depart for Liberia, black abolitionists were not so easily persuaded that her call for African emigration was for them an acceptable solution. At the annual meeting of the American and Foreign Anti-Slavery Society in Rochester, New York, on May 11, 1852, fugitive slave and prominent black abolitionist George T.

Downing led the black delegates in condemning the chapter of *Uncle Tom's Cabin* that dealt favorably with colonization. He urged that some measure be introduced to minimize the influence of a resolution that had been initiated earlier in the meeting by black physician and abolitionist Dr. McCune Smith praising Stowe's novel.[22] Free black educator and abolitionist William G. Allen echoed Downing's disapproval of the colonization theme in the novel when he wrote a letter to *Douglass's Paper* on May 20, 1852, in which he denounced Stowe's colonization chapter: "I have one regret, with regard to the book and that is, that the chapter favoring colonization was ever written" (3).

In response to the criticism blacks leveled against her colonization theme, Stowe wrote a note which was read by her friend, the Reverend Leonard Bacon of Boston, to the convention of the American and Foreign Anti-Slavery Society in New York City in 1853. Bacon claimed that she had told him that "she was not a colonizationist and that if she were to rewrite the novel, she would not send the blacks to Africa."[23] Despite this claim, Stowe again wrote favorably of colonization in her novel *Dred*, published in 1856.

Stowe's denial of colonizationist sympathy did not curb black opposition. In an editorial in the September 10, 1852, issue of his *Paper*, Douglass criticized *Uncle Tom's Cabin* because "the closing chapter urges [colonization] forcefully" (2). Black minister and abolitionist agent for the Refugee Home Society, C. C. Foote, also criticized Stowe's colonization theme.[24] In his regular column, "The Refugees' Home Society," in *Douglass' Paper* for April 22, 1853, he noted that *Uncle Tom's Cabin* had been a principal cause of an increase in procolonization sentiment:

> For the past two years my whole time has been spent listening to the views of all classes of people. . . . A sentiment . . . is now . . . developing itself with certain and accelerated growth that has for its object the ultimate removal of the colored people from the northern states to the shores of Africa. It will not be traveling far out of the record, to say, "Uncle Tom's Cabin" comes in for a large share in the growth of this sentiment. (2)

The most intensive and sustained response to Stowe's favorable treatment of African colonization can be seen in the letters exchanged between Frederick Douglass and militant black abolitionist Martin B. Delany, which were published in *Douglass' Paper* from April 1, 1853, to May 6, 1853. In his book *The Condition, Elevation, Emigration, and*

Destiny of the Colored People of the United States (1852), Delany had pointed out that "the whites, have always presumed to think for, dictate to and know better what suited colored people, then they know for themselves."[25] Delany recognized this same presumption in *Uncle Tom's Cabin* and was outraged. Therefore, in a letter written to Douglass and printed in *Douglass' Paper* on April 1, 1853, he excoriated Stowe's novel not only because of its colonizationist theme, but also because of Douglass' consultation with Stowe and Stowe's promised philanthropy on behalf of blacks:

> Frederick Douglass, esq., Dear Sir:
>
> I notice in your paper of March 4 an article in which you speak of having paid a visit to Mrs. H. E. B. Stowe, for the purpose . . . of consulting her, "as to some method which should contribute successfully and permanently to the improvement and elevation of free people of color. . . ." Now I . . . wish to say, that we have always fallen into great errors in efforts of this kind, going to others than the intelligent and experienced among ourselves; I beg leave to say, that she [Stowe] knows nothing bout us, the free colored people of the United States. Her colonization plan is cause for alarm. As God lives, I will never, knowingly, lend my aid to any such work while our brethren groan in vassalage and bondage. (2)

Douglass's angry reply to Delany's letter was printed in the same April 1 issue of *Douglass' Paper*. Douglass pointed out that some whites can help blacks, and furthermore, that Delany had not himself offered a "plan for benefiting blacks":

> That colored men would agree among themselves to do something for the efficient and permanent aid of themselves and their fate, "is a consummation devoutly to be wished," but until they do, it is neither wise nor graceful for them or for anyone of them to throw cold water upon plans and efforts made for that purpose by others. To scornfully reject all aid from our white friends, and to denounce them as unworthy of our confidence, looks high and mighty enough on paper: but unless the background . . . is filled up with facts, what use is such display of self consequence? Why, then, should any man object to the efforts of Mrs. Stowe . . . or anyone else who is moved to do anything on our behalf.

In a letter headed "Mrs. Stowe's Position" printed in *Douglass' Paper* on May 6, 1853, Delany confronted Stowe's colonizationist views head on:

Frederick Douglass, Esq.: Dear Sir:

Is not Mrs. Stowe a colonizationist? Having so avowed, or at least subscribed to, and recommended their principles, in her great work of Uncle Tom. . . . Although Mrs. Stowe has ably, eloquently and pathetically portrayed some of the sufferings of the slave, is it any evidence that she has any sympathy for his . . . semi-free brethren anywhere or of the African race at all: when in the same . . . work she sneers at Hayti while at the same time holding up . . . Liberia in high estimation? (2)

Angered by Stowe's favoring of a colony in Liberia over a free and independent black nation like Haiti, Delany perceived Stowe's gestures as racist and concluded: "I must be permitted to draw my own conclusion, when I say that I can see no other cause for this singular discrepancy in Mrs. Stowe's interest in the colored race, than that one is independent of, and the other subservient to white men's power."

In response to Delany's scathing condemnation of Stowe's procolonizationist stance, Douglass wrote this eloquent defense in the same issue:

This letter is premature, unfair, uncalled for, and withal needlessly long; but happily, it needs not a long reply. . . . The letter is premature, because it attacks a plan the details of which are yet undefined. He says she is a colonizationist: and we ask, what if she is; names do not frighten us. We recognize friends wherever we find them. Whoever will bring a straw's weight of influence to break the chains of our brother bondmen, whisper one word of encouragement and sympathy to our proscribed race in the North shall be welcomed by us to that philanthropic field of labor. We shall not, therefore, allow the sentiments put in the brief letter by George Harris, at the close of Uncle Tom's Cabin, to vitiate forever, Mrs. Stowe's power to do us good.

Like Delany, other blacks were troubled and even angered by Stowe's favorable view of African colonization. For example, George Downing's letter to *Douglass' Paper* in 1854 expressed his strong disapproval of Stowe's exporting of George Harris: "Mrs. Stowe lands and leaves one of her main heroes in Africa." The rest of Downing's letter denounced emigration as a viable alternative for blacks:

> Whither would we fly if we would escape the life which man is heir to? Where, but that we will find something to encounter, to endure—but the same spectre will arise and point to responsibilities skulked—some work left undone—run away from. These are among the thoughts that arise while listening to the declamations of . . . colonizationists who would have us go to Africa as they allege, to avoid the life we here have to endure, to be benefitted; but we look upon difficulties to surmount these. (May 10, 1854: 2)

The response that came from a correspondent of the black abolitionist journal the *Provincial Freeman* was angriest of all. In a letter headed "George Harris" printed in the paper on July 22, 1854, the correspondent explained: "Uncle Tom must be killed, —George Harris exiled! Heaven for dead negroes . . . Liberia for living mulattoes! Neither can live on the American continent! Death or banishment is our doom, say the slaveowners, the colonizationists, and, —save the mark, —Mrs. Stowe!" (2). This letter attacks all who participate in the heinous scheme of African expatriation—slaveowners, the colonizationists, and Harriet Beecher Stowe. For, in the view of many blacks, Stowe had proven herself to be an enemy of justice and equality for blacks by preferring colonization over immediate emancipation.

Just as troubling for many blacks was Stowe's use of racial stereotypes. For in *Uncle Tom's Cabin* she dramatizes the prevailing notion of black subjugation through her depiction of blacks as naturally obedient, Christian, childlike, and forgiving. And while these qualities are found in many of Stowe's blacks—including Andy, Topsy, and Sam—and are not limited to Tom, it is the latter's characterization that most offended blacks. As Thomas F. Gossett points out, "Blacks recognized that it was the submissive personality of Tom, channeled through Christian piety, which represented the long-range dangerous effects of the novel's influence."[26] From the beginning of the novel, Stowe portrays Tom as childlike, Christian, and submissive, a combination that prevents him from resisting slavery outright through forceful action. Compared to the "hard and dominant Anglo-Saxon race, Tom had the gentle domestic heart, which . . . was a peculiar characteristic of his unhappy race" (152), Stowe tells her readers, adding elsewhere that he "had the soft, impressible nature of his race, ever yearning toward the simple and childlike" (231). When Tom offers a final prayer before leaving the Shelby plantation, Stowe notes that "nothing could exceed the touching simplicity, and childlike earnestness of his prayer" (79).

"The negro is naturally more impressible to religious sentiment than the white," St. Clare declares (342)—a "truth" that the novel seeks to promote especially through the character of Tom. As a Christian leader, Tom ministers to blacks and whites. When St. Clare grieves over little Eva's death, Tom begs him to look to God for strength. St. Clare claims to do just that: "Ah, Tom! I do look up, but the trouble is, I don't see anything" (435). Still, he confesses that "it seems to be given to children, and poor, honest fellows like you, to see what we can't" (435). And finally, when Tom is brutally beaten by Legree and his evil lieutenants, Sambo and Quimbo, and lies mortally wounded, he continues his evangelism by forgiving all three and praying for the salvation of the two slaves.

Tom's Christian piety caused antebellum blacks much consternation. William G. Allen wrote a letter to *Douglass' Paper* on May 22, 1852, in which he criticized the novel for its racist delineation of black characters. He was especially troubled by Tom's excessive piety: "Uncle Tom was a good old soul, thoroughly and perfectly pious. Indeed, if any men had too much piety, Uncle Tom is that man." Allen was quick to point out that he himself did not subscribe to Stowe's brand of docile piety. Allen found a more militant theology more compatible with his personal dictum:

> I confess to more of "total depravity." More shame to me, possibly, but nevertheless, such is the fact. My non resistance is of the Douglass, Parker, and Phillip's school. I believe, as you do, that it is not light the slaveholder wants, but fire, and he ought to have it. I do not advocate revenge, but simply, resistance to tyrants, if it need be to the death. (3)

Tom's submissive character, too, caused much resentment. On December 10, 1852, William G. Nell wrote a letter to William Lloyd Garrison's *Liberator* protesting against *Uncle Tom's Cabin* for its emphasis on Tom's willing submission to slavery (5). On March 22, 1853, Douglass's Brooklyn correspondent William J. Wilson wrote his disapproval of Tom's docility: "Uncle Tom—good old Uncle Tom—ever going about doing good and no harm" (2). The Reverend J. B. Smith of Rhode Island, whose father died resisting slavery, condemned

Tom's submission to tyranny and concluded that "obedience to God is resistance to tyranny."[27]

In a letter to *Douglass' Paper* on July 22, 1854, George T. Downing expressed his objection to Tom's obsequious character, writing that "he preferred George Harris because he was the only one that really betrays any other than the subservient, submissive Uncle Tom spirit which has been the cause of so much disrespect felt for the colored man" (2). As we have seen, a correspondent of the *Provincial Freeman* for July 22, 1854, took perhaps the strongest stand by declaring that "Uncle Tom must be killed"—in other words, the image of black subservience that Tom's character engendered must be discouraged, done away with. Because the submissive, docile quality embodied by Tom was perceived by many blacks to be subversive to black progress, the spirit and the image would have to be "killed." For many black readers of the novel, the character of Tom was a telling sign that Stowe's racism lined up perfectly with the general sentiment of mainstream nineteenth-century America.

What blacks suspected as racial ambivalence in Stowe's novel was confirmed for them in her personality, particularly in her personal response to blacks. Although she had come in contact with a number of blacks in her hometown of Litchfield, Connecticut, in Cincinnati, Ohio, and during her brief tour of a Kentucky slave plantation, and though she was often patronizing and benevolent toward blacks, Stowe felt they occupied a subservient position to whites as chattel and wage slaves.[28] In this regard, she was like Ophelia in *Uncle Tom's Cabin:* she detested slavery, but could not accept blacks as her equal. Stowe was never as committed an abolitionist as were her contemporaries Lucretia Mott, Lydia Child, or the Grimke sisters. She remained on the periphery of abolitionism. Perhaps she had inherited this conservative abolitionism from her father, the Reverend Lyman Beecher. But whatever the motivation, Stowe dealt with slavery from a distance, and with a distinct racial ambivalence.

On occasion, Stowe had demonstrated this marked insensitivity towards blacks. Martin Delany reported such an incident in a letter published in *Douglass' Paper* on May 6, 1853, under the heading, "Mrs. Stowe's Position":

In May last, 1852, a colored man,—humble and common placed, to be sure—chanced to meet with Mrs. Stowe at the house of Mr.—, in the city of N——, state of N——: where he had called with some articles for sale. He informs me that Mrs. Stowe was very indifferent towards him – more than any of the several persons present; and hearing him speak on his elevation in the United States, she asked, very seriously, what he expected to gain by any efforts that could be made here; and when he referred to the West Indies, and South America, etc., as an alternative, she at once asked him, "why he did not go to Liberia." (2)

Stowe's suggestion to the peddler proves that her endorsement of Liberia as an alternative homeland for American blacks extended beyond mere fictional license. Apparently she sincerely felt that blacks could develop their potential more fully in Africa than in the United States. But for Delany and other African Americans, Stowe's behavior clearly embodied a mixture of abolition sentiment and racist doctrine – a combination which helped to prohibit the fulfillment of liberty and equality for nineteenth-century blacks.

The key to understanding the complex nature of the racial ambivalence in Stowe's novel and in her personality, and the particular responses blacks made to the novel, lies in the historical moment that inspired the novel and these reactions. For Stowe was as much influenced by her race, moment, and milieu when she created *Uncle Tom's Cabin* as the black readers who responded to it were affected by theirs. Black responses to *Uncle Tom's Cabin* were like Stowe's views on race – ambivalent. Initially, blacks eagerly heralded it and were optimistic about the impetus it would give to the abolitionist cause. But as blacks became increasingly aware that Stowe's novel had an equivalent power to foster certain images of black inferiority and could therefore be used to bolster the proslavery argument, their early enthusiasm often changed to skepticism and then to anger. Understandably, black responses changed with black perceptions of the complex dynamics of the novel and the power it had to increase or to retard freedom and equality for blacks. Thus, what initially appeared as a blessing to convert the hearts of the nation to abolitionism became for black readers, responding to *Uncle Tom's Cabin* in the context of racist and procolonizationist ideology at midcentury, a curse that encouraged continuation of the doctrine of white supremacy in America.

Notes

1. Eric Foner, *America's Black Past* (New York: Harper, 1970) 142.

2. Ibid. 143.

3. Leon Litwack, *North of Slavery* (Chicago: U of Chicago P, 1961) 114.

4. Foner, *America's Black Past* 143.

5. Litwack, *North of Slavery* 114.

6. The Fugitive Slave Act, a component of the Missouri Compromise, enacted first in 1793 and revised in 1800, 1807, 1813, 1819, and 1820, was designed to make more stringent the original 1793 law.

7. Thomas F. Gossett, *"Uncle Tom's Cabin" and American Culture* (Dallas: Southern Methodist UP, 1985) 87.

8. Kenneth Stampp, *The Peculiar Institution* (New York: Oxford UP, 1956) 130.

9. James Baldwin, "Everybody's Protest Novel," *Notes of a Native Son* (Boston: Beacon, 1984) 20.

10. Ibid. 16, 14.

11. "Uncle Tom's Cabin," *Frederick Douglass' Paper* April 8, 1852: 2. Subsequent references to this and other contemporary periodicals appear in the text.

12. Several months earlier, Douglass had described Wilson as a "keen observer and an honest adviser of his people" (*Frederick Douglass' Paper* March 11, 1853: 3).

13. Charles H. Foster, *The Rungless Ladder* (Durham: Duke UP, 1954) 34.

14. Ibid. 59.

15. J. C. Furnas, *Goodbye to Uncle Tom* (New York: Sloan, 1956) 50.

16. Frederick Douglass, "The Colored Population," *Frederick Douglass' Paper* April 15, 1853: 3.

17. Litwack, *North of Slavery* 26.

18. Thomas Jefferson, *Notes on the State of Virginia* (Chapel Hill: U of North Carolina P, 1955) 130.

19. Harriet Beecher Stowe, *Uncle Tom's Cabin*, ed. Ann Douglass (New York: Penguin, 1985) 609. Subsequent citations appear in the text.

20. Litwick, *North of Slavery* 255.

21. Jean Yellin, *The Intricate Knot: Black Figures in American Literature, 1776–1863* (New York: New York UP, 1972) 147.

22. "Minutes of the Eighteenth Annual Meeting of the American and Foreign Anti-Slavery Society," *Frederick Douglass' Paper* May 27, 1852: 3.

23. *Thirteenth Annual Report of the American and Foreign Anti-Slavery Society* (New York, 1853) 193.

24. The Refugees' Home Society was a black organization located in Detroit that assisted fugitive slaves and black emigrants in securing homes in Canada.

25. Martin B. Delany, *The Condition, Elevation, Emigration and Destiny of the Colored People of the United States* (1852; New York: Arno, 1968) 5.

26. Gossett, *"Uncle Tom's Cabin" and American Culture* 172.

27. *Proceedings of the Meeting of the American and Foreign Anti-Slavery Society* (New York, 1853) 112.

28. John R. Adams, *Harriet Beecher Stowe* (New York: Twayne, 1963) 52.

Reading before Marx: Margaret Fuller and the *New-York Daily Tribune*

CHRISTINA ZWARG

> The Newspaper promises to become daily of more importance, and if the increase of size be managed with equal discretion, to draw within itself the [audience] of all other literature of the day.
>
> MARGARET FULLER, *New York Daily Tribune*, September 24, 1845

Margaret Fuller was well known during the nineteenth century as one of the most prodigious readers of her day. Her father's insistence that she be trained in a medley of foreign languages meant that she had access to a wide variety of texts normally unavailable to young women in this country. Yet Fuller's love of reading far exceeded her father's expectations. Early perceiving the critical edge that a knowledge of literature and history had given her, Fuller came to view reading as an important site for significant social change. Even in her early translations, Fuller began to show a unique interest in transforming the reading habits of her culture.[1] Indeed, a preoccupation with reading permeates all of Fuller's writing, including her work as editor for *The Dial* and her "Conversations" with women. Significantly, Fuller's visit to the Midwest in 1843, where she saw the terrible effects of Western civilization on Native American cultures, rendered her faith in reading problematic. Yet writing *Summer on the Lakes*, her account of that crisis, enabled her to sophisticate her thinking about social change in a productive manner.[2] In the process she found a way to incorporate the thinking of one of the more radical readers of Western civilization, the popular if controversial French theorist Charles Fourier.[3] It was no accident that Fourier's vision of social change depended upon the role of women in society. Thus Fuller's interest in reading did not wane when she returned to the topic of women. Alice Jardine's idea of "Woman" as "reading effect" can be said to characterize Fuller's most famous text, *Woman in the Nineteenth Century*, written one year later.[4] Still, it was only at the close of 1844, when she began to write for the *New-York Daily Tribune*, that Fuller actually began to elaborate her theory of reading and social change. Strangely, that evolving theory has been overlooked by even the most discerning of Fuller's critics.

Greeley's paper, which he founded in 1841 with the hope of raising the "masses," matched Fuller's interests beautifully. Determined from the beginning to avoid the sensationalism of the average New York newspaper (of which there were twenty-one at the time), Greeley created a literary section for his front page.[5] Initially Henry Raymond, the future founder of the *New York Times*, handled the literary material, before taking a more lucrative position with the *Courier and Enquirer* in 1843. Greeley had encouraged Albert Brisbane to develop a column on the social vision of Charles Fourier for the same section of the paper, establishing a precedent for the mix of social and literary concerns that would soon distinguish the columns of Margaret Fuller. Unfortunately, Brisbane's dull translation of Fourier's satiric wit brought more boredom than edification to the paper, and his column eventually dropped from its pages. As a result, Greeley began looking for another writer who could assume responsibility for the work handled by Raymond and Brisbane. Because Molley Greeley, during an extended visit to New England, had been impressed with Fuller's ability, she suggested to her husband that Fuller be given the job. The critical and literary skills that Fuller exhibited in *Summer on the Lakes*, including her provocative allusions to Fourier, made it easy for Horace Greeley to heed his wife's advice. Already familiar with her work as editor of *The Dial*, Greeley greatly admired Fuller's writing in *Summer*, calling it "unequalled" as "one of the clearest and most graphic delineations, ever given, of the Great Lakes, of the Prairies."[6]

Greeley expected a great deal from Fuller, and she received fair compensation for her labor as one of the first women to work as a salaried newspaper writer.[7] Fuller apparently wrote some essays anonymously, but while in New York she signed nearly 250 with a large asterisk (or "star" as Greeley was fond of saying, often calling her "the 'star' of the *New-York Tribune*").[8] If Greeley occasionally complained about the time it took Fuller to write her columns, he greatly admired her work, and he insisted that she continue her affiliation with the paper as a foreign correspondent when she embarked on a trip to Europe in late 1846.

Without a doubt, Fuller's fascinating columns helped the paper achieve a respectable readership; by the end of the decade the *Tribune* had gone from being a competitive local newspaper to being one of national and international status (so much so that when invited only a year after Fuller's death to write a column for the paper, Karl Marx welcomed the opportunity to do so, calling it the "foremost English language American newspaper").[9] From December 1844 until August 1846, Fuller filled the pages of the *Tribune* with an enormous array of essays including reviews of books, concerts, and operas; translations from foreign newspapers; and a generous range of social commentary. Later in 1846, after Fuller began her duties as foreign correspondent for the paper, her dispatches from England and France continued to provide commentary on social and cultural matters. From 1847, when she traveled to Italy, until 1850, her letters to the *Tribune* focused almost exclusively on that country's gathering national revival, the Risorgimento.

Because scholars have assumed that the letters from Italy formed a rough outline of the lost manuscript of Fuller's history of the Italian Revolution, they have tended to overvalue them. According to Larry Reynolds, the most recent commentator on this material, the dispatches from Italy demonstrate "more artistry and power than any of her other writings," including Fuller's first *Tribune* letters from England and France, because they focus "upon the fate of the socialist republican cause in Europe" and are "polished, objective and elevated."[10]

Reynolds's admiration for the Italian correspondence rests on the consistency of Fuller's political position, which he describes as a "new ideological commitment." Had Reynolds addressed Fuller's earliest *Tribune* work, however, he would have seen more continuity in Fuller's thinking; at the very least he would have found considerable evidence that Fuller's critique of America and her interest in socialism were already quite advanced while she was still in New York.[11] Bell Gale Chevigny did take the time to review some of Fuller's early *Tribune* writings, noting Fuller's habit of translating accounts of political and social events abroad from immigrant and foreign newspapers. In August 1845, for example, Fuller translated a column from the German immigrant newspaper *Deutsche Schnellpost* entitled "The Social Movement in Europe," which called for an end to the conflicts between Marx and Ruge in Germany and included some passages from Engels's recently published *Condition of the Working Class in England*.[12] This column was one of the earliest English notices of Marx and Engels in America.

Although she acknowledges Fuller's radical disposition in these early pages of the *Tribune*, Chevigny finds troubling the unpredictable nature of Fuller's rhetorical position in her columns, calling her work "naive" and "condescending" as often as she calls it "moving or advanced." In this way, Chevigny dismisses the large bulk of Fuller's *Tribune* work as "apprentice exercises" for her later "more informed, critical, and independent role of foreign correspondent."[13] Like Reynolds, Chevigny obviously is in search of a unified political perspective in Fuller's writing, which only begins to occur, according to Chevigny, in Fuller's last Italian letters. Though she is more attentive to Fuller's earlier *Tribune* writing than Reynolds, Chevigny is no less impatient with the nature of that material. Agreeing with Reynolds that "Fuller's new sociopolitical concerns . . . resulted . . . in the best writing she ever did," Chevigny slights the enormous range of Fuller's work in those early years.[14]

The unfortunate result of this criticism, which seeks to establish Fuller's "political" credentials, has been a crude thematization of her writing in New York and her early dispatches from England and France. In the process, the real contribution of these writings, their elaboration of a radical theory of reading, has remained obscure. Conceding that Fuller did write "about" such controversial matters as prostitutes, Indians, slavery, insanity, prison reform, poverty, and growing class conflict, Chevigny and Reynolds nonetheless dismiss the manner in which she wrote, attributing Fuller's style to her old preoccupation with aesthetic concerns. In effect, both Reynolds and Chevigny are impatient with the enormous range of book and cultural reviews that fill Fuller's early column. Yet Fuller's aesthetic concerns are precisely what lend complexity to her approach to social issues in the early *Tribune* work: her skill as a reader, particularly her interest in literary discourse and the problematic of translation, gives her an enlarged sense of the vast network of ideological discourse through which we all function. These very concerns help Fuller to elaborate a radical theory of reading for the culture, one meant to develop a form of political agency that would include a more diverse group of people than those who traditionally hold power.

According to Chevigny, Fuller's European "change" entails a rejection of the "specialness and autonomy of American destiny" for a "multiple and morally dialectic" sense of the culture, one acknowledging how "nations change under the pressure of challenges posed them by other societies."[15] But Fuller's belief that cultural change is "multiple and morally dialectic" begins to emerge long before her trip to Europe: it originates with her early interest in translation and the study of comparative literature. Her determination to support a "multiple and morally dialectic" view of culture develops steadily from the moment she encounters the clash of Anglo and Native American cultures during her trip to the Midwest.

Thus, there is clearly another way to frame our understanding of Fuller's *Tribune* work. Instead of viewing the material written early in New York as her "transition" period (a position which reinforces the idea that she would require the "liberating" factors of Europe to gain true political insight), we should see them as essays dedicated to the "transitional" state of the culture. What in Reynolds's opinion constitutes a "structural" weakness in Fuller's writing, her tendency to cover a "multitude of topics related only by the fact that they happen to engage her interest at the time,"[16] may instead be seen to comprise a more sophisticated political strategy, one designed to observe the multiple fronts through which real social change must be negotiated. As we will see, this strategy becomes articulated through Fuller's constant return in her writing to the political efficacy of a certain type of reading.

My interpretation of Fuller's early *Tribune* writing is aided by Antonio Gramsci's distinction between political hegemony and domination. Gramsci was one of the first political theorists to move away from the limited understanding of ideology as "false" consciousness.[17] Against the strain in Marxist thinking emphasizing inexorable economic forces, Gramsci underscores the importance of cultural and intellectual factors.[18] In a move anticipating Althusser, Gramsci defines ideology as the horizon "on which men move, acquire consciousness of their position, [and] struggle."[19] This idea allows Gramsci to posit that an ideological consensus, aptly described as hegemonic activity, may be reached among various classes. Gramsci believes that the success of any revolutionary idea depends upon such hegemonic activity. This complex process of consent, a process working through a variety of intellectual and educational channels, distinguishes hegemonic power from the power of domination essentially realized through the "coercive machinery of the state."[20] At the same time, the concept of hegemony also helps to explain the success of certain counterrevolutionary forces. Gramsci's analysis shows how an uneven consensual process can result in a "passive revolution" and the ascendancy to power of political reactionaries. Chantal Mouffe supplies a useful description of the two methods of hegemony that Gramsci develops: "If hegemony is defined as the ability of one class to articulate the interest of other social groups to its own, it is now possible to see that this can be . . . articulated so as to neutralise them and hence to prevent the development of their own specific demands, or else they can be articulated in such a way as to promote their full development leading to the final resolution of the contradictions which they express."[21]

Rather intriguingly, much of Gramsci's theory of hegemony develops through his analysis of the Risorgimento, the same historical event that Fuller analyzes in her late *Tribune* dispatches. Nor is it coincidental that Fuller's assessment of the political transformations in Italy tends to support Gramsci's later evaluation. For Gramsci, the movement begun in 1848 by Mazzini (and what would become the "Action Party") failed to displace the more dangerous Moderate Party because it was too restricted in its approach.[22] Confined largely to the upper and middle classes, the hegemonic activity eventually advanced by the Moderate Party "became merely an aspect of the function of domination."[23] For her part, Fuller is also suspicious of Gioberti and the members who would make up the so-called Moderate Party criticized by Gramsci. And while her support for Mazzini is strong, she understands what Gramsci will later fully elaborate when she criticizes Mazzini's failure to pay attention to a host of social issues: "Mazzini sees not all: he aims at political emancipation; but he sees not, perhaps would deny, the bearing of some events, which even now begin to work their way. Of this more anon, but not today nor in the small print of *The Tribune*. Suffice it to say, I allude to that of which the cry of Communism, the systems of Fourier, etc. are but forerunners."[24]

That we can draw this parallel between Fuller and Gramsci in their thinking about the Italian revolution also confirms Chevigny's analysis of Fuller's later *Tribune* writing. But it is important to see how Fuller's analysis draws its sophistication from her long engagement in the project of developing contact between various sectors of her society, including its subaltern constituents. Though her work in this area is uneven, all of her *Tribune* activity can be said to work toward the construction of a new consensus aimed at creating an "expansive" hegemony. The terms which Mouffe uses to describe Gramsci's notion of hegemonic transformation fit the method that Fuller herself defines for her audience in the *Tribune*: "The objective of ideological struggle is not to reject the system and all its elements but to rearticulate it, to break it down to its basic elements and then to sift through past conceptions to see which ones, with some changes of content, can serve to express the new situation. Once this is done the chosen elements are finally rearticulated into another system."[25] As we shall see, Fuller develops a theory of reading that follows this same pattern. Moreover, Fuller can be said to have adopted within her columns what Gramsci would later call a "war of position" rather than a "frontal attack" to accomplish this transformation in her audience. Aware that the issues with which she deals are often highly volatile, Fuller chooses to engage in a protracted trench warfare. The consistency of her goal may be obscured by the enormous variety of her approach; yet the efficacy of such a strategy has gained considerable support among cultural critics who have begun to observe the radical dispersion of power in the variety of discourses through which we make our daily negotiations. Fuller's critical writings reveal an awareness of the complex overlay of ideological frames through which we are forced to "read" our lives as well as a willingness to shift those frames to make some conversation or translation between them possible.

Realize Your Cant, Not Cast It Off[26]

Two years after Fuller's death in 1850, Marx began to write his own column for the *Tribune*. This provocative coincidence was undoubtedly behind Chevigny's traditional Marxist approach to Fuller, with its emphasis on Fuller's growing interest in material and economic concerns. But such a focus reduces the elaborate complexity of Fuller's early *Tribune* writing and its unusual anticipation of the theoretical revisions now in play in social theory. In looking over the enormous range of writing produced by Fuller from 1844 until her death in 1850, one could argue that Fuller prepared a space for Marx even as she exceeded him in framing reading formations that he would find difficult to pursue. Such an argument must consider both the problematic split between aesthetic and political concerns besetting much of our reading and the way that feminism can supply an important conversation between the two.

Hired in 1844 to review books and artistic public performances, Fuller immediately extended the review format to include her reading of the culture. As in her other work, Fuller came to invest the reader with enormous significance in these pieces. Because it was now the space where those who had been denied access to the dominant forms of power could reassert themselves, reading became the privileged site of cultural change. The fact that Fuller was a woman certainly enhanced her interest in reading. Moreover, her rigorous training in several classical languages—unusual for most American women of the day—had widened her access to history. Yet the clash of historical sensibilities that she experienced in the Midwest had the stronger effect of setting into motion a transvaluation of the historical itself. For Fuller, the historical became radically enmeshed in reading, and her *Tribune* articles were the proving ground for this thesis.

Beginning her work for the *Tribune* just after completing *Woman in the Nineteenth Century*, Fuller naturally sustained an interest in issues relating to women, though it is interesting to see the subtle way in which Fuller incorporates a feminist critique into her developing theory of reading. Two projects were uppermost in her mind during her tenure in New York: the "importance of promoting National Education by hightening [*sic*] and deepening the cultivation of individual minds, and the part which is assigned to Woman in the next stage of human progress in this country."[27] Fuller's way of articulating her goal reveals the complex double strategy that she had learned to adopt in her other work. One aspect of this strategy, the promotion of "National Education" through the "cultivation of individual minds," appears to echo the familiar strategy of the transcendentalists: the education of the country by turning each citizen into a cultivated reader.

Yet Fuller's additional comment about the "part" to be assigned to "Woman" (not "women") in this project alters that familiar individualistic frame by invoking what would have been recognized as a Fourieristic strain. Fourier had made it quite clear that the place of Woman in culture formed the "pivot" of all cultural reform. And by 1844, Fuller certainly had found in Fourier's work an important counterbalance to the developing trends of the day, as her strategic references to him in both *Summer on the Lakes* and *Woman in the Nineteenth Century* indicate. In effect, Fuller problematizes the project of National Education with her reference to the role of Woman in the "next stage of human progress." In so doing, she alters the normative cultural understanding of the reader.

This is not the same as arguing that Fuller aspired to turn the nation into a nation of women readers. Indeed, her concern for the place of Woman is the result of her recognition that "cultivation" as such had been a vehicle of dominance and control. Fuller was well aware that women were often trained to read uncritically and therefore were badly prepared as readers. Yet Fuller also believed that the position of woman in culture, at once inside and outside its dominant discourses of power, could be instrumental in changing the act of reading itself. By 1844, in other words, Fuller understood all too well the strange alterity of woman's place; she saw how, in the words of Biddy Martin, "women are faced . . . with the challenge of refusing to be the Other of male discourse and an equally important refusal to be integrated as Same."[28] Introducing the idea of Woman was Fuller's way of transforming the project of cultivation to include the project of social change. For Fuller, "Woman" represented the irruption of difference into the project of "National" Education.

Fuller had always been comfortable with this type of double strategy. In her earliest translations, she had been determined to show that both cultures benefited in the process of converting one language into another; by translating works by Goethe and Bettina von Arnim, for example, Fuller sought not to appropriate knowledge from Germany but to put the German and North American "way of knowing" into conversation. The same goal manifested itself in her "Conversations" and throughout the writing of "The Great Lawsuit": in both, Fuller sought to put into circulation the idea that social change could have shared but different origins. However, Fuller's confidence in the power of such exchanges was tested by the conflict of European and

Native American cultures which she viewed during her trip west. The idea that reading was itself a Western "tool" or standard gave Fuller pause, chiefly because she had seen how the theory of Progress itself had been used to destroy entire cultures.[29] As a result, she began to seek a theory of reading which could engage the various constituents of a culture (or cultures) without appropriation and domination. Fuller drew from Fourier's critique of Western civilization in which "transitional" formations were crucial to establishing a social critique, and the idea of Woman represented its most significant transitional formation. Fourier's idea of the universal subjection of women (or the transhistorical nature of that subjection) became Fuller's way of identifying a space outside the local effects of cultural bias. In this way, Fuller came to view reading from the position of the strangely excluded and those who, like women, were not always part of the Western way of viewing the world. Conceived in this way, reading became for Fuller another way of interpreting, one which, if put into conversation with traditional ways of doing things, might alter the way the world was read and understood.

When Fuller writes that one of her goals is to discover the "part which is assigned to Woman in the next stage of human progress in the country," she is less interested in having women participate in the "Progress" of North America as it has already begun (indeed, after viewing the cruel path of Progress on the frontier, Fuller came to loath the very notion), than she is concerned to find ways in which the idea of Woman—offering an insight into alterity—might help to transvaluate the meaning of Progress.

In this way, the idea of Woman supplies Fuller with a sense of the importance of ideological positioning. Paying attention to gender now becomes a means of signaling the range of subject positions available in any social cluster or conflict of cultures.[30] Thus, in an important way, Fuller's "feminist" focus becomes enlarged throughout her *Tribune* columns. While she continues to refer to specific conditions relating to women in her writing, notably in her discussion of prostitution and the working conditions of the poor, her interests also turn to the variety of social effects that a consideration of gender yields.[31] Gender offers the most visible sign of the efficacy of what Fourier had called "transition" and shifting frames of reference, offering in turn a new model of reading and "cultivation."

This relationship between gender and a changing model of reading is neatly demonstrated in one of Fuller's more innovative columns, entitled "Some Items of Foreign Gossip." In these columns Fuller inserted assorted news items which she had translated from European newspapers. Of course, all of Fuller's reviews extol the benefits of translation and language skills, emphasizing that we must "learn from all nations."[32] Fuller continually encourages her audience to read foreign newspapers and, as an incentive, she occasionally translates directly from the French and German newspapers that she recommends to her readers, notably *Deutsche Schnellpost, Revue Française,* and *Courrier des Etats Unis.* As we shall see, the items which she culls from foreign and immigrant newspapers tend to be more overt in their political commentary, concerned with the developing interest in communism and socialism throughout Europe.[33] In making these translations, Fuller demonstrates a far more sympathetic and advanced sense of the European struggle for social and political transformation than many of her North American contemporaries. Yet Fuller's decision to segregate one segment of these translations under the title "Items of Foreign Gossip" bears our immediate attention, for within these columns gender intersects politics in provocative ways.

This is certainly the case in the column under that heading which begins with a description of three cases of transgendered behavior, or what Fuller calls an "exchange of parts between the two sexes."[34] In her account Fuller first describes a man in France who had both dressed and acted the part of a woman to be in the company of men. As Fuller tells the story, this person had held the attention of "many admirers" until "denounced by the Police as a man and a notorious offender against justice." The next example Fuller gives her readers involves the case of a woman who had played the part of a man throughout her life. According to Fuller's account, the woman—who went by the name of "Mr. Douglass"—had received a great deal of praise for his generosity as well as his "mildness of disposition" (an attribute noted particularly when he had allowed his wife to desert him for another man without prosecution). The third case described by Fuller concerns a woman named Maria Schellynk, who had served actively for seventeen years in the French army under Napoleon. Rather significantly, in her telling, Fuller lists the three examples in order of their "success." While the first instance of gender shifting had been discovered very early and openly scorned, the "sex" of the second person had been discovered by the larger public only at her death, with little or no public criticism. Finally, Fuller shows how the last person's "sex" was discovered yet made irrelevant by the honors that Napoleon and her fellow soldiers bestowed upon her. Thus, in the process of telling her reader about these three unusual lives, Fuller enacts an important transformation of focus. If the reader would be inclined to echo the disdainful response which greeted the story of the first transvestite (and Fuller had every reason to expect that her reader would be so inclined), Fuller is able at the end to activate a different response. In other words, she shows her reader not only alternative modes of behavior, but more importantly, alternative modes of interpreting that behavior. As usual, her focus on gender becomes the most efficient way to demonstrate the shifting ideological constraints binding her audience.

Yet gender was merely the most obvious reminder of a whole range of subject positions which Fuller intended to have her reader understand and explore. For central to Fuller's concern is the development of a broadly based cultural critique. Thus, it follows quite naturally that she end this column on "Social Gossip" with a description of the value of newspapers, for she sees the newspaper as the site of an important cultural transition: the meeting of high and low cultures and the place where conversation among various constituencies can begin.[35] Fuller's opening story from "Items of Social Gossip" on the "exchange of parts" made by men and women allegorizes her sense of the need for an active exchange of parts among the various constituents of a society at large.

One of Fuller's earliest columns gives a rather clear indication of her ambition to mix the project of national cultivation with cultural critique. In an essay meant to commemorate Thanksgiving in 1844, Fuller takes the opportunity to admonish her readers to remember those less fortunate who are still subject to the vagaries of "ignorance, corruption and wo [*sic*]." While there was nothing particularly unusual about this type of charge, Fuller's holiday column is remarkable for its affiliation of political and artistic change. Fuller describes a "movement of contrition and love" that had called "the King from his throne of gold, and the Poet from his throne of Mind to lie with the beggar in the kennel, or raise him from it." According to Fuller, this movement had said "to the Poet, 'You must reform rather than create a world,' and to him of the golden crown, 'You cannot long remain a King unless you are also a Man.'"[36] Fuller makes it plain from the start, in other words, that she is determined to establish a relationship between the political and literary changes which she sees everywhere around her. For Fuller, the political transitions of Europe, particularly those involving the shift away from monarchies to some form of representative government, are being matched by a transition in the idea of "genius" and artistic achievement. Evidence of this transformation occurs relatively early in Fuller's *Tribune* writing, marking the most interesting development of her thinking during her tenure with the paper. Not only does it show her growing sympathy for the implicit critique of individualism embedded in European socialist thought, but it also demonstrates her growing desire to assign the task of reading a central role in that critique.

Genius and Practical Power

Fuller seems to have taken to heart Emerson's paradoxical claim that the "true Romance which the world exists to realize, will be the transformation of genius into practical power."[37] Certainly the discourse of social change begins to pervade all her literary criticism in the *Tribune*. With the traditional hierarchies of political structures being put into question, it follows that for Fuller the traditional hierarchy of elite and popular literature must also come under scrutiny. Without a doubt, the articles which she translated from European and immigrant newspapers encouraged her to pursue this line of inquiry.

One of the most influential of these essays was by Gottfried Kinkel, entitled "Popular Literature in Germany," which she found in the *Deutsche Schnellpost* and published in January 1845.[38] According to Kinkel all literature depends upon "the spiritual tendencies of its time." Thus, the social and political transformations of Europe, including the communist and socialist "tendencies," generate a "new interest in the life of the common people." By Kinkel's account, it was imperative, therefore, to promote an interest in what he called "popular literature" because "the writer, educated among the cultivated, [can] rarely translate his thoughts to the mind and manners of the peasant and burgher."[39] Though Kinkel's idea of popular literature (and social change) remains largely circumscribed by an elitism in which ideas flow only in one direction, his articulation of the imbrication of political and literary concerns proves immensely valuable for Fuller. She seems to have been particularly taken by his argument that "belles lettres[,] . . . once the property of these educated classes, have condescended a step to those whom we designate by the strange name of *the people*, as if we ourselves were no part of the people. – In this sense is rising among us a popular literature that may easily begin a revolution in the literary world."[40]

More than anything else, the affiliation of social and political change with literary transformation complicates Fuller's way of addressing artistic "genius." While she continues throughout her criticism to distinguish between two types of writing, "high" and "low," the relationship between the two becomes increasingly volatile. For example, on March 4, 1845, Fuller introduces her column "English Writers Little Known Here," with the declaration that "the office of Literature is two-fold. It preserves through ages the flowers of life which came to perfect bloom in minds of genius. . . . A small part of literature has a permanent value. But the office of the larger part is temporary, as affording the means of interpreting contemporary minds to each other on a larger scale than actual conversation in words or deeds furnishes." Significantly, Fuller goes on to write: "The common and daily purposes of literature are the most important. It cannot, and will not, dispense with the prophecies of genius, but the healthy discharge of its functions must not be disparaged to exalt these."

Fuller's growing desire to turn reading into the site of social agency makes it increasingly difficult for her to separate her understanding of the "common and daily purposes of literature" from the offices of "prophecy." Fuller never completely relinquishes her faith in works of genius, believing that an important type of cultural agency may be generated from them. Perhaps her most succinct sense of that agency appears in a review of Plato in May 1845, where she writes that "it is impossible to read or repeat him with absolute servility. It is impossible to get at the outmost sense of his speech without some action of one's own intelligence."[41] Indeed, Fuller struggles to support two conflicting types of agency: that which the great work of literature can yield to the reader by the intellectual challenge it offers and that which popular literature might supply by providing another significant perspective on the culture.

Fuller's way of avoiding this conflict is to shift her attention from the author to the reader. This shift coincides with her interest in transitional modes spawned by the social criticism of Fourier. As Fuller came to believe in the importance of a hegemonic transition in culture, she also came to believe in the efficacy of what she called transitional texts. Her interest in literary and artistic works begins to focus, then, on the way in which any work can generate a new dynamic relationship between disparate groups. While she finds in works of genius a more accomplished and immediate sense of empowerment, it is an empowerment that works through the reader, who becomes the most important agent of social transition.

Fuller's focus on reading enlarges in the summer of 1845 when she reviews the poems of the British laborer William Thom. Once again she begins with an attempt to designate two types of literature. Intriguingly, however, her description of literature turns out to be more a description of the critical method used to read literature:

> There are two ways of considering Poems, or the products of literature in general. We may tolerate only what is excellent, and demand that whatever is consigned to print for the benefit of the human race should exhibit fruits perfect in shape, . . . enclosing kernels of permanent value . . . [or] *literature may be regarded as the great mutual system of interpretation between all kinds and classes of men. It is an epistolary correspondence between brethren of one family, subject to many and wide separations, and anxious to remain in spiritual presence one of another* [emphasis mine].[42]

In her analysis, Fuller goes on to suggest that both "schools" of criticism have their dangers: the danger of the first is "hypercriticism" and "pedantry," and the peril of the second is an "indiscriminate indulgence and a leveling of the beautiful with what is merely tolerable." While she expresses the hope that "these two tendencies" can be "harmonized," she makes obvious her support for the second excess. Once again, Fuller's preference carries a political value: "The spirit of the time, which is certainly seeking, though by many and strange ways, the greatest happiness for the greatest number . . . declares that the genial and generous tendency shall have the lead." There is no question that Fuller's understanding of the "spirit of the time" has been strongly influenced by the transitional modes of socialism and communism. Nor is it a coincidence that her review of Thom's poems comes out just two weeks after her translation of "The Social Movement in Europe," the article from the *Deutsche Schnellpost* which includes an excerpt from *The Condition of the Working Class* by Engels.[43] With these developing social concerns, Fuller's literary criticism becomes heavily focused on the social agency of reading.[44]

Fuller's address for January 1, 1846, tells a great deal about how completely she has internalized this way of viewing things. As was routine for Fuller, she takes the occasion of the first of the year to critique the state of the union. Fuller is particularly disappointed with the events of 1846:

> What a year it has been with us! Texas annexed, and more annexations in store; Slavery perpetuated, as the most striking new feature of these movements. Such are the fruits of American love of liberty! Mormons murdered and driven out, as an expression of American freedom of conscience. Cassius Clay's paper expelled from Kentucky; that is American freedom of the press. And all these deeds defended on the true Russian grounds: "We (the stronger) know what you (the weaker) ought to do and be, and it *shall* be so."

Although Fuller glumly reports that another "sign of the times" was that "there are left on the earth none of the last dynasty of geniuses," her choice of the word "dynasty," with its negative political connotations, is deliberate, since she sees a positive side to the eclipse of genius. Earlier in the essay Fuller endorsed "Associative" and "Communist principles" as useful antidotes to the dangerous "individualism" of American culture. Thus, Fuller finds it easy to end her discussion of genius with the argument that "the time of prophets is over, and the era they prophesied must be at hand; in its conduct a larger proportion of the human race shall take part than ever before."[45]

By the summer of 1845, Fuller had essentially outlined the theory of reading that would guide her thinking for the remainder of her *Tribune* writing. Her description of literature as "the great mutual system of interpretation between all kinds and classes of men" is less a theory of literature than a theory of cultural interaction that anticipates Gramsci's notion of hegemonic transformation. Notably, her emphasis is on the wide separations that the offices of reading are expected to cross and bring into communication. For Fuller, a certain type of reading can foster an interaction among people who are manifestly different by developing some form of equality between them. As her columns amply show, such differences can be of gender, race, or class.

This formulation helps to explain why in the same summer in which she reviews Thom's work and translates the piece "The Social Movement in Europe," Fuller is also happy to review Thomas Arnold's

Introductory Lectures on Modern History. For Fuller, Arnold's "toler-ance" of other men and their way of life raises him above a host of other thinkers. It is clear from her column that she reviews Arnold's book for the sole purpose of emphasizing his maxim that one should keep one's "view of men and things extensive[;] . . . he who reads deeply in one class of writers only, gets views which are almost sure to be perverted."[46]

In other words, Fuller makes a direct correlation between the activ-ity of reading and the process of social change, for reading can offer a way to disrupt certain ideological assumptions. Throughout her col-umns, she is always working to open a space of negotiation and com-munication between cultural and social differences. Her columns on care for the insane, prison reform, prostitutes, the repression of the Jews, and even certain health issues, notably the water cure, reflect her continual effort to establish a hegemonic discourse to replace some of the more repressive forms of dominance and control throughout soci-ety. For Fuller it makes sense to argue that a subaltern position could offer an important new perspective on life. She frequently emphasizes the idea that the poor are in a unique position to "read" the cruelties of class differences.[47] Her excellent series on the Irish character clearly promotes this position, harshly criticizing the spurious notion that the Irish are "ungrateful" for the help being extended to them by their employers. Fuller gives a particularly vivid example of the failure to consider the perspective of the employee when she writes:

> Only a day or two since, we saw, what we see so often, a nursery maid, with the family to which she belonged, in a public convey-ance. They were having a pleasant time, but in it she had not part. . . . No inquiry was made as to *her* comfort—no entertaining re-mark, no information as to the places of interest we passed was ad-dressed to her. Had she been in that way with that family ten years, she might have known *them* well enough, for their characters lay only too bare to a careless scrutiny, but her joys, her sorrows, her few thoughts, her almost buried capacities, would have been as unknown to them and they as little likely to benefit her, as the Emperor of China.[48]

For Fuller, the need to translate from class to class, an idea first sum-moned in Kinkel's essay, is no less imperative than the need to translate across cultural differences. America proves this point most strikingly, for the crisis of urban and frontier living almost always reflects the lack of understanding among various cultural differences. Accordingly, in a review of Commander Wilke's expedition to the South Seas, written in the summer of 1845, Fuller focuses on the confused contact between explorer and native and quickly draws a parallel to contact between Anglo and Native American Indians at home:

> Not only those who come with fire and sword, crying "Believe or die," "understand or we will scourge you"—"understand *and* we will only plunder and tyrannize over you"; not only these ignorant despots, self-deceiving robbers, have failed to benefit the people they dared esteem more savage than themselves, but the good and generous have failed from want of patience and an expanded intelligence.—Would you speak to a man, first learn his language![49]

Thus by the time she goes to England in the latter half of 1846 and begins to observe the oppressive nature of industrialization, Fuller already is well prepared to describe her reaction to the Castle of Stirling in the following manner:

> We were shown its dungeons and its Court of Lions, where, says tradition, wild animals, kept in the grated cells adjacent, were brought out on festival occasions to furnish entertainment for the court. So, while lords and ladies gay danced and sang above, prisoners pined and wild beasts starved below. This, at first blush, looks like a very barbarous state of things, but, on reflection, one does not find that we have outgrown it in our present so-called state of refined civilization, only the present way of expressing the same facts is a little different. Still lords and ladies dance and sing, unknowing or uncaring that the laborers who minister to their luxuries starve or are turned into wild beasts. Man need not boast his condition, methinks, till he can weave his costly tapestry without the side that is kept under looking thus sadly.[50]

The Difference of Reading

It would be a mistake, however, to assume that Fuller always reduced the aesthetic to the political in her *Tribune* writing, or that she drained all meaning to one simple ideological reading. Her dual focus on cultivation and social change, working as it does through her easy affiliation of literature, translation, and social commentary, provides us with a deeper sense of the way we are all framed by a bewildering grid of ideological formations. The value of Fuller's position on reading is not simply that we should read *about* different things, but that we should begin to read in a different way. We should read more, not simply to accumulate knowledge, but to transform *how* we know. This agenda proves to be the most rigorous and complex aspect of Fuller's *Tribune* project, and, sometimes, the most confusing.

As I have already shown, Fuller published a number of her most fascinating articles in the summer of 1845, including "Irish Character," "Asylum for Discharged Female Convicts," "The Social Movement in Europe" and two scathing critiques of America. But, as we have seen, her social criticism in these articles is not restricted to political or social issues; often, her most subtle critical assessments of important cultural problems occur in her reviews of literary texts, including works by Frederick Douglass, Bela Marsh, Mrs. Norton, Thomas Hood, P. J. Beranger, John Critchley Prince, Eugene Sue, and Benjamin Disraeli.[51] One of her most provocative essays is one entitled "Story Books for the Hot Weather" (June 20, 1845). Fuller's stock of "hot weather" reading includes Disraeli's *Sybil; or, The Two Worlds of the Rich and the Poor*, Eugene Sue's *De Rohan*, *Self* by an unnamed author, and *Dashes at Life* by the American writer N. P. Willis. Significantly, Fuller's column is more about the unsettling nature and productive work of reading than about the novels themselves. More an allegory about social crisis than a story about passing the summer days in leisure, the essay also confronts and brackets the idea of leisure in its odd affiliation with the work of reading.

The complex paragraph that opens her review is worth quoting in full because it provides a strong sense of how quickly she directs herself to the problematic of reading and its cultural significance:

> Does any shame still haunt the age of bronze—a shame, the lingering blush of a heroic age, at being caught in doing anything merely for amusement? Is there a public still extant which needs to excuse its delinquencies by the one story of a man who liked to lie on the sofa all day and read novels, though he could, at times of need, write the gravest didactics! Live they still, those reverend signiors, the object of secret smiles to our childish years, who were obliged to apologize for midnight oil spent in conning story books, by the "historic bearing" of the novel, or the "correct and admirable descrip-

tions of certain countries, with climate, scenery and manners therein contained," wheat for which they, industrious students, were willing to winnow bushels of frivolous love-adventures? We know not—but incline to think the world is now given over to frivolity so far as to replace by the novel the minstrel's ballad, the drama, and worse still, the games of agility and strength in which it once sought pastime, for indeed, *mere* past-time is sometimes needed. The nursery legend comprised a primitive truth of the understanding and the wisdom of nations in the lines—

> "All play and no work makes Jack a mere toy;
> But, all work and no play makes Jack a dull boy."

We having reversed the order of arrangement to suit our present purpose. For we, O useful reader, being ourselves so far of the useful class as to be always wanted somewhere, have also to fight a good fight for our amusements, either with the foils of excuse, like the reverend signiors above mentioned, or with the sharp weapons of argument, or maintenance of a view of our own without argument, which we take to be the sharpest weapon of all.

Fuller's writing is difficult to read here precisely because of the burden it takes upon itself. The column enacts a cunning play on fading protocols of reading. Fuller creates a reader "out of her own image" to provide an analysis of the paradoxical impossibility and necessity of "past-time." Ending her column with the statement "God has time to remember the design with which he made this world also," Fuller turns her own imitation of God (making a reader in her own image) back upon itself, creating an image of God as a good "reader" also. In effect, Fuller takes the redundancy of value in the familiar narrative of creation to focus upon reading, showing how it is not merely the initial moment of inscription (in the beginning there was the Word) that we must value, but also the consequences of that inscription; God needed his "leisure" or "past-time" to "remember the design with which he made this world." In the end, it is important for God to take the time to "read" and imitate us in the process.

The extremely transitional nature of Fuller's argument highlights her interest in the complexities of reading. The emphasis on transition is her way of highlighting the complex ideological formations which we all negotiate. Consider for a moment the "reverend signior" in her introductory comments. Is he the representative reader of leisure? If so, it is interesting that the words "reverend" and "signior" traverse several discourses—crossbreeding the clergy with jaded aristocracy—and that the behavior of this hybrid male is made an "object of secret smiles" by children. These shifts force the reader to ask a number of important questions. Who, for example, is really watching this troubled male figure of reading in their early childhood? Fuller avoids reference to women of leisure, since the essay is far to the left of that prescription (it is, indeed, no small accident that a reference to the transformation of English women into "work tools" in British factories occurs toward the end of the essay). For Fuller there is no leisure in reading if the slow perusal of texts must be "apologized" for with the idea that "didactics of writing" are the "official" work of the "reverend signior." Yet there is pleasure, somehow, in the smiles of childhood, the auxiliary space of reading, which fosters a special insight into the codes of the didactic, the "correct" and the "admirable." However, even as the reader settles on this position from which to interpret her view of the "reverend signior," that reader is forced by the very structure of Fuller's complex sentence into a new position, that of the "industrious students" grateful for the historical information interspersed among love stories. While Fuller was herself such a student of history, a fact known by the reader of her daily column, it is not the case that she is casting blame on the reader of love stories. Fuller finds a way, instead, to critique the division between the two forms. Indeed, when she goes on to review the books that she selected for her "hot day," she demonstrates the interdependence of the historic with the love story.

The point to emphasize is that Fuller's readers are not given a stable subject position in the entire opening paragraph. Instead, they slide along a shifting series of positions, places from which they might read. This shifting is affected by the tension within phrases that would find a more complacent "reading" if allowed to flow back to their usual oppositional valences, particularly the oppositional valence based on gender, which tends to subsume all others.

The inclusion of the "nursery legend" works just this way. Once again, Fuller mixes discourses, that of the nursery rhyme with that of legend, bringing the domain of women and children (understood but not stated by the absence of the phrase "nursery rhyme") into the domain of history or legend.

As usual, Fuller does not take the leisure to describe her method and materials; instead, she industriously puts them to use, without apology. Hence, there is an inevitable compounding and confounding of meaning in her work. She goes on to use the nursery legend to gloss the "primitive truth of the understanding and the wisdom of nations" (a truth left intentionally vague) and in so doing again challenges (without the "leisure" of argument) the idea that "primitive" truth should be held in opposition to understanding. Instead, the nursery legend works to make primitive sense, following the smirks of childhood, out of the leisure of the "reverend signior."

But, of course, there is more to this, for if the nursery rhyme reporting Jack's dullness has become a legend, it has done so by reversing the usual order of enunciation. The reversal does far more than exchange one hierarchical formation for another. If, initially (ending with "all play and no work makes Jack a mere toy") the emphasis was on keeping Jack sharp, warning him against easy manipulation through stupefying and lazy behavior, Fuller's transformation of the "legend" (ending with "all work and no play makes Jack a dull boy") emphasizes the terrible accomplishment of that manipulation: Jack has become a drone to the forces earlier warned against. Turning the "legend" around, the nursery rhyme becomes the legend, the "history" of industrialization to which Fuller goes on to refer in her reading of Disraeli, Sue, and Willis in the remainder of her piece.

Fuller, however, inserts that history as a legend for her "work" of reviewing: "Jack" becomes a potential reference for both the "reverend signior" and Fuller. This double association does not mean that Fuller and the signior merge as one figure through Jack. Quite the contrary, Fuller remains divided from the signior by her method. For the signior, the foil of "history" is an excuse for his leisure, and Jack is the labored figure of that excuse. For Fuller, by contrast, the "absence of argument" is precisely her tool for reading history, and Jack the playful vehicle of that reading.

Fuller's opening paragraph thus brings into play the ideas of amusement, work, and "past-time." In one sense she means to show how pastime could be productive leisure, allowing time for reflection, memory, thoughts of times past and time passing. Leisure is work in this sense, but useful work that can make her readers members of the "useful class." They can be inducted into this class if they are "useful reader[s]," though by so doing they also are condemning themselves to a struggle, which consists in learning how to uncoil the argument,

as Fuller tells her audience, from a "view of your own" in order to battle the forces changing the face of Jack's world encoded in her reading
of the nursery legend.

Fuller's opening paragraph is unsettling in the extreme, and meant
to be. The reader's position is radically destabilized by her conscious
denial of argument, allowing a form of "unconscious" writing to take
control. Her sharpest weapon is thus an intense invitation to the
unconscious, manifested in the movement toward such complexities
of a phrase as "mere pastime," which test through the word *mere* concepts as remote and connected as "boundary," "purity," "limitation,"
and "mother." What after all is "mere" pasttime for the culture determined to make pastime both effeminate and impossible? Fuller's division between the conscious intention of the word *pastime* and its
unconscious play of possibility in the hyphenated version of that
word exposes a crucial division in her work, a division marking the
gap in reading that she uses with such facility. This division is intended to show her reader how very complex an analysis of culture
must be.

Fuller's review of four books in her column reflects this same division. She praises Disraeli for attempting to "do justice to the claims of
the laboring classes," in his *Sybil; or, The Two Worlds*, yet she finds fault
with the limits of his perspective, writing that "D'Israeli shows the
stain of old prejudice in the necessity he felt to marry the daughter of
the People to one not of the People." Yet Fuller's review of Disraeli does
not call for a simple ideological rendering of the growing class conflict
in England. Rather, her review of Sue suggests something of the complexity that she was seeking. Although Fuller admires Sue, observing
that he holds "clearer notions of what he wants" than Disraeli, she criticizes his narrow rendering of the character of Louis XIV in his novel
De Rohan. Agreeing with Sue that the "Great Marnarque was really brutally selfish and ignorant," Fuller nevertheless cautions that the "illu-
sion" the king "diffused" is worth considerably more artistic investment
than that which Sue supplied. Fuller's critique is astute: "It is not by an
inventory of facts or traits that what is most vital in a character and
which makes its due impression on contemporaries can be apprehended or depicted." The same resistance to such reductive renderings
informs Fuller's review of a work entitled *Self, by the author of Cecil*,
whose focus remains "the very dregs, in a social life, now at is lowest
ebb." Fuller also finds fault with the work of N. P. Willis, claiming that

his novel *Dashes at Life* falls short of the goal she had set for American writers: to be "rooted to the soil." Yet Fuller hesitates to dismiss Willis altogether as she does the author of *Self*, supposing that the former's work may well be viewed as one of the "mongrel products" from the "transitive state we are in now." In reviewing these books together, Fuller subtly makes the point that a simplistic rendering of the venality of the aristocracy is no more effective than cheap sensationalism in descriptions of poverty. For Fuller, the purpose of literature—whether depicting a character of the highest aristocracy or looking instead at the lowest ranks of the social scale—is to assist in "unlearning the False, in order to arrive at the True." Such a project requires a variety of skills, and all of the works that Fuller reviews require an active yet "leisurely" reader. Significantly, it is a reader now enlisted in a larger social project, as suggested by the close of the column: "All these story books show even to the languor of the hottest day the solemn signs of revolution. Life has become too factitious; it has no longer a leg left to stand upon, and cannot be carried much farther in this way."[52] With her provocative statement that "God has time to remember the design with which he made this world also," the column ends.

The Efficacy of Reading

Over time, Fuller obviously began to feel a certain confidence in the efficacy of her focus on reading. We see this most strikingly in the way she finally attempts in her writing about the North American Indians to change the rhetoric of the Vanishing American. Upon her arrival in New York, with memories of the Midwest still fresh in her mind, Fuller makes a point of recalling the Indian crisis to her reader in a number of reviews, including her New Year's Day critique. ("We are not fitted to emulate the savages in preparation for the new fire. The Indians knew how to reverence the old and the wise.")[53] One of her early *Tribune* articles even sustains the fatal view that it is already "too late" to change the terrible course of events.[54] However, through her increasing awareness of both the newspaper's extraordinary ability to affect public opinion and the *Tribune*'s success in developing a faithful and growing readership, Fuller begins to think that some hope might remain for a change in the Indian policy. Hence, a month before her departure to England, she reviews T. L. McKenney's "New Book on the Indians," his *Memoirs*.[55] Claiming that she deliberately read McKenney's book on Independence Day, Fuller openly uses her review to critique the enormous range of wrongs troubling the country, from slavery to the War in Mexico. Yet, for Fuller, the "conduct of this nation toward the Indians" is the most egregious sign that the United States has failed to live up to its "fundamental idea" of equality. Fuller's review becomes less an endorsement of McKenney's "civilizing" project than an appeal for her readers to take the Indian crisis to heart and act upon it. Indeed, Fuller makes a subtle critique of McKenney's idea of "civic life," particularly as it relates to his personal dealings with several Indian children and men. Breaking from the discourse of the Vanishing American demonstrates her own faith (however qualified by her distress over the state of the country) in the possibility of significant social exchange. And it is a faith, I would argue, based on hegemonic activity rather than on the sheer acts of dominance that had characterized Indian-White relations until that time. Fuller's faith was not rewarded, of course. Yet this shared cultural failure should not diminish our appreciation of her early effort to produce a theory of reading that, if taken seriously, might have made possible such a break from the old rhetoric of Progress.

Notes

1. I have discussed this subject in some detail in "Feminism in Translation: Fuller's *Tasso*," *Studies in Romanticism* 29 (1990): 463–90.

2. I address *Summer on the Lakes* in "Foot-noting the Sublime: Margaret Fuller on Black-Hawk's Trail," *American Literary History*, forthcoming.

3. For an excellent analysis of Fourier and his influence in America during this period, see Carl J. Guarneri, *The Utopian Alternative: Fourierism in Nineteenth-Century America* (Ithaca: Cornell UP, 1991).

4. Here I am thinking of Jardine's description of the encounter between two "reading effects," which is found in her *Gynesis: Configurations of Woman and Modernity* (Ithaca: Cornell UP, 1985). See especially the chapter entitled "The Woman-in-Effect."

5. The early editions of the *Tribune* were only four pages long, the last two pages covered with public notices and advertising. Political and national news filled the second page until the Mexican War, when some of the dramatic headlines produced by the war suddenly shifted to the front page. For a good description of the newspaper see Catherine Casto Mitchell, "Horace Greeley's Star: Margaret Fuller's *New York Tribune* Journalism, 1844–1846," diss., U of Tennessee, 1987.

6. Greeley's comment continues: ". . . and of the receding barbarism, and the rapidly advancing, but rude, repulsive, semi-civilization, which were contending with most unequal forces for the possession of those rich lands." *Memoirs of Margaret Fuller Ossoli*, ed. R. W. Emerson, W. H. Channing, and J. F. Clarke (1884; New York: Franklin, 1972) 2:152–53.

7. Greeley expected Fuller to share editing tasks with him and two other members of his fledgling staff.

8. This was done to make it clear that someone other than Greeley was composing the literary section of the paper. In "Horace Greeley's Star," Mitchell argues that in her role as "editor" of the literary section, Fuller may have authored a number of pieces without signing them (53–58).

9. Karl Marx, *On America and the Civil War*, vol. 2 of *The Karl Marx Library*, ed. and trans. Saul K. Padover (New York: McGraw-Hill, 1972) xv. Because his English was not yet good enough, Marx asked Engels to write the first set of articles for the *Tribune* (*Revolution and Counter-Revolution in Germany*), which he did under Marx's name. Marx first began writing for the *Tribune* in August 1852, his first piece being "The Elections in England: Tories and Whigs" (though Marx at first depended upon Engels to translate his work). See *Karl Marx, Friedrich Engels: Collected Works*, 46 vols. (London: Lawrence, 1975–88) 11: 629–30nn1–2. See also Padover, Introduction, *On America and the Civil War*.

10. Larry Reynolds, *European Revolutions and the American Literary Renaissance* (New Haven: Yale UP, 1988) 61, 77.

11. Ibid. 67. Reynolds cites Fuller's eighteenth letter, "written to appear in the United States on New Year's Day, 1848," where she "uses the European scene as the basis for a severe indictment of American society," as an example of her shifting ideological focus (65). Yet Fuller had chosen New Year's Day (and other notable holidays, including Christmas and the Fourth of July) to critique American society from the very first. See, for example, the following articles from the *New-York Daily Tribune*: "Thanksgiving," December 12, 1844; "Christmas," December 25, 1844; "New Year's Day," January 1, 1845; "St. Valentine's Day–Bloomingdale Asylum for the Insane," February 22, 1845; "The Fourth of July," July 4, 1845; "1st January, 1846," January 1, 1846; "Colonel McKenney's New Book upon the Indians," July 4, 1846; "Memoirs, Official and Personal by T. L. McKenney," July 8, 1846. See especially "First of August, 1845" (the anniversary of the emancipation of slaves in the West Indies), in which Fuller mentions Emerson's address of the previous year.

12. Bell Gale Chevigny, *The Woman and the Myth: Margaret Fuller's Life and Writings* (Old Westbury, Conn.: Feminist, 1976) 294. Fuller translates the title "On the Situation of the Laboring Class in England" (*New-York Daily Tribune* August 5, 1845). *The Condition of the Working Class in England* was first published in German in March 1845 (Leipzig). In *Karl Marx, Friedrich Engels: Collected Works*, the

Schnellpost is described as an "organ of the German moderate democratic emigres in the USA published twice weekly in New York from 1843 to 1851. In 1848 and 1851 its editor was Karl Heinzen; in 1851 Arnold Ruge was also on its editorial board" (11:750). Marx mentions the *Schnellpost* often in his early writings, most notably in "The Great Men of Exile," where he argues that Karl Heinzen "very quickly manage[d] to ride the New York *Schnellpost* to death" (11:279), suggesting that the earlier paper from which Fuller drew her material was more radical.

13. Chevigny, *Woman and the Myth* 292.

14. Reynolds, *European Revolutions* 61. Not surprisingly, Chevigny's *Woman and the Myth* supplies brief selections from only ten essays between 1844 and early 1847.

15. Chevigny, *Woman and the Myth* 376.

16. Reynolds, *European Revolutions* 63.

17. Thus Gramsci's thinking has recently received considerable attention, particularly in its relation to Althusser's work on ideology. Both Gramsci and Althusser viewed ideology as the inevitable medium through which all social organization occurred. Unlike Gramsci, who believed that some form of "agency" could emerge through ideological formations, Althusser insisted that agency could occur only through the development of a theory of ideology, which he called "science" (see "On the Materialist Dialectic" and "Marxism and Humanism," *For Marx*, trans. Ben Brewster [London: Verso–New Left, 1986] 161–247). Still, Althusser's equivocal view of art, as somehow outside the realm of ideology, yet in a tandem relationship with both ideology and science, bears an important affinity to Gramsci's notion of "hegemony"; and it is at this provisional intersection that I would situate my reading of Fuller. For more on Gramsci and ideology see Chantal Mouffe, "Hegemony and Ideology in Gramsci," in *Gramsci and Marxist Theory*, ed. Chantal Mouffe (London: Routledge, 1979). For an interesting reading of Althusser's position on "science" and "art," see Michael Sprinker's *Imaginary Relations: Aesthetics and Ideology in the Theory of Historical Materialism* (London: Verso–New Left, 1987).

18. It is not that Gramsci, as some have averred, reversed the classic Marxian axiom that base determines consciousness by returning to the idealist notion that consciousness determines everything, but rather that he made a subtle analysis of the way in which a material and economic base might determine "what forms of consciousness are possible" (Joseph V. Femia, *Gramsci's Political Thought: Hegemony, Consciousness, and the Revolutionary Process* [London: Clarendon–Oxford UP, 1981)] 121).

19. From *Prison Notebooks*, quoted in Mouffe, "Hegemony and Ideology in Gransci" 185.

20. Femia, *Gramsci's Political Thought* 24.

21. Mouffe, "Hegemony and Ideology in Gramsci" 183.

22. Antonio Gramsci, *Selections from the Prison Notebooks*, trans. and ed. Q. Hoare and G. Nowell Smith (New York: International, 1971) 60, 76. See also Walter L. Adamson, *Hegemony and Revolution: A Study of Antonio Gramsci's Political and Cultural Theory* (Berkeley and Los Angeles: U of California P, 1980) 185–96.

23. Quoted in Femia, *Gramsci's Political Thought* 48.

24. Letter 24, *At Home and Abroad: or, Things and Thoughts in America and Europe by Margaret Fuller Ossoli*, ed. Arthur B. Fuller (1856; Port Washington: Kennikat, 1971) 320; this letter appeared in the *New-York Daily Tribune* on June 15, 1848.

25. Mouffe, "Hegemony and Ideology in Gramsci" 192. This type of strategy is everywhere apparent in Fuller's *Tribune* work. Her opening paragraphs of "The Rich Man—An Ideal Sketch" (February 6, 1846) provide just one example:

> All benevolent persons, whether deeply thinking on, or only deeply feeling, the woes, difficulties and dangers of our present social system, are agreed either that great improvements are needed, or a thorough reform.
>
> Those who desire the latter, include the majority of thinkers. And we ourselves, both from personal observation and the testimony of others, are convinced that a radical reform is needed. Not a reform that rejects the instruction of the past, or asserts that God and man have made mistakes till now. We believe that all past developments have taken place under natural and necessary laws, and that the Paternal Spirit has at no period forgot his children, but granted to all ages and generations their chances of good to balance inevitable ills.—We prize the Past; we recognize it as our parent, our nurse and our teacher, and we know that for a time the new wine required the old bottles to prevent its being spilled upon the ground.
>
> Still we feel that the time is come which not only permits, but demands, a wider statement, and a nobler action. The aspect of society presents mighty problems, which must be solved by the soul of Man "divinely intending" itself to the task, or all will become worse instead of better, and ere long the social fabric totter to decay.

26. A quote from John Sterling which Fuller uses in "The Great Lawsuit. Man versus Men: Woman versus Women," *The Dial* July 1843: 9 and again later in *Woman in the Nineteenth Century*, facsimile ed. (Columbia: U of South Carolina P, 1980) 17.

27. "Farewell," *New-York Daily Tribune* August 1, 1846.

28. Biddy Martin, "Feminism, Criticism and Foucault," *New German Critique* 27 (1982): 2.

29. She readily found herself in agreement with Henry R. Schoolcraft, who wrote that "books, and the readers of books, [had] done much to bewilder and per-

plex the study of the Indian character." See her essay "*Oneota; or, The Red Race of America* by Henry R. Schoolcraft," *New-York Daily Tribune* February 12, 1845.

30. In a review of Mrs. Jameson's *Memoirs and Essays*, for example, Fuller justly praised Jameson's critique of "the unthinking, willfully unseeing million, who are in the habit of talking of 'Woman's sphere' as if it really was, at present, for the majority, one of protection and the gentle offices of home." Fuller made clear her admiration for the way that Jameson exposed how "rhetorical gentlemen and silken dames" forgot "their washerwomen, their seamstresses, and the poor hirelings for the sensual pleasures of man that jostle them daily in the streets" in order to "talk as if Woman need be fitted for no other chance than that of growing like a cherished flower in the garden of domestic love" ("Mrs. Jameson's Memoirs and Essays," *New-York Daily Tribune* July 24, 1845). At the same time, Fuller found fault with Jameson's essay entitled "On the Relative Social Position of Mothers and Governesses." For Fuller, Jameson's advice "to the governesses reads like a piece of irony, but we believe it was not meant as such—Advise them to be burnt at the stake at once rather than to this slow process of petrifaction. She is as bad as the reports of the 'Society for the relief of distressed and dilapidated Governesses.' We have no more patience. We must go to England ourselves and see these victims under the water torture."

31. Fuller's concern for the "other" perspective of the working woman, though general, was genuine; she tended to focus on domestic servants, washerwomen, and prostitutes, in part because in the 1840s there was no visible organization among other female laborers in New York City. There was apparently one moment in March 1845 when a "major organizational effort, the Ladies' Industrial Association" was launched by a cross-section of New York women "from all ranks of trade," including "shirt sewers, plain sewers, tailoresses and dressmakers, fringe and lace makers, straw workers, the comparatively prosperous book folders and stitchers and the lowly cap makers and shoe crimpers" (Christine Stansell, *City of Women: Sex and Class in New York, 1789–1860* [New York: Knopf, 1986] 145). But, according to Stansell, the organization fell apart by the late spring, and nothing more was heard of it. Fuller, who was visiting a variety of city charities at the time, including the Bellevue Alms House, the Farm School for Children, the asylum for the insane, and the penitentiary on Blackwell's Island (see her review on March 19, 1845), did not take note of the event. Stansell writes that the "short-lived, fragile tradition of female labor organization was buried in reformers' well-intentioned efforts and in workingmen's rhetoric of the working-class home" (152).

32. "French Gayety," *New-York Daily Tribune* July 9, 1845.

33. See esp. *New-York Daily Tribune* December 16, 1844; January 6, 1845; January 11, 1845; January 25, 1845; January 27, 1845; February 4, 1845; February 24, 1845;

March 12, 1845; June 7, 1845; July 9, 1845; July 25, 1845; August 5, 1845; January 8, 1846; April 1, 1846; April 25, 1846.

34. "Items of Foreign Gossip," *New-York Daily Tribune* September 24, 1845. Even the heading under which Fuller places this account has a transformative value, since it is in this "gossip" column (a site heavily coded as "effeminate") that traditional gender expectations end up being thwarted.

35. Fuller's faith in the newspaper no doubt drew its power from her own memory of her very first publication, which was a letter to the editor of the *Boston Daily Advertiser* ("Brutus," 1834). There Fuller had made a bold and provocative start for her publishing career by criticizing the historical method of George Bancroft.

36. "Thanksgiving," *New-York Daily Tribune* December 2, 1844.

37. Ralph Waldo Emerson, "Experience," *Essays, The Second Series*, vol. 3 of *The Collected Works of Ralph Waldo Emerson*, ed. Joseph Slater et al. (Cambridge: Belknap–Harvard UP, 1983) 49. Fuller's first review for the *Tribune* was a review of Emerson's *Second Series*; see "Emerson's Essays," *New-York Daily Tribune* December 7, 1844.

38. "'Popular Literature in Germany' by Gottfried Kinkel," *New-York Daily Tribune* January 25, 1845.

39. "'Popular Literature in Germany' by Gottfried Kinkel," *New-York Daily Tribune* January 27, 1845.

40. Ibid.

41. "*Plato Against the Atheists* by Taylor Lewis," *New-York Daily Tribune* May 14, 1845.

42. "Thom's Poems," *New-York Daily Tribune* August 22, 1845. Fuller thought highly enough of this piece to republish it as "Poets of the People" in *Papers on Literature and Art* (New York: Wiley, 1846) 2:1–21.

43. "The Social Movement in Europe," August 5, 1845.

44. Thus, the second mode of criticism that she described in her review of Thom was shown in her argument to be superior for its method, which, rather than "crushing to earth without mercy all the humble buds of Phantasy," instead "enters into the natural history of every thing that breathes and lives . . . believes no impulse to be entirely in vain, which scrutinizes circumstances, motive and object before it condemns, and believes there is a beauty in each natural form, if its law and purpose be understood" ("Thom's Poems").

45. "First of January 1846," *New-York Daily Tribune* January 1, 1846.

46. *New-York Daily Tribune* August 28, 1845.

47. See, for example, her essay "Asylum for Discharged Female Convicts," *New-York Daily Tribune* June 19, 1845, where Fuller writes that the poor "are, usually,

the most generous. Not that they are, originally, better than the rich, but circumstances have fitted them to appreciate the misfortunes, the trials, the wrongs, that beset those a little lower down than themselves."

48. "The Irish Character," *New-York Daily Tribune* July 15, 1845.

49. "United States Exploring Expedition," *New-York Daily Tribune* June 28, 1845.

50. Letter 6, *At Home and Abroad* 161.

51. *New-York Daily Tribune*: "Narrative of the Life of Frederick Douglass," June 10, 1845; "The Nubian Slave," June 24, 1845; "Thomas Hood," July 18, 1845; "The Child of the Islands by the Hon. Mrs. Norton," July 26, 1845; "Prose and Verse of Thomas Hood," August 9, 1845; "Prince's Poems," August 13, 1845; "Thom's Poems," August 22, 1845.

52. In the end, Fuller's particular focus remains England: "England must glide, or totter or fall into revolution—there is not room for such selfish Selves, and unique young Dukes in a country so crowded with men and with those who ought to be women, and are turned into work-tools." Yet because she also reviews works by French and American writers (Sue and Willis), Fuller's focus includes the insight into the "difficulty of the era" provided by such eclectic "leisure" reading.

53. "New Year's Day," *New-York Daily Tribune* January 1, 1845.

54. Fuller writes: "Mr. Schoolcraft says, 'The old idea that the Indian mind is not susceptible of a high, or an advantageous cultivation, rests upon very questionable data.' He might have added, that the experiment has never been tried. . . . In every [other] instance where any fidelity was shown to the duty of reconciling two races opposed to one another in every characteristic of organization and manners, surprising success has ensued. We mention this merely to do justice in word and thought; it is too late for act; the time is gone by when the possessors of the soil might have been united as one family with their invaders; nothing remains but to write their epitaph with some respect to truth" (*"Oneota; or, The Red Race of America"*).

55. Fuller made a symbolic gesture by giving notice of T. L. McKenney's "New Book on the Indians" on July 4, 1846. Her review occurred four days later: "Memoirs, Official and Personal," *New-York Daily Tribune* July 8, 1846.

Responding to the Text(s): Women Readers and the Quest for Higher Education

SUSAN K. HARRIS

Pretext I:

We have not only the common saying for it, but the word of God also, that Man and Wife are ONE; they were intended for each other, and coming together form one perfect being. When, therefore, a woman, who in her attributes is constituted differently from man, attempts to assume the attributes of man, she injures herself, impairs her own attributes, and renders herself unfit to fill that position for which she was created, 'an help-meet for man.' . . . Let not a woman endeavor to rule by authority as a man. Let her use her influence and power by those means appropriate to her sex. Let her feminine character be such as to convince man that there is one place which is a refuge from the cares and toils of the world—a woman's society. To man belongs the labor, to woman the duty of preparing man for labor!

"Women," in *The Present* (1850)

Pretext II:

If woman is accountable to God alone, for the improvement and use she makes of her various capabilities, she must have entire freedom of action in all directions, or the responsibility is assumed by the party who restricts her. . . . Doom the wife and mother to the cares of home life, sacred and beautiful as it is, and her nature is never satisfied, because it is never fully aroused and employed.

"Reasons Why Woman Should Define Her Own Sphere," *The Una* (1853)

A cultural debate consists of a multitude of voices, often cacophonous, speaking about a subject—or subjects—of great cultural concern. It is a dialogue in which all writers or speakers on the subject participate, consciously or not; speaking out of the matrix, the thick placenta of prior voices, they repeat, challenge, or transform the words that have come before them.

In *Rhetorical Power*, Steven Mailloux discusses "cultural conversations" as the term has developed through V. L. Parrington, Lionel Trilling, and Kenneth Burke, defining it as essentially another word for "culture, that historical conversation of multiple voices engaged in continuing rhetorical conflict."[1] My term "cultural debate" is indebted to these prior critics, but departs from them in that it focuses on a particular issue or set of interrelated issues and emphasizes opposition. In addition, analysis of a cultural debate as I see it must take into account time, historical time, and changes that occur in the terms of the debate as a consequence of time's passing. A methodology for assessing a cultural debate must therefore be flexible enough to encompass individual works, both published and unpublished, and the historical trace record these works leave over time. It must also be flexible enough to allow for the fact that any document can function as a response as well as a pretext. The categories "production" and "response," in other words, are not fixed: within the scope of the debate taxonomic boundaries are fluid.

I have found Hans Robert Jauss's essay "Literary History as a Challenge to Literary Theory" most useful here; its observation that one of literature's functions in the social realm is to imagine new possibilities, thus "introducing" them within the relative safety of a known story, provides the bridge between measuring individual readers' responses and assessing cultural transformations. In Roland Barthes's terminology, within the scope of a "readable text" (analogous to Jauss's "consumable text"), a "writable" one functions to lay the foundations—first in individual readers' consciousnesses, eventually in the group's—for shifts in cultural values that will eventuate in social change.[2]

In addition to the work of Jauss and Barthes, Wolfgang Iser's essay "The Reading Process" provides insights useful for creating a methodology to examine a cultural debate. Responding to Roman Ingarden, Iser posits a "virtual dimension," the place where a reader's imagination comes together with a literary text.[3] As we read sentences, we form "illusions"; that is, we respond to each sentence—make sense of it—by creating an idea of its meaning, an idea predicated both on the sentences of that text already read and our own experience of the world that we bring to them. We are, in other words, continually creating stories as interpretive parallels to the sentences we are processing. But our narrative creativity also is deflected repeatedly by the additional information new sentences force upon us; we continually have to shift gears, to recreate the illusions. Iser, following Ingarden, calls the results of these shifts "gaps." As readers, we fill these gaps with what we already know: from the text we are processing, from other texts, from our experience of the world. "For this reason," contends Iser, "one text is potentially capable of several different realizations, and no reading can ever exhaust the full potential, for each individual reader will fill in the gaps in his own way, thereby excluding the various other possibilities; as he reads, he will make his own decision as to how the gap is to be filled."[4]

Viewed through a fusion of Barthes's structuralist and Iser's phenomenological perspectives, the "gaps" that open up when writable texts disrupt readable ones thus create the virtual dimension where the text and the readers' imaginations interact creatively, making new ideas possible. Looking at the process again from Jauss's historical perspective, we can see how minor voices, heretical and often denigrated in texts produced early in a cultural debate, slowly become major voices, first challenging the hegemony of the dominant voices, then becoming dominant voices themselves. Over time, repetition of these heretical texts makes them increasingly readable and consequently increasingly acceptable to individual readers. Over time, writers respond to the heretical segments of prior texts, producing new ones that increasingly foreground heretical ideas. Ultimately, these become "readable"; they have achieved the status of legitimate ideas; they are stories the culture tells about itself easily, without conflict.

How can we use this methodology to examine nineteenth-century women's responses to documents about women and education? To measure changes in cultural values—one of the tasks of historians of consciousness—we have to choose pretexts, aware that the activity is almost arbitrary; we choose because we must start somewhere. For the mid-nineteenth-century debate over higher education for women, choosing the ideologically opposing passages quoted above from the popular giftbook *The Present, or, A Gift for the Times* and the feminist paper *The Una* proves useful because they reflect the opposing sides in the closely related issue of the nature of the feminine. The debate over women and education, then, is framed by the epistemological debate over women. Any document focusing on the question of women and education produced within that cultural debate reflects one side or the other. I will argue that most reflect both, and that published materials are as much responses to prior texts as are diary entries. As additional speakers enter the debate, they also add to it their own interpretations, colored by their own experiences and desires; in this way the terms of the debate are transformed even while the debate is being conducted. This "conversation" is not static; it is an ongoing dialectical process that fuels both production and response.

Keeping in mind our "pretext"—the opposing definitions of women's nature and possibilities—we can look at the records left us by women diarists and correspondents as they revealed their own desires and ambivalences about acquiring education, improving their intellects, and—most importantly in this controversy—dealing with the power that education was seen to impart, power that one side in the debate, long dominant, claimed would destroy femininity.

Mary Ann Parker, for instance, was a wealthy married woman who frequently noted that "I would rather be out of this fashionable society than in it."[5] Not only did she dislike fashionable society; she liked solitude, a predisposition that made her nervous: "I think I was made to live alone," she noted in her diary on January 15, 1850, "or else to submit to a constant discipline in enduring that which is not agreeable—having people about . . . consuming my time . . . fret[s] me very much." Because she also wanted to conform to her culture's definition of a good wife and mother, she felt guilty about her solitariness: "At times my heart seems turned to stone," she had noted, regretfully, two weeks earlier. "Is it temptation?—What is it? I believe I am strangely constituted and have many trials in my inward life, which all do not know" (Dec. 31, 1849). Parker's reading in history, biography, and travel literature suggests one way she tried to fulfill her solitary bent: during the months in which she kept her diary she recorded reading "Cuzon's Monasteries in the Levant, which I like," a life of William Wirt, and Coleman's *Letters from England,* as well as a "life of Calvin" and Hawthorne's *Scarlet Letter* (March 24, Apr. 2, Feb. 21, and Feb. 28, 1850). She also embarked on a course in Latin in an "essay" to "improve" herself (Nov. 22, 1849).

Parker, who is also often sick and/or depressed, nicely illustrates the tensions women experienced between the culturally constructed definition of "woman," as expressed in our pretext from *The Present*, and their own desires, as expressed in our pretext from *The Una*. Wealthy, educated, living in the fashionable world, having as she admits "all I want – every attention" (Oct.14, 1849), Parker nevertheless seeks something else, and seeks it through her reading. The hardness of heart that disturbs her is the dilemma of a woman who has absorbed the culture's dictum that she constantly live through others but who, for herself, prefers a life of the mind. Her "essay" at Latin is a grasp at the basics of the culture's wisdom, a means of ameliorating her frustration at the way her life was being frittered away.

Similarly, Julia A. Parker Dyson's diary illustrates the conflict women experienced between their private desires to participate in their culture's intellectual power structure and their culturally induced conviction that women's function is to live for others. An unmarried teacher in her early twenties in 1841, Dyson was a voracious reader, especially of books about prominent women, many of which she also shared with her young women students. Yet her diary entries show that she was caught between conflicting impulses: one, to imitate heroic women, and the other, to conform to the cultural demand that women limit their intellectual functions to teaching moral values. For instance, several diary entries indicate her fascination with the late-eighteenth-century French feminist and political influence Madame de Staël: "I cannot contemplate a mind like hers without the most ardent longing to turn aside from the beaten track of life, and explore those rich fields of observation, those secret recesses of thought, that the gifted *few* alone may enter," she wrote on July 24, 1841. "I feel immortal longings rise within me. I would consecrate my life, yea, my whole life, to improvement – to the perfection of my whole nature. Would that I were the favored child of knowledge, placed in the midst of her treasures, initiated into her deep mysteries. Surely I would be what I am not."[6]

Here, Dyson's response to de Staël suggests that the French author inspired her desire both for the deep wisdom – the kiss of divinity – that canonical learning is supposed to impart and for the political power that de Staël wielded. For the writer of this entry, intellectual accomplishments such as de Staël's constitute power—individual power enabling the self to transcend the commonplace.

At the same time, however, Dyson agrees that the sphere of the feminine is sharply defined and cannot be abandoned without "unsexing" the adventurer. Commenting on an editorial about women's education in the popular magazine *The Lady's Book*, she reports, concurringly, that "the writer speaking of the advancement of society, remarks, that in nothing is it so strikingly manifest, as in the fact, that during the last 15 or 20 years, more has been written on the subject of female education, than all that has been written previously by any nation . . . and that, too, in a style, and from motives so entirely different. One being to make her the theme of ridicule and satire; the other from a desire to elevate her as a social and moral being, preparing her for the high destiny assigned her by heaven, to be the gentle minister of virtue, the guide and director of the mind from its first opening, and through its successive developments."[7] Here, Dyson lets her reading of the call for women's power go only so far; despite wanting to be "what I am not," she can countenance women's education as a tool only for the good of others, never for the individual woman.

These two entries illustrate the contradictory impulses, or themes, motivating women who desired to participate in their culture's system of intellectual authority. On the one hand, they sensed its power, both socially and spiritually—they suspected that if they could attain it, they would be transformed into "what I am not." On the other hand, they understood—and often agreed—that education for a woman was legitimate only if it helped her help others: it was not for herself, for "the perfection of my whole nature"; rather, it was for improving others—to make her "the guide and director of [other] minds." The emphasis in the first case is on the self, culturally defined as the male prerogative; the emphasis in the other case is on service, culturally marked as the sphere of the female.

Despite the ambivalence expressed by diarists such as Dyson and Parker, it is clear that American women did feel the need for intellectual power. Many sought to educate themselves to achieve some status beyond that of wife, mother, or daughter—to exist in some kind of individuality in a culture that celebrated individuality but restricted its manifestation to white men. American women's responses to Elizabeth Barrett Browning's feminist poem *Aurora Leigh*, which diarists and correspondents mention more frequently than any other text, show that American women applauded women who exercised cultural authority. Early in 1856 Ada Parker wrote to a friend to ask: "Have you seen 'Aurora Leigh,' Elizabeth Browning's last book? . . . I long to possess her poems—to have them by my pillow with the most precious of my books, as a personal inspiration to faith and courage. She drinks at a fountain whose waters cannot fail, and her words are full of hope and healing."[8] Eleven months later Lydia Maria Child, herself a successful American novelist, wrote to her friend Marianne Silsbee: "I am charmed with Mrs. Browning's *Aurora Leigh*. It is full of strength and beauty; and it strikes at the artificial distinctions of society with a boldness that delights me. Verily, great is Elizabeth Browning! A Milton among women! How glad I am that genius is under the *necessity* of being ever on the free and progressive side! How I delight in having old fogies tormented, always and everywhere!"[9] Eleven years later Olivia Langdon (later to become Mrs. Samuel L. Clemens), reread *Aurora Leigh* and reminded her correspondent, "What a favorite it is of mine."[10]

The records nineteenth-century women left of their reading suggest that with their desire to educate themselves, they also searched for role models: examples of other women who stood out as powerful individuals. Between 1869 and 1871 Julia Newberry, a young women of the leisure class, recorded her determination "to study hard this Winter, and do *something* . . . 'Be somebody, July,' Papa always used to say, and be somebody I WILL."[11] Although travel and illness had disrupted Newberry's formal education to the point where she recorded, "I really am not well enough to read anything *deep*," in 1870 she noted that she had read "'Lamb,' 'Tuckerman's book on American artists,' 'Young's Night Thoughts,' 'Chemistry,' 'Pickwick,' and the book of 'Genisi' [*sic*] . . . some of Disraeli's 'Curiositys [*sic*] of literature,' with biographies of 'Mrs. Sigourney,' 'Ristori,' 'Theodosia Burr,' 'Mad. Necker,' 'Lady Anne Lindsey,' 'Maximilian' and others" (75). Books that she considered "particular friends . . . that I read all the time and over and over again" include "Jane Eyre. And all that Charlotte Bronte ever wrote . . . Vanity Fair. Haslitt's Essays . . . All Byron's decent poems . . . Hawthorne's house with the seven gables. Longfellow's Hyperion. Old Town Folks by Mrs. Stowe. King Henry the IV and V . . . Ruskin's book of beauties . . . Bacon's Essays . . . Hope Leslie" (153–55).

Unlike many of her older contemporaries, Newberry mixed in a number of novels with her nonfiction reading: interestingly, of the ones written by women all either argue for women's education, as does Stowe's *Oldtown Folks*, or feature deeply individualistic, icono-clastic heroines, as do Sedgwick's *Hope Leslie* and Brontë's *Jane Eyre*. In trying to improve her education, Newberry was also acquiring a canon of female heroes. Similarly, Hannah Maria Washburn, who kept a list of the books she read between 1861 and 1870, recorded "Mrs. Stowe's 'Pearl of Orr's Island,' the 'Life of the Last Mrs. Judson,' 'Beu-lah' [by Augusta Evans], 'Villette,' 'The Rebels' [by Lydia Maria Child], and 'Helen,' [by Maria Edgeworth]," sandwiched between such works as "The Last Days of Pompei," "Les Miserables," and Shakespeare's "Anthony and Cleopatra."[12]

Newberry and Washburn's diaries not only show that even casual readers could accumulate a canon of female heroes; they also show that these readers were in continual contact with discussions about female education. Virtually all of the women's texts that they read reflected the debates about women's nature and the amount of formal education appropriate for women. As they accumulated models of female achievement, then, mid-nineteenth-century women were also constantly confronted by forms of the debate itself. Moreover, be-cause they came to the texts as women aspiring for expanded oppor-tunities themselves, they responded to those aspects of the debate that spoke to their own predispositions. In "The Reader's Construction of Meaning: Cognitive Research on Gender and Comprehension," Mary Crawford and Roger Chaffin discuss the implications of personal and gender history for reading, suggesting that individuals bring to texts schemata, or organizing structures, that direct the ways they process texts.[13] These frameworks guide both interpretation (in Iser's formula-tion, the stories we create as we decode sentences) and memory of what has been read. Coming to women's writings that contain hereti-cal subtexts arguing for women's education, Newberry and Washburn bring with them schemata privileging that theme.

The diary of Maud Rittenhouse, a young woman who was later to become a writer and a women's rights activist, suggests how such sche-mata function. In 1881 Rittenhouse read one of Augusta Evans's novels and found herself both repelled and compelled by it.

The book I read the day before[,] *Vashti, or Until Death do Us Part*, by Evans, was the funniest thing I ever saw. The main object of the writer seems to be to compose a book as entirely different from anything else ever written as possible and I think in that she succeeds. Her girls of 16 talk philosophy, quote poems and the "maxims of cynical Rochefoucauld." Everybody in the book save one old maid is in love, not a person finds that love reciprocated, everybody dies but two, one the hero, whose "true love" has died, the other a glorious girl, hopelessly in love with aforesaid hero, nobody gets married, and the book stops without really ending. I suppose it did me good for it kept me running to the Dictionary or to an encyclopedia to see who Joubert is, or where the "cheerless temple of Hestia" stands or stood, or to find what "a wan Alcestis" and "a desperate Cassandra he had seen at Rome," indicated.[14]

Here Rittenhouse brings more than one schema to Evans's text: her framework for processing *Vashti* aesthetically rejects it: she is repelled by Evans's lush prose and lavish plotting. But because she has intellectual ambitions herself, she also responds to the text as a challenge: she goes to her dictionary because as an aspiring writer she knows that she should be familiar with Evans's references. This schemata privileges *Vashti*'s assumption that women can participate in the culture's literary history, and by responding to it as she does, Rittenhouse shows her own affirmation of women's capabilities for assuming intellectual power.

Let us look at one of Evans's works—not *Vashti*, but one that problematizes the issue of women, education, and power: *St. Elmo* (1866). Bearing in mind the concerns articulated by the diarists quoted above, what opportunities does *St. Elmo* grant individuals to, in Iser's terms, "realize" the text in ways that it might not at first seem to invite?

St. Elmo is a romance, with a bitter, Byronic hero who is ultimately Christianized and a pious but proud heroine who brings him to his knees. Some contemporary reviewers evaluated it on that score: for instance, a *New York Times* reviewer attacked the book for featuring yet another "charlatan of literature, . . . the gloomy being who lives in a mysterious chamber filled with Chaldee manuscripts, Turkish scimetars, and Eastern relics."[15] The review for *Scott's Monthly Magazine*, on the other hand, lavished praise on Evans's taste, "cultivated and refined by a thorough knowledge of classical and modern belles-lettres,"[16] and at least one early-twentieth-century critic noted Evans's "deep love of scholarship."[17] These last responses give us insight into an alternate way of processing this text. In addition to presenting a

Byronic love story, *St. Elmo* also presents a story about language and power, and about women's appropriation of that power. Edna, the heroine, is obsessed with learning: through the course of the novel she becomes a full-fledged, if academically uncertified, classical scholar. Even as a rural orphan she had read Plutarch's *Lives* and Anthon's *Classical Mythology*; the plot device that introduces her to the hero, St. Elmo, is, as the narrator carefully tells us, a copy of Dante, in "Cary's translation, with illustrations designed by Flaxman";[18] and by the time she is an adult—living in St. Elmo's mother's house and tutored by his old tutor—she has mastered Latin, Greek, Hebrew, and Chaldee, and has read through European and Near Eastern classical texts. Her major interest is ethnology, and she contributes to the ongoing nineteenth-century debate over the origins of languages and cultural myths by writing a book that traces their evolution through the central figure of a female taxonomer and hermeneut. She becomes internationally known and respected for her work—before she gives it all up to marry the reformed St. Elmo.

Edna's story perfectly illustrates nineteenth-century women's conflicts about gender, learning, and power. She is trapped between passions: sexual passion for St. Elmo, a misogynist who is threatened by her erudition, and intellectual passion for canonical wisdom. For most of the novel, her intellectual passion is foregrounded, not only because St. Elmo goes off on long journeys, but also because most of the conversations between characters focus on women and education or, even more fundamentally, on women and language. Edna's manuscript is at first rejected by the editor to whom she had sent it, simply because a woman wrote it: "The subject you have undertaken is beyond your capacity—no woman could successfully handle it," he writes, advising her to burn it and "write sketches of home life—descriptions of places and things that you understand better than recondite analogies of ethical creeds and mythologic systems" (197–98). In a debate between Edna, St. Elmo, and Estelle (interestingly, Edna's sexual rival) even the antiheroine argues—learnedly—against St. Elmo's fulminations against "strong-minded (that is, weak-brained but loud-tongued), would-be literary females" (220). In her defense of educated women Estelle marshals references to the Chevalier Bayard, Cuvier, Mill, and Ruskin; and even her reservations are constructed to display her own erudition, as when she criticizes "the Corypheus of the 'woman's rights' school" (219–21). Earlier, when Edna had declared her intentions of becoming a scholar, her guardian had hesitated lest Edna become a "blue-stocking"; her mentor, a minister, champions female learning and argues that "where one woman is considered a blue-stocking, and tiresomely learned, twenty are more tiresome still because they know nothing" (70).

Edna's progress through the stages of acquired wisdom mark turning points in her life; she goes from wanting to prepare herself to teach primary school to wanting to be famous. The last, of course, lies well outside woman's sphere: Edna's "ambition" for "a victory that would make her name imperishable" (109) should mark her as a wicked woman who defies her culture's prescriptions.

But somehow that is not what happens. *St. Elmo* works in curious ways, effecting itself through the conflict between the novel's narrative design and its implicit thematizing of a woman's struggle to appropriate intellectual authority in a culture that denies female intellectual power.

The narrator of *St. Elmo* is fully as erudite as her protagonist; perhaps we can even see her as the role model that Edna strives to emulate. The first page, for instance, places the young Edna in the country, nature's child—but the narrator describes her as standing in "ancient, classic Caryatides attitudes" and "chanting the prayer of Habakkuk" (1); in her late adolescence she is described as standing "on the line, narrow and thin as Al-Sirat, that divides girlhood and womanhood [when] all seemed to her fresh, pure heart as inviting and bewitching as the magnificent panorama upon which enraptured lotophagi gazed from the ancient acropolis of Cyrene" (87). The narrator presents Edna's scholarly awakening within similarly abstruse references:

> The hoary associations and typical significance of the numerous relics . . . seized upon Edna's fancy, linked her sympathies with the huge pantheistic systems of the Orient, and filled her mind with waifs from the dusky realm of a mythology that seemed to antedate all the authentic chronological computations of man. To the East, the mighty *alma mater* of the human race . . . her thoughts wandered in wondering awe; and Belzoni, Burckhardt, Layard and Champollion were hierophants of whose teachings she never wearied. As day by day she yielded more and more to this fascinating nepenthe influence . . . the wish strengthened to understand the symbols in which subtle Egyptian priests masked their theogony. (109)

Such references serve two functions: to place Edna among the classic figures that she will, in time, come to represent as the most recent manifestation, and to prove the author's right to authority by displaying her own erudition. In other words, the narrator's claim to authority— to power over her reader—rests on her own possession of the culture's high canonical history. With this, she projects both a readable and a writable text: her high canonical framework depends on readers' familiarity with the story of Western culture; her situating a woman as its principal interpreter demands that readers reconfigure their concept of the relationship of gender to cultural authority.

At the same time that she establishes her own and her character's cultural power, however, the narrator also develops a story that contradicts itself: a story about an active, learned, and powerful woman who declares that woman's nature is passive and that her place is in the home. Edna defends Tennyson's *The Princess* over Barrett-Browning's *Aurora Leigh* because although "I love and revere Mrs. Browning, and consider her not only the pride of her sex but an ornament to the world, . . . I find it difficult to forgive the unwomanly inconsistency into which she betrays her heroine" (335), the problem being, apparently, that in the last book of the poem Aurora tells Romney that she loves him without waiting for him to speak first. Despite the fact that Edna is by this time internationally famous—she makes this speech at a dinner party attended by some of the most influential literati of Britain and the United States—she also chooses to attend to a sick child rather than to remain at the dinner. Through the course of the novel she also develops angina from overwork, and at the end, when St. Elmo reappears, converted and presumably tamed, she accedes to his demand that she give up writing and become his wife. In all of this, the narrator roundly affirms Edna's ideology.

In the story she tells (as opposed to the way she tells it) then, Evans's narrator capitulates to the cultural demand that a heroine, to be approved, must be intellectually and emotionally subordinate to a man and must find her highest being not in satisfying her own ambitions, in cherishing her own ego, but in supporting his. And yet the narrator's own language—her participation in the multireferencing that links the living to the authorities of the past—carries out the theme that the story's plot attempts to deny. Although the plot has Edna develop heart disease as a consequence of her work, this narrator generally refrains from moralizing about it. Nor does she cease placing Edna within a high cultural context. Most importantly, she communicates Edna's fascinations with her studies and her gratification at her own renown not only without censorship of her protagonist, but with a fascination into the process of historical scholarship equal to the character's own. In fact the narrator's high canonical intertextuality establishes a countertheme to the one suggested by the novel's narrative design, a theme that valorizes self-sufficient women who have seized verbal authority and act successfully in the world. In effect, the narrator gives readers the choice between two stories about women: that told by the text's language and that told by its design. Which one they choose to read will depend on their own frameworks for processing this and prior texts, including the "text" of their own life experiences. Mary Parker and Julia Parker Dyson, one suspects, would have had difficulty reconciling Edna's ambitions with her claim to femininity; Julia Newberry and Maud Rittenhouse would have had difficulty reconciling Edna's ideology of womanly self-effacement with her claim to cultural authority.

This fictional text, then, is as much a response as it is a pretext; it embodies, rhetorically as well as thematically, the opposing sides of the cultural debate.

Documents concerning women and education produced during the latter half of the nineteenth century reflect the cultural debate rhetorically even in the rare cases when they do not reflect it thematically. Rhetorical history, in other words, embodies intellectual history; the result is texts presenting arguments that can be interpreted as supporting either side of the debate. Juxtaposing heretical minor themes to conservative major ones, documents focusing on women and intellectual power create gaps that offer readers a choice. Or, in the words of *St. Elmo*'s narrator, "indolent, luxurious readers, who wish even their thinking done by proxy" (the audience for Barthes's readable text? For Jauss's consumable text?)—those who use fiction *only* as reconfirmation of the stories they already know (the narrator of *St. Elmo* refers to this process as the "hasty, careless, novel-reading glance")—will see only the cover story, the narrative, fictional or other, that reflects the dominant theme, that women should not possess effective verbal authority in realms beyond the domestic. Other readers—those to whom Herman Melville, writing in a similar context, refers as "eagle-eyed"—those struggling with their own desires to operate outside the boundaries of women's social roles, will respond to the covert story, the one that opposes and ultimately disrupts the overt text. These readers, seeking wisdom as their culture defined it, will bring to the text schemata that privilege the story about intellectual power.

What was intellectual power in the nineteenth century? In *Professing Literature*, Gerald Graff has pointed out that the most prestigious professions for American men were the ministry and law, and that in the universities curricular preparation for these fields required the study of history, classical philology, and biblical studies. On a less formal level—that is, not as a formal part of the curriculum—a well-educated man was expected to be familiar with the best of Anglo-European literature, from classical times to his own.[19] Most men acquiring this knowledge did not actively use it professionally; then as now, the study of belles lettres was primarily a social one, to mark students as members of a class that could afford to keep its sons out of the marketplace during their early adulthood. What it did do, however, was to embellish their verbal lives—that is, to create a context for oral and written discourse that signaled, first, the socially significant fact that they *had* a college education; second, the culturally significant fact that they could place their own discourse within the discourse of their culture's past; and third, the hierarchically significant fact that in so doing they could appropriate the power and prestige of their predecessors. In social terms, the whole purpose of a canon is to give a culture a rhetorical and thematic history and therefore models; as historical models become shrouded by the past, they assume the power of semi-divinities. Calling on the gods yields something of their power to the caller. Moreover, if those who habitually call on the past also happen to be born into the group that wields effective power—social, political, financial—the two forms of authority become fused in the popular mind. Hence the amount of quotation in nineteenth-century discourse: in speeches and essays—argumentative modes—especially, but also in fiction. Hence the common practice of keeping commonplace books—storing up quotations for future use. Hence also, of course, the practice, among satirical writers such as Charles Webb or Mark Twain, of littering their work with fabricated or inappropriate quotations, an impulse to carnival among the serious official culture.[20] In a society whose entire fabric was intertextual—from its interior decoration to its architecture, from its music to its rhetorical modes—the ability to draw at will on the canonical writers of the past was the ticket first, to intellectual power, and second, to effective power.

A concomitant of such practices was the fear of educating marginal groups: in nineteenth-century America, women and African Americans. To know the wisdom—the mysteries—of the past was to prepare oneself to appropriate power. And power is the ability to act, to act as an individual, to have an impact on others in what the nineteenth century called the public—by which it meant white male—sphere. For women or nonwhite males to lay claim to such power was to threaten the foundations of a system that conceived of the ability to act as the prerogative of white men who saw themselves as descended—sexually, racially, and spiritually—from the canonical heroes of the past.

Women understood that situation, and they developed a multiplicity of rhetorical modes and thematic arguments to deal with it. Women writers wrote in the reflection of the debate as much as their audience read in it. Like *St. Elmo*, formal documents written by nineteenth-century women that focus on women's education tell two stories at once. These essays frame their arguments for women's educational opportunities by raising other kinds of questions, a rhetorical device calculated to create a dual text for a dual—at times a schizoid—readership. For instance, in *Woman Suffrage and Woman's Profession*, a collection of speeches published in 1871, Catharine Beecher, perhaps the most prominent advocate of education for women in the nineteenth century, argued for "the establishment of *woman's* [sic] *universities*, in which every girl shall secure as good a literary training as her brothers, and then be trained to some profession adapted to her taste and capacity, by which she can establish a home of her own, and secure an independent income—*this* is what every woman may justly claim and labor for, as the shortest, surest, and safest mode of securing her own highest usefulness and happiness, and that of her sex."[21] But *Woman Suffrage and Woman's Profession* is prefaced by an appeal "To The Ministers of Religion in the United States"—in other words, to the men Beecher sees as the most influential watchdogs of women's behavior—and it strongly suggests that the essays themselves will be about teaching women how to care for themselves physically. Although some attention is given to the apparently deplorable state of women's health, especially in the last essays, the major part of the collection focuses on the development of a women's university—run by and for women.

Similarly, in an essay that rejects female suffrage, Beecher also claims unequivocally that women have a right to equal advantages with men, have never had them, and therefore should fight to get them: "It is the right and the duty of every woman to employ the power of organization and agitation, in order to gain those advantages which are given to one sex, and unjustly withheld from the other."[22] Beecher's tone has a double intention here that can only be read in light of her own and her readers' ambivalence about the final intentions of women's education: on the one hand, she advocates moves that, if successful, will clearly propel women into the mainstream of intellectual power in the United States; on the other, she denies that that is her intention. Consistently maintaining that her interest in women is *only* to improve their welfare in the private realm, in fact her program for them lays the groundwork for their emergence into the public realm of "organization and agitation" and, finally, into full political and social equality. The result is a document offering readers two mutually exclusive readings, according to the schemata they bring to it: those, represented by the "Ministers of Religion," who want to ameliorate women's problems but not radically shift the status quo can read about a plan to make women into healthier and more effective wives and mothers; those who look for avenues to effective power in the public realm can read about a plan for a women's university offering women an education equal to a man's.

Writing forty years later, but with equal zeal and a similar framework, Anna Julia Cooper, foremost advocate of higher education for African American women, also argued for women's participation in the sphere of intellectual power. Younger than Beecher by nearly two generations and much more radically outspoken, Cooper nevertheless employs similar rhetorical contexts for her call for women's, and especially black women's, full educational equality. Like Beecher's *Woman Suffrage and Woman's Profession*, Cooper's collection of essays, *A Voice from the South*, begins with an address to an audience of ministers. Unlike Beecher's preface, Cooper's is a full essay that argues for women's rights. In composing it, Cooper, an extraordinarily well-educated woman for her time, black or white, displays the full range of literary references: she begins her talk with a discussion of the position of Muslim women, then quickly moves to Western cultural ground, citing, in rapid order, Macaulay, Tacitus, Guizot, Bascom, Emerson, de Staël.[23] In her opening pages then, Cooper uses conventional rhetorical means—the call to the culture's great figures of the past and the implicit assumption of their authority—to inform her male audience that she is their intellectual equal.

But as she argues for black women's education, she also carefully avoids claiming that educated women will challenge male authority. In other essays, Cooper notes, astutely and at times acerbically, that black men's attitudes toward black women are tantamount to white men's attitudes toward black men. Here, however, Cooper carefully claims that the reason black women should be better educated is, first, to make them better Christians, and second, to further the elevation of the race. Citing Jesus Christ as the originator of "the idea of the radical amelioration of womankind," she fuses the Christian ideal with the racial imperative: "Now the fundamental agency under God in the regeneration, the re-training of the race, as well as the ground work and starting point of its progress upward, must be the *black woman*." Later she discusses the church's "oversight" in "not developing Negro womanhood as an essential fundamental for the elevation of the race, and utilizing this agency in extending the work of the Church."[24]

Cooper's Christian and racial arguments function as do Beecher's Christian and domestic ones: both deflect attention from the fact that women who had been educated like men would be likely—as both Beecher and Cooper certainly did—to move out of the private sphere of the approved feminine and into the male social and political arena. Calling on the same canonical authorities as men—from the Bible to Emerson—they present themselves as fully equal, fully capable. Yet both know the threat their arguments pose, and both carefully locate their proposals to educate women within other pressing cultural concerns: for the white audience, the question of female health and family moral cohesion; for the black audience, the question of the future of the Negro race. While white and black women can process the arguments for educating women, white and black men can process the assurance that educated women will not threaten the male power structure, whether of white men who possess power, or of black men who are struggling for a share of it.

Evans's, Beecher's, and Cooper's texts present the dualities of the debate about women and cultural power most clearly, but other women's texts present the possibilities for alternative readings as well. Over time, these texts first highlight, then foreground, the push for equal education and, hence, authority. In many, such as *St. Elmo*, protagonists' desires for education constitute one end of a polarity established between conventional heterosexuality—presented as the story of a woman who subordinates herself intellectually to her husband—and independence, presented as a woman who, in the words of Elizabeth Stuart Phelps's heroine in *The Silent Partner* (1871), tells her suitor: "If I married you, sir, I should invest in life, and you would conduct it. I suspect that I have a preference for a business of my own."[25] Some of Harriet Beecher Stowe's characters—though not many—reject the female role altogether; *My Wife and I* (1871) features one woman who claims: "I don't demand anything of any man, I only want to be left alone. I don't want to wait for a husband to make me a position. I want to make one for myself; I don't want to take a husband's money, I want my own."[26] The novels of E.D.E.N. Southworth, which do not thematize higher education for women but do explore women's possibilities for financial and psychological autonomy, often echo *The Una*; in *The Deserted Wife* (1850), for instance, Hagar, the heroine, cries out to her repressive husband: "I have a will! and tastes, and habits, and propensities! . . . that all go to make up the sum total of a separate individuality, a distinct life! For which *I alone* am accountable, and *only* to God!"[27]

In addition to problematizing the question of female autonomy, many mid-nineteenth-century American women's novels either focus on women's educational ambitions or include significant minor characters who thirst for canonical knowledge. Stowe's New England novels, for instance, tend to fall into the second category. In *Oldtown Folks* there is Grandmother Badger, whose spare time is given to reading; the narrator remembers her "always as a reader." "In her private chamber was always a table covered with books; and though performing personally the greater share of the labors of the family, she never failed to have her quiet hour every afternoon for reading. History and biography she delighted in, but she followed with a keen relish the mazes of theology."[28] The heroine of *The Minister's Wooing* fortifies her sanctity with Jonathan Edwards's sermons. Most of Stowe's novels call for women's rights to study subjects such as Greek, Latin, higher mathematics, and astronomy.

But even Stowe's novels do not admit the logical ends of her call. The character from *My Wife and I* who asserts her independence is unusual in Stowe's works; more often, Stowe militantly asserts women's need to continue studying, but rationalizes it as making them

intellectual companions for their husbands and giving them something to think about besides clothes. Stowe's female exemplars manage
spotless houses in the mornings and devote their afternoons to study—
to self-improvement. Stowe's Puritanism is nowhere better illustrated
than in her desire to encourage women to be serious: thoughtful, informed, able to discourse upon all subjects and in all company. Her
ostensible goal, however, is, like her sister Catharine's, to make women
better wives, mothers, and Christians. Her novels participate in the
debate about higher education for women by subordinating the call to
"more important" social questions dealing with women's roles. Her
acceptance of traditional roles lies uneasily with her call for women's
education; the structure of her novels, in other words, reflects once
more the conflict between socially constructed concepts of gender
and what she perceives as a pressing need for individual women. The
value of her novels, then, again lies with the schemata brought to
them by individual readers.

Written late in the century, Frances W. Harper's *Iola Leroy* (1892), a
novel focusing on racial regeneration, contains an argument for women's education and independence that is similarly enfolded in a concern for the upward progress of the newly emancipated African American population. Both Iola, the mulatta heroine, and Lucille Delany,
the heroine of "unmixed blood," are educated, independent, and determined to make a place for black women in the intellectual as well as
the economic world. Yet like Anna Julia Cooper's and Catharine
Beecher's essays, Harper's novel places these characters' aspirations
within both a Christian and a culturally defined "feminine" frame, a
frame that lays claim to the equality of Christians, on the one hand,
and to the equality of womanhood on the other. Because the white
community did not regard African American women as feminine—
that is, dependent, frail, chaste—black women writers labored under
the additional onus of proving their heroines to be as "womanly" as
white women even while they were arguing that women in general
were as fully capable as men. Many of their portrayals of black women
strive to project their subjects within white canonical frames of reference: when Iola is rescued from her brief sojourn in slavery, she is referred to as "the beautiful but intractable girl who was held in durance
vile," who is "taken as a trembling dove from the gory vulture's nest
and given a place of security." Moreover, the Union general who meets
her is impressed by the fact that in America such a girl would have

been "a chattel, with no power to protect herself from the highest insults that lawless brutality could inflict upon helpless and defenseless womanhood."[29] To create a heroine acceptable to an audience that read within the culture's definitions of true womanhood, Harper projected her protagonist within the imagery of fair damsels from the Middle Ages—a readable text designed to appeal to a nineteenth-century audience for whom white medieval culture conveyed historical status and legitimacy. The alternate black heroine, Lucille, on the other hand, is the character whom Iola herself most admires—she is, as Iola remarks, "my ideal woman. She is grand, brave, intellectual, and religious."[30] She also runs a school for black women and is capable of organizing and undertaking large programs for racial uplift. She is, in fact, one of the most autonomous characters in the novel, but she is also the one seen in the least direct way. Her power is deflected by being reported through other characters and by constantly being projected in terms of implicitly feminine self-abnegation; she runs a school to help the poor, to uplift the race, but not to achieve intellectual power for herself. And she, too, is eventually married—to a man who is not her intellectual superior but is, within the iconography of racial coloration, her racial superior. Iola's brother, he is so fair as to be able to choose his racial identity. Though he is praised for choosing to marry "black," no mention is made of the consequences for Lucille of marrying "white." The unwritten cultural text, however, would suggest that Lucille will never get the upper hand in the marriage. Like Stowe, then, Harper disguises, and disempowers, her educated female characters by subordinating their individual abilities and needs to a "more important" social goal and, ultimately, to the power hierarchy of conventional heterosexuality and racial coloration. Nevertheless her unwritten texts raise issues that have the potential for radical shifts in cultural values; readers bringing to them schemata encompassing the implications of empowering black women will recognize the possibilities that a Lucille Delany presents.

Women's participation in the nineteenth-century debate about higher education for women constitutes both a response to and a reflection of the arguments and the anxieties that characterize the debate as a whole. Women's responses are especially poignant because they show the dilemma of contradictory impulses; in both their private and public writings, women reveal how deeply their self-perceptions were created by the culture's construction of gender and, as a consequence, how troubled they were when they recognized within themselves conflicting imperatives. Evidence of their conflicts appears in all the genres in which they write: in the contradictions inherent in fiction that insists that they subordinate intellectual ambition to the needs of others while at the same time valorizing intellectuality; in learned essays that demonstrate the writer's own education while arguing that women be trained only so that they can serve others; in diaries and letters in which women furtively express their desires to know more than they do, to do more than their culture tells them they should, and to be what they are not.

Nevertheless, these readers and writers also show that women who sought to participate in the culture's idea of intellectual power did exist in the nineteenth century, both historically, as evidenced in their diaries and letters, and imaginatively, as evidenced in the fiction featuring them. In addition, the diaries and fiction show them responding, actively, to the terms in which the debate was couched, while the essays show that their authors produced texts that could be processed according to more than one schemata. None of the writers, public or private, are cultural radicals. Even Anna Julia Cooper accepts American culture's basic premises; her radicalism consists of her demand that African Americans, and especially African American women, have a piece of the pic. But most importantly here, we should recognize that protesting voices did exist, that they heard and responded to each other, and that they have left a trace record of desire that we can read as the precursors of genuine boundary-breaking in the cultural image of women's capabilities and place. In Jauss's terms, these are documents that anticipate unrealized possibility, eventuating in new paths for future experience. Beginning about the mid-1870s, novels such as Elizabeth Stuart Phelps's *The Story of Avis* (1877) begin to question openly the assumption that talented women should give up their personal ambitions upon marriage; Phelps's novel also seriously questions the structure of marriage relations. Additionally, Phelps creates a feminist canon to frame her protagonist's story: the would-be artist discovers her vocation while reading *Aurora Leigh* and realizes her failure while reading to her daughter—significantly named "Wait"— Spencer's story of the grail quest. Phelps's earlier publications, such as *The Gates Ajar* (1868), had contained their feminism within an adamantly Christian frame; publication of *The Story of Avis* signals her emergence into a secular and far more radical consciousness.

The likelihood is that she took her readers there, too. In 1878 Olivia Langdon, now Olivia Clemens, the wife of Mark Twain, wrote to her sister Susan Crane: "I am reading some short stories now of Miss Phelps[;] they are sensational as all her stories are." It is not inconsequential that in the same letter she reported:

> I told Mr. Clemens the other day that in this day women must be everything. They must keep up with all the current literature, they must know all about art, they must help in one or two benevolent societies, they must be perfect mothers, they must be perfect housekeepers and graceful gracious hostesses, they must go and visit all the people in the town where they live, they must always be ready to receive their acquaintances, they must dress themselves and their children becomingly and above all they must make their homes charming and so on without end—then if they are not studying something their case is a hopeless one.[31]

Clearly, while they were reading and studying, they were also thinking about the way their culture shaped their lives, and the works written for them addressed their concerns. The women of Olivia Langdon Clemens's generation were the mothers of the New Woman, whose texts and activities redefined the image and status of women in the early twentieth century. Like Julia Newberry, these women used their reading to formulate their ambitions to "be somebody"; like Phelps's protagonist, they willed their ambitions to their daughters, who in their own generation refused any longer to suppress, subordinate, or wait.

Notes

The epigraphs are from "Women," in *The Present; or, A Gift for the Times*, ed. F. A. Moore (Manchester, N.H.: Moore, 1850) 42–45; and "Reasons Why Woman Should Define Her Own Sphere," *The Una: A Paper Dedicated to the Elevation of Women* 1 February 1853: 9.

1. Steven Mailloux, *Rhetorical Power* (Ithaca: Cornell UP, 1989) 58.

2. Hans Robert Jauss, "Literary History as a Challenge to Literary Theory," *Toward an Aesthetic of Reception*, trans. Timothy Bahti (Minneapolis: U of Minnesota P, 1982) 3–45. For Barthes's discussions of scriptable and lisable texts, see *Writing Degree Zero*, trans. Annette Lavers and Colin Smith (New York: Hill, 1967).

3. Wolfgang Iser, "The Reading Process," *The Implied Reader: Patterns of Communication in Prose Fiction from Bunyan to Beckett* (Baltimore: Johns Hopkins UP, 1974) 279.

4. Ibid. 280.

5. Mary Ann Parker Diary, 1849–50, ms., New-York Historical Society, New York City, December 27, 1849. Subsequent citations appear in the text.

6. Julia A. Parker Dyson, *Life and Thought: or, Cherished Memorials of the late Julia A. Parker Dyson*, ed. E. Latimer, 2nd ed. (Philadelphia: Claxton, Remsen, Hafflefinger, 1871) 62.

7. Ibid.

8. *Letters of Ada R. Parker* (Boston: Crosby and Nichols, 1863) 154.

9. December 9, 1856, Lydia Maria Child Letters, 1845–80, American Antiquarian Society, Worcester, Mass. Some of these letters have been reprinted in *Lydia Maria Child: Selected Letters, 1817–1880*, ed. Milton Meltzer and Patricia G. Hollands (Amherst: U of Massachusetts P, 1982).

10. June 7, 1867, Olivia Langdon Letters, microfilm copies, Clemens Family Letters, Mark Twain Archives, Elmira College. Originals are at the Mark Twain Memorial, Hartford, Conn.

11. Julia Newberry, *Diary*, with Introd. by Margaret Ayer Barnes and Janet Ayer Fairbank (New York: Norton, 1933) 32.

12. Hannah Maria Washburn Diaries, 1861–70, ms., New York Public Library, Astor, Lenox, and Tilden Foundations.

13. Mary Crawford and Roger Chaffin, "The Reader's Construction of Meaning," in *Gender and Reading: Essays on Readers, Texts, and Contexts*, ed. Elizabeth A. Flynn and Patrocino P. Schweickart (Baltimore: Johns Hopkins UP, 1986) 4.

14. Maud Rittenhouse, *Maud*, ed. Richard Lee Strout (New York: Macmillan, 1939) 26.

15. Quoted in William Perry Fidler, *Augusta Evans Wilson, 1835–1909: A Biography* (University: Alabama UP, 1951) 134.

16. Quoted ibid. 145–46.

17. Ibid. 133, 236.

18. Augusta Evans [Wilson], *St. Elmo* (Chicago: Donohue, n.d.) 15; subsequent citations are given parenthetically in the text.

19. Gerald Graff, *Professing Literature: An Institutional History* (Chicago: U of Chicago P, 1987) 19–46. For the history of women's colleges, see Barbara Miller Solomon, *In the Company of Educated Women: A History of Women and Higher Education in America* (New Haven: Yale UP, 1985). Solomon's book, however, does not address the implications of college curricula as fully as Graff's. A useful set of primary documents are the Elmira Female College Catalogues, 1856–74, available at Elmira College, Elmira, N.Y. Chartered by New York State as a baccalaureate-

granting institution in 1855, Elmira offered women a classical curriculum.

20. I am thinking particularly of Twain's chapter headings in *The Gilded Age*. Charles Webb also published a parody of *St. Elmo*, entitled *St. Twel'mo; or, The Cuneiform Cyclopedist of Chattanooga*. See Fidler, *Augusta Evans Wilson* 138–39.

21. Catharine Beecher, *Woman Suffrage and Woman's Profession* (Hartford: Brown and Gross, 1871) 52.

22. Ibid. 4.

23. Anna Julia Cooper, *A Voice from the South*, The Schomburg Library of Nineteenth-Century Black Women Writers (New York: Oxford UP, 1988) 9–13.

24. Ibid. 14.

25. Elizabeth Stuart Phelps, *The Silent Partner*, ed. Mary Jo Buhle and Florence Howe (New York: Feminist, 1983) 263.

26. Harriet Beecher Stowe, *My Wife and I; or, Harry Henderson's History* (New York: Ford, 1872) 104.

27. E.D.E.N. Southworth, *The Deserted Wife* (Philadelphia: Peterson, 1855) 299.

28. Harriet Beecher Stowe, *Oldtown Folks* (New Brunswick: Rutgers UP, 1987) 28.

29. Frances W. Harper, *Iola Leroy; or, Shadows Uplifted* (Boston: Beacon, 1987) 38–39.

30. Ibid. 242.

31. November 30, 1878, Olivia Langdon Letters.

Notes on Contributors

MARVA BANKS, associate professor of English and modern languages at Albany State College, has written on Alice Walker and Francis Harper. She is currently working on the writings of Mary Ann Shadd Cary for the Shomberg Library of Nineteenth-Century Black Women Writers.

WILLIS BUCKINGHAM is professor of English at Arizona State University. He is the editor of *Emily Dickinson: an Annotated Bibliography* and *Emily Dickinson's Reception in the 1890s: A Documentary History*. Currently he is at work on Dickinson's relationship to the reading culture of her generation.

ROBERT DALY is Distinguished Teaching Professor of English at the State University of New York at Buffalo. He is the author of *God's Alter: The Word and the Flesh in Puritan Poetry* and is at work on a book-length manuscript, *American Visionary History: The Literary Creation of a Usable Past*.

WAI CHEE DIMOCK, associate professor of literature at Brandeis University, is the author of *Empire for Liberty: Melville and the Poetics of Indi-*

vidualism and the forthcoming *Symbolic Equality: American Literature, Law, Political Culture.* She is also co-editor of the forthcoming volume *Class and Literary Studies.*

SUSAN K. HARRIS is professor of English at Pennsylvania State University. Her publications include *Nineteenth-Century American Women's Novels: Interpretive Strategies* and *Mark Twain's Escape from Time: A Study of Patterns and Images.* She is at work on a book on Twain's domestic reading circle.

RAYMOND HEDIN is associate professor of American literature at Indiana University. His articles on black American literature have appeared in such journals as *American Literature, Callaloo,* and *Novel.* At present he is completing *Married to the Church,* an ethnographic study of men who attended St. Francis Seminary in Milwaukee in the 1960s.

JAMES L. MACHOR is associate professor of English and American literature at Kansas State University and a former Senior Fulbright Fellow. He is the author of *Pastoral Cities: Urban Ideals and the Symbolic Landscape of America* and is at work on a book tentatively entitled *Informed Reading and the Interpretive Contexts of American Fiction, 1820–1865.*

STEVEN MAILLOUX, professor of English and comparative literature at the University of California, Irvine, is the author of *Interpretive Conventions: The Reader in the Study of American Fiction* and *Rhetorical Power,* and is co-editor of *Interpreting Law and Literature: A Hermeneutic Reader.* He currently is writing a book on cultural reception and rhetorical hermeneutics and is editing a volume entitled *Rhetoric, Sophistry, Pragmatism.*

STEPHEN RAILTON is associate professor of American literature at the University of Virginia. His most recent book is *Authorship and Audience: Literary Performance in the American Renaissance.* He is currently working on a study of Twain tentatively entitled *The Artist as Performer.*

JOHN CARLOS ROWE is professor of English at the University of California, Irvine, where he teaches the literatures and cultures of the United States and critical theory. His numerous publications include *Through the Custom House: Nineteenth-Century American Fiction and Modern Theory, The Vietnam War and American Culture* (co-edited with Rick Berg), and the forthcoming *At Emerson's Tomb: The Politics of Literary Modernism in the United States.*

CHRISTINA ZWARG, associate professor of English at Haverford College, has published articles on Emerson and Margaret Fuller in *Studies in Romanticism*, *Cultural Critique*, and *American Literary History*. Her forthcoming book is entitled *Feminist Conversations: Fuller, Emerson, and the Task of Reading*.